The Cambridge Companion to Hippocrates

Hippocrates is a towering figure in Greek medicine. Dubbed the 'father of medicine', he has inspired generations of physicians over millennia in both the East and West. Despite this, little is known about him, and scholars have long debated his relationship to the works attributed to him in the so-called *Hippocratic Corpus*, although it is undisputed that many of the works within it represent milestones in the development of Western medicine. In this *Cambridge Companion*, an international team of authors introduces major themes in Hippocratic studies, ranging from textual criticism and the 'Hippocratic Question' to problems such as aetiology, physiology, and nosology. Emphasis is given to the afterlife of Hippocrates from Late Antiquity to the Modern period. Hippocrates had as much relevance in the medieval Islamic world as in the fifth century BC Greek world, and he remains with us today in both medical and non-medical contexts.

PETER E. PORMANN is Professor of Classics and Graeco-Arabic Studies at the University of Manchester. His main research interests are the transmission of Greek medical and scientific knowledge into the Islamic tradition, as well as the engagement over the centuries of Jews, Christians, and Muslims with the classical heritage. His recent publications include *The Arabic Commentaries on the Hippocratic 'Aphorisms'* (*Oriens*, with Kamran I. Karimullah; 2017), *Medical Traditions* (*Intellectual History of the Islamicate World*, with Leigh Chipman and Miri Schefer-Mossensohn; 2017–18) and *Philosophy and Medicine in the Formative Period of Islam* (with Peter Adamson; 2017).

For Dmitri with love in Christ Bishop Seglas Pentecost 2020

Continued at the back of the book

The Cambridge Companion to Hippocrates

Edited by

PETER E. PORMANN
University of Manchester

CAMBRIDGE
UNIVERSITY PRESS

CAMBRIDGE
UNIVERSITY PRESS

University Printing House, Cambridge CB2 8BS, United Kingdom

One Liberty Plaza, 20th Floor, New York, NY 10006, USA

477 Williamstown Road, Port Melbourne, VIC 3207, Australia

314–321, 3rd Floor, Plot 3, Splendor Forum, Jasola District Centre, New Delhi – 110025, India

79 Anson Road, #06–04/06, Singapore 079906

Cambridge University Press is part of the University of Cambridge.

It furthers the University's mission by disseminating knowledge in the pursuit of education, learning, and research at the highest international levels of excellence.

www.cambridge.org
Information on this title: www.cambridge.org/9781107068209
DOI: 10.1017/9781107705784

© Cambridge University Press 2018

First published 2018

Printed in the United States of America by Sheridan Books, Inc.

A catalogue record for this publication is available from the British Library.

Library of Congress Cataloging-in-Publication Data
Names: Pormann, Peter E., editor.
Title: The Cambridge companion to Hippocrates / edited by Peter E. Pormann.
Description: Cambridge, United Kingdom ; New York, NY : Cambridge University Press, 2018. | Includes bibliographical references and index.
Identifiers: LCCN 2018018142 | ISBN 9781107068209 (Hardback) | ISBN 9781107695849 (Paperback)
Subjects: LCSH: Hippocrates. Works. | Hippocrates – Influence. | Medicine, Greek and Roman – History. | Medical literature – Greece – Criticism, Textual.
Classification: LCC R126.H8 C36 2018 | DDC 610.938–dc23
LC record available at https://lccn.loc.gov/2018018142

ISBN 978-1-107-06820-9 Hardback
ISBN 978-1-107-69584-9 Paperback

Contents

Notes on Contributors

Véronique Boudon-Millot is Research Director at the Centre National de la Recherche Scientifique (CNRS) and director of the research group Orient et Méditerranée (CNRS, University of Paris – Sorbonne). Apart from numerous articles and conference proceedings, she has produced four critical editions with French translations of works by Galen for the prestigious series *Collection des Universités de France: Exhortation to the Arts* (2000): *On My Own Books* and *On the Order of My Own Books* (2007), *Avoiding Distress* (2010) and *On Theriac to Piso* (2016).

David Cantor is a historian in the Office of History at the National Institutes of Health, Bethesda, Maryland and teaches at the University of Maryland, College Park. Apart from books and articles on the history of medicine in the twentieth century, such as *Stress, Shock, and Adaptation in the Twentieth Century* (co-edited with Edmund Ramsden; 2014); *Meat, Medicine, and Human Health in the Twentieth Century* (co-edited with Christian Bonah and Matthias Dörries; 2010) and *Cancer in the Twentieth Century* (2008), he edited *Reinventing Hippocrates* (2002). He is the series editor (edited collections) of *Social Histories of Medicine*.

Elizabeth Craik is Honorary Professor at the University of St Andrews. She has published widely on tragedy, social history, and history of medicine in ancient Greece, focussing in particular on Hippocrates and the *Hippocratic Corpus*. She produced critical editions and translations of four Hippocratic treatises, *Places in Man* (1998), *On Sight* and *On Anatomy* (2006), and *On Glands* (2009), and recently published an influential monograph, *The 'Hippocratic' Corpus* (2015).

Lesley Dean-Jones is Associate Professor of Classics at the University of Texas at Austin. She has published on female patients and practitioners in ancient Greece; her books include *Women's Bodies in Classical Greek Science* (1994) and *Ancient Concepts of the Hippocratic: Papers Presented at the XIIIth International Hippocrates Colloquium, Austin, Texas, August 2008* (co-edited with Ralph M. Rosen).

R. J. Hankinson is Professor of Philosophy and Classics at the University of Texas at Austin. He has published numerous articles on many aspects of ancient philosophy and science; his books include *Cause and Explanation in the Ancient Greek World* (1998), *Galen on Antecedent Causes* (1998), *Simplicius: On Aristotle, On the Heavens 1* (2002–6), and the *Cambridge Companion to Galen* (2008).

Brooke Holmes is Robert F. Goheen Professor in the Humanities, Professor of Classics and the director of the Interdisciplinary Doctoral Program in Humanistic Studies at Princeton University. Her publications include *The Symptom and the Subject: The Emergence of the Physical Body in Ancient Greece* (2010), *Gender: Antiquity and Its Legacy* (2012) and *The Frontiers of Ancient Science: Essays in Honor of Heinrich von Staden* (co-edited with Klaus-Dietrich Fischer; 2015).

Jacques Jouanna is Emeritus Professor at the University of Paris – Sorbonne and a member of the Institut de France (Académie des inscriptions et belles-lettres). He founded the Research Group Greek Medicine in Paris and instituted the *Colloque Hippocratique*, a series of international meetings now in its fifteenth iteration. He has received numerous awards for his groundbreaking work, especially in editing Hippocrates (Officier de la Légion d'Honneur, Commandeur de l'Ordre des Palmes académiques and Chevalier des Arts et Lettres). His recent critical editions and translations for the *Collection des Universités de France* include *Prognostic* (with A. Anastassiou and C. Magdelaine; 2013), *Epidemics* 1 and 3 (2016), and *Hippocratic Problems* (with A. Guardasole; 2017). The second edition of his monumental monograph on Hippocrates (*Hippocrate*; 2017) has just appeared.

Karl-Heinz Leven is Professor of Medical History and director of the Institute for the History and Ethics of Medicine at the Friedrich-Alexander University of Erlangen – Nürnberg. He has published widely on both the ancient and modern history of medicine, notably on infectious diseases and Hippocratic ethics and their reception. His works include *Antike Medizin: Ein Lexikon* (A Dictionary of Ancient Medicine; 2005) and *Geschichte der Medizin: Von der Antike bis zur Gegenwart* (History of Medicine from Antiquity to the Modern Age; 2008).

Daniela Manetti is Professor of Classics at the University of Florence. She has published widely on ancient Greek medicine, including the history of medical exegesis and Greek medical papyri. She is co-editor of the series *Corpus dei Papiri Filosofici*. She produced critical editions of the Hippocratic *Epidemics* 6 (with Amneris Roselli; 1982) and the so-called *Anonymous of London, On Medicine* (2011), an introductory treatise on medicine.

Lorenzo Perilli is Professor of Classics at the University of Rome Tor Vergata and the director of the research centre Forms of Knowledge in the Ancient World, specialising in the history of science and medicine. His works include the critical edition of Galen's *Hippocratic Glossary* (2017), an edited Festschrift for two veterans in the field of Hippocratic studies (*Officina Hippocratica: Beiträge zu Ehren von Anargyros Anastassiou und Dieter Irmer*; 2011), an edited volume on the concept of Greek *lógos* (2013), and a collection of fragments of the empiricist physician Menodotus of Nicomedia (2004).

Peter E. Pormann is Professor of Classics and Graeco-Arabic Studies at the University of Manchester. Recent publications include two special double issues: *The Arabic Commentaries on the Hippocratic 'Aphorisms'* (*Oriens*, co-edited with Kamran I. Karimullah; 2017) and *Medical Traditions* (*Intellectual History of the Islamicate*

World, co-edited with Leigh Chipman and Miri Schefer-Mossensohn; 2017–18) and three edited books: *La construction de la médecine arabe médiévale* (with Pauline Koetschet; 2016), *Philosophy and Medicine in the Formative Period of Islam* (with Peter Adamson; 2017), and *1001 Cures: Contributions in Medicine and Healthcare from Muslim Civilisation* (2017).

Amneris Roselli is Professor of Classics at the University of Naples. She has published widely on ancient Greek medicine, especially the Late Antique tradition. She has edited a number of Greek texts, including the Hippocratic *Epidemics* 6 (with Daniela Manetti; 1982), *On the Sacred Disease* (1996), and Aristotle's *On Breath* (1992).

Chiara Thumiger is Wellcome Trust Medical Humanities Fellow at the University of Warwick, working on ancient histories of *phrenîtis*. She has published widely, including on topics at the intersection between literature and history of medicine in the ancient world. Her main publications are *Hidden Paths: Self and Characterization in Greek Tragedy: Euripides' 'Bacchae'* (2007), *Erôs in Ancient Greece* (co-edited with Ed Sanders, Christopher Carey and Nick Lowe; 2013), *Homo Patiens: Approaches to the Patient in the Ancient World* (co-edited with Georgia Petridou; 2015), *A History of the Mind and Mental Health in Classical Greek Mental Thought* (2017), and *Mental Illness in Ancient Medicine: From Celsus to Paul of Aegina* (co-edited with P. Singer; 2018).

Laurence M. V. Totelin is Senior Lecturer in Ancient History at the University of Cardiff. Her work focusses in particular on the history of pharmacology and botany. Her publications include *Hippocratic Recipes: Oral and Written Transmission of Pharmacological Knowledge in Fifth- and Fourth-Century Greece* (2009) and *Ancient Botany* (with Gavin Hardy; 2016).

Mathias Witt is a surgeon, jurist, classicist, and historian of medicine. He is Associate Professor (*Privatdozent*) for History, Ethics, and Theory of Medicine at the medical faculty of the Ludwig-

Maximilian University of Munich. His research focusses on ancient medicine and its afterlife, in particular on ancient surgery. His publications include a collection of fragments of the Hippocratic treatise *Wounds and Missiles* (2009). An edition of Arabic and Greek fragments of the surgical manual by Antyllus, one of the most important surgeons from second century AD Alexandria, is forthcoming.

Preface

Hippocrates, the 'father of medicine', inventor of the famous Hippocratic Oath, from whom and in whom all medicine originated. There can be no doubt that Hippocrates is the most famous physician from antiquity, and possibly of all time. In the five years preceding publication of this book alone, some 300 articles in medical journals have discussed various aspects of Hippocrates, often portrayed as embodying Greek medicine in general. To this day, in ethical debates Hippocrates looms large. On the subject of abortion, for instance, the Oath has been scrutinised to see whether it allowed the practice or not. The judgment by the US Supreme Court in the landmark case *Roe v. Wade* refers to scholarly debates about it. Hippocrates plays his part even in the popular media, with the Oath referenced in various episodes of the US television series *Star Trek*.

Already in his lifetime, Hippocrates appears to have been the most famous physician. For both Plato and Aristotle, he is *the* physician par excellence, and soon after his death, many legends about his life were told and myths forged, which enhanced his quasi-God-like reputation. Hippocrates allegedly refused to cure the king of Persia, but treated Democritus for melancholy. Whether it is in Late Antiquity, the Middle Ages, the Renaissance, or the early modern period, Hippocrates emerged as a model, and the most modern and progressive physicians claimed to be his heirs: one has, for instance, a 'second Hippocrates' in the eleventh-century Arabic writer Ibn Abī Ṣādiq and an 'English Hippocrates' in Thomas Sydenham (1624–89), also seen as the 'father of English medicine'. Hippocrates' appeal also transcends the confines of country and creed. Christians, Jews, and Muslims appropriated him in various ways. His influence in Arabic is arguably greater than in Latin, and his fame reaches all the way to India and China.

Therefore, Hippocrates and the works attributed to him clearly deserve an easy guide to a topic that can appear extremely baffling to the uninitiated. In spring and summer 2012, Michael Sharp, my commissioning editor at Cambridge University Press, discussed with me the possibility of producing such a guide in the form of a *Companion to Hippocrates*, and I was immediately enthusiastic about the idea. I had just moved to Manchester and begun my project on the 'Arabic Commentaries on the Hippocratic *Aphorisms*'; I had time on my hands, and a great desire to provide an easy introduction to a fascinating, yet difficult and recondite topic. I put together a proposal and a team of contributors, and in May 2013, the Syndics approved it. Progress remained good and steady, and all the contributors and I met as a group in September 2014 to discuss pre-circulated papers. The workshop was incredibly fruitful, and on the fringes, we also planned the fifteenth *Colloque Hippocratique*. A year later, during the Hippocratic Colloquium, we came again together in Manchester, although quite a few of the authors had not yet produced their final version, and my dream to have the *Companion* ready for this meeting was squashed. As always is the case, some authors took longer than others, but I am glad to have handed over the manuscript just as my *Aphorisms* project draws to a close at the end of July 2017.

A project of this nature would not have been possible without the generous support of many different individuals and institutions. First and foremost, I would like to thank the contributors for their willingness to embark on this journey and their readiness to put up with my editorial interference; in one case I had to cut a chapter to a third of its length. My team in Manchester also deserves my profound gratitude, especially my administrators Drs Steven Spiegl, Michelle Magin, and Melissa Markauskas, all of whom helped compile and edit the chapters in the various iterations. Michelle in particular helped organise the workshop and colloquium and Melissa compiled the appendix and bibliography. Other team members such as Drs Nicola Carpentieri, Kamran Karimullah, Hammood Obaid, and Elaine van Dalen all helped in various ways. Moreover, I am grateful to

Professors Manfred Horstmannshof, Helen King, Vivian Nutton, and Philip J. van der Eijk for their advice in the initial phase of the project. Institutional support came in many guises. First and foremost, I would like to thank the European Research Council, who made this endeavour possible. The British Academy and the Leverhulme Trust also provided a small grant in connection with the *Colloque Hippocratique*, which allowed us to discuss our work-in-progress further. Finally the University of Manchester, our School of Arts, Languages, and Cultures, and my own Department of Classics and Ancient History have provided an extremely congenial environment in which to compile, write, and edit this *Companion*, and, to name but two for many, my current Head of Division, Professor David Langslow, and my current Head of School, Professor Alessandro Schiesaro, have lent many a helping hand and facilitated things that would probably have been impossible elsewhere. My gratitude also goes out to my commissioning editor at Cambridge University Press, Dr Michael Sharp, without whom this project would never have seen the light and whose flexibility, forbearance, and intellectual involvement helped it come to fruition; and to my copy editor, Ms Theresa Kornak, for her professionalism and meticulous attention to detail. Dr Hammood Obaid compiled the index with great care and also corrected many an error.

Finally, I would like to thank my wife, Dr Nil Özlem Palabıyık, for her forbearance and help with many aspects of this book. Shortly after I delivered it to the Press, she delivered our first daughter, Julia Helena.

Notes on Citations

Classicists value precision and love Latin abbreviations. There are few fields in the humanities in which scholars have established a comprehensive system that allows them to refer not just to the pages of a text in a certain edition, but also to the line of that text in numerous editions. Classicists have achieved this: they can refer to each line of Homer and Hesiod, Plato and Aristotle, Hippocrates and Galen, and the fragments of Presocratic philosophers. This in itself is great, and I am going to explain in a moment how this is achieved. Likewise, classicists have created well-established abbreviations, so that most would readily understand that 'A. *A.* 689' (first 'A.' in Roman font, second in italics) refers to line 689 in Aeschylus' *Agamemnon*; or 'Hp. *VM*'' refers to the treatise *On Ancient Medicine* attributed to Hippocrates. 'Why *VM*?,' you might ask. The answer is simple: from the Renaissance onwards, a tendency to refer to Greek works by their Latin titles developed. *VM* stands for *De Vetere Medicina* ('On Ancient Medicine'), just as 'Gal. *QAM*'' stands for Galen's treatise *The Capacities of the Soul Depend on the Mixtures of the Body*, called *Quod Animi Mores corporis temperamenta sequantur* in Latin. In the last title, the Latin word *mores* ('manners'; 'character') is a particularly misleading translation of the Greek *dynámeis* ('capacities') and goes back to the Middle Ages.

How do these references work? Let me explain by looking at the five examples that are most relevant to this *Companion*. For Plato, Aristotle, Hippocrates, and Galen, there are standard editions. Plato's *Complete Works* were printed in Geneva in three volumes by Henri Estienne, Latinised as Henricus Stephanus, in 1578. Each page has two columns, a Latin and a Greek one, and in the space between the two columns there are four to five letters (A–E) that further divide the text. Therefore, the reference 'Pl. *R.* 617e4–5' refers to Plato's *Republic*,

p. 617, 4–5 lines down from the marker 'E' in the Stephanus edition, Volume Two (the volume is not given, but the title tells us where to look). Most scholars will not consult the Stephanus edition, but a modern one such as that by S. R. Slings in the *Oxford Classical Texts* series, which has the Stephanus pagination in the margins. Likewise, for Aristotle, the standard edition was produced under the auspices of the Prussian Academy by August Immanuel Bekker (1785–1871). It appeared between 1831 and 1870 in five volumes; the first two volumes contain the Greek text and have a continuous pagination, with each page comprising two columns, a and b. So, 'Arist. 980a21' refers to page 980, first column, line 21 (which happens to be in Volume Two). For Presocratic philosophers, the standard edition is by Diels and Kranz, two German scholars. Hermann Alexander Diels published the first edition (with German translation) in 1903, then Walther Kranz further improved text and translation with new additions until the fifth edition (1934–7) and a sixth was published after both editors' deaths in 1952. They divide the fragments into a (accounts), b (verbatim quotations), and c (imitations), and each philosopher has a number. Therefore, DK24B3 refers to author number 24, Alcmaeon, and there the third verbatim quotation.

Throughout this *Companion*, there are occasional references to Plato, Aristotle, and the Presocratics, yet Hippocrates and Galen figure much more prominently. The standard Hippocratic edition is that by Émile Littré (1839–61) in ten volumes; it is often just abbreviated as 'L.', and here, we shall use the following two formats: '2.636 L.' refers to Volume 2, p. 636 and '2.636.1–2 L.' to Volume 2, p. 636, lines 1–2. For Galen, the bilingual Greek-Latin printing in twenty-two volumes by Karl Gottlob Kühn (1819–33) remains standard; it is abbreviated as 'K.'. So, '1.64 K.' refers to Volume 1, p. 64 of Kühn's edition, and '1.64.1–2 K.' to Volume 1, p. 64, lines 1–2.

Precision and concision are often achieved at the expense of clarity and easiness. Although Stephanus and Bekker references are quite standard in most modern editions and translations, and are often indicated in the margins, the same cannot be said for references to

Littré or Kühn. The older Loeb editions (with English translations), for instance, do not have Littré page numbers; nor does, for instance, the English translation of Galen's *On the Sects for Beginners* by Michael Frede (1985: 3–20) have Kühn numbers. Therefore, to identify a Littré or Kühn reference, one has to go to the Greek text and then find the corresponding translation, which is not so easy without knowledge of Greek.

Another way of referring to classical texts in general and the *Hippocratic Corpus* in particular is to give titles, books and chapter numbers. Some texts in the *Corpus* are short and comprise only one book, such as *Art*; others have more than one, such as the *Aphorisms* and *Epidemics* (both in seven books). Therefore, *Art* 1 refers to chapter one of *Art*, whereas *Epidemics* 6 or *Aphorisms* 5 refers to the sixth book of the *Epidemics* or fifth book of the *Aphorisms*; in different Hippocratic texts, there are further subdivisions. Therefore, the famous phrase 'to help, or at least to do no harm' occurs in *Epidemics* 1.11 (*Epidemics*, book one, chapter eleven in the Loeb edition), corresponding to 2.634.8–636.1 L. (Volume 2, p. 634, line 8 to p. 636, line 1 in Litre's edition), to ed. Smith (1923) 164 (the Loeb edition with facing English translation), and Jouanna (2016), 18, line 1 (Jouanna's latest critical edition with facing French translation). In other words, there are many ways of referring to the same passage in Greek, and this looks more complicated than it is. In practice, we have favoured book and chapter references here, as well as references to the Loeb translations, now also available online.[1] Sometimes, however, the individual authors felt that further references, either to Littré as the standard edition or to the latest and most authoritative critical edition, were needed.

Moreover, to make the book even more user-friendly, I have included an appendix with all the Hippocratic works, their titles in English and Latin (full and abbreviated forms), as well as English translations. There are two very helpful lists of Hippocratic and Galen

---

[1] www.loebclassics.com (accessed 26 July 2017).

works, respectively, originally compiled by the late and lamented Gerhard Fichtner, and now updated by the Corpus Medicorum Graecorum (Fichtner 2016, 2017); they are available also from their websites.[2] If an uninitiated reader comes across recondite abbreviations in the notes, then these Fichtner lists will help, and anyone who wants to engage with the more detailed scholarship on Hippocrates and the *Hippocratic Corpus* will need to learn this scholarly apparatus in any case.

[2]   http://cmg.bbaw.de/online-publications/hippokrates-und-galenbibliographie-fichtner (accessed 26 July 2017).

1 Introduction

Peter E. Pormann

Hippocrates remains a figure shrouded in mystery. We have next to no indubitable facts about his life. Although a large number of texts attributed to Hippocrates have come down to us, we cannot be certain that any one of them was written by the historical Hippocrates. One of the most eminent historians of medicine, Philip J. van der Eijk, has recently argued that we should abandon the moniker 'Hippocratic' and simply talk about early Greek medicine, as the so-called *Hippocratic Corpus* is so diverse and contains writings from the fifth century BC to the first and second century AD. Not everybody, of course, would agree with this view, yet it shows that Hippocrates remains a hot topic of debate, which attracts an ever growing amount of scholarship.

Hippocratic studies have grown enormously since the late nineteenth century. In the early twentieth century, there was a clear focus on editing texts according to the latest philological methods. The great editorial project *Corpus Medicorum Graecorum* began in 1904 with the publication of a manuscript catalogue by Hermann Diels (1904–5). One of the questions that scholars hotly debated since antiquity is the so-called Hippocratic Question: what texts in the *Hippocratic Corpus* were written by the historical Hippocrates? Already in the nineteenth century there emerged a view that one can divide the treatises of the *Hippocratic Corpus* into Coan and Cnidian, the former more rational or characterised by prognostic, the latter more empiric and diagnostic. In the second half of the twentieth century, a number of scholars tried to discern certain Coan and Cnidian layers within individual treatises, notably by paying close attention to language and style.

The great French editor of Hippocrates, Émile Littré (1801–81), placed the treatise *On Ancient Medicine* at the beginning of his

Complete Works, arguing that it exemplified the outlook of the true Hippocrates: an aversion to theorisation and an emphasis on practical experience and own observation. This was a strange reversal of fortune, as Galen of Pergamum (ca. 129–216), the greatest and most influential commentator on Hippocrates, had dismissed this text as spurious. Nowadays, few scholars would say that they can confidently identify even a single treatise in the *Hippocratic Corpus* that was undoubtedly written by the historical Hippocrates. Nor do they still uphold the distinction into Coan and Cnidian treatises. Yet, an eminent Harvard historian of Greek science and medicine, Mark Schiefsky (2005), argued that *On Ancient Medicine* is our best bet, if we want to find a truly Hippocratic text, just as Littré did more than a century and a half later.

The richness and growth of Hippocratic studies can perhaps best be illustrated with a short overview of a conference series, called *Colloque Hippocratique* or *Hippocratic Colloquium* that began in 1972 in Strasburg and has since taken place every three to four years. From their inception, these were truly international and interdisciplinary meetings, with scholars coming from different countries and traditions.[1] The first meetings still focussed on the *Hippocratic Corpus* and its place in medical history or Hippocratic medicine more generally.[2] Soon, however, special topics emerged such as the history of ideas,[3] the Hippocratic *Epidemics*,[4] nosology,[5] philosophy,[6] therapy,[7] and the normal and pathological.[8] The first decade of the new millennium witnessed three colloquia with a greater English-speaking presence, focussing on the context of the *Hippocratic Corpus*,[9] medical education,[10] and the idea of the Hippocratic.[11] In 2012, the Colloque Hippocratique returned from Texas to Paris,

---

[1]   See Jouanna and Zink (2014), i–iii, who reviews the history of these encounters.

[2]   Université des sciences humaines de Strasbourg (1975); Joly (1977); Grmek and Robert (1980); López Férez (1992).

[3]   Lasserre and Mudry (1983).   [4]   Baader and Winau (1989).

[5]   Potter, Maloney, and Desautels (1990).   [6]   Wittern and Pellegrin (1996).

[7]   Garofalo (1999).   [8]   Thivel and Zucker (2002).   [9]   van der Eijk (2005b).

[10]   Horstmanshoff (2010).   [11]   Dean-Jones and Rosen (2016).

France[12] and in 2015 was held in Manchester, England, exploring the commentary tradition, both East and West.[13] The next meeting will take place in Rome on 25–27 October 2018 and is organised by three of our authors, Lorenzo Perilli, Daniela Manetti, and Amneris Roselli, as well as two other scholars.

In Hippocratic scholarship in general, we can see a movement towards greater awareness of and concern with the social setting in which it took place. Concepts such as the medical marketplace in which practitioners of various types competed became more prominent, as did the place of women. Over the last thirty years or so, one can also note a greater interest of historians of philosophy in the *Hippocratic Corpus*. Of course, the overlap between so-called Pre-Socratic (or perhaps better, Early Greek) philosophy and Hippocratic thought had been known for a long time, yet more and more proper philosophers are paying close attention to Hippocratic writings, just as they do to medicine more generally. Three areas that have proved particularly fertile are epistemology (how to know whether treatments work); the anatomy of the body (how the different parts function); and the body–mind interface, for instance, how the body influences the mind, how mental illnesses come about, and how physiological processes such as mixtures interact with psychological ones such as moods.

The aim of the present *Cambridge Companion* is to provide the uninitiated reader with a first overview of the rich topic that is Hippocrates and the *Hippocratic Corpus*; and to provide easy and multiple ways into it. The 'Hippocratic Corpus' and Hippocrates are not mere synonyms, as we have already seen, and they exist in a creative tension that is felt throughout this volume. The *Corpus* encompasses many different and often widely divergent treatises that tell us a lot about early Greek medicine. Many of the chapters included here explore their plurality, but also the common features that one can find among them. Likewise, the powerful attraction that

---

[12]   Jouanna and Zink (2014).   [13]   Pormann (in press).

the figure of Hippocrates exerted over generations and generations of patients and practitioners also deserves full scrutiny. Hippocrates was constructed and reconstructed across time and space in myriad ways. This lavish legacy often surpassed the historical and textual record. Hippocrates became a symbol, a token for the ideal physician, who already in a Greek (often mythical) past prefigured contemporaneous best practice. For this reason, in temporary terms, this *Cambridge Companion* pays a great deal of attention to what one could call the afterlife of Hippocrates, beginning in Hellenistic times and continuing nearly until today.

Both Hippocrates and the *Hippocratic Corpus* are multifaceted; similarly, the approach taken here is equally diverse. The different authors all tackle the topics from their particular viewpoint, which are often diverse. The first two chapters, both written by extremely eminent scholars from different traditions, already illustrate this; generally speaking, I have not tried to impose doctrinal unity or impose one interpretation. The different approaches can stand next to each other. Likewise, the authors of the chapters come from different countries and traditions, and are at different points of their academic career. There sometimes is, or at least is perceived to be, a substantial divide between 'continental' and 'Anglo-Saxon' scholarship, the former more focussed, for instance, on philology and the latter on social history and critical theory. This difference in approach can nicely be discerned, for instance, in the two chapters on 'aetiology' by Jim Hankinson and 'epistemologies' by Lorenzo Perilli: whereas the former is clearly indebted to a more analytical tradition, the latter sometimes waxes lyrical in its metonymies and metaphors in the style of continental philosophy.

This *Cambridge Companion* is written in English, the lingua franca of modern science and scholarship, and encroaching more and more even in the field of the humanities. Yet, there can be no doubt that anyone who wants to delve deeply into scholarly debates and make his or her own original contribution needs to read French, German, and Italian; possess excellent knowledge of Greek and

Latin; and ideally also master some of what our continental colleagues call the 'Oriental' languages (e.g., Arabic, Hebrew, Syriac). This, in a way, was one of the challenges in editing this *Companion*: to make what is often very recondite scholarship in languages other than English accessible to the general reader without any previous knowledge – linguistic or otherwise. To this end, four chapters included here were translated, from French (Jouanna, Boudon-Millot), German (Leven), and Italian (Perilli). In the case of the chapter on the textual history, I myself abridged and simplified a much longer contribution (now published as Jouanna 2017), and translated it into English. I am personally particularly pleased that I was able to include this chapter, as it is the first time in a *Cambridge Companion* that textual history and criticism, and the branch of philology concerned with producing critical editions – what the French call 'ecdotique' – is fully explained and explored in a separate chapter.

Most specialists refer to Hippocratic works by their Latin titles and abbreviations, which, in a way, is strange, as they were written in Greek and have titles in Greek. Here, however, we have used English titles throughout. For ease of use, however, the appendix lists all treatises in the *Hippocratic Corpus* according to their English titles together with their standard Latin ones in full and abbreviated format. Therefore, those who want to venture further can easily understand the somewhat recondite nomenclature used in specialist scholarship.

Elizabeth Craik opens the volume with an overview chapter of both what we know (or rather, do not know) about the historical Hippocrates and about the structure and content of the *Hippocratic Corpus*, or, as she prefers to call it, the *Hippocratic Collection*. Craik begins by reviewing briefly the information about Hippocrates, and argues that although many later sources are clearly apocryphal, we should perhaps pay greater attention to them. Internal evidence from the *Hippocratic Collection* for Hippocrates' life is virtually nonexistent; however, one can glean some information about the authors of individual treatises such as *Epidemics* from their content.

The difficulty, however, remains, that one cannot be sure who this author was – whether the historical Hippocrates or someone else.

Craik then surveys the *Hippocratic Collection* and emphasises its diverse nature in terms of themes, styles, and date of composition. She discusses various methods of classifying the texts: Littré, for instance, had eleven categories; some scholars distinguished between Coan and Cnidian works; others used subject matters. Yet, ultimately all these systems are flawed, and modern scholarship has largely abandoned them. Despite these caveats, it is possible to group certain texts together and show that they were probably written by the same person, or at least come from the same milieu. She also cautions us against following previous fads and favouring some treatises over others: the Oath, for instance, is so unique in its impact that it has wrongly removed other ethical (or 'deontological') treatises from people's attention.

Despite all the diversity within the *Hippocratic Corpus* and all the difficulties to discern the historical Hippocrates from among a mass of later legends and stories, Craik pleads against the idea of abandoning the notion of Hippocrates. The long tradition clearly saw a unifying principle that somehow binds the various texts together; and these texts cannot be separated from the historical Hippocrates, who, in a way, marks the beginning of the Hippocratic tradition. She sees the present *Cambridge Companion to Hippocrates* as evidence for this assessment.

Any study of the *Hippocratic Corpus* needs to be based on a sound understanding of the texts within it. One can come to such an understanding, however, only through an awareness of how the texts were transmitted. Why do we read the Greek texts as printed in our modern editions; how did the editors arrive at their choices when deciding between variant readings; and how did the texts survive over a period of more than 2,500 years? Jacques Jouanna provides answers to these questions by approaching the textual history of the *Hippocratic Corpus* in a twofold way. He first tells the story of the Hippocratic text from the earliest time, the late fifth century BC until the Middle Ages and the Renaissance. He shows what we know, but also hints at the great loss of information that characterises so much of classical Greek culture. Both Plato and Aristotle mention Hippocrates, but then for the next 300 years, we have only the most limited information about the transmission of the *Hippocratic Corpus*. Yet, we can learn about the first Alexandrian editions and the many commentaries, which are so crucial to textual scholarship.

Jouanna also recounts how the editions of our time are the product of a long tradition, beginning with the Renaissance printings in the early sixteenth century. The most accepted Greek text resulted from the first editions by the Aldine Press, and later editors often followed their text, even when they had access to better manuscripts with superior readings. As it happened, this was also the case for the great French editor of Hippocrates, Émile Littré, whose edition and French translation of the *Complete Works of Hippocrates* (1839–61) remains the standard reference. It is only with the development of textual criticism and stemmatics in the late nineteenth century that things changed. A science emerged that endeavoured to understand how the different manuscripts related to each other, in order to reconstruct the earliest form of the text, the so-called archetype. To do so, it is important to distinguish between the direct tradition – the Greek manuscripts and papyri containing works by Hippocrates – and the indirect tradition, consisting of the many quotations in commentaries, glossaries, and other works. The last century and a half then saw many critical editions, often the result of large-scale projects and international collaborations.

Brooke Holmes then takes us into debates about the Hippocratic body. Taking her cue from discussion in contemporary debates in critical theory, she shows that the concepts of the body in general, and in the *Hippocratic Corpus* in particular, are constructed. There is not just the body as an objective reality that is described in its complexities; rather, we conceptualise the body through our own assumptions, be they cultural, societal, sexual, personal, or otherwise. Holmes then traces ideas about the body (Greek *sôma*) from Homer to the *Hippocratic Corpus*, and then looks at how the different Hippocratic writers conceptualise it as a space that can be mapped and as a dynamic entity that fulfils various functions.

The inside of the human body was largely hidden from Hippocratic authors. They conceived of it in terms of receptacles such as the bladder and vessels, which carried the various bodily matters, including the humours, from one receptacle to another. The texture of the bodily parts also played an important role: some are spongy and porous, others hard and dense. These attributes were also used to distinguish between men and women, the latter having looser and more porous flesh.

The humours such as phlegm or bile occupy a prominent place in many Hippocratic treatises; when one prevails, this may lead to certain character traits and bodily disorders: phlegm, for instance, can cause epilepsy. Various powers (or 'faculties', Greek *dynámeis*) also play an important part: different organs possess different powers contributing to the overall function of the body as a whole. Some powers counter others, and the body becomes the arena of conflict between competing elements, both internal and external. Digestion is a case in point: the innate heat concocts the food, a necessary phenomenon, that, when it goes wrong, can again lead to disease. Therefore, one needs to take care of the body in its complexity to maintain health (and life itself).

In his chapter on 'aetiology', Jim Hankinson discusses views about the causal origins of disease (and by extension of conditions of health), and causal theory more generally construed. He shows the many competing and often conflicting accounts of how disease comes about that we find in the *Hippocratic Corpus*, which itself, as we have seen, contains texts composed over a period of several centuries and written from a variety of different, and at times incompatible, theoretical standpoints. He focuses on the treatises dating to the fifth and fourth centuries BC, especially those concerned with theoretical debates, such as *Epidemics; Prognostic; Ancient Medicine; Art; Nature of Man; Regimen; Sacred Disease; Breaths; Airs, Waters,*

Places; Affections; Diseases; and *Places in Man.* These treatises differ very widely from one another in their understandings of the origins of diseased conditions and the type of theoretical entity any responsible aetiology needs to posit. Despite their differences, however, these texts share a general commitment, notably a belief in the physical causality of disease and a corresponding rejection of any appeal to divine intervention, at least in specific cases. Hankinson discusses the various methods by which the different theorists seek to commend their own particular views, in particular in regard to their relations with empirical evidence and confirmation. He does so by frequently letting the texts speak for themselves, thus providing a wonderful flavour of the debates that raged in the medical circles of classical Greece.

Aetiology is closely linked to the topic of the next chapter, epistemology: after all, the theory of causation, aetiology, also involves knowing the causes, something that falls within the compass of the theory of knowledge, epistemology. Yet, Perilli, who tackles the latter topic, approaches it quite differently from Hankinson. Perilli begins his discussion with the key episode from the *Iliad* around the wrath of Achilles, the greatest Greek hero: he is angry with Agamemnon, who leads the expedition against Troy, and is minded to withdraw from combat and return home. Achilles says about Agamemnon that he 'does not know how to look/think/understand (*noêsai*) before and after'. This ability to classify events in order to learn from the past to predict and influence the future is what Perilli calls 'Achilles' paradigm'. He argues that although the medical writings of the *Hippocratic Corpus* are manifold and diverse, we find here for the first time a critical self-reflection about one's own methods, a realisation, so to speak, of Achilles' paradigm. The intellect (Greek *noûs*) creates knowledge (*epistémē*), and this is a crucial part of the medical art (*téchnē*). Yet, equally important is the practical knowledge, the 'astute intelligence' (*mêtis*) that is a key attribute of the eponymous hero of the other Homeric epic, Odysseus. Whereas Achilles exemplifies the virtuous hero able to know the past, act in the present, and be aware of future consequences, Odysseus, the anti-hero, uses his many wiles (*polýmētis*) to his advantage. Hippocratic medicine, Perilli concludes, encompasses both: knowledge (*epistémē*) and practical intelligence (*mêtis*).

He arrives at this conclusion after a rollercoaster ride through the epistemological aspects of the *Hippocratic Corpus*. At the origin of medical knowledge stands observation: the physician sees the signs of health and disease, and records them faithfully. The next step is to classify the data, to arrange it, in order to make sense of it. This then allows one to identify diseases ('diagnosis') and to foretell their course ('prognosis'). Moreover, treatments are developed on the basis of these classifications. The Hippocratic physician records not only positive cases, but also negative ones; the error and the awareness about it is crucial to the progress of medical knowledge. Perilli also emphasises the fact that many Hippocratic texts such as *Sacred Disease* make a clear distinction between natural and supernatural agency, and reject the latter as an explanation for health and disease. This said, other texts remain in the previous paradigm and employ magical remedies.

Like epistemology, ethics is a topic that generally comes under the heading of philosophy. In the next chapter, Karl-Heinz Leven explores the ethical aspects of Hippocratic medicine. Of course, the most famous ethical text within the *Corpus* is the Oath. It is the most famous medical text from antiquity, and casts an enormous shadow. And yet, as Leven argues, it only became famous from the first century AD onward, and is, in many ways, at odds with other treatises in the *Corpus*. Therefore, it is unlikely that it dated back to Hippocrates' lifetime, nor does it reflect the medical ethics of the fifth and fourth centuries BC. For this reason, Leven begins by considering the question of medical ethics from a different vantage point. He first gives an overview of the other treatises on medical deontology within the *Corpus*, namely *Law, Art, Physician, Decorum* and *Precepts*; many of these texts, too, are of a rather late date, and therefore not a reliable guide to the situation in classical times. It is therefore necessary to consult other treatises in the *Hippocratic Corpus* as well as other texts from the fifth and fourth centuries BC.

By combining these different sources, Leven highlights the main topics of medical ethics in Hippocratic medicine. The injunction 'to help and not to harm' occupies a prominent position, as does the concern to preserve one's own reputation and that of the medical art more generally. For instance, the ability to predict the course of a disease allows the physician not to take on desperate cases that would end in failure, although the *Epidemics* contain quite a few notes on cases that did result in the death of the patient. Leven also cautions us against reading modern concerns into the texts from the past. For instance, the debate about when to discontinue life support did not play any role in Graeco-Roman times, as medicine was much more limited in its abilities.

In the last part of his chapter, however, Leven discusses the Oath and the debates surrounding it in some detail, as no discussion of Hippocratic ethics could overlook this highly influential text. It is both mysterious and imbued with religion, and therefore contrasts sharply with the secular tendencies that we find throughout the *Hippocratic Corpus*. Leven dismisses Ludwig Edelstein's idea that the Oath originated in a Pythagorean milieu, and ponders the problem of why surgery is forbidden, although it featured within the *Corpus*. Likewise, the injunctions not to provide lethal or abortive drugs remain puzzling, especially because we find recipes for the latter in certain gynaecological works. Ultimately, the Oath is an oddity within the *Corpus*, and a text that came to exemplify medical ethics only from the Renaissance onwards. We should therefore not use it as a guide to this topic in classical times.

The next two chapters deal with the question of what a disease is and how to treat it. In her chapter, Amneris Roselli begins by pointing out that the term 'nosology' (like so many others such as 'aetiology' or 'epistemology') is derived from Classical Greek, but is actually a modern invention. Yet, although the Hippocratics had no word for 'nosology', they certainly discussed the nature of diseases and how to classify them. Within the *Hippocratic Corpus* we find a group of what one could call 'nosological' texts, the most important being *Diseases 1–4; Regimen in Acute Diseases,* and *Affections,* the last composed with a lay audience in mind.

Roselli begins by explaining the different ways in which the Hippocratics classified disease. The place where an illness occurred offered a prime criterion (already used in Mesopotamian medicine), and we find an arrangement of diseases from 'tip to toe', that is, from the top (the head) to the bottom of the human body. The division of diseases into acute and chronic largely postdates the *Hippocratic Corpus,* although there are clearly a number of works specifically dealing with acute diseases. Another opposition is that of common versus specific to a certain location, such as so-called 'epidemic' diseases.

Roselli then discusses the nature of the nosological treatises, and shows in particular how they were composed and what material they share. Then she lists the elements of which the description of each disease is generally composed (although not all are always present); they are the name, symptoms, aetiology, treatment, and prognosis. She then ponders the problem of two opposing tendencies: to differentiate and to find common features. Apparently the lost *Cnidian Sentences* contained a proliferation of closed lists of diseases according to certain categories; 'closed lists' here refers to a list with a specific number, such as 'seven diseases of the bile' and so on. Yet the author of *Regimen in Acute Diseases* rebukes this proliferation. Finally, Roselli closes with a reflection on the relationship between Mesopotamian and Hippocratic nosology. Although there are some common elements (such as the arrangements of diseases 'from tip to toe'), Greek texts are generally freer and more innovative, whereas the Mesopotamian material is more controlled and conservative.

The treatment of diseases is the topic of the next chapter by Laurence Totelin, or rather, the treatment of diseases through medicinal substances and diet, as opposed to surgery, which is discussed in the following chapter. Totelin begins with a long quotation from

Disease of Women 2 that illustrates the great variety of therapeutic options, ranging from drugs to diet, and includes fumigation. This example also illustrates that the division of therapy into drugs (*phármaka*) and regimen (*díaita*) is often blurred in the *Hippocratic Corpus*.

In the *Corpus*, we do not have any work specifically dedicated to pharmacology, although it is clear that in the fifth and fourth centuries, pharmacological writings, or at least drug files, did exist. The treatises with the most practical drug recipes in the *Corpus* are the various gynaecological treatises, such as that quoted at the beginning of the chapter. *Regimen* and *Nutriment* offer advice on diet as a means of treating diseases. Further, unsurprisingly, the nosological treatises already also discuss therapy, as we have seen.

Totelin then argues that rather than distinguishing drugs as internal and external, it is more appropriate to classify them by their entry point into the body. The mouth is obviously the most important orifice, but the skin, nose, anus, and vagina also all play their parts. Drugs had a huge variety of different effects, and these effects were later used to classify them. The most important drug actions related to the four primary (or cardinal) qualities of drying or moistening and warming or cooling. In general, the principle of 'opposites cure opposites' – known in Latin as '*contraria contrariis curantur*' from the Greek 'τὰ ἐναντία τῶν ἐναντίων ἐστὶν ἰήματα' and nowadays called 'allopathy' – dominated the Hippocratics' therapeutical thinking.

Physicians and other medical practitioners operated in a competitive medical marketplace and often argued about the best (or even just the right) treatment. We can trace these debates through a variety of Hippocratic texts, such as *Sacred Disease*, which inveighs against charlatans and faith healers. Importantly, the boundaries between folk remedies and the learned remedies of the Hippocratic doctors are not always so clear cut. In fact, Totelin concludes that the latter undoubtedly often drew on the former, not, of course, without modifying them and integrating them into their own medical system.

In this way, Hippocratic therapeutics were not stagnant or conservative, but an interesting locus of innovation and change.

Hippocratic surgery has been a somewhat neglected topic over the last 100 years, and was perceived as rather basic. In his chapter on the topic, Mathias Witt, a clinically trained surgeon himself, rectifies this perception. He does so by drawing not just on the surgical treatises in the *Hippocratic Corpus*, but also on the rich later tradition from the first century AD onwards, which preserves many important fragments of Hippocratic material. He argues that one can use modern criteria and divide Hippocratic surgery and the treatises contained in the *Corpus* into trauma and non-trauma surgery. Trauma surgery is well represented in the *Corpus*, with works dealing both with bones, notably the setting of dislocated bones, and soft tissue injuries. Yet non-trauma or elective surgery is represented only by *Haemorrhoids* and *Fistulas*, two rather short works. This has led some scholars to link lack of non-trauma surgery in the *Corpus* to a reluctance to cut in non-emergency cases.

Witt argues, however, that the many fragments from the otherwise lost treatise *Wounds and Missiles* demonstrate that non-trauma surgery was part and parcel of Hippocratic practice. He concedes that the principle 'to do no harm' was of paramount importance, to protect not just the patient, but also the reputation of the practitioner. This said, in the fifth and fourth centuries, there was a body of Hippocratic treatises – or possibly one large work possibly representing a file of various materials – that as a whole encompasses all areas of surgery performed in antiquity. It is only through the vagaries of transmission that non-trauma surgery is rather poorly represented. Witt also discusses the injunction in the Hippocratic Oath not to cut stones, arguing that it should be seen in the light of the principle of doing no harm and preserving the reputation of the physician. Yet, there were no specialist barber surgeons as in the Middle Ages, and most Hippocratic physicians will also have performed some surgery.

Throughout his chapter, Witt provides examples of surgical procedures, which remain rather basic by modern standards. Given that there was no anaesthesia or asepsis, deep or invasive surgery was not attempted. The area of bone surgery, for instance, focussed on setting dislocated bones, and some of the procedures described in the *Corpus* still continue to be used today and are even called Hippocratic. He closes the chapter with a brief discussion of gynaecological surgery, focussing on obstetrics and operations on the female genitals, which, again, remained rather basic.

Lesley Dean-Jones then looks at the topic of women in Hippocratic medicine more generally. A main topic of contention is whether *in general* women need different treatments from men. In other words, the question is whether apart from childbirth, menstruation, and purely female conditions sex played a role for the Hippocratic doctor. Within the *Corpus*, there are a number of treatises devoted specifically to gynaecology and obstetrics, such as the various works contained in *Diseases of Women* 1–4, *Sterility*, *Nature of Women*, and *Generation* and *Nature of the Child*. Yet, the *Corpus* also includes many case histories, especially in the *Epidemics*, and roughly a third of them have female patients.

In the gynaecological treatises, the treatments often have a popular or folk element to them, and not a few form part of what the Germans call '*Dreckapotheke*'—a pharmacology that relies heavily on waste products of various sorts, including excrements and urine. Smell in particular was a potent remedy, created both through fumigations and in various pessaries, inserted, for instance, into the vagina. Hippocratic doctors apparently dealt only with problematic births, and one would assume that midwives routinely delivered babies. Male physicians undoubtedly drew on the knowledge of such midwives and other female practitioners and patients, the latter describing their own experiences which men cannot share.

The Hippocratics, like many other contemporaneous Greek thinkers, saw strong differences in male and female physiology. Women were thought to be softer and moister. Menstrual blood is necessary for childbearing. Yet, when the blood is not used for procreation, then the excessive blood needs to be expelled through regular periods. When menses are retained, however, the excess of blood in the body has a detrimental effect. Therefore, young girls are encouraged to marry (and by implication engage in sexual intercourse with their husbands) and to have children, in order to counteract any excess blood and its harmful consequences. Although there is only limited evidence, it would appear that male physicians diagnosed and treated women differently from men. How exactly they related to their female patients is unclear, but in certain situations, they must have transgressed the normal boundaries of shame that existed in Greek society, where most women were secluded from men.

The relationship between patient and physician is addressed extensively in the next chapter by Chiara Thumiger. She begins by reviewing the sources and what they can tell us about this relation. The most important one is undoubtedly the *Epidemics*, a composite text with three main parts: Books 1 and 3 contain the most rhetorically elaborated case histories; Books 2, 4, and 6 are characterised by widely divergent material ranging from scattered notes to coherent accounts; and Books 5 and 7 include numerous long narratives. These case notes, to be sure, are written by doctors and reflect their perspective, but they give us numerous insights into the patients' perspectives as well; at times, we can even discern the patients' voices across the clinical accounts.

From the *Epidemics* and other Hippocratic treatises, a complex picture emerges. In the fifth and fourth centuries, physicians were mostly itinerant, and therefore did not have lifelong relationships with their patients, even if we find many cases where doctors follow patients over extended periods of time and seem to have known them well. During the consultation, physicians used their own perception of the patients to predict their current condition and its future path. Yet, they also questioned them to take their medical history, and the subjective experience of patients shows through a number of clinical accounts.

Scholars have long argued that Hippocratic medicine appears to be centred on physicians who seem to have little regard for, and empathy with, their patients. Repeatedly, texts in the *Corpus* emphasise the need of the patient to defer to the physician; and the case histories can appear detached and devoid of compassion. Yet, Thumiger offers another reading of these clinical accounts that allows us to see how patients shared their experiences, including their fears and anxieties with their doctors, thus suggesting a more nuanced picture of the doctor–patient relationship in Hippocratic times.

The final four chapters deal with the reception of Hippocrates and the Hippocratic Corpus in later times, beginning with Véronique Boudon-Millot's chapter on his most important exegete, Galen of Pergamum (ca. 129–216 AD). Galen lived in a highly competitive age when different medical schools vied for the attention of patrons and patients. These rival schools used Hippocrates to advance their own agenda, and therefore, interpreting Hippocrates in the light of one's own medical doctrine proved particularly important. Galen began to write commentaries on Hippocrates first for private consumption, for himself and a small coterie of friends and colleagues, but later composed them for publication. In this he was animated by the same desire to shape Hippocrates in his own image and to refute rival interpretations. Galen wrote not only commentaries, but also other works devoted to different aspects of Hippocrates' works, such as *On the Elements according to Hippocrates*, an introductory work, or *On the Doctrines of Hippocrates and Plato*, a massive attempt to harmonise the physician's and philosopher's ideas.

The principles (*archaí*) of Hippocratic thought occupied a pivotal place in Galen's mind, and they were first, anatomy is of paramount importance in medicine; second, two different types of heat, innate and acquired, play a central role in human physiology; and third, health consists of a balance of the four humours, linked to the four primary (or cardinal) qualities, dry and moist, and warm and cold. Through his oeuvre, when Galen interprets Hippocrates, he reads these ideas into the Hippocratic text, even where, from a modern point of view, he clearly cannot be right. Finally, Galen insists that the *Best Physician Is Also a Philosopher*, as his work with this programmatic title argues. And Hippocrates, in Galen's portrayal at least, emerges as the physician who embodies this ideal.

Although in the second century AD Galen still operated in a world characterised by competition between rival schools, Galen's own interpretation of Hippocrates and his own medical doctrine came to dominate Late Antiquity. Daniela Manetti traces the story of Galen's growing dominance, beginning with the stories about Hippocrates. His fame grew through the centuries, and more and more undoubtedly apocryphal stories were told about him: he cured a Persian king of lovesickness; refused a high salary to go to the Persian court; cured the Athenian plague, and so on. Not just stories about his life, but also his witty sayings gained increasing popularity and were often quoted outside medical circles. Some of these witty sayings can be found in the *Hippocratic Corpus*, such as the first aphorism, 'Life Is Short, the Art Is Long ... '; others do not appear in any extant Hippocratic works. In the age after Galen, Galen's Hippocratism, as we have said, became dominant. This is true, for instance, for the encyclopaedic tradition, whose main exponents are Oribasius, personal physician to Emperor Julian, the Apostate (reigned 361–3); Aetius of Amida and Alexander of Tralles (both sixth century), and Paul of Aegina (seventh century). All these writers had strong links to Alexandria, where the iatrosophists (or professors of medicine) taught a syllabus of Hippocrates and Galen in the amphitheatres. We also have a large number of Hippocratic commentaries, written in Greek as lecture notes, dating from the fifth to seventh centuries. They offer us a unique insight into how Hippocrates was taught in Alexandria. One important feature is the increasing importance of Aristotelian and Neoplatonist philosophy during the medical lessons.

In the Latin West, Galenism did not dominate to the same extent, but here, too, we find traces of Hippocrates in various guises. There are, for instance, a number of Latin translations from Late Antiquity, often originating in Northern Italy. Likewise, some of the lecture note commentaries travelled from Alexandria to Ravenna, and were translated there into Latin. And the popular stories about

Hippocrates also find their way into the Latin tradition, all the way to North Africa, where they appear in the works of St Augustine and in mosaics surviving in what is now Algiers.

This Late Antique tradition with all its ramifications had a profound impact on the Arabo-Islamic world, which I explore in my own contribution, focussing on both Hippocrates as a legendary figure popular among the Muslims, and on the *Hippocratic Corpus* as translated into Arabic. I begin by studying the many legends and reports of Hippocrates' life that enjoyed great popularity in Arabic. Much of this material goes back to Late Antiquity (as previously discussed by Manetti). Not only did reports about Hippocrates' life entertain Arab readers, but also the many utterances that were attributed to him. Some came from texts such as the *Aphorisms*, whereas others do not have any specific provenance that can be traced. In this way, the figure of Hippocrates loomed large in the medieval Islamic world, and stories and sayings found their way into works of literature.

I then turn to how the *Hippocratic Corpus* was transmitted into Arabic. Generally speaking, one can say that it came in the wake of Galen, and notably Galen's many commentaries on Hippocrates' work. The main translator was Ḥunayn ibn Isḥāq, a Nestorian Christian living in ninth-century Baghdad. His powerful patrons commissioned Arabic translations, which he produced with the help of his collaborators in his 'workshop' or 'school'. Importantly, the translation from Greek into Arabic often involved a Syriac intermediary translation (Syriac is an Aramaic dialect used by Christians in the Middle East and beyond; it is, in a way, the language that Jesus would have spoken).

Generally speaking, the legacy of Late Antique Alexandria was incredibly powerful for the reception of Hippocratic works in Arabic. It comes, therefore, as no surprise that the Alexandrian curriculum also dominated later developments. For this reason, I close with three case studies on Hippocratic texts that proved to be particularly popular in both Alexandria and Baghdad, namely the *Aphorisms*, the *Prognostic*, and the *Epidemics*. The *Aphorisms*, for instance, spawned more than a dozen extant Arabic commentaries, and others that are lost now. All three texts, moreover, played a crucial role in the education for many generations of medical students in the medieval Islamic world.

My chapter clearly shows that Hippocrates and more generally the Greek medical tradition exerted an enormous, formative influence over developments in the medieval Islamic world. It is therefore fair to say that the Arabo-Islamic medical tradition is as much heir to the Greeks as is Christian Europe. Moreover, the links between medicine in Latin Christendom and the Arabo-Islamic world are not limited to a shared heritage. Medicine in the 'Latin West' developed largely through contact with the 'Arabic East', notably the many translations of medical texts that not only dominated the nascent European universities in the Middle Ages, but continued well into the Renaissance.[14] Therefore, it makes no real sense to speak of a 'Western medical tradition' or 'Western medicine' to the exclusion of the Islamic heritage; the latter was part and parcel of the former. Therefore, when scholars at the (now defunct) Wellcome Institute for the History of Medicine in London compiled a survey of *The Western Medical Tradition: 800 BC to AD 1800*, they rightly included 'the Arab-Islamic medical tradition'.[15] One has to bear this caveat in mind when reading the last chapter by David Cantor on 'Western Medicine since the Renaissance'. Cantor here explores how Hippocrates and the *Hippocratic Corpus* continued to be of relevance in Europe and North America ('the West'), while being fully aware that 'Western' medicine did encompass the legacy of the Islamic world.

In the Renaissance, Hippocrates first was very much read and understood through the prism of Galen, and only slowly emerged from his shadow. As challenges to Galen multiplied, for instance because of the discovery of new anatomical features and new diseases, Hippocrates morphed into a chameleon-like figure that could be used to justify diametrically opposed positions. He stood

[14] For a recent exploration of this topic, see Hasse (2016), with further literature.
[15] Conrad et al. (1995).

for practical medicine and observation and against theoretical speculation; and then again, as the model of the philosopher-physician whose medical insights are steeped in theory. Adherents of the new chemical medicine of Paracelsus could claim Hippocrates as their model against mainstream medicine; and the medical and scientific establishment, for instance in the form of the Royal Society, could view him as the figurehead of the empiricism advocated by Francis Bacon (1561–1626) and dominant for much of the seventeenth and early eighteenth centuries. In Leiden, Hermann Boerhaave (1668–1738) advocated a medical chemistry according to Hippocratic principles, and in France, Philippe Pinel (1745–1826), the pioneer of psychiatry, erected Hippocrates as a model to follow.

This trend to remodel Hippocrates in the image of one's own convictions continued throughout the nineteenth century. In the United States, for instance, Hippocrates was used on different sides of the arguments leading to the American Civil War (1861–5). And perhaps the last generation of physicians trained in the Classics who lived towards the end of the century regarded Hippocrates as the antithesis to emerging modern medicine that, with its technical apparatus, tests, laboratories, and mechanisation, lost sight of individual patients with their idiosyncrasies.

Over the course of the twentieth century, Hippocrates lost relevance in medical debates, and few practitioners nowadays would claim to follow him in their theoretical and practical approach, although some still do. Yet, Hippocrates increased in importance in the area of medical ethics, and especially after the Second World War and the crimes of the German National Socialists, including in the field of medicine, modern Hippocratic Oaths proliferated in many medical schools, following on from the Declaration of Geneva, which is a rewritten version of the Hippocratic Oath produced in 1948. Hippocrates also continues to live on in popular culture, as cartoon characters, rap creations, or *Star Trek* personas: A *Deep Space Nine* episode, 'Hippocratic Oath', sees Dr Bashir grapple with

Hippocrates' legacy, and elsewhere in the *Star Trek* universe, Hippocrates and Galen appear.

These chapters in this *Companion* cover a large array of topics in Hippocratic studies. And yet, one could have added many more; this is the nature of any such enterprise. But there are two chapters that I would particularly have liked to add to this collection: (1) on the pre-history of Hippocratic medicine and its contact with surrounding traditions; and (2) on the interplay between philosophy, especially Pre-Socratic and Aristotelian, and Hippocratic medicine. As they are missing here, let me just provide a few thoughts on both topics and suggest further readings.

In the past, we had the notion of a 'Greek miracle' or 'miracle grec': from the seventh to the fifth century BC, a highly sophisticated Greek culture emerged as if out of nowhere, a truly miraculous occurrence. Another notion was that of the transition from 'myth (*mŷthos*)' to 'reason (*lógos*)', which was largely completed by the fifth century BC. For medicine, take the famous example of *Sacred Disease*, a treatise that advocates that epilepsy has natural causes just as any other disease. It argues in particular against the prevalent opinion that the gods are specifically to blame for it, and that it is somehow linked to spiritual contamination or ritual pollution. Therefore, so the story goes, without any precursor, we see a fully formed rational approach to medicine appear all of a sudden, and this is due to the Greek genius.

Over the past thirty years, this view has seen a number of challenges, the two most important being the following. First, it is wrong to characterise the Hippocratic medicine of *Sacred Disease* and other similar treatises within the *Hippocratic Corpus* as rational and what came before as irrational.[16] Magic, for instance, can function according to its own rational system that is internally coherent – even if, from a modern perspective, we do not believe in it. Nor, to stay with *Sacred Disease*, is Hippocratic theory rational in the sense of rejecting

---

[16]   See the pioneering work of G. E. R. Lloyd (e.g., 1979, 2003) on this issue.

all supernatural agency: all natural phenomena are 'divine (theîa)'. Moreover, the basic explanation of epilepsy in this work – that it is caused by an excess of phlegm in the brain – is hardly underpinned by what modern medicine would call 'evidence'. With this in mind, when we look at the pre-history of Hippocratic medicine, we find important predecessors, the two most important being ancient Egyptian and ancient Near Eastern cultures, to which Hippocratic medicine was indebted.[17]

The relationship between early Greek (or Pre-Socratic) philosophy and Hippocratic medicine is an intimate, yet complex one.[18] For instance, the physician and philosopher Alcmaeon, who probably lived towards the end of the sixth century BC, stressed the importance of balance, a concept very prominent in many Hippocratic texts. Likewise, many Hippocratic texts resonate with debates in early Greek philosophy; a good example is the discussion of téchnē ('art', 'craftsmanship', 'expertise') in Ancient Medicine.[19]

Likewise, Aristotle's biological works and the so-called Shorter Works on Nature (known by their Latin title of Parva Naturalia) pick up many of the themes discussed in the Hippocratic Corpus. As some of the treatises date from the fourth century BC, they are roughly contemporaneous with Aristotle and reflect common debates at the time. Therefore, this topic, too, is fertile ground for scholarly enquiry.[20]

Despite the inevitable gaps that an enterprise like the present will undoubtedly have, I sincerely hope that this Companion will introduce a new generation of readers and students to Hippocrates and the Hippocratic Corpus. Both loom large not just in the so-called 'Western' tradition of medicine, but also in intellectual and popular culture more generally, both East and West. Greek medicine in general and the Hippocratic tradition in particular offer fertile ground for

[17]   van der Eijk (2004a) gives a concise and lucid summary of the debates with further literature.
[18]   See van der Eijk (2008) for a general discussion.   [19]   See Schiefsky (2005).
[20]   van der Eijk (2014).

future scholarship on all levels, from detailed philology and editorial technique to social and theoretical approaches that provide fresh readings. Yet, it is perhaps in the area of Hippocrates' afterlife, beginning with Galen, that the most still remains to be done. Let us not forget that we have neither a critical edition nor a translation into any modern language of Galen's *Commentary on Hippocrates' 'Aphorisms'*, the most read and debated Hippocratic text. And most of the Arabic Hippocratic tradition still remains to be edited. Therefore, may this *Companion* be a contribution to current debates, and a stimulus and springboard for future research.

2 The 'Hippocratic Question' and the Nature of the *Hippocratic Corpus*

Elizabeth Craik

HIPPOCRATES, LIFE AND TIMES

In *The Cambridge Companion to Galen*, the first chapter is entitled 'The Man and His Work'; the first sentence of the chapter records the date and place of Galen's birth (information regarded as established: AD 129, in Pergamum) and the second records the date and place of his death (information regarded as probable: second decade of the third century, in Rome); the first paragraph continues with an account of Galen's output, based on his own autobiographical listing of his writings.[1] The second chapter is entitled 'Galen and His Contemporaries'; here, the focus is on Galen's reactions, recorded in personal comment or, frequently, criticism, to the works of others.[2] The contrast with the paucity of reliable evidence for the life, work, and intellectual stance of Galen's revered predecessor Hippocrates is stark – and this despite the rich and extensive resource of the *Hippocratic Corpus*, which extends to ten volumes in the standard nineteenth-century edition of Littré.[3]

We may begin with an epitaph. 'Here lies Thessalian Hippocrates, a Coan by descent, born of the immortal race of Apollo. By the arms of Hygieia he achieved many victories over disease, and won great repute not by chance but by art.' In other epigrams too the healing powers of Hippocrates are lauded.[4] Epitaphs are not necessarily models of biographical veracity and cannot even be taken as proof of their subject's existence. But coincident content in an extensive

My book (Craik [2015]) will be found to complement and amplify this chapter.
[1]   Hankinson (2008).   [2]   Lloyd (2008).   [3]   Littré (1839–61).
[4]   See *Anthologia Graeca* 7.135 for epitaph; also 9.53, 16.268, and 269 for other epigrams.

biographical tradition (admittedly late and of unknown or dubious origins) and in varied epistolary and anecdotal traditions (admittedly supposititious and marked by fanciful embellishment) as well as a few fifth-century pointers (admittedly tangential and allusive in character) do combine to corroborate some salient points. Hippocrates was born in Cos and lived in Thessaly; he had a special relationship with gods of healing (descent from Apollo and an alliance with Hygieia); and he was a successful physician, a practitioner of the 'art' or 'craft' of medicine.[5]

It has become unfashionable to place much credence in ancient biographical data and the prevailing climate with regard to evidence, for the life of Hippocrates, as that of other ancient figures, is one of extreme scepticism.[6] In truth, many major figures of Greek intellectual life are no less elusive than Hippocrates and mistrust of external evidence, typically 'late', has considerably diminished the available sources of information. In some cases, the internal evidence of a writer's oeuvre comes to our aid. Thus, from the prologues to their work we know something of the aims and objectives pursued by the historians Herodotus and Thucydides; from the choral *parabasis* of several comedies we can reconstruct the political stance of Aristophanes; and there is some apparently autobiographical content in the lyric verse of tragedy. However, no Hippocratic work gives a clue, far less lays a claim, to authorship by any named person, whether Hippocrates or another. Two writers are mentioned critically by name, but these allusions are fleeting and incidental: Empedokles in *Ancient Medicine* and Melissos in *Nature of Man*. There is, nevertheless, a considerable degree of self-reference in the works of the corpus, and the use of the first person by an author is always potentially illuminating. Some suggestions on authorship follow in the final section in this chapter.

The philosophers Plato and Aristotle both allude to Hippocrates as a prominent contemporary figure, implying that he was well known

---

[5]　On the epistolary and biographical traditions, see Smith (1990) and Pinault (1992).

[6]　Lefkowitz (1981) was influential in setting this sceptical trend.

to them.[7] The comic poet Aristophanes seems to suggest, in apparent parody of the doctors' Oath, that Hippocratic practices were familiar in Athens of his day.[8] There is ample evidence of a two-way process of influence, not only between Hippocratic medicine and ancient philosophy but also between medicine and a range of other genres: the literary intertextuality is formidable in its extent and complexity. There is much reference to or elucidation of Hippocrates in later writers, most obviously in the lexicographer Erotian and at greatest length in the doctor Galen, and there is valuable information also in the medical content of such writers as Celsus and Pliny. By and large, these later writers are basing their observations on the same texts, or at least some of the same texts, as are available to us; they are asking some of the same questions and reaching similar or different conclusions by interpretation of the same material.

A recurrent question relates to the reasons for Hippocrates' move from the southern island of Cos to northern Greece: on the evidence of the case histories detailed in *Epidemics* he spent time in Thrace and on the island of Thasos, as well as Thessaly, where he apparently died. Questions are commonly asked also of personal and political loyalties, both to Greek communities and in reaction to the great powers in Persia and, of increasing importance, Macedon. Some of the documents transmitted with the *Hippocratic Corpus* seem to be invented to furnish evidence, where evidence is lacking, for such communication. In this material, some depict Hippocrates as a philosopher-physician of supreme integrity, resisting blandishments of the Persian king and holding his own with the Macedonians; some depict Hippocrates as coming to the aid of the Athenians at the time of the great plague.

In addition, an extensive group of letters purports to be a correspondence between Hippocrates and Democritus. Although little in this exchange provides independent evidence for actual contact – much being a demonstrable pastiche of extant

---

[7] Plato, *Protagoras* 311b–c; *Phaedrus* 270c–d; and Aristotle, *Politics* 1326a15–16.
[8] Aristophanes *Women at the Thesmophoria* 270–74.

Hippocratic and partially extant Democritean texts – the letters nevertheless surely reflect the reality of intellectual interaction in fifth-century BC Thrace. Democritus of Abdera was a most prolific writer on a great range of scientific subjects, including biology and comparative anatomy. The great early 'sophist' Protagoras came from the same region. It is pertinent to note that the historian Thucydides, who displays a conspicuous familiarity with medical ideas and terminology, originated in Thrace also. The cultural vitality of Abdera and adjacent cities evidently matched their economic prosperity, which was based on an extensive trade in grain. Thasos was a rich and vibrant capital city, and the island played a significant part in the political and military history of the Aegean.

The peripatetic lifestyle of doctors is matched by the similar mobility of itinerant poets and sophists. All gravitated to prosperous places in search of patronage or prestige. Sophists, unlike poets and physicians, required a democratic market for sale of their skills and Athens provided this. Although there were doubtless doctors in Athens, it was not in the fifth century – and indeed never became – a place where medicine flourished. Much more important were the western Greek cities of Italy and Sicily; the southern regions of Libya, especially Cyrene; the northern areas of Thessaly and Thrace; and the eastern Greek seaboards of Cos and Cnidus. These constituted the intellectual world of Hippocrates. The development of Greek medicine may be seen in the context of the development of other forms of expository prose. Various forms of *historía*, 'enquiry', were the common generic genesis of the subsequently differentiated 'history' and 'philosophy'. Early prose, deeply imbued with antecedent poetic and especially epic traditions, used the Ionic dialect (well known as literary dialect of the historian Herodotos). This convention in expression, generally abandoned with the growing prominence of the Attic dialect of Athens, had a peculiarly long future in medical writing.

THE 'HIPPOCRATIC QUESTION': A LONG CONTROVERSY

There was a Hippocratic Question before there was a *Hippocratic Corpus*. That is to say, a corpus could not take shape until the matter of its constituent content arose. But the process was much less formal and much more random than the term 'corpus' suggests; the word 'collection' would be more apt. Rather than the formation of a definite corpus, far less the foundation of a definitive canon, there was the gradual collection and agglomeration of material viewed by consensus as having common authority and authorship. It is likely that copies of early medical works arrived in Alexandria piecemeal and that some were then lumped together, whether by chance or by choice, and came to be regarded as a Hippocratic collection. There was, however, continuing fluidity in views of what constituted true Hippocratic character and authenticity.

The first evidence for this process lies in glossography. It is a prerequisite of an attempt to explain the terminology of an author that the works of that author can be identified. There were many early Hippocratic glossographers, most known to us by little more than name and most with a bent more philological than scientific. An important but shadowy figure was Baccheius (third century BC), whose lists were abridged and re-ordered by the equally shadowy Epicles (first century BC). In a valuable lexicon, which has survived, Erotian (first century AD) cites these predecessors and uses their format as a basis of his own. Although Erotian in a full preface explicitly lists the titles of works to be glossed, his practice in the glossary is not totally consistent with this preliminary list and, despite an extensive knowledge of medical writing and much acuity in interpretation, he does not explore questions of authorship or authenticity. An uncritical, or simply unconcerned, stance on this is apparent in that he includes the patently spurious epistolary material. Also, while expressing doubt that one work (*Prorrhetic*, probably intending *Prorrhetic* 1 only) is genuinely by Hippocrates, he does so without explanation. The influence of Erotian on the subsequent tradition was immense. His overall view of Hippocratic material was adopted by Renaissance editors and conditioned the approach of Littré also: despite dismissing the biographical tradition as invented 'fables', Littré followed earlier editorial practice in his inclusion of the *Letters*.[9]

Paradoxically, it may be that the spurious biographical and pseudo-historical material, some of it perhaps composed as early as the fourth century BC and so before the advent of lexicography, gave impetus to the notion of a Hippocratic collection; it may even have lent an air of authenticity to those medical works to which it was attached. Lists of Hippocratic works are contained in several versions of the life of Hippocrates. The earliest of these versions seem to be based on *Lives* written by Soranus (second century AD). The most full and striking catalogue is contained in the so-called 'Brussels Life'; its great interest is that, with many works readily identifiable and recognisable as belonging to 'our' Corpus (*Oath*, *Joints*, *Fractures*, *Aphorisms*, among others) are listed many works now lost and unknown to us. These include treatises on a whole series of diseases such as dropsy, gout, jaundice, and others. On the evidence of Galen, his recent predecessors Dioscorides and Artemidorus Capito (early second century AD) addressed questions of genuineness; it appears that their judgements tended to privilege works regarded as 'useful' – that is, of practical rather than theoretical content – such as *Prognostic* and *Regimen in Acute Diseases*. Even on Galen's somewhat hostile account of his predecessors it may be seen that they made some remarkably perceptive observations on the uneven or bipartite character of certain works, such as *Nature of Man* and *Diseases 2*. However, excessively explicit and fanciful explanations were sought in terms of authorship imputed to different Hippocratic relatives.

Galen's own part in categorising works viewed by him as totally genuine (as, above all, the surgical treatises *Joints* and *Fractures*); as authentic but subject to accretions (as *Aphorisms*); and as spurious (as

---

[9]   For Erotian, see Nachmanson (1917, 1918).

Glands) laid the foundations for the views of subsequent generations. Although many of Galen's views have stood the test of time – notably his realisation that the books of *Epidemics* might be grouped in three categories as 1 and 3; 2, 4, and 6; and 5 and 7 – many are now regarded as misleading and slanted attempts to foist his own ideas on his ideal and idealised predecessor. Thus, Galen had an excessively favourable view of *Nature of Man* because its clear expression of humoral theory meshed with his own; similarly, his citations of *Surgery* are disingenuously given the seal of approval on the basis of notional but objectively non-existent teleological content. Galen too had a strong notion of family participation, attributing some works to Hippocrates' sons Thessalus and Dracon or son-in-law Polybus. But it is important to recall that already Aristotle – close in time to Hippocratic composition – regarded Polybus as the author of certain works, or parts of certain works, including a section of *Nature of Bones*.[10]

The earliest editors and translators of the sixteenth century, following the translation of Calvus (1525) and the *editio princeps* of Asulanus (1526), aimed to present 'all' the works of Hippocrates; exceptionally Zwinger (1579) selected only twenty-two Hippocratic treatises for comment and elucidation.[11] Cornarius (1538), Mercurialis (1588), and the influential Foesius (1595) knew of inconsistencies in the lists of works attributed to Hippocrates and of complexities in the process of transmission, but through their collections an emerging canon appeared.[12] Van der Linden (1665) followed in presenting the same works, but innovated and clarified by arranging their content in numbered sections.[13] Mercurialis had attempted to categorise the works in four broad classes on the basis of rudimentary stylistic criteria; he distinguished treatises written by Hippocrates, notes edited by others (supposedly relatives), works written by others (supposedly relatives or pupils), and, finally, works with no

---

[10] On Galen's interpretations, see Smith (1979); on Dioscorides and Artemidorus Capito at 234–40.

[11] Calvus (1525); Asulanus (1526); Zwinger (1579).

[12] Cornarius (1538); Mercurialis (1588); Foesius (1595).   [13]   van der Linden (1665).

Hippocratic character. A succession of critics made judgements along similar lines, notably (from a medical standpoint) the distinguished and versatile physician Haller and (from a more literary point of view) the Homeric scholar Grimm.

The nineteenth century brought great progress in Hippocratic scholarship; landmarks were the great editions of Littré and Ermerins, the insightful translations of Adams and Petrequin, and the perceptive (though now overlooked) encyclopaedic contributions of Greenhill.[14] All of these, in different ways, discussed the problems of authorship and attribution. The most elaborate scheme propounded is that of Littré. Littré's Introduction, occupying almost all of his first volume, culminates in a lengthy detailed itemised discussion of the entire Hippocratic collection, arranged in eleven classes determined by supposed authenticity and relative dating. These are 1, works by Hippocrates; 2, works by Polybus; 3, pre-Hippocratic works; 4, works not by Hippocrates but of his school; 5, notes and extracts; 6, several works by a single unidentified author, not Hippocrates; 7, one work by a single identified author; 8, post-Hippocratic works; 9, works not cited in antiquity; 10, works now lost but all or part by Hippocrates; and 11, apocryphal pieces.[15]

In the course of the twentieth century, the focus of debate shifted somewhat and, following the ground-breaking study by Jouanna and Grensemann, classification of Hippocratic works as 'Coan' or 'Cnidian' became current.[16] However, the validity of this apparent geographical divide has been increasingly questioned. Although it is recognised that a real distinction can be made between works concerned with the classification of diseases, primarily diagnostic in approach (regularly viewed as 'Cnidian'), and works concerned rather with theories of therapy and medical ideology,

---

[14]   Littré (1839–61); Ermerins (1859–64); Adams (1849); Pétrequin (1877–78); Greenhill (1862–64).

[15]   1.292–439 L.

[16]   See Jouanna (1974) and Grensemann (1975); also Lonie (1965) and, expressing a change of mind, Lonie (1978) and, for continuation of the debate, Lloyd (1975) and Thivel (1981).

primarily prognostic in approach (regularly viewed as 'Coan'), there is awareness of much crossing between these categories. There is also an increasing awareness of the important part played in medical history by other regions of the Greek world.

There is consciousness too of the importance of other doctors and other texts, notably of the medical traditions glimpsed in the Menoneia, also known as the 'Anonymus Londinensis' papyrus, and in the fragments of the early philosophers collectively known as 'Pre-Socratics'.[17] Recently, some scholars have begun to suggest that the 'Hippocratic question' is meaningless and the concept of Hippocratic medicine is itself flawed; that the *Corpus* has no ancient sanction or inherent authority, being merely a 'Renaissance construct'.[18] However, the planning of this volume is testimony to the continued validity and indeed vitality of a more traditional view.

THE NATURE OF THE HIPPOCRATIC CORPUS

How many works are there in the Hippocratic collection? This apparently simple question has a complex answer, as different editors list and enumerate in different ways.[19] In my work on the collection, I list fifty-one works and arrange them in alphabetical order, using the standard Latin abbreviation for title.[20] It is seen that titles were not contemporaneous with composition but were attached – often with manifest inconsistency – later, and in some cases much later. This simpler list may serve as a useful adjunct to the fuller formulation of Jacques Jouanna.[21] It is important to recognise that the Hippocratic material remains in some sense fluid and open to different lines of description and analysis.

It will be clear from my list that some works are discussed together sequentially, as is the case with *Fistulas* and *Haemorrhoids*; *Fractures* and *Joints*; and *Crises* and *Days of Crisis*.

---

[17] Sources for the 'Anonymus of London' are Jones (1947) and, with bibliography, Manetti (2010); for the 'Pre-Socratics', Diels and Kranz (1964).

[18] See especially van der Eijk (2015). [19] See Anastassiou and Irmer (1997–2012).

[20] See Craik (2015). [21] Both lists are included for comparison in the appendix.

Similarly some works are discussed together and treated as a unity, as is the case with *Generation* and *Nature of the Child*; *Nature of Man* and *Regimen in Health*; and the *Seven Months Infant* and *Eight Months Infant*. The judgements underlying this arrangement are not seriously controversial. Other groupings are more difficult and there is a degree of arbitrariness in the table presented. Thus, the seven books of *Epidemics* are treated in simple numerical sequence, though there is a scholarly consensus that three groups can, as Galen recognised, be distinguished: Books 1 and 3; Books 2, 4, and 6; and Books 5 and 7. Similarly, the three books of *Diseases of Women* are treated in sequence, though Book 3 is sometimes regarded as separate with the title *Sterility*. The four books of *Regimen* are treated as an organic unity, though Book 4 is sometimes regarded as separate with the title *Dreams*. By contrast, the four treatises *Diseases* 1, 2, 3, and 4 are clearly entirely separate and distinct from one another.

As noted earlier, attempts to classify the works by putative authenticity (by Hippocrates, by a member of his extended family, or of some other provenance) or by supposed date (pre-Hippocratic, Hippocratic, or post-Hippocratic) have long been abandoned; and attempts to classify the works by Coan or Cnidian content and affiliations have proved scarcely more generally acceptable. But classification of some sort would enhance understanding of the component parts and so of the collection as a whole. We might attempt to classify by subject matter. Most treatises can be grouped under one of the following heads: scientific principles, anatomy and physiology, nosology and pathology, surgery, therapy and prognosis, gynaecology and embryology, and deontology. Many works, however, resist classification, being quite mixed in content.[22] We might attempt to classify by genre and most works can be categorised as one of the following: scientific treatise, instruction manual, handbook, manifesto, series of case records, and collection of personal memoranda or notes. But, again, many are quite mixed in type and so resist classification;

---

[22]   Erotian pioneered an approach by a series of topics. Phillips (1973), 38–121, uses broad headings in discussing the content of the collection.

further, the very concept of generic distinctions is anachronistic. We might attempt instead to classify by form or format, beginning with the ancient distinction between treatises proper and more disjointed collections of material. But this does not take us very far.

There is enormous stylistic variation also. Some works are polished and marked by conspicuous use of techniques of rhetorical composition, marked by devices such as alliteration, assonance, anaphora, asyndeton, and antithesis. Some, by contrast, are loosely composed in an artless or careless fashion. In some there are features suggesting elements of an oral tradition. There is much interpenetration of content, passages being repeated verbatim, or almost so, in different works. Many treatises are the result of the activity of a compiler or an editor rather than an author. Frequently, after a personal prologue, the content degenerates into an impersonal amalgam of material with an occasional personal interjection inserted. There is evidence of collaboration but also of rivalry.

Classification by medical content, though useful for readers interested in some particular aspects, is of limited use in overall grouping. It emerges that in treatment by surgery some physicians have recourse to cutting (bloodletting, phlebotomy) and others to burning (cauterisation), and in treatment by regimen some doctors confine their prescriptions to dietary practice whereas others stress the importance also of exercise and baths; also different drugs are recommended by different practitioners. These differences in therapeutic practice are matched by significant variation in theoretical views of anatomy, physiology, and pathology. In anatomy, different accounts are given of the course of the blood vessels; in physiology, different versions are found of the significance of bodily components, such as bile and phlegm; in pathology, different causes of disease are postulated. But distinct categorisations in the collection as a whole cannot be established on the basis of such similarities and differences in the theory and practice of medicine.

Can we identify the voice of Hippocrates in the *Corpus* that bears his name? A strong case can be made for Hippocratic authorship of *Fractures* and *Joints*. A separate but also strong case can be made for *Prognostic* and *Prorrhetic* 2; and perhaps, with them, for *Epidemics* 1 and 3. These authoritative texts are quarried, quoted, and summarised in a body of lesser works, including *Mochlicon, Nature of Bones, Anatomy, Use of Liquids*, and *Surgery*, derivative pieces that may come from a time of intellectual revision and consolidation, perhaps mid fourth century BC. It may be possible to hear echoes of Euryphon in the many nosological works apparently based on a common model, such as *Affections, Internal Affections,* and *Diseases* 2. It is certainly possible to identify an author or redactor of unknown name, one dominant physician responsible for a substantial sub-section of the *Corpus*, a large group of related physiological and gynaecological texts, concerned especially with theories of reproduction and embryology: *Generation, Nature of the Child, Diseases* 4, *Diseases of Girls, Glands*, and certain parts of both *Diseases of Women* (especially Book 3) and *Nature of Woman*.

To understand the *Corpus* as a whole in its formidable diversity it is necessary to examine and contextualise its component parts. It is necessary also to disabuse oneself of some widespread prejudices and predispositions, particularly with regard to the status of certain favoured works. Everyone who has heard of the *Hippocratic Corpus* – or even of Hippocrates – has heard of the Oath. But that document is very commonly misquoted, its content and its history being alike misunderstood and misrepresented. And there are other deontological texts, notably the *Law*, unreasonably passed over by comparison. In the same way, the collection *Aphorisms* takes complete precedence over the similar *Coan Prognoses*. Then a few sentences from the treatise *Sacred Disease* are constantly paraphrased and selectively cited as proof of the 'rational' character of Greek medicine. But this allegedly rational aspect is exaggerated both with regard to the treatise (where the author's stance is arguably quite traditional) and to Greek medicine in general (where irrational attitudes persisted even in the time of Galen). Another treatise commonly privileged in modern discussion is *Ancient Medicine*, a work that is certainly important, but not uniquely so; it owes its reputation simply to the assessment of Littré, who gave it pride of position in Book 1 of his edition.

The Western medical tradition claims Greek roots and has tended to read its own contemporary ideas and attitudes into the past, to the exclusion or downgrading of theories that do not 'fit'. One example is the focussing of attention on the theory of four bodily humours and postulates of humoral imbalance, ideas that dominated Western medicine from the Renaissance to the nineteenth century and that are commonly believed to have a Hippocratic origin. However, the four-humour theory makes only a sporadic appearance in the *Corpus*; it is seen in *Nature of Man* and (a conflicting version) in *Diseases* 4. By contrast, theories of flux and fixation of peccant matter, ubiquitous in Hippocratic physiology and pathology, are little discussed elements in the tradition. Another example relates to understanding of the vascular system. It is difficult for the modern reader to forget Harvey. But if, instead of measuring the 'accuracy' of ancient views against the precise detail of Harvey's discoveries (and inevitably finding them wanting), we scrutinise ancient perceptions of the general principles of blood flow, pulsation, and circulation, there are genuine insights to be appreciated. The multifarious *Corpus* must be viewed on its own terms and the terms of its day, rather than as a monolithic foundation for later European medicine.

3 Textual History

Jacques Jouanna

INTRODUCTION

What we nowadays call the *Hippocratic Corpus* (or *Hippocratic Collection*) comprises the medical treatises transmitted under the name of Hippocrates. Hippocrates, an eminent physician of the fifth and fourth centuries BC, hailed from a family of Asclepiades and achieved great fame already during his own lifetime. The modern term *Hippocratic Corpus* implies that these treatises cannot all have been written by the historical Hippocrates, as Elisabeth Craik has shown in Chapter 2. The medieval manuscripts, however, simply attribute these texts to 'Hippocrates', without being concerned with the 'Hippocratic Question'. Likewise, since the Renaissance, the various editions generally preserve the traditional name of 'Hippocrates', including the modern editions in the great collections of Greek texts such as the *Corpus Medicorum Graecorum*, Loeb Library, and the *Collection des Universités de France*. This means that even today, Hippocrates can refer both to the historical personality and to the texts transmitted under his name.

The current number of treatises within the *Hippocratic Corpus* results from the history of the editions, from the first Greek edition (*editio princeps*), the so-called Aldine edition of 1526, to the great nineteenth-century edition that still exerts enormous influence, namely that by Émile Littré (1839–61); Ermerins' later edition (1859–64) has not replaced Littré's. Because none of the three great projects to edit the Hippocratic Corpus – in Germany (*Corpus Medicorum Graecorum*), in the United States (Loeb Library), and in France (*Collection des Université de France*) – is yet completed, volume and page references to Littré's edition remain standard. For instance, the Index Hippocraticus[1] and the electronic Thesaurus Linguae Graecae refer to Littré's edition. Therefore, references to Littré's edition will remain standard, even if more recent editions mark progress by improving the critical text through enhanced understanding of both the direct and indirect textual traditions.

GENERAL OVERVIEW

In its current form, the *Hippocratic Corpus* comprises seventy-two treatises, more than the sixty mentioned in the entry on Hippocrates in the Byzantine dictionary known as the *Souda*. There are, however, other ways of counting these treatises – Elisabeth Craik, for instance, lists fifty-nine, as can be seen from the appendix. The modern conception of the *Hippocratic Corpus* goes back to Renaissance editions, but differs from the situation in the medieval manuscripts, where additional treatises are attributed to Hippocrates, as we shall see.

Some editors, such as Jones (1931) and Littré (1849, 6.72–87), give *Regimen in Health* as a separate treatise, but in reality, it is part of *Nature of Man* (and thus transmitted in the oldest manuscripts). Likewise, Littré separated *Eight Months Infant* into two treatises (*Seven Months Infant, Eight Months Infant*), following a medieval manuscript, whereas other modern editions have it as one. The list of seventy-two titles also comprises five titles not part of Littré's edition, namely the metrical version of the Oath, *Remedies*, the spurious version of *Seven Months Infant, Testament*, and *Wounds and Missiles*. This corpus of seventy-two texts is also used in the *Index Hippocraticus*[2] and its various supplements.[3] Yet the list in the appendix, which one could regard as canonical, does not include all the texts attributed in the medieval manuscripts to Hippocrates. Already in his influential catalogue of Greek medical writers, Diels did not just list the manuscript copies of the texts contained in Littré's edition (1905, 3–38; 1907, 25–9), but also those manuscripts

---

[1]   Kühn and Fleischer (1986–9); Anastassiou and Irmer (1999, 2007); Anastassiou (2014).
[2]   Kühn and Fleischer (1986–9).
[3]   Anastassiou and Irmer (1999, 2007); Anastassiou (2014).

containing other texts attributed to Hippocrates (1905, 39–57). In the nineteenth century, a number of scholars edited some of these additional texts,[4] yet in the twentieth, few have followed their lead. Exceptions include Delatte (1939), who published two treatises on different nourishments attributed to Hippocrates, and Deichgräber (1970), who published the *Testament*. Two versions of a pseudo-Hippocratic letter to King Ptolemy are preserved in numerous manuscripts,[5] but have still not been edited, probably because it is historically impossible that the fifth-century BC Hippocrates wrote to the third-century BC Ptolemy. In one old manuscript, however, one version of the letter appears straight after the *Aphorisms* and the *Prognostic*, and this shows that the scribes and patrons did not consider the letter out of place among the most famous Hippocratic writings.

Therefore, one has to be careful not to be too restrictive in what one considers as belonging to the *Hippocratic Corpus*, for the image of Hippocrates has undergone numerous mutations in different circles: the 'Christian' Hippocrates[6] differs greatly from that projected by Galen and recovered during the Renaissance. Thankfully, in recent times, a number of Hippocratic writings that were previously considered marginal have been edited, notably texts from the corpus of so-called *Hippocratic Problems* and treatises dealing with humoral pathology.[7]

TEXTUAL HISTORY FROM ANTIQUITY TO THE RENAISSANCE

The textual history of the *Hippocratic Corpus* in general terms obviously needs to be written chronologically, that is, from the oldest to the most recent witnesses, thus explaining the main periods until the production of the oldest surviving witnesses. Not counting the papyri, these are the extant medieval manuscripts from the tenth

---

[4]   Boissonade (1831), 422–8; Dietz (1834); Ermerins (1840), 279–97; Ideler (1841); Ruelle (1898).

[5]   Diels (1905), 40–1; Diels (1907), 27.   [6]   Temkin (1991).

[7]   Jouanna (2005a, 2005c, 2006b).

century onwards, and the Latin translations of texts that are not transmitted in Greek. One ought first to establish the archetype of the direct textual tradition, and then to use the indirect tradition, in order to reconstruct the oldest variant readings. On the basis of these readings, one can then endeavour to reconstruct the original with the greatest assurance. Let us therefore first review the main stages in the transmission of the Hippocratic texts, and then discuss the history and techniques of critical editions from the Renaissance until today.

Classical Period

From the fifth and fourth centuries BC, we have only a few witnesses to the texts of the *Hippocratic Corpus*. In the *Phaedrus*, Plato clearly appears to have known Hippocrates' output, for he alludes to a passage where Hippocrates stated that one cannot know the nature of the body without knowing the nature of the whole (*Phaedrus* 270 c). Much ink has been spilled about the meaning of this statement and to what text in the *Hippocratic Corpus* it belongs. Be that as it may, we can be certain that it is not a literal quotation that one could find in the *Hippocratic Corpus*.

By contrast, in his *History of Animals* (3.3, 512a12–513a7) Aristotle quotes nearly verbatim a fairly long passage from chapter 11 of *Nature of Man* dealing with blood vessels, and attributes it to Polybus.[8] Therefore, it is fair to assume that at least part of this treatise was not written by Hippocrates, but by his son-in-law Polybus. Because there are only minor textual differences between these two independent witnesses – Aristotle's *History of Animals* and the Hippocratic *Nature of Man* – we can be certain that the medieval manuscripts transmit the texts quite faithfully. This passage also appears in *Nature of Bones*, probably quoted from *Nature of Man*.

Moreover, there is yet another parallel. Beforehand, Aristotle had also quoted a shorter description of blood vessels and attributed it to Syennesis of Cyprus, a disciple of Hippocrates according to the

---

8   Anastassiou and Irmer (2006), 363, n. 4.

Life of Hippocrates preserved in a Brussels manuscript. This latter passage also appears in *Nature of Bones*, where it is quoted anonymously. This second parallel can illustrate the importance of the indirect textual tradition. We find two variants: in some modern editions of Aristotle's text, the blood vessels originate in the navel (*omphaloû*) and run along through the loins (*osphûn*), whereas the Hippocratic parallel shows that the reading 'eye (*ophthalmoû*)' and 'brow (*ophrûn*)' are clearly correct.[9] For according to Aristotle (513a11), his predecessors argued that the blood vessels originate in the head – and not the navel – whereas he himself thought that they originate in the heart (513a22).

Hellenistic Period

The Hellenistic period from the third century BC onwards is marked by an incredible loss of Greek medical literature in general and references to Hippocrates and the *Hippocratic Corpus* in particular.[10] For instance, the first substantial extant references to a treatise from the *Hippocratic Corpus* date as late as the first century BC. They appear in the so-called lemmas (source text quoted in a commentary and subsequently explained) by the empiricist physician Apollonius of Citium on *Joints*. The gap between Aristotle in the fourth and Apollonius in the first century BC is due to the great loss of medical literature that has not come down to us; and yet, this was the time when the Library of Alexandria emerged as a major intellectual centre, and when celebrated physicians such as Herophilus, Erasistratus, and their pupils practised in that city.[11] Although Herophilus and others innovated substantially, notably in the area of anatomy, and therefore criticised Hippocrates (whom Apollonios of Citium still called 'the very divine Hippocrates'), a rich commentary tradition on the *Hippocratic Corpus* flourished in Alexandria; this tradition goes back to the classical age and the exegetical traditions that emerged on the island of Cos.

---

[9]   Ibid., 397, n. 2.   [10]   Roselli (2000).   [11]   von Staden (1989).

In third-century BC Alexandria, it was not only physicians who commented on Hippocratic texts, but also grammarians; the latter composed a number of glossaries and commentaries. The most important glossary is that composed by a pupil of Herophilus, Bacchius of Tanagra; it comprises three books and explains difficult and rare technical terms occurring in at least eighteen treatises in the *Hippocratic Corpus*.[12] His contemporary Philinos of Cos, the founder of the empirical school of medicine, composed in his turn a glossary in six books, and Apollonius of Citium wrote one in three. These glossaries often were a locus for fierce philological debates. For instance, Apollonius argued against Bacchius and reproached him for having misunderstood the ancient compound verb *amphisphállō*, which occurs in the treatise *Mochlicon*, dealing with bone setting. Bacchius explains this verb as meaning *peribállō*, 'to envelop'. Yet in reality, it means 'to rotate' (a dislocated joint). For in the context of the passage, the treatment of the dislocated joint takes three steps: first to lift it up, second to stretch it, and third to *rotate* it. This dispute between two glossographers could seem trivial and the difference slight – *amphisfállō* versus *peribállō* –, yet it also shows that philological questions had real-life medical consequences. For the empiricist Apollonius rebuked the Herophilean Bacchius for his lack of experience affecting medical practice; and it also shows that rivalries between different medical schools, such as that of the empiricists and the rationalists.

Roman Period

We know only indirectly of the intense exegetical activity of the Alexandrian glossators, mostly through two glossaries dating back to the Roman period. The first was composed by Erotian and dedicated to the chief of physicians Andromachus during Nero's reign (54–68); it survives only in a later redaction.[13] The famous physician Galen of Pergamum (ca. 129–216) authored the second roughly a century later,

[12] Ibid., 484–500.
[13] Nachmanson (1917); see also Ilberg (1893); Nachmanson (1918).

when he was still relatively young. It so happens that these two glossaries are the oldest surviving Greek glossaries. They are of crucial importance for two reasons. First, their prefaces provide precious information about the earlier glossographical tradition, as does Erotian, through whom we know of Apollonius of Citium's previously mentioned glossary. Second, the words that figure in these glossaries are often very rare and the explanations therefore of great value.

Galen was undoubtedly the most important person in the transmission and circulation of Hippocratic works.[14] His glossary has obviously made its mark, but it is through his many extant Hippocratic commentaries and the many Hippocratic quotations in his works that he had such a long-lasting effect. Galen provides valuable information about the textual history in his commentaries by talking about previous glossographers and commentators whose works are now lost. For instance, Galen discussed the two first known editors of the *Hippocratic Corpus*, Dioscorides and Artemidorus Capito, who lived in the first or second century AD; he often inveighed against them for allegedly replacing good ancients readings with newer, yet inferior ones. Then Galen frequently mentioned variant readings that appeared in the manuscripts of his time and how he endeavoured to trace the most ancient ones. Finally, Galen's commentaries are of crucial importance for the transmission of the Hippocratic texts, because in them, he regularly quoted the source text first; the technical term for these quotations is 'lemmas'. There is an important interplay between the direct manuscript tradition, that is, the text transmitted in the medieval manuscripts produced by anonymous scribes, and this indirect tradition of the Hippocratic lemmas in Galen's commentaries. Sometimes these lemmas are so important that a whole Hippocratic treatise can be reconstructed from the lemmas, which are extracted from the commentary, be it (rarely) in the Greek source, or (more frequently) in the Syriac, Arabic, and Hebrew translation. Some editors have favoured the

---

[14] See Chapter 13 by Véronique Boudon-Millot on 'Galen's Hippocrates' in this volume; and Manetti and Roselli (1994); Flemming (2008).

evidence from the lemmas over that from the medieval manuscripts containing the Hippocratic texts, but that is a very curious procedure, based on the exaggerated notion of Galen's philological skills as an editor of Hippocrates. Today, by contrast, we consider the medieval manuscripts as the direct (and primary) tradition, whereas Galen's lemmas represent the indirect (and secondary) tradition.

Byzantine Period

Alexandria in the sixth and seventh centuries witnessed a flourishing of exegetical engagement with the *Hippocratic Corpus*. One can therefore designate this period as a second 'Alexandrian Renaissance'. During this period, three commentators gained prominence: Palladius, Jean of Alexandria, and Stephen of Alexandria. All belonged to a group of teachers of medicine called 'iatrosophists'. Therefore, the commentaries often reflect classroom teaching.[15] The *Aphorisms* was the most fundamental treatise, and stood at the beginning of the medical curriculum, as it was considered to provide a general overview of all branches of medicine; Stephen's commentary on the *Aphorisms* survives,[16] as does that of Theophilus the Protospatharios, a Byzantine physician of the ninth or tenth century. It has recently been shown that Palladius' *Commentary on Hippocrates' 'Aphorisms'*, thought to survive in part in an Arabic translation, is unfortunately lost, apart from a few quotations.[17] Stephen's commentary on the *Prognostic* also survives, as do the commentaries on *Epidemics*, Book 6, by Palladius and John, and on *Fractures* by Palladius and Stephen.

The study of these Alexandrian commentaries has greatly progressed over the last few decades, not least through the production of critical editions and translations. For instance, it is clear now that they share important features, such as the division of the introductions into eight 'headings': (1) the aim, (2) usefulness, (3) authorship,

---

[15]   Horstmanshoff (2010).
[16]   Ed. and trans. Westerink (1985 [2nd. edn. 1998], 1992, 1995).
[17]   Pormann et al. (2017).

(4) title, (5) place within the works by Hippocrates, (6) division into parts, (7) genre, and (8) exegetical method. Likewise, the commentaries are often divided into lessons (*práxeis*), each consisting of a general overview ('*theōría*') and explanation of the passage (or 'lemma') in question ('*léxis*').

Book Production and Textual Transmission

Originally, the Hippocratic works were written on papyrus rolls, each book occupying one roll. To ensure that the books were placed in the right order, scribes used so-called catchwords: they wrote the beginning of the next book (and roll) at the end of the previous one. The book as we know it today, where one can turn pages, is called a codex, and codices became fashionable from the third century AD onwards. Sometimes, however, scribes made mistakes when copying the rolls onto codices, as the famous case of *Epidemics* Books 1 to 3 illustrates. For a variety of reasons, there can be no doubt that originally *Epidemics*, Book 1 must have been followed by *Epidemics*, Book 3. Yet, in most of the medieval manuscripts and modern editions, Books 1 and 3 are separated by Book 2, undoubtedly because the rolls got mixed up. (This said, we do find the right order in one medieval manuscript, most likely going back to a different branch of the tradition preserving the correct order.)

Another source of error was the passage from Greek upper to lowercase letters. Until the ninth century AD, Greek was written in uppercase or capital letters (formerly call 'uncials'), but then a minuscule cursive developed and became dominant within a relatively short period of time. This transition led to a number of errors, for instance, in the area of word divisions. The earlier capital script did not have any word divisions, which were added when writing in small letters.

Middle Ages and Renaissance

In the Latin Middle Ages, Hippocrates' works were known chiefly through the so-called *Articella* (or 'Small Art'), a collection of medical works produced in the School of Salerno in the twelfth century; it included Latin renderings of the *Aphorisms* and the *Prognostic*, both extracted from the lemmas of Galen's commentaries translated into Arabic.[18] A third text, the *Regimen in Acute Diseases*, was also added in a Latin translation produced from an Arabic intermediary. To be sure, there had been some Latin translations that were based directly on the Greek original, such as those by Burgundio of Pisa (twelfth century), Bartholomew of Messina (thirteenth century), or Niccolò da Reggio (fourteenth century), but these new Latin renderings had no impact on the medical curriculum in the nascent European universities. Generally speaking, people consulted the Latin translations without being too concerned about whether they were produced from the Greek original or an Arabic intermediary translation.

It is for this reason that whole swathes of texts belonging to the *Hippocratic Corpus* have been saved from oblivion during the Renaissance, such as the greater part of the *Epidemics*. The first edition of the 'complete works' (*Opera Omnia*) of Hippocrates appeared in 1525 in Rome and was produced by Calvus. One year later, Francisco Asolano of the Aldine Press in Venice prepared the first Greek edition of Hippocrates' 'complete works'. Both of these editions provided readers with more Hippocratic works than the most comprehensive medieval manuscripts. This thus constituted the rediscovery – first indirectly in Latin translation and then directly in the Greek original – of the core of Hippocrates' 'complete works', and this at a time when the Arabo-Latin medicine exemplified by Avicenna's *Canon* still dominated the medical discourse. From that time onwards, more and more Hippocratic editions appeared, striving to retrieve Hippocrates' own words.

EDITING THE HIPPOCRATIC CORPUS

Let us now turn to the second part of this chapter, the 'reverse' textual history, that is, the history of the text from the vantage point of the

---

[18]   O'Boyle (1998); Arrizabalaga (1998).

modern editor, who establishes the critical text by first taking the direct tradition into consideration, and then the indirect tradition. In this way, through the use of all available witnesses, one can go back as much as possible to the original text. From the outset it should be made clear that each Hippocratic treatise has its own problems, and that editors cannot simply transfer the insights gained from one treatise to another.

The textual tradition of each Hippocratic treatise comprises two elements: the direct and the indirect traditions. By 'direct tradition' one generally understands the medieval manuscripts and the papyri which provide direct access to the Greek source text. 'Indirect tradition' refers to information about the Greek text that one obtains indirectly, through quotations in later authors, such as glossators and commentators. The Latin, Syriac, Arabic, and Hebrew translations can in principle belong to either the direct or the indirect tradition, depending on whether they attest to the Greek source text or later quotations.

To establish a truly critical edition, one needs to consider all these elements, allocate them their place within the transmission of the text, evaluate them, and select the significant witnesses. On the basis of these witnesses, one can then establish the text and compile the critical apparatus, using the methods of textual criticism, generally referred to as the method of Lachmann (1793–1851), a famous German classicist. For the Hippocratic texts, this method has been refined over the course of the centuries with the different editions of Hippocrates from the Renaissance until today. To gauge the progress in editing the *Hippocratic Corpus*, we shall review the main stages in this editorial project.

Editions from the Renaissance until Today

During the Renaissance, the editors generally relied on a single manuscript in order to produce their printed editions. This is true for the first Greek edition, the *editio princeps* of 1526 by the Aldine Press, which comprises fifty-nine Hippocratic treatises. This initial choice of a single manuscript determined the later history of the printed text. For subsequent editors generally followed this first edition and corrected it only occasionally, as did for instance, Cornarius in his 1538 edition of the Greek text. What thus emerged is a generally accepted text, a so-called vulgate, which dominated the Hippocratic editions for the next 300 years. The Latin translations printed during the Renaissance, those by Calvus in 1525, Cornarius in 1546, and Foes in 1595, had a far greater impact in propagating the ideas of Hippocrates than the Greek editions.

The second major stage in editing Hippocrates is nineteenth-century France. For the first time, scholars did not just confine themselves to offering corrections to the 'vulgate' text, but began to collate all the available manuscripts afresh. Although there were some forerunners in this endeavour such as Adamance Coray (1748–1833), originally from Asia Minor but then doctor of medicine at the Faculty in Montpellier, it was Émile Littré (1801–81) who produced the first critical edition of the *Hippocratic Corpus*. This edition, in ten volumes with Greek text and French translation on facing pages, was based on the collation of all the Greek manuscripts available in what was then the Royal Library in Paris (later to become the French National Library, or Bibliothèque nationale de France). He collated these Greek manuscripts extremely carefully, and his collations remain a rich source of information until today. F. Z. Ermerins used them for his edition of the Greek text with facing Latin translation. Moreover, J. E. Pétrequin (1877–8) produced a critical edition of the surgical treatises. In all these nineteenth-century editions, however, textual information was merely accumulated and no attempt made to group the manuscripts through the methods of textual criticism. Moreover, the power of the 'vulgate' text was tremendous, even if it was not always known on which manuscripts it was based. Even Littré adopted 'vulgate' readings, although all the manuscripts that he consulted offered a different reading.

Only in the late nineteenth century did the third stage of editing Hippocrates begin, when a number of German philologists applied the methods of textual criticism to the Hippocratic text. The great German classicist Johannes Ilberg (1860–1930) was a pioneer in this respect, and produced so-called stemmas for both the direct and the indirect traditions in the preface to the 1894 edition of Hippocrates. A stemma is a branch diagram, a sort of inverted tree, in which one shows how later manuscripts relate to earlier ones, the aim being to go back to the archetype, the text closest to that of the author. During this golden age of editing Hippocrates, some Hippocratic texts even penetrated German schoolbooks: in his Greek reader for secondary schools, arguably the greatest German classicist, Ulrich von Wilamowitz-Moellendorff, included extracts from *Airs, Waters, Places* and *Sacred Disease*; first printed in 1902, this textbook saw numerous editions and remained popular until the 1930s and beyond.

The great editorial project of the *Corpus Medicorum Graecorum* is largely attributable to the meeting of two classicists, the German Hermann Diels and the Dane Johan Ludvig Heiberg at a congress of the International Association of Academies in 1901 in Paris. With the support of the Berlin and Copenhagen Academies, the project began with the publication of Diels' (1904–5) catalogue of Greek manuscripts and continued with the publication of Heiberg's edition of Hippocrates in 1927. It continued over the years, and owing to philological progress, earlier editions were sometimes replaced by later ones. For instance, H. Diller's 1970 edition of *Airs, Waters, Places* replaced an earlier one produced by Heiberg in 1927. The project continues today, although its main focus has shifted towards Galen.[19]

France witnessed a veritable second Renaissance of Hippocratic studies (after the first, nineteenth-century one discussed earlier), and the Parisian publisher Les Belles Lettres remains at the centre of Francophone scholarship. For instance, the late and lamented Jean Irigoin (1920–2006) published two seminal studies on the Greek

[19]   http://cmg.bbaw.de (accessed 16 May 2017). Examples of Hippocratic editions include Jouanna (1975; 2nd edn. 2002); Potter (1980); Joly (1984; 2nd edn. 2003); M. Hanson (1999); and Overwien (2014).

textual history of the *Hippocratic Corpus*.[20] Most importantly, however, between 1967 and 2017, fifteen volumes of Hippocratic critical editions (with French translations) appeared in the series *Collection des Universités de France (CUF)*, the last two volumes being *Epidemics I and III* and *Hippocratic Problems*.[21]

In the United States, the Loeb Library began to publish editions of Hippocrates in the 1920s.[22] Here the Greek text, with a very restricted apparatus, is accompanied by an English translation. This project, too, is ongoing, and new texts and translations are published regularly.[23] A number of Italian scholars also published editions of Hippocratic texts in a variety of places.[24] Finally, British scholars have also contributed to editing Hippocrates in recent times.[25]

The Older Greek Manuscripts

The manuscript tradition for each Hippocratic treatise is somewhat different, yet it is possible to make some general remarks about the older manuscripts. The two oldest and most complete manuscripts are

- Venice, Biblioteca Nazionale Marciana, MS gr. 269 (col. 533), a tenth-century manuscript generally referred to by classicists as *Marcianus gr. 269* and designated in many Hippocratic editions by the abbreviation 'M';[26] and
- Rome, Vatican Library, MS gr. 276, dating to the eleventh or twelfth century (*Vaticanus gr. 276*, or 'V').

---

[20] Irigoin (1997, 2003). [21] Jouanna (2016); Jouanna and Guardasole (2017).

[22] Jones (1923a, 1923b, 1931); Withington (1928).

[23] Potter (1988b, 1988c, 1995, 2010, 2012); Smith (1994).

[24] Manetti and Roselli (1982); Roselli (1996); Andò (2000); Giogianni (2006); Lami (2007).

[25] Craik (1998, 2006, 2009).

[26] Classicists generally designate manuscripts by a Latin adjective, a Latin language descriptor, and a number. This adjective can refer to a city (e.g., 'Parisinus' for Paris, 'Hauniensis' for Copenhagen, 'Vindobonensis' for Vienna); a library (e.g., 'Marcianus' for the Biblioteca Nazionale Marciana, named after the evangelist Mark); or a collection (e.g., 'Palatinus' referring to the Palatine collection that was taken from Heidelberg in the Palatinate region of Germany and brought to the Vatican in 1622 after the sack of the city). In the following, we shall provide a place name, library name, and shelfmark for each manuscript, but also give the Latin term for the manuscript, as this is the one most commonly used in the secondary literature.

Both of these manuscripts have a list of contents (the so-called *pínax*) at the beginning, listing sixty and sixty-two individual treatises, respectively, although neither comprises all the treatises mentioned in the list of contents, owing to the vagaries of textual transmission. Neither of these old manuscripts was used in the Aldine edition of 1526, nor by Littré in the nineteenth century, as he did not have direct access to them. This said, there is a more recent manuscript of the fifteenth century that was copied from 'M' and that served as the basis for much of the Aldine edition of 1525. This manuscript is

- Paris, Bibliothèque nationale de France, MS 2141 (fonds grec) (*Parisinus gr.* 2141, 'G').

Another old manuscript, dating to the twelfth or thirteenth century, is used to fill gaps in 'M', on which it depends:

- Paris, Bibliothèque nationale de France, MS 2140 (fonds grec) (*Parisinus gr.* 2140, 'I').

Likewise, although Littré did not have access to 'V', there is a later manuscript that is based on it to which he did have access and that he used for his edition:

- Paris, Bibliothèque nationale de France, MS 2146 (fonds grec) (*Parisinus gr.* 2146, 'C').

Two important manuscripts from the eleventh century that contain only a smaller part of the *Hippocratic Corpus* are the following:

- Paris, Bibliothèque nationale de France, MS 2253 (fonds grec) (*Parisinus gr.* 2253, 'A'); and
- Vienna, Österreichische Nationalbibliothek, MS med. gr. 4 (*Vindobonensis med. gr.* 4, 'θ').

These two old manuscripts appear not to have had any effect on the subsequent textual tradition, as we do not know of any copies made of them. Other old and important manuscripts exist for individual treatises. Generally speaking, manuscripts 'M' and 'V' belong to the same branch of the stemma, whereas the other old manuscripts represent a different one. The type of mistakes in these two fundamental branches of the stemma clearly show that they must have branched off before the advent of Greek minuscule (or lowercase) script, that is, before the ninth century.

Finally, let us mention three more manuscripts all going back to the tenth century, which preserve only a part of the *Hippocratic Corpus*, but which owing to their age and position in the stemma, are of crucial importance. They are

- Florence, Biblioteca Medicea Laurenziana, MS gr. 74, 7 (*'Laurentianus gr. 74,7*; 'B'), containing the surgical treatises
- Paris, Bibliothèque nationale de France, MS 446 (supplement grec) (*Parisinus suppl. gr.* 446, 'C''), containing *Aphorisms* and *Prognostic*
- Rome, Vatican Library, MS Palatinus gr. 398 ('b'), containing the *Letters*.

More Recent Greek Manuscripts

It is impossible to give a detailed account of the great number of more recent manuscripts, most of which are listed in Diels' (1904–5) catalogue, treatise by treatise. Generally speaking, scholars agree on how to group the more recent manuscripts (also called '*recentiores*'), yet there is some uncertainty of those deriving from M. As we have already stated, the tradition is divided into two branches, one deriving from M and the other from V. Manuscript I, mentioned earlier, was copied from M, as was the first part of:

- Paris, Bibliothèque nationale de France, MS 2142 (fonds grec) (*Parisinus gr.* 2142, 'H').

This first part is called Ha, and dates back to the twelfth century, whereas the second part, Hb, dates to before 1310, the date of the watermark on the paper. In the sixteenth century, a copy of I was made, namely

- Copenhagen, Royal Library, MS 244 Old Royal Collection (*Hauniensis ant. fund. reg. 244*, 'Haun').

For his edition, Littré used a number of more recent Paris manuscripts that derive from M, and other more recent manuscripts in Italy, England, and Germany derive from I.

There are fewer manuscripts in the V branch of the stemma, and they are often younger than those belonging to the M branch. Let us just mention two that had an effect on the early printing of Hippocrates during the Renaissance, namely

- Oxford, Bodleian Library, MS Holkam Gr. 92 (*Bodleianus Holkam. gr. 92*, 'Ho').
- Munich, Bayerische Staatsbibliothek, MS cod. gr. 71 (*Monacensis gr. 71*, 'Mo'), dating to 1470–80.

The Holkam manuscript was used in the Aldine edition where M had textual gaps, and Mo was employed by Cornarius in his 1538 edition of Hippocrates.

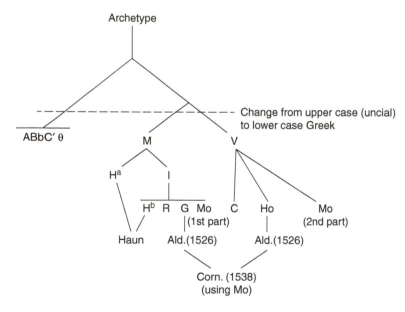

This is a simplified version of the so-called 'stemma' for the Greek textual history of the Hippocratic Corpus. This stemma shows how the main manuscripts (A B b C C' θ H Haun Ho G Mo) are descended from the archetype – the oldest text that can be reconstructed on the basis of the manuscript evidence– ; how they relate to each other; and how they influenced the earliest two Greek editions, that of the Aldine Press (Ald. 1526) and that by the Renaissance hellenist Janus Cornarius (Corn. 1538).

The stemma (or branch diagram of the textual tradition) on the opposite page can illustrate the interdependence of the manuscripts discussed here; it is, of course, simplified, but provides the reader with a general outlook.

Greek Papyri

We know of papyri for twenty-one Hippocratic treatises. These papyri preserve either the texts themselves, therefore belonging to the direct textual tradition, or quotations, and thus are part of the indirect tradition.[27] The oldest papyri date back to the first century BC for the direct tradition and the third century AD for the indirect tradition; the youngest belong to the sixth and seventh centuries AD. Therefore, these papyri are roughly a thousand years older than the manuscripts, and therefore testify to a much older stage of the textual tradition. Unfortunately, however, they are often very short and badly damaged, so that their use is limited. Moreover, one has to be wary of modern editions of these papyri, as editors are sometimes quick to restore readings; one therefore should rely only on clearly visible readings.

The papyri also provide important information about how the Hippocratic texts were used in antiquity. For instance, we have the most papyri, ten, for the *Aphorisms*, and this underscores the fact that it was by far the most popular text. Next is the *Prognostic* with five papyri, and *Nature of Man*, both again very popular texts. Other popular topics included gynaecology and surgery, and the Hippocratic *Letters* are also well represented.

Translations and the Source Texts

The evidence from translations can also be divided into two: relating to the direct and indirect traditions, respectively. What matters is the Greek source text: if it is a Hippocratic text, then the target text

---

[27] Marganne (2014); see especially the appendices on pp. 300–302 listing the various papyri. Adorno et al. (2008) no. 18 (Hippocrates), 77–233, also provides information about the papyri. An important research tool is provided by the CEntre de DOcumentation de PApyrologie Littéraire (CEDOPAL) in the form of the Mertens-Pack 3 (MP3) online database; see http://web.philo.ulg.ac.be/cedopal/en/ (accessed 18 May 2017).

belongs to the direct tradition; if, however, it is a Greek text merely quoting Hippocrates (for instance, in the form of lemmas), then it belongs to the indirect tradition.

The most numerous translations of the *Hippocratic Corpus* are in Latin. They can usefully be divided into three periods: early translations of Late Antiquity; medieval translations of the eleventh to fourteenth centuries; and Renaissance translations. For the textual history, age matters: it is the earliest translations that provide the most useful evidence for the Greek textual tradition, but one should not neglect the medieval and Renaissance translations either. Another point is very important: whether the Latin translation was produced directly from the Greek source text, or whether there were other intermediary translations, for instance in Syriac and Arabic.

The earliest translations of the fifth and sixth centuries were produced directly from a Greek source text. Moreover, this source text predates the Greek manuscript tradition by some 500 years, not counting papyri. Therefore, these old translations are of prime importance for the history of the Hippocratic text: they allow us to reconstruct the archetype (the oldest layer) of the direct tradition. We have these old Latin translations for a number of treatises: *Airs, Waters, Places; Aphorisms; Prognostic; Nature of Man; Regimen;* and *Diseases of Women*. Two Latin manuscripts of the ninth century preserve many of these old translations, and are therefore particularly important; they are

- Milan, Biblioteca Ambrosiana, MS Gr. 108 (*Codex Ambrosianus* G 108)
- Paris, Bibliothèque nationale de France, MS 7027 (fonds latin) (*Parisinus lat.* 7027).

The Latin translations become even more important when the Greek original is lost. This is rare for Hippocratic texts, although there is the example of *Weeks*, the Greek text which was consumed in the great fire of the Escorial Library near Madrid in 1671.

As previously mentioned, the later translations are less important for the reconstruction of the Greek textual tradition, but deserve study in their own right. For instance, the medieval translations of treatises such as *Airs, Waters, Places; Aphorisms; Nature of Man;* and *Regimen* replaced the older ones. Likewise, during the Renaissance, scholars endeavoured to retranslate various Hippocratic texts into more elegant and more classical Latin, and these new versions gradually replaced the old ones.

Whenever one is faced with a Latin version that has an Arabic intermediary, one should try to find the Arabic translation on which the Latin one is based. The Arabic translations of Hippocrates often derive from the indirect, not the direct tradition, as they are frequently extracted from the lemmas in Galen's commentary. For these, they provide precious evidence, and should therefore be exploited to the full. It is only recently, however, that the Arabic and Syriac evidence has been taken into consideration.[28] The complexities of the indirect evidence from the translation of the Arabic and Syriac lemmas have recently attracted intense scholarly attention.[29]

Indirect Tradition

The indirect tradition comprises all the evidence about the text that does not come directly from the text. We have already mentioned the indirect tradition on a number of occasions, but it is useful to give a more thorough account here. In the *Hippocratic Corpus*, the indirect tradition differs greatly from treatise to treatise. Yet, one can distinguish four categories, to be discussed in turn now.

PARALLEL REDACTIONS

One of the features of the *Hippocratic Corpus* is that for certain treatises there exists parallel content. In other words, passages in two texts are so similar that they cannot have arisen independently from one another by coincidence. The degrees of closeness vary from case to case. One can explain these parallels in two ways: either one of the texts was copied from the other; or they both go back to the same source, which is now lost. The first alternative, that one text was

---

[28]   Jouanna (2013); Overwien (2014); both editions contain German translations of the Arabic translation to give the reader an impression of what the Arabic has to offer.

[29]   Barry (2016); Mimura (2017); Karimulla (in press).

copied from another, is the most likely explanation in the case of treatises that are themselves compilations, such as the *Aphorisms* or the *Coan Prognoses*, and even more so in case of the short treatises that are so-called centos, that is, made up entirely of quotations from other works such as *Nature of Bones*, *Crises*, and *Days of Crisis*. The second alternative is more likely in the nosological and gynaeco-logical treatises such as *Diseases* and *Diseases of Women*: here the parallels can be explained through a common source that is now lost. Whatever the right explanation for these parallels may be, modern editors should always point them out, even if they cannot fully explain them, and include significant variants in the critical apparatus.

LEXICOGRAPHERS

The most frequently used indirect tradition is that of the lexicogra-phers. We basically have the glossaries of Erotian from the first and Galen from the second century AD, as previously discussed; a later one was composed by Hesychius of Alexandria in the fifth or sixth century.

It is helpful to explain what the usefulness of the two main glossographers consists of for the establishment of the Hippocratic text. The rare words that feature in Erotian and Galen also appear in a good number of Hippocratic treatises. For Erotian's glossary, it is easier to determine from which Hippocratic texts he extracted his entries. For Erotian composed his glossary by reading through the various Hippocratic texts one by one; therefore in the original version the words are not in alphabetic order, but in the order in which they appeared in the Hippocratic source. Of course, this original version is now lost, and we only have a later version, arranged alphabetically; yet even there, within each letter, the original order is maintained. We can therefore nearly always deter-mine whence a particular entry was taken. By contrast, Galen composed his glossary straight away according to the alphabet, and this makes it much more difficult to know from which treatise his entries were taken. There are, however, two exceptions: when

Galen explains a word that appears only once in the whole Hippocratic corpus (a so-called *hapax*); and when Galen himself mentions the source, although he does so only rarely.

Erotian drew on more than forty treatises for his glossary. How then can these entries be used to establish a critical text? Given that the words in the glossary are normally quite rare, they can be a criterion for gauging how much or how little the Hippocratic text has evolved. Some of these words are only partially preserved in the medieval manuscripts. They thus offer a measure of how 'conservative' the manuscript in question is, that is, whether it endeavours to preserve the text, even when it no longer makes any sense. Older words have been replaced by more current ones; this is a well-known principle in textual criticism: the more difficult reading (the '*lectio difficilior*') is replaced by the easier reading (the '*lectio facilior*').

COMMENTARIES

We have already discussed the commentaries on Hippocrates earlier. Here, the aim is to show how these commentaries are to be used when editing the various Hippocratic texts. One can distinguish three groups of commentaries: (1) the older ones pre-dating Galen of Pergamum, (2) Galen's commentaries, and (3) the Late Antique Alexandrian commentaries.

Apollonius of Citium wrote a commentary on *Joints* in the first century BC, and it is the oldest surviving Hippocratic commentary. Because of its age, it allows us to go back to a state of the text before the archetype of the manuscripts belonging to the direct tradition (namely B M V), but also before the lemmas contained in Galen's commentary. It thus shows us the development of the Hippocratic text from the first century onwards.

Galen's commentaries are equally important, although they attest to a text that is three centuries younger than Apollonius'. Editors of Hippocrates must consult them, because they contain not only the text as available in the second century AD, but also numerous ancient variant readings in manuscripts and the two ancient editions by Dioscorides and Artemidorus Capito, which Galen often quoted and discussed.

There are, however, some pitfalls that editors need to avoid. They must distinguish between the lemmas that Galen himself adduces, that is, the Hippocratic text that he himself quotes (to be designated as 'GalL'), and other citations adduced by Galen inside the commentary itself ('GalT'). For the lemmas are more likely to be contaminated with the direct tradition than the quotations within the commentary. For the lemmas, one ought to determine whether Galen himself copied the lemma, or whether this was done later by one of his scribes, who were more likely to use the direct tradition. The editors should strive to distinguish clearly between the direct and the indirect traditions, despite the large amount of cross-contamination between the two traditions. The commentaries of Late Antique Alexandria, from the so-called second Alexandrian Renaissance, do not have the same full lemmas as Galen's commentaries, nor are they as old; yet, one ought to consult them and they occasionally offer interesting textual evidence.

QUOTATIONS OUTSIDE THE COMMENTARY TRADITION

We also find a great number of quotations of Hippocratic works outside the commentaries and glossaries discussed in the foregoing. Anastassiou and Irmer (1997–2012) have surveyed this rich tradition in their monumental work, gathering all the relevant evidence in their *Testimonien zum Corpus Hippocraticum*. Galen remains the main source for such quotations (collected in volume ii.2 of the *Testimonien*), but there are also many quotations in two anonymous doxographies, the so-called *Anonymous of London* and the *Anonymous of Paris*, as well as in later Greek encyclopaedic writers such as Oribasius (fourth century), Aëtius of Amida (sixth century), Alexander of Tralles (sixth century), and Paul of Aegina (seventh century).

DIALECT

The *Hippocratic Corpus* is written in a Greek dialect called 'Ionian'. Generally speaking, this was the preferred dialect for scientific enquiries, and even non-Ionian speakers would use the Ionian dialect to compose their works. For instance, Herodotus, the great Greek historian, wrote in Ionian, although he came from Halicarnassus in Asia Minor, where people spoke Doric Greek. Likewise, on the island of Cos, whence Hippocrates hailed, the dialect was Doric. Scholars have traced Doric tendencies in the Ionic *Hippocratic Corpus*, and this is explained by the background of the author. The situation is further complicated by the fact that the Attic dialect, that of Athens, dominated in later times and was at the basis of the 'common' (*koiné*) Greek language that spread over parts of Africa, Asia, and Europe in the wave of Alexander the Great's conquests.

Editors of Hippocrates are faced with a real problem: what to do about the dialect. Generally speaking, the manuscripts do not offer a coherent picture. Some later manuscripts display more 'Ionic' readings, probably resulting from the desire of the scribes to present a consistent Ionic text. Sometimes in their quest for Ionic forms they even make up new ones that never really existed; scholars speak here about 'hyperionisms', in other words, hyper-correct Ionian forms.

Editors of the nineteenth and early twentieth centuries strove for consistency and probably chose more 'Ionic' readings than necessary. Yet each treatise has its own history, and even within the Ionic dialect, different forms co-existed; after all, Herodotus knew of four varieties of the Ionic dialect.[30] Therefore, modern editors should exert caution and not try to impose a certain variety of Ionic, nor should they correct dialect forms silently, as has often happened in the past. Because of this, we are still in a very difficult position regarding the dialect, because the critical editions do not always tell us what readings the manuscripts displayed. Therefore, it would be better to

---

[30]   *Histories* 1.142.

present the state of the text with its dialect variants, and thus to restore the archetype through thorough textual criticism. This archetype, to be sure, is still hundreds of years removed from the time of Hippocrates. But it is better to be aware of this situation than to correct the text and provide the illusion of going back to an original that exists only as a figment of the editor's imagination.

CONCLUSION

Let us close this chapter about the textual history of the *Hippocratic Corpus* by restating this fundamental principle: any study of Hippocrates and the works attributed to him must begin with the constitution of the text. To produce critical editions of the Hippocratic text that are based on all the available evidence – of both the direct and indirect traditions – and translate this text thus constituted into modern languages is the starting point for all subsequent investigations or interpretations. We have seen that the Hippocratic vulgate, the text commonly printed until the nineteenth century, was based on late manuscripts that do not offer the best text. Even by collating the various Paris manuscripts, Littré could not produce a truly critical text. Therefore, although the references to Littré's edition will remain standard for the foreseeable future, we cannot rely on his edition to reach a precise understanding of the texts contained in the *Hippocratic Corpus*; we must consult the most recent critical editions. This is an absolute necessity in order to make progress in the investigation and interpretation of the ancient medical tradition in general, and Hippocratic thought in particular.

4 Body

Brooke Holmes

THE BODY AND THE HIPPOCRATIC BODY

What is the body? The answer to this question might seem obvious. In point of fact, however, when we take up the subject of the Hippocratic body, we are inquiring into the origins of the very idea of the body. For the writings of the *Hippocratic Corpus* offer something like the first appearance of a concept of a physical or biological body within the Western medical and philosophical tradition.[1] By this I do not mean that the Hippocratic writers discovered the foundations of a science of the body to oppose superstition and crude empiricism. Rather, by using 'the body (*sôma*)' to organise and guide their perceptions of disease and the theories they developed of human nature and its malfunctioning, the Hippocratic writers lay the groundwork for understanding the body not just as an object of medical knowledge, but also as a philosophical problem that would persist for the next two millennia. When we ask what 'the' body, or the 'Hippocratic' body is, we are participating in this tradition even as we try to gain critical distance on it.[2] The body whose representations we seek to map and whose realities we (i.e., historians of ancient medicine and classicists, but also anthropologists, philosophers, sociologists, cultural critics, biologists, and so on) assume in reading the Hippocratic texts is in some fundamental sense always already a product of classical Greek medicine, always already 'Hippocratic'.

By addressing 'the body' in the *Hippocratic Corpus*, this chapter responds to recent scholarly trends inside and outside the history of

---

[1] I defend this claim and the basic line of argument in this chapter at greater length in Holmes (2010b).

[2] For some general but perspicacious remarks on the difficulty of getting outside a theoretical framework informed by our own understanding of nature and the body, see Descola (2012, 2013), writing from within anthropology (and taking the nineteenth century as especially consequential for these concepts as meta-concepts).

medicine and the classics. For several decades now, the body has attracted considerable research and theoretical speculation across a range of disciplines in the humanities and social sciences. Part of the attention in the Anglo-American context comes from the rise of academic feminism and gender and sexuality studies in the 1970s, 1980s, and 1990s. Taking aim at the idea of the body as the biological bedrock of human nature and sexual difference, many scholars in these fields have argued that the language of 'the body', understood as the biological body, has succeeded in masking the assumptions, biases, and fears that have silently and often perniciously shaped how the body, especially the sexed body, has been understood through the history of medicine and science. Moreover, insofar as these assumptions, biases, and fears continue to determine how bodies are understood today, we need further scholarship on how representations of the body are influenced by cultural and social factors as much as by empirical research or everyday experience. Within the field of ancient medicine, in the 1990s the cultural turn to the body produced, most notably, a series of important studies on the female body in early medical writing (and gynaecology has played an important role in broader work on sex and gender in antiquity during the past few decades).[3] These studies have amply demonstrated the many ways in which ingrained cultural assumptions about the female and sexual difference persist within Hippocratic gynaecology under the cloak of new physiological and pathological models. By and large, however, they left the category of 'the body' unexamined.[4]

---

[3]   See esp. Dean-Jones (1994), Hanson (1990, 1992a), King (1998), and Sissa (1990), as well as the earlier work of Manuli (1980, 1983) and Rousselle (1980). See also Flemming (2000) on the female body in Galen and other imperial-era medical authors.

[4]   Porter (1999), in the introduction to an important edited collection on the classical body, flagged the need for an inquiry into the category of 'the body', which is 'generally assumed, not queried' (3–4). See also Bynum (1995), on the looseness of the semantic field of 'the body' as it operated in the mid-1990s, and the incisive critique of the assumed category of 'the physical body' in Mol (2003), 7–12. But although work across the loose field of new materialism outside the classics has developed more sophisticated accounts of physicality and the body, old habits die hard. Even recent work on 'the body' in the classics and ancient history tends to assume the category as self-evident.

The body, however, is not just a representation. In the early decades of the twenty-first century, interest has grown across the humanities and social sciences in overcoming the entrenched dualism of mind (or soul) and body, and in rethinking embodiment, materiality, and the physical conditions of life. Fields such as the philosophy and history of medicine and biology, medical anthropology, medical sociology, and bioethics, as well as growing areas of interdisciplinary research sometimes grouped under the heading 'new materialisms', are flourishing. These developments have great potential to inform new paradigms and research questions for historians of early Greek medicine, encouraging them to see their material in different ways and with different aims while building on rich traditions of scholarship. In the context of these larger trends, we stand to gain much from examining the ancient Graeco-Roman roots of concepts such as 'body', 'nature', and 'matter' in classical antiquity, and, within such a project, the *Hippocratic Corpus* has an important role to play.

Nothing I have just said, however, should be taken to imply that the body in the *Hippocratic Corpus* is *only* a scholarly construct or an artificial imposition. For one thing, that would misleadingly imply that some frames of analysis are *not* products of their historical, intellectual, and national contexts. Rather, these contexts always influence the questions we ask of our texts, even though under the best circumstances the texts surprise us with the answers they yield.[5] One such product is the term 'Hippocratic' itself, though it has a long history. The descriptor 'Hippocratic' can wrongly imply more homogeneity among the texts of the *Corpus* than they in fact possess, and so I adopt it here advisedly. I believe, nevertheless, that these writers share enough common ground when it comes to their views on the body (*sôma*) to merit the use of the term. Perhaps most fundamentally, the Hippocratic writers place *sôma* at the heart of what they know and how they practice. In writing that the starting point of medical reasoning is the nature of the body, the author of *Places in Man* makes

---

[5] The comments in King (1998), 54–74, on the 'Hippocratic research programme' are especially useful here.

explicit what many other texts take for granted.[6] What can we say by way of introduction to this body?

Unfortunately, we have little evidence to guide us in the meaning of *sôma* prior to the Hippocratic texts, and interpretations of the evidence that we do have are contested. In the *Discovery of the Mind*, Bruno Snell claimed that Homer lacks a word for the unified living body: *sôma*, he argued, is used only to designate a corpse.[7] On the basis of this philological argument, Snell concluded that Homer thus lacks a *concept* of the unified living body. The argument has been widely criticised on both philological and philosophical grounds, but though flawed in some respects, as I have discussed elsewhere, it throws into dramatic relief our ingrained habit of taking 'the body' for granted as a category, rather than as a historically emergent concept.[8] The classical era medical texts, as I have already suggested, can help us understand its emergence and dismantle its obviousness. In the Hippocratic treatises, *sôma* describes the three-dimensional object that you can touch and see and smell, enveloped by skin and articulated by bone.[9] Of course, the medical writers are unusually well acquainted with this object, but we can hardly explain their investment in the *sôma* only through reference to their constant handling of the sick. After all, healers had been handling the bodies of patients for a long time before the fifth century BC. I would emphasise instead that the Hippocratic body is much more than what meets the eye or the hand. Indeed, what evades being seen or touched directly can be credited with endowing the *sôma* with its remarkable explanatory power in the work of the Hippocratic medical writers, inspired as they are by a more general revolution in imagining the 'unseen' dimensions of reality in Pre-Socratic philosophy and its turn away from anthropomorphic gods and daemons as causes.

---

[6]   See *Places in Man* 2 (6.278 L.).   [7]   Snell (1953), 1–23.

[8]   See esp. Renehan (1979); Williams (1993), 21–49; and Gill (1996) for critiques of Snell. For a fuller discussion of Snell's argument, the evidence from Homer, and other pre-Hippocratic evidence for *sôma*, see Holmes (2010b), 6–8, 29–37.

[9]   We have to be careful, however, not to assume that three-dimensionality as a formal concept is an integral part of the definition of *sôma* prior to Aristotle: see Lang (2015).

These more mysterious aspects of *sôma* can be classified into two categories, which I use to structure the two latter sections of this chapter. On the one hand, the hidden body refers to its interior spaces, especially the chest cavity, but also a host of other cavities and places enfolded in the flesh. In these cavities, the processes of disease unfold not just out of sight, but often largely below the threshold of the embodied person's perception and sensation. In Hippocratic writing the hidden space within the body takes over much of the ground of gods and daemons in magico-religious accounts of disease, as I discuss in more detail in the text that follows. To the extent that the body, like nature in the famous dictum of Heraclitus, 'is wont to hide', the work of the physician is rigorously semiotic, organised by the interpretation of the signs produced out of the depths of the body and analogous to the hermeneutic labour of the diviner.[10] The tacit prohibitions on cutting open the body in the fifth and fourth centuries BC only exaggerate the semiotic work of the Hippocratic physician.

The hidden body includes, on the other hand, the panoply of forces acting on each other within the interior. If the inner spaces and places inside the body can come to light with the scalpel, as the systematic dissection of human beings in Ptolemaic Alexandria will prove, the forces animating the body can be seen only through their effects. In the Hippocratic texts, the most important forces are associated with the constituent, fluid stuffs of the body, conventionally referred to as humours by modern scholars (though not all ancient authors call them *chymoí*). In health, these forces support life by counterbalancing one another. But one force often grows too strong and disrupts the body's economy of power, tilting it towards disease and eventually death. The body is so susceptible to these upsets of power because it has to constantly negotiate the external world – taking in food and drink, enduring changes of weather and season, and expending energy through movement.

---

[10] Heracl. DK22B123.

Besides the humours, other important 'players' within the body include breath, core heat, and the body's nature. In short, the Hippocratic body is fundamentally *dynamic*, animated by forces in an agonistic relationship with one another and always engaged with a teeming mass of external forces (winds, foods, etc.) that it struggles to resist or conquer. Despite being imagined, usually implicitly, as self-regulating, then, the body is not fully self-sufficient, thereby creating the very need for medicine. The work of the Hippocratic physician, and to a lesser degree the patient, is to manage a body that cannot always manage itself.

Much of the 'Hippocratic' body, we have just seen, is unavailable to direct perception. The physician or the medical researcher relies on the symptoms of disease and other signs produced by the body to build hypotheses about events in the interior, the nature of the forces involved, and the nature of the body itself. Neither a biological given nor a purely ideal or imagined object, the body in the work of the early medical writers can be described as a 'conceptual object' that demands both inferential reasoning and hands-on engagement from the physician, much as it still does today. By going back to the early formation of the physical body in the work of the Hippocratic authors, we are in a better position to grasp its complexity, and the consequences of its classification as physical and biological, in the present.

In what follows, I elaborate the two aspects of the Hippocratic body that I have just sketched out: *sôma* as a largely hidden inner landscape of parts connected by channels and flesh of different densities and textures and *sôma* as dynamic, populated by a range of impersonal forces and, in some texts, animated by a tendency towards life. I take account of the fact that 'the' Hippocratic body is always, by default, the male body, while some features mark the female body as different. I want to begin, however, by giving a little bit more background to the Hippocratic body, so that its distinctive aspects can better come into focus.

BEFORE THE HIPPOCRATICS

The surface of the body for the Hippocratic authors conceals a variegated landscape of bones, sinews, hollow spaces, denser flesh, and channels. These descriptions, though owing something to glimpses inside the body and the opening up of animal bodies, enact a speculative understanding of the internal anatomy of the body informed primarily by the physiology and the pathology of the humours. It is as receptacles and channels for the humours that the parts of the body come into focus most sharply.[11]

By conceptualising what is inside a human being in terms of the movement of fluids and also breath, the medical writers show themselves to be heirs to an earlier imaginary. What little we know of this world comes primarily from Homer's two epics, in which life-forces and emotions pool and seethe and course through the hero.[12] At the same time, the medical writers depart radically from early poetry by conceptualising interior space in terms of parts and stuffs with natures that are known primarily through objective inquiry, carried out under the auspices of medicine as an art (*téchnē*), rather than through embodied experience.[13] Let us take a closer look at the difference between these two ways of knowing what is inside a person.

It is very difficult for us to imagine a person, and especially the inside of a person, without relying on a concept of the physical body. Not surprisingly, then, the topic of what is usually called 'Homeric psychology' together with its relationship to Homer's anatomical knowledge has been a vexed issue since at least the mid-nineteenth

---

[11]   Gundert (1992), 453.

[12]   See Padel (1992), esp. 78–98 and Clarke (1999), esp. 80–109.

[13]   One might object that the difference of perspective is due to genre: Homer is poetry; the *Hippocratic Corpus* is technical prose. The objection helpfully points to the role played by the rise of medical writing and competitive oral performance in changing conceptualisations of the body and the subject position of the physician, on which see Holmes (2013), esp. 249–59. But it does not undermine arguments for the historical novelty of these new ways of imagining the bodily interior, in that the prose treatise and epideictic speech are themselves products of the fifth century BC. Goldhill (2002) is a helpful introduction to the rise of prose; on the genre of medical prose more specifically, see van der Eijk (1997).

century. I do not have the space here to deal with the problems at any length. Given how easily we naturalise the body in Hippocratic medicine, however, we should at least flag some of the differences between early Greek ways of conceptualising the insides of a person and those of the Hippocratic writers.

The Homeric epics and other archaic poems most frequently describe the behaviours of the substances responsible for life, feeling, and thought, together with the space in which they move, in phenomenological terms, rather than from the perspective of things and events that are potentially observed. Such descriptions are not metaphorical; they do not assume a literal (physical, objective, anatomical) idea of the body.[14] For the various parts of the Homeric person are not parts of a body, understood as a stand-alone physical object, but rather parts of a self that are known primarily as loci of thought and emotion, pleasure and pain, and so known primarily through felt experience. What happens to the self *may* be visible to others. So an observer may see energy surging up in a warrior by the glint in his eyes, and some of the parts of the self spoken of as seats of cognitive and emotional activity are imagined as concrete entities that could be seen under extreme conditions (in the *Iliad*, the skin is often breached in scenes of combat). The *phrénes* (sometimes identified with the diaphragm by modern scholars), for example, are at one point removed by a spear.[15] They become, at that moment, part of the shared 'seen' space defined primarily by the surface of the person. The dynamics of wind and water observed in the outside world inform the imagination of mental life as 'ebb and flow', as Michael Clarke has thoroughly demonstrated.[16] What a person feels inside is part of a continuous feedback loop within the self that does not take place in an objective or 'literal' space that is best understood by physicians, nor are such experiences referred to expert knowledge about the nature of the structures and stuffs that lie beneath the skin. In early Greek texts, we

---

[14]   As Clarke (1999) rightly emphasises: what he calls the 'psychology' in Homer 'is not easily reducible to what we can apprehend on the basis of our modern understanding of the physical body' (77). See also Holmes (2010b), 41–83.

[15]   Homer, *Iliad* 16.504.   [16]   Clarke (1999), esp. 79–109.

can see instead a robust, first-personal mode of knowing the inside of a human being.

We can better grasp these different ways of conceptualising a human being (in the first person and third person, 'felt' and 'seen') by thinking for a moment about the boundaries of the person in early Greek poetry. These boundaries are created, first, by skin. 'Neither stone nor iron', the skin is damaged primarily by being broken, and its repair is entrusted to the physician.[17] By contrast, the boundaries of the person function differently in the case of a disease such as the plague. Here, Apollo's arrow does not work by piercing the skin but instead represents or symbolises the transfer of the god's anger to its mortal victims, whose sufferings are produced directly by the god's intention to harm. The 'felt' space of the person is in this respect contiguous with the domain of the gods and other disease-causing agents. The boundary between the two domains is marked primarily by the person's perception of something 'other' erupting into conscious experience.[18] The intruding foreign agent resembles a weapon in many respects. Crucially, however, the agent of disease transgresses not the boundary of the skin but the boundary between the conscious self and the daemonic realm.

The damage wrought by an intrusive daemonic agent seems to have fallen outside the expertise of the average physician. When Achilles calls for an expert to give advice about the plague that strikes the Achaean army in Book 1 of the *Iliad*, he asks for a seer, a holy man, or a dream interpreter – not a doctor.[19] In fifth-century texts we do find references to a figure called the *iatrómantis*, the

[17]   'Neither stone nor iron': Homer, *Iliad* 4.510. On the physician and wounds to the skin, see, e.g., Homer, *Iliad* 11.515, where the physician is worth many men for his ability 'to remove arrows and apply soothing medicaments'. See also Pindar, *Pythian* 3.40–55, where skill in the recitation of charms is added to the physician's expertise, creating what Émile Benveniste called the 'doctrine médicale des Indo-Européens': see Benveniste (1945).

[18]   For cross-cultural evidence of perceptions of otherness objectified as daemonic or divine agents, see Csordas (1990), with a sophisticated analysis of embodiment that draws primarily on Maurice Merleau-Ponty and Pierre Bourdieu. On such objectifications as 'abductions of agency', see Gell (1998).

[19]   Homer, *Iliad* 1.62–4.

'healer-seer'.[20] But what is emphasised here is the application of expertise in communicating with the realm of gods and daemons to the care of the sick. The special vision of the expert does not involve seeing inside the person.[21]

A number of factors contribute to changes in the conceptualisation of medical expertise and *téchnē* in the sixth through fourth centuries BC, including, importantly, the rise of the 'inquiry into nature' and changing ideas about the unseen powers at work in the cosmos. Here it is worth emphasising simply that the inquiry into nature has a powerful impact on the medical writers who, in the fifth century BC, begin mapping the inner landscape in terms of structures, channels, and substances that are envisaged as existing first and foremost as concrete entities whose natures can be known *only* by medical inquiry and training, in part because so much of what happens inside the body does not cross the threshold of perception and in part because even what a patient does feel, he fails to make sense of, at least intuitively, in terms of natures and causes. By positing unfelt space within the body, the medical writers quite literally make space for the daemonic realm, which lies beyond the boundaries of the self in Homer and other early poetry, *inside* the person. Moreover, what is experienced is referred back to substances and powers that are properly impersonal, cut off from the forms of communication and social reciprocity that characterise relationships between mortals and immortals or between the parts of the Homeric self and the 'I'. These natures have to be manipulated by the physician – or the patient carrying out the orders of the physician – acting on the body externally, with drugs and regimens. If they are left unmanaged, they

---

[20] See Aeschylus, *Eumenides* 62 and *Suppliants* 263, with Parker (1983), 209–12.

[21] But see also fr. 1 (Davies) of the *Sack of Troy* attributed to Arctinus, where Machaon has skill in dealing with wounds while Podaleirius has the gift of 'diagnosing unclear things'. The division of labour may represent changing ideas about medical expertise in the sixth and fifth centuries BC: see further, on the dating of the fragment, Davies (1989) 3, 5–6, 11 n. 6, 65, 77. The comparative Assyrio-Babylonian evidence regarding the division of labour between the seer and the doctor is intriguing, though the difference between their areas of expertise remains a subject of debate: see Scurlock (1999).

produce a wide range of diseases, most of which had been seen previously in terms of the agency of gods.

In short, then, the medical writers reimagine what used to be seen as a boundary between the self and an absolute other in terms of a split within the human being between the conscious, experiencing, mindful self and a hidden, largely unfelt inner space and the impersonal powers that determine what happens there. The *sôma* becomes Hippocratic – and, hence, familiar to a long Western tradition of thinking about the body – through its identification with this space and these powers: alien and daemonic, but also available to objective inquiry and technical control. Let us turn, then, to some of the most important aspects of the inner landscape: vessels, flesh, and the *schēmata*, the 'forms' which will come to be called 'organs' after Aristotle.

THE INNER LANDSCAPE

It is worth stressing once again that anatomical research cannot be held responsible for changes to the conceptualisation of the inner landscape in the *Hippocratic Corpus*. Rather, we need to pay attention to how inner parts and stuffs function within new systems for explaining health and disease and how they participate within the broader imaginary being developed around the physical body, especially as it is conceptualised as unseen, unruly space *and* as an interconnected, living unity.

I have used the Greek word *schēmata* and not the English word 'organs' because the latter term reflects an Aristotelian analysis of body parts in terms of their functions within a broader teleological model of the body. For Aristotle, function determines structure. By contrast, for the Hippocratic writers, while structure determines how parts function, 'there is never any hint that [sc. parts] have particular structures in order to fulfil given roles'.[22] The major parts of the body, including what we would call organs, are usually analysed

---

[22]   Gundert (1992), 465.

in terms of how their shape and texture affect the humours. The author of *Ancient Medicine* writes:

> I hold that one must also know which affections come upon the human being from powers and which from structures. What do I mean by this? By "power" I mean the acuity and strength of the humours; by "structures" I mean all the parts inside the human being, some hollow and tapering from wide to narrow, others also extended, others solid and round, others broad and suspended, others stretched, others long, others dense, others loose in texture and swollen, others spongy and porous.[23]

The shape of a part thus determines its ability to attract fluids within the body. Hollow and tapering structures, for example, excel at attracting and retaining moisture, a fact that the author establishes by appealing to an analogy with 'evident things outside the body', such as cupping glasses, common bell-shaped instruments that were heated and placed on the skin to draw up fluids to the surface.[24]

Notice here the interchangeability of the internal part and an object that exists out in the world, which is justified by the fact that they share a shape whose nature determines the effect of the part on fluids. In the human body, the best examples of hollow and tapering parts are the bladder, the uterus ('for women'), and the head. Indeed, the head often functions in Hippocratic nosology like a giant cupping instrument; as a likely site for the attraction of excess fluid, it is especially prone to disease. What matters here is building a working model of the inside of the body as a system for understanding the mechanics of the fluids that determine health and disease and, accordingly, whether the embodied subject feels well or unwell. The system is known via an analogical, objectified way of seeing, rather than through embodied perceptions.

---

[23]   *Ancient Medicine* 22, 1.626 L., trans. Schiefsky (2005).
[24]   *Ancient Medicine* 22 (1.626–28 L.). Interestingly, the listener can also observe his own body transformed into an object: he is invited to form his mouth into an 'o' in order to draw up liquid via a straw.

Not only shape but also texture affects how parts of the body participate in the circulation of humours. Those that are spongy and porous, such as the spleen and the lungs, readily drink up fluids, making them especially vulnerable to becoming overly saturated when there is excess moisture in the body. If they grow too saturated, parts that were once spongy become hard and dense. They dilate and touch other parts of the body, and they suffer pain at the pressure of winds. The spongiest parts of the body are the glands, the subject of an entire treatise, where they are said to be distributed throughout the body's cavities and joints. By virtue of being loose textured, the glands can absorb a considerable amount of moisture before becoming diseased, meaning they do not typically 'suffer together' with the rest of the body. When they do become oversaturated, however, the entire body suffers.[25]

Just as texture differentiates one part from another, it also differentiates one sex from the other. The medical writers generally believed that the flesh of the female body is looser and so more porous than the flesh of the male body, especially after the physiological changes brought about by menarche, sex, and pregnancy loosen up the vessels of the female body. Because it is porous, female flesh absorbs moisture easily, as at least one gynaecological author thought was simple enough to prove analogically through an experiment with non-human bodies. He recommends the following experiment: place wool and a closely woven cloth over water; after a few days, remove the fabrics. You will find, he says, that the wool is much heavier than the cloth because it has absorbed more of the liquid. The experiment ostensibly demonstrates that 'a woman, being more porous, draws more moisture from the belly to her body and draws it more quickly than a man does'.[26] To the extent that they absorb so much moisture, female bodies come to require regular evacuation, which according to the standard Hippocratic analysis is the very purpose of menstruation.

[25] *Glands* 1 (8.556 L.). [26] *Diseases of Women* 1.1 (8.12 L.).

By describing the female body as unarticulated and excessively moist, the medical writers are doing more than just drawing on broader cultural ideas about the lability of women, their susceptibility to disruption, and their incapacity for ethical agency: they are also providing new justification for those ideas.[27] The female body is differentiated from the male archetype (and, by extension, female nature from male nature more broadly) not only by the texture of the flesh but also by the presence of the uterus. The medical writers notoriously imagine the uterus as a source of problems – in fact, they tend to trace most symptoms in their female patients to uterine events – because it travels through the body in search of moisture.[28] Here again, cultural beliefs about the instability of women and the conceptualisation of the female body reinforce one another.

When we speak of 'the' Hippocratic body, then, we are speaking of a male body that shares some features with the female body but is not the same as it. The imagination of the female body, in particular, reminds us that descriptions of the body in the *Hippocratic Corpus*, especially the inner body and the natures of its parts, are never just explanatory in relationship to health and disease but also support and reflect a larger set of ideas about the body and human nature. So, for example, the sponginess of the glands or female flesh, like the hollowness of the head or womb, expresses the difficult relationship of the Hippocratic body to fluids, which are seen as both life-sustaining *and* susceptible to disequilibrium, thereby putting even the everyday life of the body at constant risk of tipping towards disease. By conceptualising the inner landscape in terms of labile fluids, the Hippocratic writers imply that bodies need physicians to control and regulate them.

In a similar way, when the Hippocratic writers describe hollows and cavities inside the body, they are not simply identifying structures

---

[27]   On the association between the articulation of the body, gender, and agency, see Kuriyama (1999).

[28]   For example, *Diseases of Women* 2.123 (8.266 L.), 124 (8.266 L.), 127 (8.272 L.), and 137 (8.310 L.). On the wandering womb see Dean-Jones (1994), 69–73, 112–19, 35–6 and, for analysis of medical and non-medical evidence together, Faraone (2011).

with important roles to play in physiology and pathology. They are vividly painting the various cavities as a network of hidden nooks and crannies that nourish disease without either the embodied person or the physician knowing that things are going wrong until it is potentially too late. Here is the author of the treatise *Art* speaking about the many cavities inside the body:

> Now such being its nature the art must be a match for the open diseases; it ought, however, not to be helpless before diseases that are less visible. These are those which are determined to the bones or to the cavity. The body has of these [sc. cavities] not one but several. There are two that take in food and discharge it, with several others besides these, known to men who are interested in these things; the parts of the body that have surrounding flesh which is called 'muscle' all have a cavity.[29] Everything in fact that is not grown entirely together, whether it is covered by skin or flesh, is hollow, and in health is filled with air, in disease with humour. Such flesh then the arms have, and so have the thighs and the legs. Moreover, in the fleshless parts also there are cavities like those we have shown to be in the fleshy parts. For the trunk, as it is called, in which the liver is covered, the sphere of the head, in which is the brain, the back, against which are the lungs – all these are themselves hollow, being full of interstices. And among these there are vessels containing many things, some of which do harm to the possessor, and some do good.[30]

Although medical writers more often speak about 'the cavity' with reference either to the entire trunk or the belly, this author multiplies the cavities inside the body as sites for diseases to flourish without the embodied person knowing what is happening.

The author of this treatise is especially concerned with exonerating physicians for apparent failures to cure disease. He strategically shifts blame onto non-compliant patients and faults, too, the 'nature

---

[29]   For the translation of *tà mélea* as 'parts of the body', see Jouanna (1988), 235, n. 4.
[30]   *Art* 10, 6.16–18 L., trans. Jones (1923b), modified.

of the body' itself for allowing 'diseases [to] live not in plain view'.[31] Confronted with a body complicit in disease, the physician has to force it to produce symptoms and thereby reveal what is happening in its concealed spaces.[32] In the mapping of an inner landscape of crevices and little rooms, the author vividly enacts what I described in the foregoing as the incorporation of erstwhile daemonic space into the *sôma*.

In addition to the structures and the flesh of the body, the Hippocratic writers spend much time thinking about and mentally tracing the vessels that connect the various parts and vein the flesh (I use the language of vessels because it is not until the Hellenistic period that we find the distinction among veins, arteries, and nerves). These vessels loom large in Hippocratic pathology, creating networks through which diseased and excess humours easily move from one part of the body to another.[33] The vessels can also cause problems when they get blocked up, as in *Sacred Disease*, where the spread of phlegm through the vessels prevents the free flow of air, producing a range of catastrophic symptoms.[34] In *Breaths*, to take another example, when breaths accumulate in the vessels they compress the blood, causing the 'thinnest part' to separate out and pool in inappropriate places that become seats of disease.[35]

The Hippocratic writers were also interested in the anatomy of the vessels and their role in sustaining health in the body, and a few treatises offer quite detailed (if also vague and confused) attempts to give a full accounting of the paths of the vessels.[36] In focussing on the interconnection of the vessels, some authors reached for the figure of the circle to describe the overall system. The author of *Places in Man*,

---

[31]   *Art* 11 (6.20 L.).

[32]   *Art* 12 (6.24–6 L.). On the author's use of language associated with the torture of slaves in the law court, see von Staden (2007b), 28–32.

[33]   Later authors will speak of the transfer of disease in terms of sympathy, though there are reasons not to project that concept too readily on the Hippocratic texts: see Holmes (2014).

[34]   *Sacred Disease* 6–7 (6.370–4 L.).   [35]   *Breaths* 10 (6.104–6 L.).

[36]   For discussion of Hippocratic descriptions of vascular anatomy, see Harris (1973) and Duminil (1983).

for example, writes in the opening chapter that 'it seems to me that there is no beginning point of the body, but every part is beginning and end alike, as the beginning point of the figure of a circle is not found'.[37] From at least the eighteenth century AD, references to the circle here and elsewhere have been read as evidence that the Hippocratics knew of the circulatory system well in advance of Harvey and that they possessed a model of the body as an 'organic machine' like those at the heart of what was called iatromechanism.[38] Neither of these interpretations has much support among historians of ancient medicine today, but they do help us recognise that the Hippocratics represent the body not just as daemonic and untrustworthy but also as a dynamic system whose parts work together for health. I would like to shift focus now to this dynamic body, starting with the humours and then moving to other, more 'vital' forces in the body, including its nature.

THE DYNAMIC BODY

We have been focussing on the inside of the body as a topographically variegated space for the circulation of the humours according to largely mechanical principles, such as the attraction of fluids into tapering, hollow spaces. But humours are dynamic in another way, too, in that they are defined and differentiated from one another by virtue of their powers.

Although the list of humours and powers varies from author to author, humours are widely understood in terms of how a stuff affects other stuffs and is itself affected (by, say, heat, cold, or acidity). In a healthy state, powers interact to maintain the conditions of life (or at least they do not interfere with physiological function). The interaction is often described by modern scholars as a quasi-

---

[37] *Places in Man* 1 (6.276 L.). See also *Nature of Bones* 11 (9.182 L.); *Regimen* 1.19 (6. 492–94 L.). See Joly (1960), 65, for further discussion of the figure of the circle in classical medical and philosophical texts.

[38] For a dismissal of the idea that Hippocratic sources anticipated Harvey in the discovery of the circulatory system, see Harris (1973), 48–9. On eighteenth-century iatromechanist receptions of the *Corpus*, see Lonie (1981).

democratic balance of powers, but we have reason to doubt whether *isonomía* was the primary model. The word appears only in a fragment of the text of the sixth century BC natural philosopher (and perhaps also physician) Alcmaeon, where it is not even clear that Alcmaeon himself used it.[39] Turning to the Hippocratic texts themselves, we find that many authors think that one humour normally prevails in a given individual, perhaps endowing the person with a certain type of character or predisposing him to certain pathological conditions; it may also be normal and not necessarily problematic for one humour to prevail in all bodies in a given season or under certain climactic or environmental conditions.[40] Still, in other cases, powers grow danger-ous precisely because they start to dominate the other powers.[41] In any event, all humours have the potential to become pathogenic when they undergo changes to their powers, as we can see especially clearly in *Affections*: 'Bile and phlegm produce diseases when, inside the body, one of them becomes too moist, too dry, too hot, or too cold.'[42] The author then offers a long list of what precipitates the humour's change: food, drink, exertions, wounds, smell, sound, sight, sex, heat, and cold. If any of these stimuli are too strong or too weak, disease results. Insofar as the body is always being subjected to changes in the weather, food and drink, exertion, and sensory experi-ence, the humours are always in a state of flux, their powers barely held in check by the parameters of what is appropriate for a given body in a given place under given environmental conditions.

What does it mean to make the humour a cause of a symptom or a disease? Here we can think back to accounts of disease that vest causal responsibility with gods or other divine agents, such as dae-mons, who act in the world primarily on the basis of intentions. Recall

---

[39]   Alcmaeon DK24B4.   [40]   See further von Staden (1999b).
[41]   See, e.g., *Ancient Medicine* 14 (1.602 L.).
[42]   *Affections* 1 (6.208 L.). It should be noted that while in the Hippocratic texts, the humours are part of the healthy body, it would seem from the doxographical Anonymous Londinensis papyrus that other classical-era writers on medicine held that the humours were substances created only under pathological conditions. In fact, the view ascribed to 'Hippocrates' by that text is that disease is produced by harmful residues created by undigested food (*Anonymous of London* 5.35–6.44).

that in the case of the plague in the first book of the *Iliad*, Apollo brings the disease about with an arrow, but the proper cause of the plague is his anger, itself triggered by the anger of his priest Chryses.[43] We have a causal chain here. The chain is, however, discontinuous at the moment that the anger of the god is transferred to the arrow. Rather than functioning like a proper instrument, which acts on the victims to produce symptoms, the arrow behaves more like a symbol that, in Ruth Padel's words, marks 'the daemonic advantage over the human'.[44] It represents the translation of Apollo's desire to harm into efficacious – indeed *uncannily* efficacious – action. After all, what defines the gods if not their exaggerated power to act in the world? The 'how' simply is not that important. What the Achaeans want to know is 'why'. By contrast, in the work of the Hippocratic writers, the question of 'how' comes to the forefront. Listen, for a moment, to an imagined heckler in the treatise *Breaths*: 'So *how* do breaths cause fluxes? *In what way* does wind cause haemorrhages in the chest?'[45] On the magico-religious model, the actual mechanics of causation matter little, given the efficacious agency of the gods. But the medical writers are trying to substitute not just different causes of symptoms, but an entirely different model of causality. As a result, they are under pressure to spell out the mechanics of the disease process.

In most early medical texts, the response to a 'how' question, whether explicit or implicit, takes the form of a causal chain quite unlike the one outlined for the plague in the *Iliad*. The chain is triggered by an external catalyst, such as the ingestion of food or a change of weather, but it unfolds largely inside the body through the humours. But rather than just transferring the efficacious agency of a god to the impersonal humour, the medical writers *fragment* the agency exercised by a god. The disease no longer represents the realisa-tion of a god's intention to harm, but becomes a series of micro-events, some of which are contingent and necessarily entail each other. We can consider as an example the account of an epileptic fit given

---

[43] Homer, *Iliad* 1.43–52.   [44] Padel (1992), 152.   [45] *Breaths* 10 (6.104 L.).

in *Sacred Disease*. The fit is triggered by the rise of the south wind, which chills the phlegm in a congenitally phlegmatic person. The phlegm then descends into the channels through which air circulates in the body, and the blocked air triggers a range of symptoms. One bad things feeds off another. Eventually, the disease – that is, an entity that does not pre-exist the causal chain but is brought into existence through it – accumulates sufficient force to cause real harm, displacing the need to blame the hand of a god. For, as the author of *Regimen* writes, diseases 'don't come upon people all at once; rather, gathering themselves together gradually, they appear with a sudden spring'.[46] Here again we are reminded of why the cavity, lying as it does not just out of sight, but below the threshold of the embodied subject's perception, poses such a threat to health. But we can now also recognise something about how disease develops in this space: it works incrementally but with all the inevitability of impersonal necessity. By orchestrating the mechanics of the symptom's production through a series of cascading micro-events, the medical writers fill the conceptual space that was once occupied by the symbol of the god's power with new agents, stuffs, and forces that do not desire to hurt anyone, but blindly, bit by bit, bring about disease and death all the same.

I have gone into some detail in describing the causal chain of disease within the Hippocratic body because it sheds light on a crucial aspect of that body as a conceptual object. If agency is fragmented, who is left to blame? Who can be held responsible for the disease? What is more, the powers involved are all impersonal, their actions determined by their natures rather than by their intentions. If the space filled by the causal chain answers the 'how' question, it seems to block the 'why' question.

One way of answering the question of the blame is to fault the body itself and its nature for disease, as we saw in *Art*.[47] Indeed, one

---

[46] *Regimen* 1.2 (6.472 L.).

[47] See *Art*. 11 (6.20 L.), cited above n. 77, and *Places in Man* 43 (6.338 L.), where the body, succumbing to malignant forces, starts to create festering.

reason that the physical body acquires such negative connotations, once it enters the medico-philosophical tradition in antiquity, may be precisely because it enters that tradition as a locus of vulnerability and the terrain of disease. Nevertheless, the Hippocratic body is, in the end, an object. It is therefore poorly positioned to absorb the blame for disease. Blame is instead deflected onto the people who are in a position to take responsibility for the care of the body. This describes the physician, of course. But for all that the Hippocratic body is constitutively dependent on medicine for its well-being, the position of responsibility is occupied primarily by the embodied (male) subject.[48] Hippocratic texts such as *Affections* and *Regimen* explicitly cast the patient as a subject who should learn enough about his body to be able to ward off disease before it sets in, and detect abnormalities before they get out of hand (the author of *Regimen* is especially interested in what he calls 'pre-diagnosis').[49] Not only medical texts, but also other late fifth- and fourth-century BC texts testify to a growing ethical imperative to take care of the body, as Michel Foucault has demonstrated in the second volume of the *History of Sexuality*.[50] Foucault, however, did not recognise the way in which the very emergence of the physical body drives the development of techniques of caring not just for the body but for the self more generally in this period. The management of the body becomes integral to the self-mastery of the male subject while also serving as a model for techniques of caring for the soul in philosophical ethics.[51] By recognising once again that the Hippocratic body is not a given but an emergent historical phenomenon, we come to recognise how it shapes the way people are thinking about not just disease but also self-mastery in the classical period.

Yet the Hippocratic body is not only seen as unstable and therefore dangerous and requiring management, and the humours do not exhaust the repertoire of forces active within it. Both explicitly and, more often, implicitly, the Hippocratic authors assume the presence

---

[48]   The female patient is not framed as an ethical agent of self-care: see Dean-Jones (1992).
[49]   See *Affections* 1 (6.208 L.) and *Regimen* 1.2 (6.472 L.), 3.69 (6.606 L.).
[50]   Foucault (1985).   [51]   See further Holmes (2010b), 192–227, and Holmes (2010a).

of an active force or forces associated with the entire body in its agonistic encounters with external forces and in its struggles against disease. These battles are primarily fought in the belly or cavity, where incoming food and drink are either conquered and converted into nourishment or else themselves master the body. In the second scenario, 'the same things that otherwise make it thrive prevail over the body and produce the opposite effects'.[52] In *Ancient Medicine*, the author describes the crucial moment in human history when people realise that they have to cook their food to break down powers that are otherwise stronger than the nature and power of a human being.[53] The same way that we use heat to break down the strength of raw food, the cavity cooks or 'concocts' incoming food further through its own innate heat – the Hippocratics anticipate the importance of innate or vital heat in Aristotle and the Stoics here – and coction is also how the body overcomes the power of rogue humours.[54]

We learn a good deal about the idea of concocting diseased matter from one group of texts, in particular, the *Epidemics*, six treatises written by different authors and dating from the last decade of the fifth century to the middle of the fourth century BC. The *Epidemics*, with their bare lists of symptoms and laconic case histories, were for a long time believed to be entirely untheoretical, their authors committed only to the impartial observation of symptoms (and so laudable by the standards of modern observational science). But few historians today fail to take note of the theoretical concepts informing how and what these authors see, among which concoction occupies an important place.[55] The authors of the *Epidemics* record symptoms with an eye not just to what is happening inside the body, but also, and more importantly, to what symptoms

---

[52]   *Places in Man* 43 (6.336–8 L.).   [53]   *Ancient Medicine* 3 (1.578 L.).

[54]   Though a number of authors seem to assume the presence of innate heat, references to it are not especially common. See *Aphorisms* 1.14 (4.466 L.), 1.15 (4.446 L.); *Uses of Liquids* 2 (6.122 L.); *Diseases* 1.11 (6.158 L.); and *Regimen* 2.62 (6.576 L.). Heat also plays a crucial role in the development of life in the embryological treatises. See Gundert (2000), 17.

[55]   On these theoretical concepts, see esp. Langholf (1990).

say about the prospects for recovery, relapse, or death. They examine the effluvia, in particular, as providing information about whether the body will achieve a crisis and expel the malignant humour(s), usually on a particular ('critical') day in the disease cycle. The frame of reference means that whether symptoms are good or bad correlates with whether the body or its nature is mastering the disease, or vice versa. Though these value assessments are not always explicit in the *Epidemics*, they are laid out categorically in prognostic treatises such as *Prognostic* and *Coan Prognoses*, which form the theoretical background to the observations catalogued in the *Epidemics*. By using symptoms to track the inner struggle between body and disease, these treatises do important work in conceptualising a tendency towards health within the body. Even if they rarely name that force or tendency the 'nature' of the body, it is insistently present as the referent of 'good' prognostic signs. One way of imagining the nature of a body in the early fourth century BC, then, is as a kind of vital force, oriented in a quasi-teleological fashion towards life and health. This 'will' to health exists alongside and in subtle tension with the conceptualisation of a daemonic and unruly body.

There is, in fact, a famous passage from one of the latest *Epidemics* texts, *Epidemics* 6, on the 'untaught' nature of the body:[56]

> The body's nature is the physician in disease. Nature finds the way for herself, not from thought. For example, blinking, and the tongue offers its assistance, and all similar things. Well trained, readily and without instruction, nature does what is needed.[57]

The author goes on to list a range of other phenomena: tears, moisture of the nostrils, sneezing, ear wax, production of saliva in the mouth, breathing in and out, yawning, coughing, hiccoughing, urinating, and so on. These phenomena were of course familiar to other medical

---

[56]   Note that *phýsis* is also the term used for what guides embryological development: *Generation and Nature of the Child* 27 (7.528 L.). For *phýsis* in the medical texts more generally, see Beardslee (1918), 31–42; Michler (1962); Manetti (1973); Ayache (1992); Andò (2002); and von Staden (2007b).

[57]   *Epidemics* 6 5.1 (5.314 L).

writers. But what we seem to be seeing here is a new level of self-consciousness about the body's own drive towards health. The idea of 'untaught' nature will be taken up enthusiastically by Galen, who happily acknowledges its Hippocratic provenance while reading the *Epidemics* passage against the background of ethical naturalism as it is developed in the Hellenistic schools, especially Stoicism. From the perspective of the reception of 'Hippocrates', not just in Galen but in the later medical tradition as well, untaught nature is therefore an integral part of the 'Hippocratic' body.

In the passage from *Epidemics* 6, the nature of the body is explicitly without thought and productive of phenomena we would call physiological. Yet for all their investment in the non-conscious, automatic body, the Hippocratics do not exclude cognition, emotion, and perception from their accounts of either disease or the healthy body. On the contrary, they incorporate these 'mental' activities into an understanding of human nature rooted in the behaviour of the humours and the other stuffs and parts within the body. On the one hand, reports of symptoms mix phenomena that we might distinguish as bodily and mental or psychic. On the other hand, some authors give fairly developed accounts of mental functions, sometimes marked explicitly as belonging to the soul (*psychē*).[58] *Regimen* devotes several chapters to how the mixture of fire and water in the soul affects cognition.[59] *Airs, Waters, Places*, working with a single set of causal factors that encompass cultural factors in addition to environmental ones, speaks of their impact on the body and soul or mind.[60] Other texts (e.g., *Sacred Disease, Breaths*) give accounts of cognition and judgement that rely on air, moisture, and the brain or the state of the blood.[61] These accounts extend materialist explanations of thought found in Pre-Socratics such as Heraclitus, Empedocles, and Diogenes.

---

[58]   For a general overview of the bodily and the psychic in the *Corpus*, see Gundert (2000), esp. 20–31. See also Pigeaud (1980), 71–112.

[59]   *Regimen* 1.35 (6.512–22 L.), with Jouanna (2012).

[60]   *Airs, Waters, Places* 16 (2.62–4 L.), 19 (2.72 L.), and 24 (2.88 L.).

[61]   *Sacred Disease* 14 (6.386–8 L.) and *Breaths* 14 (6.110–12 L.). For a fuller discussion of the location of cognitive process in the Hippocratics, see van der Eijk (2005a), 119–38.

At the same time, medical writing of the fifth and fourth centuries BC clearly took physiological accounts of human nature in all its aspects to a new level of ambition and complexity. By the fourth century BC, these accounts were seeking to explain not just mental activities, but, in some cases, different types of human character. The very success of these medical or physiological accounts of human nature seem to have helped spur on competitive attempts, most obvious in Plato's early dialogues, to give an account of the human that privileged not the *sôma* but the *psychē* as the determinative part of the human being.

At the same time, the striking monism of the Hippocratic texts is not the whole story. For despite their physiological or materialist accounts of human nature, they also enact, in subtle but powerful ways, a sharp difference between the body and mind or soul. We see this most notably in the presentation of the physician as a knower whose knowledge or thought bears no explicit relationship to the state of his body, but also in the presentation of patients whose beliefs, motivations, fears, and desires affect their health by causing certain behaviours, without those mental states ever being targeted therapeutically.[62] In a number of different ways, then, the Hippocratic body also plays a decisive role in the rise of body/soul dualism in the Western tradition.

The Hippocratic body, then, is not just a physical object, even less an object that was there all along to be discovered by the classical Greek medical writers. Largely hidden, it emerges into visibility as physicians and patients interpret its signs and symptoms in terms of events involving impersonal stuffs acting out their natures in an unseen and largely unfelt space within. The inner landscape of this body is one dominated by differently shaped hollows, flesh of different textures, and interconnected vessels. The medical writers describe more than physiological or nosological systems. They develop a corporeal imaginary, shaped by long-standing cultural beliefs about daemonic agency, the mechanics of fluids, and the figure of the circle.

---

[62] See Gundert (2000), 35; Holmes (2010b) (on patients); and Holmes (2010a) (on physicians).

Within this space, the humours shape a new causal narrative of disease, one driven by a chain of micro-events, rather than by a divine agent. In showing up the body's unstable commitment to its own flourishing, such narratives encourage not just a belief in the need for medicine in health as well as in disease, but also a new form of subjectivity organised around the care of the body.

Yet the Hippocratic body is not only an object of care. It also has a nature actively oriented towards life and health. Life and health here are not limited terms, but encompass all aspects of a human being, including thought, emotion, and judgement. The totalising physiological and materialist accounts of human nature that we find in the Hippocratic authors gave rise to a lively and unresolved debate in antiquity about the extent to which the body determines the mind, and indeed, how much of 'me' is determined by the body. At the same time, the very creation of the physical body as an object, accomplished not just in medical writing but through the intersection of medical theory and medical practice, is part of what has left us with the idea of a subject who is not reducible to the body. If the Hippocratic body is still in a crucial sense 'our' body, it is because these questions continue to haunt us.

5   Aetiology

Jim Hankinson

Medical aetiology is concerned with the causes of health and disease. It is a relatively modern term, appearing in medical contexts in the late seventeenth century. Yet, the reflection on how diseases are caused is an ancient one: we find it in Pre-Socratic philosophy and notably the *Hippocratic Corpus*. In this chapter, I shall briefly look at philosophical texts and then explore the study of causation within the *Hippocratic Corpus*. Balance plays a prominent role, as does human nature, which is characterised by humours and various qualities such as dry and wet, and hot and cold. In particular, I shall show that 'natural' (or what one would nowadays call 'physiological') processes occupy a prominent place in the explanation for the causes of disease. Yet, although there are many common features throughout the *Corpus*, we shall also encounter quite different modes of explanation and expression. Moreover, I shall discuss how the authors of the various treatises combine the various factors leading to health and disease into a system that allows them to recognise and combat the causes of disease in more complex settings. Finally, I shall explore the role of the environment, which includes both geographical and climatic features. But let us begin by looking at one of the most famous fragments of medical content among the Pre-Socratic writings.

CONCEPTUAL ORIGINS

It is a truism that the development of both Pre-Socratic thought and of the medical views we associate with the *Hippocratic Corpus* is characterised by the emergence of a new taste for naturalised explanation. A particularly widespread notion is that of balance and harmony: a good condition (of just about anything) consists in the proper

89

proportion of its fundamental constituents, a bad one in some corresponding imbalance. The idea is already present in Anaximander (DK12B1); but more importantly for our purposes it is championed by Alcmaeon of Croton, an early fifth-century BC Pythagoreanising doctor:

> Alcmaeon says that health is preserved by equality among the powers – wet and dry, hot and cold, bitter and sweet, and the rest – while monarchy among them causes disease, since the monarchy of either member of a pair is destructive. Disease comes about *by* an excess of hot or cold, *from* a surfeit or deficiency of nutriment, and *in* the blood or the marrow or the brain. Health is the proportionate mixture of the qualities.[1]

Apart from the political metaphors of equality and monarchy, it is unclear how much of that semi-technical vocabulary is authentically Alcmaeonian; although the carefully-chosen prepositions I emphasised may well be significant, as indicating respectively the general types of efficacious cause, their proximate vehicles, and the locations in which they have their effects. But what is clear is that he elaborated a physiology (and an associated pathology) based on the idea of balance between an indefinite number of opposites:

> He said that most human things come in pairs, speaking not like them [sc. Pythagoreans] of a determinate list of oppositions, but rather of any kind of opposition whatever, such as black and white, sweet and bitter, good and bad, big and small.[2]

Whether Alcmaeon really thought that absolutely any case of opposition figured potentially among the causes of health and disease (the re-iteration of the opposition sweet/bitter from text 1 is perhaps significant) does not greatly matter. What does is that, among the general conceptual apparatus relating to health and disease, there appears a set of related notions which are to be of the utmost importance:

---

[1]   DK24B4; [Plutarch] *Opinions of the Natural Philosophers* 911a; emphases mine.
[2]   Aristotle, *Metaphysics* A, 986a, 29–34.

opposition, balance, imbalance, hot and cold, excess and deficiency, mixture, power, quality. Almost all of the classical Hippocratic theoretical texts make use of some, indeed usually most, of these categories; and their influence can also be discerned in the more empirical and descriptive texts (such as *Epidemics*) as well. Equally, nutrition (as mentioned in 1) is of prime importance, both for the maintenance of health and in the treatment of disease, a general commitment which unifies theoreticians as otherwise divergent as the authors of *Ancient Medicine* and *Nature of Man*.

THE NATURE OF NATURE

'Nature', *phýsis*, is a fundamental, if many-faceted, concept, and may refer, among other things, to the constitution of the world as a whole, and to the individual natures of the things which make it up. In the latter sense, *phýsis* is close in meaning to *ousía* (in the sense of essence), and is sometimes, as frequently in Aristotle, identical with it. And in the sense of the general natures which different types of things share, the concept is also basic to the overall Hippocratic approach (and indeed to anything that can properly be called science). Even diseases have them: 'each of them comes to be in accordance with its own nature.'[3] But the Hippocratics are equally concerned with particular natures, differences in the individual make-up of different individuals of the same general natural type, differences which will account (at any rate in general) for their widely differing susceptibilities to types of disease. Thus the author of *Nature of Man* is concerned both with the question of what the fundamental constitution of human beings consists in, as well as with the explanation and significance of their particular variations. This, too, is a basic Hippocratic preoccupation. But the explanations of particular variations from the general, perhaps ideal, norm will themselves involve generalisations, covering the types of things responsible for those variations. Science consists in providing robust, explanatory, and

---

[3]   *Airs, Waters, Places* 22 (Jones [1923a], 128).

empirically responsible generalisations which are based on, and responsive to, observation. This is what many Hippocratics at least aimed at. How empirically responsible they actually managed to be is of course another question.

The protean nature of 'nature' is usefully summed up, albeit in characteristically enigmatic and paradoxical language, by the author of *Nutriment*:

> Secretions in accordance with nature, of the stomach, of urine, of sweat, of sputum, of mucus, by way of haemorrhoids, warts, skin eruption, swellings, carcinomas; from the nostrils, lungs, stomach, anus and penis, both in accordance with nature and contrary to nature. The differences in these things vary according to individuals, in times, and otherwise. All of these things are one nature, and not one. All these things are many natures and one.[4]

For all its Heraclitean obscurity, the main point does emerge reasonably unequivocally: these various type fluxes share a (very) general definition, but they vary as to their particular natures and as to whether they are natural or unnatural, for which read healthy or unhealthy. Moreover, their particular qualities are relative to particular individuals too; what would be a healthy excretion for one person might be a fatal sign for somebody else. This is a perfectly general Hippocratic point: what is good for you may be bad for me, but if so, that fact is to be accounted for in terms of some difference between us, either of natural, in the sense of a more or less permanent constitution, or of particular contingent circumstances and dispositions. But, or so the implicit argument goes, even these will be, up to a point, susceptible to explanatory generalisation. Similar points are made concerning the nature of nutriment itself:

> Nutriment and the form of nutriment are one and many; one insofar as its kind is one; differing in form by moisture and dryness; and in these are forms and quantity; they are for something and a certain

---

[4] *Nutriment* 17 (Jones [1923a], 348). *Nutriment* is almost certainly a later text, although there is no consensus as to when it was composed. For all that, it provides a useful point of entry to the general issues with which this article is concerned (it was considered to be genuine, and of great importance, by most ancient commentators, including Galen).

number of things. It increases, strengthens, and makes fleshes, and makes both similar and dissimilar [to it] what is in each part, according to the nature of each part and the original power. It makes [it] similar to the power when what enters in wins out, and whenever what was there before is overcome.[5]

There is a single general class, of the nutritious, that has the capacity to nourish (in a very general sense: for our author, the category includes air); but it comes in various forms distinguished by degrees of wetness and dryness. Depending on the relative strength of the nutritive power and of what it is working on, sometimes the power itself alters the underlying material, but sometimes (presumably in the better cases) it is assimilated into that which it nourishes.

A few more dark passages are worth brief consideration:

There are many varieties of power. Humours which destroy the whole or a part, which come from outside or within, and which are both spontaneous and not spontaneous, spontaneous as far as we are concerned, but not spontaneous as to their cause. Of the causes, some are clear and some obscure, some within our power and some not. Nature is sufficient for all things and in all things.[6]

Here causes are explicitly mentioned (although the notion of a power, too, is obviously a causal one: 1, 4), along with the important idea that although some things may seem to arise spontaneously, in fact everything has a cause, even if one that escapes our limited faculties. This is a recurring theme: 'every phenomenon will be found to have some cause, and if it has a cause, chance will be no more than an empty name'.[7] Indeed, 'spontaneous' often means, as it does here, without any *obvious* cause, or in the natural run of events, or without any intervention on the part of the doctor.[8] Congruently with this, although some texts allow that doctors may achieve beneficial results

---

[5]   *Nutriment* 1–3 (Jones [1923a], 342).   [6]   5: *Nutriment* 13–15 (Jones [1923a], 346).

[7]   *Art* 6 (Jones [1923b], 198–200). Also edited with commentary and English translation in Mann (2012).

[8]   See Lo Presti (2012).

by good luck (and equally unluckily cause harm), this is due to their incompetence, and in any case the 'lucky' results will be in principle explicable on the basis of a correct pathology.[9]

Nutriment, chapter 25, enumerates the ways in which diseases differ, according to nutriment, breath, heat, blood, phlegm, bile, and 'humours', and the different sorts of tissue and organs involved, and chapter 27 notes that there is a difference between having the power to produce sweetness and actually being sweet (to the taste). All of these issues, in particular the role and multiplicity of powers and natures, their multiply relative characters, the difference between internal and external causal factors, and between evident and non-evident causes, will be of paramount importance. The 'humours' mentioned here (and at 5) are not the canonical four, the fundamental constituents of human physiology that we will meet with in *Nature of Man*, nor any variant thereof. Rather the term covers (as it often does) a loosely defined range of fluids, often distinguished by taste ('sweet', 'bitter', etc.), which may or may not have harmful (or healthful) effects, but which are at any rate implicated in a proper account of the physiology of metabolism.

DISEASE AND NATURE: THE CASE OF SACRED DISEASE

'Sacred disease' was the name given by the Greeks to epilepsy and other types of seizure disorder, because of its striking, not to say terrifying, symptoms and its apparently random incidence; but the author of the text of that name emphasises that it too has its own determinate (and determinable) nature:

> I shall discuss the so-called sacred disease.[10] In my view it is no more divine or sacred than any other disease,[11] since it has its own

---

[9]   *Diseases* 1.7–8 (Potter [1988b], 114–18); see also 1.1 (Potter [1988b]), 98; *Places in Man* 46 (Potter [1995], 92–4). *Places in Man* is also edited with English translation and notes in Craik (1998).

[10]   For this terminology see also *Airs, Waters, Places* 3 and 4, ed. and trans. Jones (1923a), 73–4, 77–8, and *Breaths* 14, ed. and trans. Jones (1923b), 250–1; *Airs, Waters, Places* is edited with German translation in Diller (1970); *Breaths* in Heiberg (1927).

[11]   *Airs, Waters, Places* 22, ed. and trans. Jones (1923a), 125–30, says the same about the endemic impotence of the Scythians.

nature and occasion; but people think it to be a divine thing because of their helplessness and its strangeness.[12]

The author vigorously rejects the idea that there is something especially numinous about this disease; it has a natural explanation like any other (it is caused, allegedly, by a build-up of excess phlegm in the brain). The 'purifiers' and other charlatans who treat it as an affliction from the gods, in addition to being illogical and inefficacious, are actually impious, as they believe (or at least profess to) that divinities can be coerced by their mumbo-jumbo. If you actually understand the nature and origin of the disease, then it is treatable, even curable, provided that it is not too deeply entrenched:

> This so-called sacred disease comes about from the same occasions as the rest of them, from things that go into and come out of the body, from cold, the sun, and from the changing and never-resting winds . . .. Each [disease] has its own *phýsis* and *dýnamis*, and none are untreatable. Most are cured by the same things from which they arise . . .. Whoever knows how to bring about wet and dry, hot and cold, in human beings can cure this disease too, if he can determine the appropriate times and what is beneficial, without purifications and magic.[13]

This confident passage asserts a general claim about the external occasions of diseases, which affect constitutions (in this case phlegmatic ones) which are primed to be so affected. To say that 'most are cured by the same things from which they arise' does not insinuate homeopathy, but rather the reverse. It is by suppressing the causal factors, in this case the excessive damp and coldness engendered in the brain by phlegm, that the condition can be combatted, typically by applying things that are opposite in quality to them. Thus this passage exemplifies the general Hippocratic commitment

12   *Sacred Disease* 1 (Jones [1923b], 138). Also edited in Heiberg (1927).
13   *Sacred Disease* 21 (Jones [1923b], 182).

to allopathy,[14] as well as the widespread, albeit not universal, reduction of general causal factors to the supposedly fundamental qualities of hot, cold, wet, and dry; and it also attests to the pathological significance of excesses of phlegm and bile. Even if the author's preferred account of the aetiology of the pathology is convoluted, fantastical, buttressed by unconvincing analogies, and in general empirically inadequate, the general rationalist commitment is striking. *Sacred Disease* is also characteristic of the general Hippocratic temper in restricting, and perhaps eliminating, the scope of any appeal to the divine.[15]

INTERNAL AND EXTERNAL CAUSES: DISPOSITIONS AND OCCASIONS

While different writers in the collection champion very different theories as to the number and nature of the qualities in balance, there is a fairly general consensus, as befits the fundamentally naturalistic mentality from which spring the vast majority of the texts in the corpus, that diseases arise when the body is pushed towards some pathological imbalance by some suitable external event, which is generally, as in the two foregoing passages, referred to as a *próphasis* (later in *Sacred Disease*, sudden heatings and coolings, changes in the winds, fears and shocks are *propháseis* of epilepsy in children: chapter 13).[16] Elsewhere a *próphasis* is often a 'pretext' (even in medical contexts it occasionally means 'purported cause'); but the various usages are unified by the idea of overtness: a *próphasis* is something which is obvious. In medicine, *propháseis* are often contrasted, as the evident antecedent circumstances attending the diseases, with the causes, what is responsible for them in some more general sense. The reference, however, can be variable. Thus, although the phrase

---

[14] Made explicit at *Breaths* 1: "If one knows the cause of the disease, one will be able to prescribe what is beneficial for the body. This sort of medicine is wholly natural.... In short, opposites are cures for opposites" (*Breaths* 1, ed. and trans. Jones [1923b], 226–7). See also *Nature of Man* 9, 13 (Jones [1931], 24–6, 36); but see *Places in Man* 31, 42 (Potter [1995], 72, 84–6) for a more nuanced view.

[15] On this issue, see Hankinson (1998).   [16] Jones (1923b), 164–6.

phanerè próphasis ('evident occasion') is very common, albeit often used negatively,[17] *aitíē* can be used in the same way: 'copious sweating occurring after sleep without any *phanerè aitíē* indicates that the body has too much food'.[18] Equally, *próphasis* sometimes simply has the general sense of 'cause': 'the cure must be created to counteract the *próphasis* of the disease'.[19]

Sometimes it is hard to tell which sense is in play:

> Stymarges' handmaid, who did not even bleed when she gave birth to a daughter, had the mouth of her womb retroverted. There was pain in the hip-joint and leg; phlebotomy in the ankle relieved it, but tremors racked her whole body. One must go to the *próphasis*, and the origin of the *próphasis*.[20]

According to Galen, the particular disease here is the tremor, its *próphasis* the retention of blood, and its origin the retroversion of the cervix. So whatever the *próphasis* is here, it can hardly be an external, possibly causally relevant circumstance. It seems rather to designate a proximate cause, of which the malformation of the cervix is the underlying responsible condition, here denoted as the origin of the condition as a whole. Elsewhere, however, the origin of the disease is the moment of its onset: 'the tongue was livid from the start; the *próphasis* seemed to be a chill after bathing'.[21] And *Places in Man* 1–2 holds that 'there is no beginning of the body', although 'the nature of the body is the beginning of medical reasoning'.[22] Indeed, 'there is no established beginning of healing, or of the art as a whole'.[23] Things, then, are somewhat messy.

---

[17] For example, at *Prognostic* 18: 'shortness of breath which abates without any other obvious *próphasis*' (ed. and trans. Jones [1923b], 36–7); and 24: 'if pain does not persist because of inflammation or any other obvious *próphasis*'; compare *Regimen* 3.70, *Epidemics* 3.2, *Aphorisms* 2.41.

[18] *Aphorisms* 4.41 (Jones [1931], 144).

[19] See also *Nature of Man* 9 (Jones [1931], 26).

[20] *Epidemics* 2.4.5 (Smith [1994], 72).   [21] *Epidemics* 7.11 (Smith [1994], 314).

[22] Potter (1995), 18–22.   [23] *Diseases* 1.9 (Potter [1988b], 118).

HUMOURS, DISPOSITIONS, AND CONSTITUTIONS

But however annoying such terminological laxities may be, the general sense is rarely in doubt. Frequently, what is the cause for some condition is a relevant disposition of the patient's, for example their being phlegmatic, naturally cold and wet, and so inclined to produce phlegm as a result, a standing condition which predisposes the individual to a particular type or types of ailment, such as epilepsy in *Sacred Disease*. But in other cases, it is an actual structure which is implicated. For instance, at *Sacred Disease* 6, it is 'the brain which is responsible for this affection, as it is in the case of other particularly serious diseases'.[24] There follows a detailed, if fanciful, description of the brain and its connection by way of 'veins' (here just vessels in general) to the rest of the body, and the ways in which various constrictions and blockages, in particular those produced by excessive phlegm, affect its functioning, by interfering with the free passage of air, in which intelligence resides (and which forms a sort of analogue of the nervous system). But obviously this too is an account of the internal causal conditions responsible for the onset of the disease in those vulnerable to it, and those vulnerabilities are determined by constitution: the disease 'arises in the phlegmatic and not the bilious'.[25] The general idea, that harmful effects are produced by the incidence of triggering causal events in those whose constitution renders them particularly prone to such pathologies, is widespread throughout the corpus, even if the particular accounts of the different constitutions, and their relevant susceptibilities, differ widely.

One may thus discern a surprisingly consistent general attitude to aetiology. A typical example may be found in *Diseases* 1,[26] which

---

[24]   Jones (1923b),152. Compare the distinction made in *Ancient Medicine* between 'diseases that arise from powers and those that arise from structures': 22, ed. and trans. Jones (1923a), 54–5; also edited, with French translation and notes, in Jouanna (1990), and with English translation and commentary in Schiefsky (2005).

[25]   8, Jones (1923b), 154.

[26]   The texts transmitted as *Diseases* 1–4 are quite distinct and the products of different hands (and approaches). Thus, *Diseases* 2 is sometimes thought to represent (or at least to derive partly from) the 'Cnidian' approach to medicine; while *Diseases* 4 is usually

starts by affirming the fundamental importance of general aetiology as a basis for proper therapeutics:

> Anyone who wants to inquire about healing in the correct manner ... must concern himself with the following things. First, from what do all human diseases arise? Then, which diseases, when they arise, are necessarily long or short, mortal or not, permanently disabling to some part of the body or not, and which, when they do arise, have outcomes which are difficult to predict, whether good or bad?[27]

The answer to the initial question is supplied shortly afterwards:

> All diseases arise for us either from things present in the body, from both bile and phlegm, or from external things: from exertions and wounds, and from heat which overheats and cold which over-chills. Bile and phlegm come into being together with our coming into being, and are always present in the body in greater or lesser amounts. They produce diseases partly because of the effects of food and drink, and partly from heat which overheats and cold which over-chills.[28]

Bile and phlegm are innate components of the human system (although they are not constitutive of it, as other theories, pre-eminently that of *Nature of Man*, held). When they are thrown out of balance they become pathological; and this is caused by ill-advised nutrition, and external heating and cooling. This is a widespread view:

> All human diseases occur as a result of bile and phlegm, which produce diseases whenever they become too wet, too dry, too hot or too cold. [They] undergo these things as a result of food, drink,

grouped with *Generation* and *Nature of the Child* as products of a school (and possibly the same author) promoting a four-humour constitutive scheme of blood, water, bile, and phlegm. See Potter (1988b), 94–7, 186–7; Potter (1988c), 3–5; Potter (2012), 97–9; and Jouanna (1999 [orig. 1992]), 381–4.

27   *Diseases* 1.1 (Potter [1988b], 98).
28   *Diseases* 1.2 (Potter [1988b], 100–2).

> exertion, wounds, smells, sights, sounds, sex, and heat and cold; and
> they do so when any of the things mentioned are applied
> inappropriately to the body, against normal practice, and when too
> much or too strong, or not enough and too weak.[29]

Here we find a particular specification of the importantly distinct factors in causal explanation already foreshadowed by Alcmaeon in the passage quoted earlier, although it does not make the same general typological distinctions. Bile and phlegm are apparently conceived of as the vehicles by means of which imbalances in the fundamental qualities are mediated in the body. A wide variety of apparently disparate occasions are noted, but significantly many of them have to do with regimen, broadly construed: food, drink, exertion, sexual activity; heat and cold are also implicated. So the human body exists in a state of more or less fragile equilibrium, which, if maintained, produces, perhaps constitutes, good health, but when disturbed by any one of a number of internal and external influences, results in weakness and ultimately disease. But how far and to what extent any of these influences will in particular cases result in injury to the patient's health will depend equally on particular facts of that patient's internal dispositions, as well as on what they are as a matter of fact accustomed to, all of which is perfectly consistent with the gnomically expressed views in the first passage from *Nutriment* quoted earlier. We shall return to the central importance in Hippocratic aetiology (and therapeutics) of the generalised notion of regimen below. But first let us explore a little further the implications of the general model of aetiology and pathology that has emerged so far.

THE ESTABLISHMENT OF EMPIRICAL CONNECTIONS

It is one thing to note the occurrence of some event antecedent to the onset of disease; quite another to establish its causal implication in any internal processes in the individual that bring the disease about:

---

[29]   *Affections* 1 (Potter [1988b], 6).

Even for good doctors, similarities cause errors and difficulties; but so, too, do differences. What kind of *próphasis* there is, is hard to figure out, even for someone familiar with the methods. For instance, if someone has a pointy head and a snub but sharp nose, is bilious, vomits with difficulty, is full of black bile, is young, and has lived a wild life, it is difficult to reconcile all of these things with one another.[30]

We are not told why this concatenation of signs and symptoms is difficult to make sense of, but the general idea is clear enough: such circumstances rarely go together, and are perhaps also difficult to account for theoretically (the interest in physiognomy is significant: certain types of morphology were supposed to indicate underlying physiological and temperamental conditions). In general, *Epidemics* avoids general theory; but what sorts of event occurred in the immediate vicinity of the onset of disease is a matter of pervasive and consuming interest throughout its various books, in spite of their manifold differences is style and subject matter.[31] Indeed, the *Epidemics* can be seen as an account of diseases, both epidemic and individual, that seeks to record for further use, reference and investigation what appeared to be the possibly relevant peculiarities in their surrounding circumstances that might allow for further significant empirical organisation and, ultimately, theoretical elaboration and understanding.

In the individual case histories in particular, a wide variety of events that occurred immediately prior to the onset of an illness is often noted, presumably with a view to attempting to develop robust, empirical causal (or at least semiotic) connections between them and their apparent consequences. Sometimes these seem to exhibit certain inchoate patterns, reflecting judgements about what, in the

---

[30] *Epidemics* 7.26 (Smith [1994], 332). This is one of the relatively rare remarks in the *Epidemics* on the difficulty of general diagnosis; but see also 6.3.12, text 12 which follows.

[31] For a brief account of the origins of our *Epidemics*, see Jouanna (1999 [orig. 1992]), 29–30.

circumstances, may have been relevant, presumably on the basis of previously observed concatenations of events. For example, drinking is quite frequently implicated, particularly in the case of young men who have a tendency towards loose-living, like the example-case just quoted,[32] while drinking associated with sexual over-indulgence (3.17.10, 16), or with unfamiliar toil and fatigue (3.1.8, 17.3), or of strong liquor is particularly dangerous (4.15). In some cases, the occasion is thought to have been exacerbated by unwise therapeutic intervention. *Epidemics* 4.11 records the case of a boy who becomes feverish after being struck in the head by a piece of pottery, but then goes on to note: '*próphasis*: after washing around the wound, the woman rubbed it, and it became chilled'.[33] A reasonably clear underlying conception emerges: acute conditions at least tend to result from external causes affecting and modifying the internal dispositions of the patients in ways which lead to illness, or alternatively external injuries provoke serious lesions, which may then be helped or harmed by further interventions, depending on how those affect the conditions in question.

But in the *Epidemics*, the conclusions offered are at best provisional. Illnesses often arise without any obvious occasion, or in the case of women, are simply generally associated with pregnancy and childbirth (1.27.4, 5, 9, 13; 3.1.10, 11, 12; 2.1.17–20; 3.17.2, 14), more rarely with menarche (1.27.14; 2.1.8; 3.17.7), and on two occasions with grief (3.17.11, 15). In one case (3.1.6),[34] the doctor says 'they said she had been eating grapes', but apparently reposes little confidence in the relevance of this. Concomitant signs and symptoms are also observed, such as loss of appetite, thirst, vomiting and nausea, diarrhoea, the condition of urine, sweats, fatigue, coma, delirium, and sleep disturbance. Sometimes these are noted in the various 'constitutions' of *Epidemics* 1 and 3, the general accounts of the prevailing diseases and associated climatic conditions in particular places and times. Occasionally, we find details that seem merely circumstantial:

---

[32]   See also *Epidemics* 1.27.2, 12; 3.1.4, 5.   [33]   Smith (1994), 98.

[34]   Jones (1923a), 230.

'In Larisa, a bald man was suddenly stricken with pain in the right thigh. Nothing prescribed did any good' (3.17.5),[35] and although it might have been aetiologically significant that the daughter of Neleus was twenty and a virgin when she was struck a blow that led eventually to her death, the fact that she was beautiful, although poignant, can hardly have been medically relevant (5.50).[36]

But for all their peculiarities and elisions, the *Epidemics* show doctors in the process of wrestling with the business of trying to understand how diseases work, of what typically goes with what, and with what to expect on the basis of which signs, as accurate prognosis, even in wholly hopeless and untreatable cases, was a signal way of underlining one's claims to expertise.[37] Thus the case histories often record the early stages of the illness, in particular where pain was first felt (hypochondrium: 1.27.11, 12; loins: 1.27.2, 7, 13; 3.1.2, 11; stomach: 1.27.4; 3.1.12; head: 1.27.6, 14; 3.1.2, 4; 3.17.4, 9; heart: 3.17.10; liver: 3.17.13). The notion of the origin of disease is relevant here: 'we need to examine the origins of the disease; if it develops rapidly it will be clear in its development'.[38] See also *Epidemics* 2.1.11, 'we need to examine the points of origin from where they began to suffer, whether the pain was in the head, the ear, or the side'. [39]

Thus the authors of the *Epidemics* were on the look-out both for general similarities between types of illness, both endemic and epidemic as well as sporadic, as well as specific differences in patterns of incidence and onset that might be made to correlate with specific differences between individuals, in terms of their age,

---

[35]   Ibid., 266.   [36]   Smith (1994), 190.

[37]   "It is best for a doctor to employ prognosis. For if he knows and tells sufferers what is happening to them, what has happened, and what will happen, filling in the gaps in their accounts, he will inspire more confidence that he understands what is actually happening to the sick, and so men will dare to entrust themselves to the doctor. And he will carry out treatment in the best manner if he knows in advance what will occur on the basis of present symptoms" (*Prognostic* 1, ed. and trans. Jones [1923b], 4–5).

[38]   *Epidemics* 2.1.6. Rapidity of onset is also an aid to diagnosis and treatment: *Nature of Man* 13, ed. and trans. Jones (1931), 35–6.

[39]   Smith (1994), 28.

sex, general habits of behaviour and lifestyle, and their exposure to specific potentially triggering events (more of the details of this will emerge shortly). But *Epidemics* is a series of scattered notes, from different and differently motivated hands, and no single, developed account of medical aetiology can be extracted from it. Still, an important if isolated note in *Epidemics* epitomises the inductive procedure implicit in it:

> The complete summary account derives from the genesis and the points of origin, and from many accounts, and from things learned gradually, when one gathers them together and fully understands them, whether they are like one another, and even in the case of the dissimilarities, whether these also are alike, so that there arises one similar type from the dissimilarities. This is the method. In this way there will be a verification of correct accounts and a refutation of the incorrect ones.[40]

'Things learned gradually' are the empirically derived and marshalled evidence, while the concentration on 'many accounts' prefigures the reliance on testimony of later Empiricist doctors. Galen refers the remarks about likeness and dissimilarity (which recall those of the two passages from *Nutriment*, quoted earlier) to the process of the division and sub-division of causally relevant types on the Aristotelian model, which may be an over-interpretation; but the writer is clearly envisioning some process of the gradual accumulation of detailed and empirically adequate information concerning the structure of diseases, information that is capable of being organised into an explanatory and predictive whole. The very possibility of such an enterprise presupposes acceptance of the basic ideas with which we started: that disease is a natural phenomenon, susceptible of a generalised, naturalistic explanation, and that the key to discovering those explanations lies in empirical research aimed at isolating the general concatenations of events that bring them about, difficult

---

[40]   *Epidemics* 6.3.12 (Smith [1994], 238–40).

though this may be because of the inherent variability of its subject matter.[41]

HOT AND COLD, WET AND DRY: QUALITIES AND HUMOURS

But beyond that, things rapidly become untidier. Different texts propound, or presuppose, significantly different theories regarding the basic constitutions of things. As we have already seen, there is no consensus about the role or significance, let alone the number and identity, of the items known as 'humours', *chymoí*, a term which originally meant simply 'juice', or 'sap', or 'flavour'. For the author of *Nature of Man*, however, they are the subsequently canonical blood, phlegm and yellow and black bile, the basic constituents of human, and indeed animal, physiology, the relative proportions between which vary both generally according to age, gender, and regimen, and individually from person to person within those normal ranges, variations which account for different susceptibilities to different types of disturbing influence, and all of which are reducible to the four causally basic qualities of hot, cold, wet, and dry:

> The human body has within itself blood and phlegm and yellow and
> black bile, and these are the nature of the body, and because of them
> it suffers and is healthy. So it is particularly healthy when these
> things maintain a balance of their power and their quantity in
> relation to one another, and when they are thoroughly mixed
> together. It suffers when one of them becomes either too small or
> too great, or is separated in the body and is not mixed with all the
> others.[42]

And, a little further on:

> I hold first of all that they are distinct according to convention, in
> that none of them bears the same name, and secondly that,

---

[41]   See also *Places in Man* 41 (Potter [1995] 80–2).

[42]   *Nature of Man* 4 (Jones [1931], 10–12). Also edited with commentary and French
translation in Jouanna (2002 [orig. 1975]).

according to nature, their forms are different, and that phlegm in no
way resembles blood, nor blood bile, nor bile phlegm ... their
colours are evidently dissimilar to sight, and nor do they appear
similar when touched by the hand; for they are neither similarly hot
or cold, or dry or wet.[43]

Phenomenal qualities are indications of fundamental causal properties, and it is in terms of the balance and imbalance of these that health
is maintained and disease engendered.

But of course one may make that latter supposition without any
commitment to the degree of theorising evident in *Nature of Man*, as
well as disagreeing about what are, in fact, the relevantly prognostically
significant phenomenal qualities, and how, if at all, they serve to reveal
underlying causal realities. A key comparison text here is *Ancient
Medicine*. It makes use of the language of humours, but in a way fundamentally (and self-consciously) opposed to the constitutive theoretical
speculations of *Nature of Man*, speaking rather about how, as a result of
long observation and experience, the relevant powers of foodstuffs to
alter and affect the body have been discovered:

they (i.e. the people of former times) suffered many and terrible
things on account of their strong and bestial regimen, eating raw
and unmixed things which possessed great powers.[44]

Later, in the course of castigating misguided moderns who repose
their confidence in some general 'hypothesis' that goes beyond the
mere aggregation of such empirical connections (in particular those
which hypothesise the fundamental importance of the four qualities),
he writes:

The powers of each of these [sc. types of flour] are great and different
from one another . . .. For man is affected and altered by each of these
things in one way or another: and the whole of regimen is based on
these things, for the healthy, the convalescent, and the sick ...

---

[43]   5 (Jones [1931], 12–14).   [44]   17: *Ancient Medicine* 3 (Jones [1923a],18).

> The first investigators, researching properly and with reasonings appropriate to the human nature, ... did not consider the dry, the wet, the hot or the cold, or any of these things either to harm or to be of any benefit to man, but rather they thought that the strength of each thing, being more powerful than the human nature which failed to overcome it, did the harming . ... The strongest of the sweet is the sweetest, of the bitter the bitterest, of the sharp the sharpest, and there is an extreme of each of these internal things. They saw that these things were internal to human beings, and were harmful to them, since there is in human beings salt, bitter, sweet, sharp, astringent and insipid, and countless others possessing powers varying in both number and strength.[45]

He defines a power (in the case of items of nutriment) as 'the extreme intensities and strength of the humours'[46]; and the humours mentioned in the last sentence are the actual flavours of foods (see also the 'sweet' and 'bitter' of Alcmaeon, above).

This is an empirical claim: relative conditions of (phenomenal) heat and cold have little or no significant correlations to healthy or harmful outcomes, a contention expanded on in chapters 16–19. By contrast, if the 'hot, cold, wet, and dry' of the theoreticians are purely theoretical constructs, we would need to know what they are supposed to refer to and how their presence or absence is to be determined, a task which, the author suggests, is both superfluous and beyond the capacity of the theorisers: chapters 13–15.[47] In fact heat and cold are spontaneously corrected for in the body, and if not spontaneously, then immediately and effectively by the actions of the patient.[48] Significantly, our author acknowledges and rejects an objection, namely that sufferers from ardent fever and pneumonia and other 'strong diseases' do not recover quickly and spontaneously:

---

[45]   *Ancient Medicine* 14 (Jones [1923a], 36–8).   [46]   22 (Jones [1923a], 56).
[47]   For differing assessments, see Lloyd (1979), 147–9, and Hankinson (1992).
[48]   16 (Jones [1923a], 42–4).

> I take to be the greatest indication in favour of my view the fact that
> men do not suffer from fever as a result of heat alone, and that this
> cannot be the sole cause of the damage, since one and the same
> thing can be both bitter and hot, or sharp and hot, or salty and hot,
> and many other things besides, and also that cold exists along with
> other powers. It is these things which do the damage. Heat is merely
> concomitant, and has the force of a leading factor, and is
> exacerbated and increases along with it, but has no power greater
> than that which is proper to it.[49]

Heat (and cold) may intensify the effects of the other factors – but
it is the powers of the latter which determine the actual outcomes.
And this is (allegedly) an empricially determinable fact. Of course,
such empirical determinations are notoriously difficult to make in
practice, as was appreciated by some at least of the doctors of the
time (compare the cautious and provisional semiotics of the
Epidemics). Moreover, some of the contributors to the corpus at
least tried to invoke specific, in some cases quasi-experimental,
observations in support of their causal accounts. In chapter 15 of
Ancient Medicine, the writer notes that one can observe the effects
of astringent or 'soothing' substances on hides and wood: 'it is not
the heat which has great power, but the astringent and the soothing
and the rest I have spoken of, both what is taken internally by the
patient in the form of food and drink, and what is applied and
administered externally'(chapter 15).[50]

But for all their theoretical differences, both this text and *Nature
of Man* are concerned with distinguishing the genuinely causal from

---

[49] *Ancient Medicine* 17 (Jones [1923a], 44–6).

[50] Jones (1923a), 40. Such empirical claims regarding the causal significance of flavours
could be, and were, controverted. The author of *Regimen* writes: "Those who have
tried to treat in general of sweet, or fat, or salty things, or of the power of any other such
thing, do not know what they are doing, since the same power does not belong to
everything sweet, or everything fat, or some other such quality. For many sweet things
are laxative, but many constipating, many dry, but many moisten; and it is the same
with everything else" (*Regimen* 2.39, Jones [1931], 306). *Regimen* is also edited with
French translation and notes in Joly and Byl (2003 [orig. 1984]).

the merely adventitious, and stress the fact that a genuinely causal account will be complex, general, and (in principle) exceptionless. The inexperienced go wrong because they mistake mere concomitance for causality, and generalize extravagantly from an inadequate basis:

> If the patient has experienced something unusual on that day [sc. when some complication has arisen], either in bathing, or taking a walk, or eating, or something else, even though all of them may be either beneficial or not, most doctors, like lay-people, assign responsibility to one of them, and in ignorance of the real cause, may well suppress something which is in fact beneficial. One should not reason like that, but should understand what is the effect of untimely extra bathing or fatigue, since it is never the same ill-effect that results from either of them, nor from over-repletion, nor from this or that foodstuff.[51]

For example, heavy drinking of undiluted wine always has similar effects, and on the same organs (although specific expert understanding of this is still required), while cheese is not equally upsetting to all who consume it. Some tolerate it perfectly well, indeed thrive upon it, while for others it is dangerous and harmful. This must be because there is something specific about those who are intolerant of it ('a humour hostile to cheese'); otherwise everyone who ingested it would be affected in the same way. This is why (and how, and the extent to which) the doctor needs to understand the nature of the human body (chapter 20).[52] Of course that general idea is a commonplace: 'The nature of the body is the starting point of medical reasoning'.[53]

---

[51]   *Ancient Medicine* 21 (Jones [1923a], 56).   [52]   Jones (1923a), 54.

[53]   *Places in Man* 2 (Potter [1995], 20–2). *Places in Man* offers a general account of the internal structures of the human body and their inter-relations in order to sketch how diseases arise, and also how they can spread from one part to another, in the form of moist fluxes. All parts of the body affect each other, none is primary; and the same is true of disease. Diseases in dry parts are more established than those in wet parts because the latter tend to move around. Even so, any disease in one part will immediately affect another (*Places in Man* 1–2, Potter [1995], 18–22). The tendency of diseases to migrate from one part of the body to another is also a commonplace: *Nature of Man* 10, ed. and trans. Jones (1931), 2–31.

So once again, behind the specific disagreements about the number and the nature and the accessibility of the fundamental constituents, there lies agreement at least that there are such constituents, and that interference with and imbalance among them, however produced, is both the cause and the form of diseases, at least those of a systemic nature. This is no less true for the partisans of the 'novel hypotheses' excoriated by the author of *Ancient Medicine* than it is for the author himself. *Nature of Man* conceptualises health and disease in terms of the four humours, and the basic qualities (hot, cold, wet, dry) they exhibit. Those qualities are just as important in *Places in Man*, although the humours as such make no appearance: the author talks vaguely of 'fluxes', and though they are sometimes associated with phlegm, phlegm appears to be, as it often does elsewhere, a pathological residue. An alternative constitutive scheme is found in *Diseases* 4 (and *Generation* and *Nature of the Child*, n. 26). *Regimen* (see n. 50) settles on the more traditional fire and water, as embodying the hot and dry, and the cold and wet, respectively. Even in highly schematic texts like *Breaths*, which makes the nature of the air we breathe the basic cause of health and disease, the same general ideas recur: air is the agent that brings about the heatings and coolings, the transfer of fluids from one place to another, as well as constrictions and dilatations beyond the normal that engender the whole panoply of diseases, whether epidemic or peculiar to particular individuals. In his account of the 'sacred disease', air is the proximate cause which affects the activity of the blood, which is responsible for intelligence[54]; much the same goes for his account of dropsy, confused and barely intelligible though it is (chapter 12, 246). Air is the most important and primary cause of health (and hence of disease: chapter 5, 232), because of the essential things we ingest (the others being food and drink) it is the one we can least do without (chapter 4, 230–32): "Breaths then are clearly the most fundamentally implicated in all diseases; all the others are auxiliary and contributory causes" (chapter 15, 252).

---

[54]   *Breaths* 14 (Jones [1923b], 250–2); this account recalls that of *Sacred Disease*, see earlier).

EPIDEMIC AND SPORADIC DISEASES: THE INFLUENCE
OF CLIMATE, ENVIRONMENT, AND REGIMEN

Breaths brings into relief three other general categories in the Hippocratic classification and explanation of disease, all of which have already been touched on: the distinction between epidemic and sporadic diseases; the impact of general ambient factors on the particular prevalence of diseases; and the role of individual regimen in the maintenance of health and the causing of disease. Consider the following passage:

> Some diseases arise from regimen, others from the air we inhale . . . . When many people are stricken with a single disease at the same time, we should assign as the cause of it whatever is the most common factor, the one which all of us make use of: this is what we inhale. For it is clear at any rate that it is not each individual's regimen that is responsible, when the disease attacks everybody one after the other, both younger and older, women and men, wine-drinkers no less than those who drink water, those who eat barley cakes and those who consume bread, and those who exert themselves greatly and those who do not. For the regimens would surely not be causes when people who have followed every different type of regimen are stricken by the same disease. But when diseases of all different types arise at the same time, clearly their individual regimens are the causes of the individuals' diseases.[55]

A common theme recurs: if the effects are the same, so too must be the relevant causal influences. The general types of cause are those of *Breaths*, as is the distinction between epidemic and sporadic diseases, which is also implicit in the general structure of the *Epidemics*, in particular 1 and 3, with its contrast between the general 'constitutions' on the one hand and the descriptions of particular cases on the other. But the passage goes further in implicating specific variations in regimen, here broadly construed to include general lifestyle in

---

[55]   *Nature of Man* 9 (Jones [1931], 24–6).

addition to diet,[56] in the genesis of particular, non-epidemic ailments. But matters are more complex than this. Different individuals will be differently disposed to respond either well or badly to variations both in their dietary and lifestyle practices and in their immediate environment, in terms of their own particular constitutions, however those are to be analysed. We should also consider why some diseases are epidemic only for particular species (although some, like the plague of Athens, are not: Thucydides 2.50):

> There are two kinds of fevers, one which is common to all and is called 'plague', the other which arises specifically through poor regimen in those who have undertaken a bad regimen; but air is the cause of both of them. Epidemic fever is for this reason the same, since everyone inhales the same air, and since the same air is mixed in the same way in the body, the fevers that arise are the same. But perhaps someone will say: 'but why then do the same diseases not afflict all animals but only some of them?' I would reply that body differs from body, nature from nature, and nutriment from nutriment, and so the same things are not well-suited or ill-suited to all kinds of animal, some are beneficial or harmful to some, and others to others. So whenever air has been infected with the sort of pollution (*míasma*) which is hostile to human nature, men become sick, but when the air becomes ill-suited to some other kind of animal, then they are the ones that fall sick.[57]

The language of hostility to nature recalls that of *Ancient Medicine* in the case of cheese-intolerance; and that of pollution also deserves a brief mention. *Míasma* is a powerful notion in the Greek tradition – it is what Oedipus suffers as a result of his actions, a divinely inflicted evil that makes him contagious to, and to be shunned by, other humans. It is obviously a model for infectious diseases. But what is striking about the Hippocratic corpus is the complete absence of any idea that disease is something that can be

---

[56]   See Jouanna (2016).   [57]   *Breaths* 6 (Jones [1931], 232–4).

transmitted from one individual to another, simply in virtue of the fact that they are afflicted by it. I have argued elsewhere that the Hippocratics' total rejection of the possibility of infectious transmission is due to the fact that it was associated with an earlier, supernatural paradigm of disease which they were concerned to distance themselves from.[58] But the idea of infectious transmissibility was still very much alive, as Thucydides' classic description of the Athenian plague makes clear (2.51): doctors were the worst afflicted, because they associated with sick (although they were of no use: 2.47). But although he acknowledges what he evidently sees as the evident fact of infectious transmissibility, Thucydides is no believer in the divine; and he tries to record the onset, spread, and eventual remission of the disease (2.48–9), as well as its symptoms (and the fact of acquired immunity: 2.48, 51), and the prevailing climatic conditions (and the incidence of other diseases) in a manner strikingly reminiscent of the *Epidemics*, although he is careful to disclaim any medical expertise himself (2.48). This disease was savagely pandemic – everyone, no matter what their age or constitution, seemed to be susceptible to it (2.51).

When confronted with such generalised diseases, our authors talk, as we have seen, of generalised harmful conditions of the environment – they will deploy terms like *míasma*, but in a way immunised of any supernatural connotations. Pollutions are for them, as they still are for us, physical facts about the nature of the air and water themselves. The author of *Airs, Waters, Places* thus distinguishes between endemic and epidemic diseases, the former being a function of the site of the city in question. South-facing cities which are sheltered from cold northerly winds have plentiful, if brackish water, and their residents tend to flabbiness (they are 'moist and full of phlegm': chapter 3),[59] in contrast with those which face north, whose water is hard and cold, and citizens lean ('they are bilious rather than phlegmatic': chapter 4, 76). These basic

---

[58] Hankinson (1995). [59] Jones (1923a), 74.

conditions (and their variations) can be used to predict the prevalence of distinct types of diseases, for men and women, young and old. The best-situated city faces east, thus avoiding extremes of heat and cold from summer and winter winds. Its water is better, because 'purified by the rising sun'; it is 'clear, sweet and soft'; and it 'particularly resembles the spring, in its moderation of both heat and cold' (chapter 5, 80). By contrast the west-facing city is subject to rapid changes of temperature and humidity during the day, particularly in the summer; and 'particularly resembles the autumn, in regard to its daily changes, since the difference between sunrise and afternoon is so great' (chapter 6, 82).

So the seasons, too, are enlisted into the general account of healthiness and insalubriousness (chapter 10). This is another general feature of the corpus. *Aphorisms* 3.1–23[60] offers a wide variety of claims about the relations between the seasons, both general and particular, and the prevalence of diseases. *Epidemics* 2.1.1–5 deals with the peculiarities of seasonal diseases, as well as with the effects of unusual weather patterns:

> In Crannon, in summer, anthrax. During the hot weather there was continuous, violent rain; it occurred more when the wind was southerly ... In hot dry weather, fevers are mostly sweat-free; but in those where [fevers] where there is any rain, there is more sweating at the beginning .... Ardent fevers occur mostly in the summer; [they occur] in other seasons too, but are drier in the summer ....
> In autumn, diseases are most acute and most fatal ... the year has a cycle of disease, just as the day has .... In stable times, and years which produce seasonal things at seasonal times, diseases are dependable and have their proper crises; but in unstable years they are unstable and hard to resolve: so in Perinthus, when there is deficiency or excess of wind or calm, rain or drought, heat or cold. But the spring is usually very healthy and minimally fatal.[61]

---

[60] Jones (1931), 122–30.   [61]   *Epidemics* 2.1.1–5 (Smith [1994], 18–20).

Such claims, both specific and general, occur throughout the *Epidemics* and elsewhere.[62]

Airs, Waters, Places creates its general typologies to assist travelling physicians (like the compilers of *Epidemics*), arriving in an unfamiliar town, in gauging the likelihood of the prevalence of diseases; but they will also need time *in situ* to form opinions as to what types of epidemic may afflict it in the course of the year as a result of particular climatic phenomena (chapter 2).[63] They will also need to know about 'the preferred regimen of the inhabitants, whether they are heavy drinkers, whether they take lunch [sc. in addition to their other daily meal: see below] and are generally inactive, or whether they are athletic and industrious, eating much and drinking little'.[64]

Regimen is here treated in general terms, as befits a general guide to the types of illnesses to expect. But this is perfectly consistent with consideration of individual variations, both in the generally preferred lifestyle of particular people, and in specific disruptions to such styles of living, and it is in these that we find another source of diagnostic (and prognostic) signs, as well as (and for obviously related reasons) of theoretical explanations of particular, as opposed to either endemic or epidemic diseases. Different people have different constitutions, and what suits them, and by extension what does not, will largely depend on those individual differences. This is precisely what was found in the passages from *Nature of Man* 9 and *Breaths* 6 quoted earlier, and is summarised in the following:

> The cure [sc. of sporadic diseases] must be devised to counteract the
> *próphasis* of the disease ... and should involve a change in regimen.
> For it is certainly clear that, whatever regimen the man is
> accustomed to adopt, either all of it, or most of it, or at least one part
> of it does not suit him. When you have discovered what they are,
> you need to change them, and you should create the cure looking

---

[62] For example, *Nature of Man* 7–8 (Jones [1931], 18–24); *Regimen* 2.37–8 (Jones [1931], 298–304).

[63] Jones (1923a), 72.   [64] *Airs, Waters, Places* 1 (Jones [1923a], 70–2).

both to the age and constitution of the patient, and the season of
the year, and the type of disease, sometimes removing things,
sometimes adding them, ... and he must pay attention, both in
dosage and regimen, to the age, the season, the constitution, and the
disease. But whenever a single disease establishes itself as epidemic,
it is clear that it is not the types of regimen that are responsible, but
rather what we breathe in is the cause, and this evidently because it
has some noxious discharge in it.[65]

The importance of regimen, both in sickness and in health, is evi-
denced in a variety of texts. It is central to the conception of medicine, and of human nature in *Ancient Medicine*. *Regimen in Acute
Diseases* 9 claims: 'this inquiry is the finest and most bound up with
the majority of the most important things in the art; it has the
greatest power of bringing health to the sick, and the preservation
of it to those who are healthy, and peak condition to those in
training: indeed, what everyone wants'.[66] *Regimen* 1.2 says that
'whoever wants to write accurately about human regimen needs to
understand and make the appropriate distinctions in human nature
as a whole', which requires understanding the nature of the fundamental constituents (for him fire and water), but also 'the particular
power which each of the things with which we make our regimen,
foods and drinks, has, both by nature and necessity, and by human
art'[67]; and after this exercise too needs to be taken into account (2.
61–6, 348–64). Finally, *Regimen in Health*, which appears in our
manuscripts as a coda to *Nature of Man*, makes similar distinctions
according to the time of year, the nature and age of the patient, their
basic physical constitution, and their customary habits: 'one should
construct the regimens in relation to the individual's time of life,
and the season, and their physical type by counteracting the heat
and cold which prevail in them, since then they will be

---

65   *Nature of Man* 9 (Jones [1931], 26); immediately follows the other passage from this
    book).
66   Jones (1923b), 70.
67   Jones (1923b), 226; these are treated in detail at 2.39–56 (Jones [1923], 306–42).

healthiest'.[68] Particular regimens, then, moderate the internal tendencies (towards hot or cold, wet or dry) that the individuals manifest as a result of the circumstances in which they find themselves, and which, if not counteracted, lead to disease.

We may add two final points. It is a commonplace that people can become accustomed to certain ways of life, even if they may not be fundamentally healthy; and in such cases these acquired dispositions, too, need to be taken into account.[69] Secondly, and relatedly, any rapid change from one state to another is dangerous. Rapid climatic changes are associated with the onset of epidemics, which is why autumn is more dangerous than spring, as its daily temperature variations are more extreme.[70] Unsettled as well as unseasonal weather is associated with epidemics.[71] This is put most generally in *Humours*: after saying that changes are responsible for diseases, in the seasons just as in everything else, the author continues: 'seasons which arrive gradually are the safest, just as are regimens ... which are directed gradually'.[72] It is a point also made in numerous places in *Regimen in Acute Diseases*, for example at 45–6: sudden exercise after prolonged inactivity is dangerous; indeed 'any change much in excess of what is moderate is harmful' (chapter 46)[73]; 'the most violent changes to our natures and constitutions are the most productive of illness' (chapter 35, 90); sudden changes from water to wine, or vice versa, are harmful (chapter 37, 92); if accustomed to two meals a day, then missing one is bad (chapters 30, 32, 86–8)[74]; and in general all changes in regimen indicated by illness should be carefully calibrated.[75] Sudden changes in circumstances, in habits, and in treatment, are all dangerous, and to

---

68   *Regimen in Health* 2 (Jones [1931], 48, with modifications). Also edited in Jouanna (2002 [orig. 1975]).

69   See also *Regimen* 2.66, on the differences between those in training and used to exercise, and those who are not: Jones (1931), 358.

70   *Airs, Waters, Places* 6 (Jones [1923a], 82).

71   See also, e.g., *Epidemics* 1.4–5, 1.13, 3.2–3 (Jones [1923a], 152–6, 164–6, 238–40).

72   *Humours* 15 (Jones [1931], 88).   73   Jones (1923b), 100–2.

74   See also *Ancient Medicine* 10–11 (Jones [1923a], 28–32).

75   Compare *Regimen in Health* 1 (Jones [1931], 44); *Regimen* 1.35 (Jones [1931], 292).

be avoided and minimised.[76] Finally, swift changes in the weather, and indeed in ambient temperature, are also dangerous.[77]

CONCLUSIONS

Behind the bewildering multiplicity of competing, indeed mutually inconsistent, theoretical (and anti-theoretical) accounts of the nature and constitution of the human body and of the origins and explanation of diseases, a number of points of general agreement emerge. First of all, there is a commitment to generality of explanation. The infinite variety of human experience of disease can be regimented and organised under certain general headings, which are significant precisely because they encode actual causal facts about the world which are themselves quite general, and hence generalisable and repeatable. Congruently with this, appeals to divine intervention and efficacy are correspondingly rare (although not for all that entirely absent). The world of disease (or at any rate the medically tractable parts of it) is a world of pathological facts which are themselves based on physiological facts, which are themselves ultimately physical in nature. Any individual variations then in the comparative incidence of particular types of illness are to be accounted for in terms of the significantly different constitutions of those who, having been subjected to the same generally causally significant influences, react in significantly different ways: suffering severe effects, less serious effects, or (at the limit) no effects at all. Indeed, what may be harmful for one individual may be positively beneficial for another,[78] but if that is the case, it will always (or at least generally) be because of the ways in which the individuals differ constitutionally. It will never simply be a matter of chance or luck; 'for on examination, there is evidently no spontaneity at all; for everything that happens will be found to happen because of something, and in this 'because of something' spontaneity will be seen to have no reality and to be a mere name'.[79]

---

[76] See also *Aphorisms* 2.51, 3.1 (Jones [1931], 120, 122).
[77] *Sacred Disease* 13 (Jones [1923], 164–8).
[78] See also *Places in Man* 41 (Potter [1995], 80–2).   [79] *Art* 6 (Jones [1923], 14–18).

6 Epistemologies

Lorenzo Perilli

To discern, to define relationships, and to gauge the prospect: *aísthēsis, lógos, prónoia*. This is the essence of Hippocratic epistemology and the mark that it left on Western knowledge. It is the actualisation of Achilles' paradigm (*Iliad* 1.343); it is, in fact, the very identity of the Greek mind, which shapes itself as such and that lives on, surprisingly uninterrupted; incorporating, absorbing, metabolising, and re-elaborating every impulse. During the ten-year siege of Troy, Agamemnon offended Achilles so much that the latter withdrew to his tent with the intention of returning home. He knew that without his help the Greek army would be bound for disaster. But the deficiency, he proclaimed, has nothing to do with muscle strength. Agamemnon, chief of chiefs, lacks the illuminating clarity of the intellect, the sole source of salvation; when Agamemnon speaks he almost blabbers (1.106–120): he does not know how to look at once before and after, and how to connect the future to the past.

To discern (*aísthēsis*) is to observe, gauging objects in relation with each other, to relate to the environment, to gather and elaborate primary information. To identify entities.

To define relationships (*lógos*) is to connect, classify, to arrange in ranks, to make the stage of the world something that can be grasped. To build identities.

To gauge the prospect (*prónoia*) is to look at the horizon of a spatial and temporal continuum, establishing links of causal and functional order. To give sense through connections.

119

The issue at stake is to elaborate a method by which to make decisions in circumstances of opacity, and to draw a map that could guide one in the realm of uncertainty.

DEFINING EPISTEMOLOGY

Medicine is the first discipline in the West to establish itself autonomously, and to reflect explicitly upon itself, its own content, and its own methodology. For the ancient *téchnai* (arts, craftsmanships), epistemology consists in laying conceptual schemes upon an empirical foundation, elaborating a tactic and a strategy to move forward in a way that will be called 'scientific', that is, the effort to understand how an opinion may become an argumentation, how to give a shape to an intuition. We must, nonetheless, agree on the meaning of this concept. For the Scottish philosopher James F. Ferrier – who coined the term in 1854 in his Institutes of Metaphysic –, 'epistemology' means to ask 'the truly first question in regard to knowing and the known', to explore 'the laws both of knowing and of the known, in other words, the conditions of the conceivable; laying out the necessary laws, as the laws of all knowing, and all thinking, and the contingent laws as the laws of our knowing and of our thinking'[1]; in other words, to answer the question: 'What is knowledge?' In the Anglo-Saxon world, to this day, epistemology equals gnosiology; elsewhere, the concept insists on the role of positive science as a model; it indicates the critical inquiry into the structures and methods of science (observation, experiment, inference), and in these terms one can speak of an epistemology of medicine as well as of an epistemology of mathematics.

The epistemology of the ancient medical art (*téchnē iatrikē*) is a conscious reflection on the 'built-in stimulus to growth'[2] of the arts (*téchnai*) themselves. These possess an innate form of prospective dynamism, a trust in a progressive growth based on critical self-awareness, a trust that activates the intellectual faculties needed to

---

[1]　　Ferrier (1854), 45–6.　　[2]　　Lloyd (1984), 424.

push the disciplines towards ever new configurations. Such a critical knowledge and trust place medical thought on a virtuous trajectory that is closed to traditional and popular knowledge, destined to an important, yet only cumulative growth. We must not, however, think of a clear break between traditional knowledge and the knowledge of the arts (*téchnai*): on the contrary, there exists an important continuity.

> Death, disease, madness, dreams, divination, and fate ... were the province of myth, religion, and ritual long before science and natural philosophy, and long after their first hesitant appearance in Greek thought. It was mainly through myth, in belief, and through ritual, in practice, that the Greeks, like others, responded to the facts of death and disease, for example, and it remained so, even after the inquiry concerning nature were some kind of going concern.[3]

FROM LOGIC TO GNOSIOLOGY

In Greek thought, the *Hippocratic Corpus* represents the accomplishment of the transition from logic to gnosiology. The paradigm shift owes much to sophistic mediation. Spontaneous logical thinking was already characteristic of archaic thought: it governed the network of immediate connections, allowing thought to think its object. It does not need to go back to the causes that make the thinkable thinkable. It leaves this task to gnosiology, a discipline that explains *how* thought may draw on *reality* and reach *true* knowledge. In the original mental attitudes of the ancients, the *true* and *real* coincide: this is the premise to the genesis of logical problems.

The 'true' does not derive from an analysis of the 'real', but is identical with it.[4] It does not reside in the judgement of a subject, but belongs to the realm of objectivity. The subjective dimension of awareness requires a passage that happens gradually, surfacing suddenly in Achilles' demand before Agamemnon in the first book of the

---

[3]   Lloyd (1987), 4.   [4]   See also Calogero (1967), 39, 73.

Iliad. It is found again in the tragedy of Sophocles, in Euripides, Thucydides, and Gorgias, and in the *Prometheus* attributed to Aeschylus ('of my own will, of my own will I erred, gainsay I will not', v. 266). It is fulfilled in the *Hippocratic Corpus* and in some treatises that may be defined 'epistemological'. Their objective is not as much truth (*alḗtheia*) but rather correctness (*orthótēs*).

EPISTEMOLOGIES

There is not only one epistemology in fifth-century medicine, as there is not one 'Hippocratic' medicine. There are different empirical approaches and theoretical developments. The 'Hippocratic' system is not coherent and unitary; it presents endless differences within itself, which range from slight variations in meaning to radical differences. The so-called *Hippocratic Corpus* is a sort of 'secret garden' born out of contaminations, in which what is inside is decontextualised, and what is left outside is doomed to oblivion, owing to its being outside the accepted canon.[5] Hippocratism is medicine as seen by the winners. It does not embrace the horizon that was once multifarious, having its own linguistic, stylistic, and operational modes, which were really modes of thinking. Rooted in history, medicine responded to the push of the changing social structure at the end of the archaic age, which saw the affirmation of new mercantile oligarchies; the search for new models of intellectual, political, and economical organisation; and new interlocutors. It is here, in the network of connections of which medicine is but one branch, that we must look for its meaning. Whosoever looks for a coherent and systematic pursuit of theoretical and programmatic objectives, shared by different works in the *Corpus*, will not find it.

AN EPISTEMOLOGICAL DECALOGUE

Yet, there are some essential traits common to a part of the treatises of the *Hippocratic Corpus*. These, in some cases, represent consciously

---

[5]   On the Hippocratic canon, see Chapter 2 by Craik and Chapter 3 by Jouanna in this volume.

elaborated methodological and theoretical issues, while, in other cases, they represent more or less institutionalised intuitions. The epistemological decalogue, for fifth-century BC 'rational' medicine, may be articulated as follows:

(1) reliance on observation and on empirical evidence, and logical coordination of data;
(2) the tendency to meticulous recording of signs, symptoms, proofs; therefore
(3) systematisation and organisation as clinical notes;
(4) the prominence of inductive-deductive reasoning towards prognostic elaboration (Achilles' paradigm);
(5) the tendency to generalisation;
(6) clear demarcation between natural and supernatural;
(7) awareness of the notion of error and its epistemological function;
(8) argumentative capacity and tendency to apodeictic statements; and lastly,
(9) the need to proffer rules, to identify a method, to reflect critically on itself.

These aspects seem inevitable for any form of medicine that would not limit itself to the uncritical accumulation of data; yet, only in Greece did they develop in a coherent and somewhat systematic manner, although with contrasting approaches. Besides, there were choices that required an explicit and almost ideological position, a deep conceptual maturation. Among these, there is the pretence to arrive at

(10) a causal explanation of pathological phenomena.

Observation, Empirical Evidence, Logical Coordination of Data

Before Plato radically altered the relationship between knowing subject and known reality, a banal though decisive concept characterised Greek thought: "Experience is the principle of learning." A so-called *schólion* (an ancient explanation) to Pindar's Isthmean ode 1.56 attributed this to the poet Alcman, perhaps confused with the Pre-Socratic philosopher Alcmaeon. The principle was also embraced by medicine;

the author of *Sacred Disease* 14 writes: 'If you cut open and observe . . . you will find'. This is the ideal of direct observation as instrument of validation, hence: 'you may learn that it is not a god but the disease which injures the body'. The physician operates on nature, he creates the conditions to have access to his object of inquiry: then there is nothing left but to observe, and the heuristic procedure is completed. He does not need abstract reasoning procedures. By observing the brain of an ill goat, a researcher will find that the brain is soft, full of liquid, and foul-smelling. The cause of epilepsy is therefore only physiological and does not require supernatural hypotheses.

This empirical approach is, however, immediately contradicted in *Sacred Disease* 11, when the Hippocratic author offers the general conclusion: "So it is also with a man." Extending the observation performed on an animal to humans is justified only by the conviction of the uniformity of nature and of the universality of its laws. A measurable nature: medicine emerges as art (*téchnē*) because of its capacity of measuring. Medicine has at its disposal an instrument, which, although not infallible, still remains the best. This is perception based on the senses. In *Ancient Medicine*, the Hippocratic author states (chapter 9): 'One must aim at a measure; but you will find no measure – nor number nor weight besides – by referring to which you will know with precision, except the feeling of the body'.

The author of *Sacred Disease* is, among the authors of the *Corpus*, the one who treats the role of cognition and the coordination of perceptions in more detail. This work is the most relevant to the process of acquiring an epistemological conscience, an awareness of the relationship between the internal and the external, between subject and object, between body and environment.[6] At this stage, there appears an encephalocentric theory that departs from cues already present in Alcmaeon of Croton (beginning of the fifth century BC). The brain coordinates perception and transforms it into knowledge,

---

[6]   Lo Presti (2016), 175.

and vice versa, the organs of the human body – including sense organs, such as the eyes – operate following stimuli from the brain: "The eyes, tongue, hands and feet carry out what the brain knows" (*Sacred Disease* 16). The brain becomes an intermediary and an interpreter of all that, through the air, reaches the body from the exterior, and penetrates it. From this purely materialistic principle – the air – which recalls part of contemporary thought (Archelaus and Diogenes of Apollonia) – is said to derive instruments of rational thought (*phrónimon* and *gnṓmē*), and also the capacity of synthetic understanding (*sýnhesis*) and the analytic faculty that allows discernment (*diágnōsis*). This simplified and yet innovative interaction between a materialistic external principle, the air, and its internal mediator within the body, the brain, poses human cognitive capacity in direct relationship with physiology, in an attempt to explain it.[7] Identifying a specific organ as the instrument of sensorial coordination was, in the fifth century BC, anything but banal.

In the operational sphere, the author does not have much to add to his rivals' works and even declares to be ready to accept some of their dietary prescriptions. He nonetheless radically turns the tables of methodology: he understands that finding and describing signs are the indispensable premises to the search for the physiological causes of any process, and that the accumulation of data from observation precedes any potential progress. This is demonstrated by *Sacred Disease* 7: "The patient becomes speechless and chokes, froth flows from the mouth; he gnashes his teeth and twists his hands; the eyes roll and intelligence fails, and in some cases excrement is discharged." The description is the result of observations of patients and data recording carried out by the physicians. Immediately afterwards, however, these data based on observations are intermingled with claims of causal order devoid of any empirical validation:

> I will now explain how each symptom occurs. The sufferer is
> speechless when suddenly the phlegm descends into the veins and

---

[7]   Lo Presti (2008, 2016).

intercepts the air, not admitting it either into the brain, or into the hollow veins, or into the cavities, thus checking respiration. For when a man takes in breath by the mouth or nostrils, it first goes to the brain, then most of it goes to the belly, though some goes to the lungs and some to the veins. From these parts it disperses, by way of the veins, into the others. The portion that goes into the belly cools it ...[8]

Many other works confirm this extraordinary capacity for observation, from the *Prognostic* to the *Epidemics*, to nosological and gynaecological treatises. Both the Hippocratic physician and the Hippocratic epistemologist – profiles that do not necessarily coincide – know that the horizon of what can be perceived by the senses contains in itself all that is necessary to know. Each detail becomes a sign, before turning into a symptom. Nevertheless, the explanations given, for instance, about the action of corporeal humours like bile and phlegm, though based on rigorous observance of a naturalistic phenomenology, cannot be proved or deducted through a procedure based on inference and observation.

It can be surprising that the author does not display any awareness of the necessity to search for a foundation to his aetiological statements. The same is true for the closing generalisations. A statement such as "The patient suffers all these things when the phlegm flows cold into the blood which is warm; for the blood is chilled and arrested"[9] comes from deeply rooted theoretical preconceptions. To the modern eye, this is a critical element; it nonetheless underscores the idea of an organism whose parts and activities are all functionally connected. With time, this will bear important fruits: the explanations of the origins of symptoms and illnesses will change, but the theoretical scheme will remain stable. The causal naturalistic explanations, or the rationalistic explanations, being devoid of empirical foundations, were based on trust, and not on a binding demonstrative argument. Nature (*phýsis*) was chosen a priori.

---

8   *Sacred Disease* 7, ed. and trans. Jones (1923b), 158–9.
9   *Sacred Disease* 10, ed. and trans. Jones (1923b), 160–1.

Moving beyond the methodological awareness redolent of contacts with the philosophical-sophistic reflection, the entire *Corpus* testifies to a proper 'art of observation'.[10] Data recording was based on well-known instruments: 'sight, hearing, smell, tact, tongue, logical connection' (*Epidemics* 6.8,17). The five senses, complemented by the governing rational component that connects data into a system in order to make sense of them, allow one to undertake the examination of the sick body.

Recording Signs

Medicine has always been the science of observation: for this, there was no need of a well-formed theoretical apparatus. Works produced in ancient Egypt are evidence of this. Not only traditional medical papyri prove it. Even an unusual work such as the *Treatise on Snakes* of the fourth century BC (roughly contemporary with the 'Hippocratic' texts, although containing more ancient materials), coming from the temple at Heliopolis,[11] is a witness to an uncommon keenness towards observation, and to an excellent capacity of classification. This medical-zoological text on snakes, which has the homogeneous structure of a technical manual, shows how the subdivision into classes and the elaboration of specific categories are the premise of any art (*téchnē*). It records, according to a regular pattern, the name of the reptile, and then its family, morphology, behaviour, shape of the bite, association with a god, prognosis, and therapeutic prescriptions. The manual is divided in two parts. In the first part, the work reports in separate sections the description of each snake and the shape of its bite, with possible consequences; in the second part, additional sections describe the treatment to be adopted. The author knew zoological classifications. He was an expert in medicine as well as in snakes (which always retained a special importance in Egypt and that even in Greece accompany the medical symbology of Asclepius), and he had practical aims. As Sauneron observed, his method 'testifies to great

[10] Jouanna (1993), 44.
[11] Pap. Brooklyn Museum, n. 47.218.48 and 85, ed. Sauneron (1985).

gifts of observation and ability to classify ... the Egyptian physician possessed an intimate and profound knowledge of snakes'.[12]

This attitude should be compared with the clinical notes of the *Epidemics*, which is a typical example of recording signs. In these clinical notes, the description of individual cases complements the *katastáseis* (descriptions of general external conditions, even environmental ones, and of the illnesses that characterise them). In this text, as opposed to the Egyptian one, the author moves from individual cases to generalisations. It is probable that the organisation of notes into sections – in the Egyptian treatise, in the texts of the *Hippocratic Corpus*, and even in sanctuaries where medicine was practised – derived from individual case notes assembled for the use of physicians, which were bound together at a later point.[13]

The systematic collection of individual cases, the description of symptoms and the identification of the illness, all followed clearly formalised procedures. *Epidemics* 1.10 provides a double general scheme of reference:

> The following were the circumstances attending the diseases, from which I framed my judgments, learning from the common nature of all and the particular nature of the individual, from the disease, the patient, the regimen prescribed and the prescriber – for these make a diagnosis more favourable or less.

These general elements are followed by the patient's constitution and by the specific symptoms:

> (Learning) from the constitution, both as a whole and with respect to the parts, of the weather and of each region; from the custom, mode of life, practices and ages of each patient; from talk, manner, silence, thoughts, sleep or absence of sleep, the nature and time of dreams, pluckings, scratchings, tears; from the exacerbations, stools, urine, sputa, vomit, the antecedents and consequents of each member in the successions of diseases, and the abscessions to a fatal

---

[12] Sauneron (1985), 206.   [13] See also Langholf (2004); Perilli (2009).

issue or a crisis, sweat, rigour, chill, cough, sneezes, hiccoughs, breathing, belchings, flatulence, silent or noisy, haemorrhages, and haemorrhoids. From these things must we consider what their consequents also will be.[14]

It is worth looking also into *Regimen in Acute Diseases* (*App.*) 9:

Patients have many aspects. Therefore, the person treating must pay attention to see that none of the immediate signs escape his notice, nor any of those that you know by reckoning ... Now, you must mark well the first day on which any patient began to be ill, observing whence and why the disease starts ... When you question the patient and examine each thing carefully, do so first with regard to the state of his head, whether it is free of pain ... observe carefully when the patient rises, too, whether he faints, or whether his breathing is adequate; observe the stools, whether anything dark is passed ... and the fever, whether it has another access on the third day. ... Signs: dark stools indicate death, whereas those like a healthy person's, when they have this appearance every day, betoken recovery. But when a patient fails to have a movement after he has received a suppository, and there is also difficulty in breathing, or if either on getting up into a chair or right in his bed he loses consciousness—when these things happen to the patient, either male or female, expect derangement. You must also pay attention to the hands, for if they tremble, expect such a patient to have a flow of blood from his nostrils. You must look at both nostrils, for if the air is drawn equally through them both, and much is carried through, a convulsion is likely; if a convulsion does occur in such a patient, death is to be expected, and it is good to predict this.[15]

Prognostic is also a mine of information about symptomatology and its interpretation, and their correlation to predict future developments. To *Prognostic* 2.13, we owe the description of the signs that

[14]   trans. Jones (1923b), 181.   [15]   trans. Potter (1988b), 247–51.

foretell the death of the patient (the so-called 'Hippocratic Face'), which became a reference for the whole history of medicine.

Greek medicine is characterised, as opposed to Egyptian medicine, by attention not only to the illness – which remains an object of study – but also to the patient. The so-called Hippocratic triangle in *Epidemics* 1.11 describes the correlation between physician, patient and illness, a collaboration which is necessary in order to reach the cure: "The art has three factors: the disease, the patient, the physician. The physician is the servant of the art. The patient must co-operate with the physician in combating the disease." Each patient is an object of observation; he is identified by name, provenance and other elements that qualify him individually. Still, the illness is not the illness of this or that patient; it does not have any individual traits, instead belonging to more general categories, as there cannot exist an illness for each patient. This fact implies the capacity, which is not a trivial one, to distinguish between those differences in patients that point to a different illness from the differences that instead point to the same nosological picture. Once again, it is not only practice that testifies to the maturity of this method, but also the explicit awareness of it. Such an awareness is patent in the critique against those physicians who did not know how to achieve unity from the totality of individualities, that is, how to overcome the fragmentation of singularities.[16] The objects of the critique were the so-called 'Cnidian' physicians, whose *Sentences* represented a model to be surpassed. Yet, their careful surveys were probably instrumental in the creation of a clinical database on which physicians continued to draw.

Regimen in Acute Diseases 1 articulates the following criticism: "The authors of the work entitled *Cnidian Sentences* have correctly described the experiences of patients in individual diseases and the issues of some of them." But this is banal, the author continues: anybody would be capable of it; it is as important to find out

---

[16] This is what Spinoza calls 'res singulares', *Ethics*, Part 2, Expl. 7: 'things ... that are finite and have a determined existence' (*res ... quae finitae sunt, et determinatam habent existentiam*).

what the patient fails to say. The Cnidian remedies, moreover, were few and ineffective, but it is above all unthinkable to consider an illness as different from another only because it has a different name: "For the number will be almost incalculable if a patient's disease is diagnosed as different whenever there is a difference in the symptoms, while a mere variety of name is supposed to constitute a variety of the illness." The Cnidians lack the intellectual instruments needed to master experience, to reduce variability to unity.

Systematisation and Organisation as Clinical Case Notes

The classification of animals for diet, therapeutic purposes, and their effects on the human body is particularly telling. Chapters 46–49 of *Regimen* 2 present a systematic catalogue of edible animals that raised the admiration of scholars. Fifty-two types of animals are identified; their dietary characteristics are indicated and sometimes the explanation of their causes. A real pre-Aristotelian zoological system emerges from it, which is an extraordinary example of systematisation of knowledge according to categories.[17] Clearly, every operation of this kind requires the existence of a definite scheme.

The author of *Regimen* 2 draws a list of animals according to more general classes (such as mammals, birds, fish, crustacea, molluscs), sometimes according to their habitat and diet, but, more importantly and systematically, according to the effect on the person who eats them, that is, their dietary properties – light or heavy, dry or wet, fat, astringent or laxative, slimming, helpful for the sight, diuretic. It is typical of an 'artist' or craftsman (*technítēs*, 'the one who exercises the art') that this classification follows the criterion of the effect of the animals as food: according to Aristotle the scientist's knowledge must rather have an epistemological perspective, not a practical one; the scientist operates not in view of any specific aim, but for the sake of knowledge (*Generation of Animals* 756a33).

---

[17]   'Coan animal system': Burckhardt (1904); 'Hippocratic animal system': Harig and Kollesch (1974); 'pre-Aristotelean animal system': Palm (1933).

The same systematic classification is applied to other substances, such as those of vegetal origin, and in a methodological chapter (*Regimen* 2.39), the author criticises precisely those who utilised more general systems of classification. Because every substance has its own effect (*dýnamis*), the author maintains, this must be the criterion to be adopted. Without a doubt, *Regimen* 2 is different from the rest of the work, as Galen observed in *On the Properties of Foodstuffs* 6.473,16 K., considering it 'truly worthy of Hippocrates'. It draws on older sources; it systematises and develops them. It is not isolated: other treatises in the *Hippocratic Corpus*, such as *Affections* and most importantly *Internal Affections* (works that are considered older than *Regimen*), without the level of detail of *Regimen*, classify animals on the basis of their characteristics in groups that are repeated regularly. It is implausible that each author proceeded autonomously: these writings testify to a shared process of systematisation.

When examining the clinical notes of each patient, recorded at his sickbed by the physician and reported in the *Epidemics*, one observes the capacity to trace the essential, and a scarce interest for the therapeutic dimension. This attitude is contrary to that of the author of *Regimen* 2, who was interested precisely in the therapeutic effect of food. In the *Epidemics*, despite being often identified by their names, patients sometimes appear to be but a test for understanding the illness, an indicator. The work done in *Epidemics* raises admiration, but, to books such as 1 and 3, which have a consistent and cohesive structure, one must add other books that share with many treatises – such as the gynaecological ones – an additional or catalogue-like structure, which sometimes is more orderly and systematic, but often confused, as if they were 'a largely unsorted chaotic database',[18] filled with notes, recipes, and clinical accounts that are not elaborated into a system.[19]

---

[18]   This expression is from Langholf (2004), 231, for works such as *Places in Man*, *Affections*, *Nature of Woman*, *Use of Liquids*, *Diseases* I, *Coan Prognoses*, *Prorrhetic* 1–2, *Nature of Bones*, *Mochlicon*, *Anatomy*, *Humours*, and *Aphorisms*.

[19]   See Langholf (2004); Smith (1983).

If one looks at the *Corpus* as a whole, the extraordinary level reached in the clinical description and in the systematisation of data becomes evident. These are 'made to talk', and to provide information about what is going to happen.

Inductive-Deductive Route for Prognostic Purposes

The concise and elegant opening statement of *Prognostic* is the programmatic declaration of medicine as the science of prevision: "It is the task of the best physician to practise forecasting" it says, and forecasting means to 'recognise immediately and to declare publicly what has happened beforehand, the present situation and what one expects to happen', that is to say patient history, diagnosis, and prognosis. The logical extrapolation of the future is the central operation for Greek epistemology in the fifth century BC, for medicine in particular—its most self-aware witness. Founded on a semiotic-inferential structure, it is identified quite simply with the correct 'scientific' procedure. The rational integration of the temporal sequence allows for any mechanical seriality to be overcome, as logical correlation takes over. Heuristic instances find their expression here, the progressive becoming of a 'new science'. As another passage will confirm (1.21), 'to elaborate (deductively) the prognosis' means to ascertain from external details (signs, which become symptoms) the future, that is, to extrapolate the development of the illness: it is the prospective angle of Greek medicine.

The epistemological construction that these physicians build is based on an evidential paradigm[20] that allows them to infer both what the patient fails to say, as well as what is to be expected. To do this, one needs data, but data are meaningless without a method that allows one to arrange them within a network.

The inferential procedure, which is superior to perception (*Art* 11.15) and to the outcome of chance (*Ancient Medicine* 12.14), reasserts a pragmatic instance of the foretelling of the future. It prevails over the patient's history and the diagnosis of the disease, but is still

---

[20]   Ginzburg (1989).

related to them. In the reciprocal integration of past, present, and expectation (*Prognostic* 1), seriality, chance, and analogical illusions surrender to the rationality of inference. The reality dominated by the physician has a causal dimension, besides a temporal development. The method of conjecture, proceeding according to clues, substitutes the foreknowledge (*prónoia*) of the diviner, based on the privilege of a direct contact with the divine, by which to interpret the sign. The unfailing knowledge that Alcmaeon thought exclusive to the god (*saphéneia*) remains unattainable for man. This method requires the active participation of a knowing subject, since the world does not disclose itself anymore, 'miraculously' offering its essence to the observer. It must instead be responsibly interpreted, indeed intellectually 'constructed': in the search for reality and truth the guiding principle of inference is epistemologically central. Single events, placed on the space–time continuum peculiar to the Greek mind, are bound to each other, and through this binding they acquire meaning.

Because, as Xenophanes preached (fr. 34 DK), 'the veil of opinion hangs upon all things', perception must be integrated and knowledge must be articulated on two levels, so that 'what the physician cannot see with the eyes nor hear with the ears, he grasps through *logismós*' (*Art* 11), with the 'eye of the mind' (*Breaths* 3.10). Although the concept surfaces repeatedly in the works of the *Hippocratic Corpus*, it is nonetheless characteristic of the whole Hellenic culture: Homer, with a brilliant intuition, states the centrality of logic-causal connections of facts for man, that is to say, the capacity of finding in them earlier and later instances, and to correlate them. This is the ability that Achilles claims for himself in the first book of the *Iliad*, denying it to the uncouth Agamemnon. The latter lacks the capacity, originally reserved to the diviners, to establish a connection between available data. He lacks an eye that sees beyond the present, connecting rationally past and future: 'he cannot coordinate (in Greek *noêsai*, a lightning-fast act of thought) what is in front and what is behind' (*Iliad* 1.343). Here, 'what is in front' is the past, visible in its entirety, whilst the future is not visible because it is hidden 'behind' the back. It is not by chance that Agamemnon, until the end of the story, cannot see where he has done wrong, and finds consolation in attributing all responsibility to the gods: "What could I do? The god carries out everything to its end" (19.90). He cannot escape the conventional schemes.

One verse thus designates Achilles as the incarnation of a burgeoning, self-aware rationality: the birth of intellect.[21] This would also designate him as an outcast, even in the use of language, to make him extraordinary in his own world: "Achilles has no language in which to express his disillusionment, ... misusing the language he disposes of. ... Achilles' tragedy, his final isolation, is that he can in no sense, including that of language (unlike, say, Hamlet), leave the society which has become alien to him."[22] But Achilles is not outside his community: he departs from it only in order to find its lost values. He has been taught to be 'a speaker of words and doer of deeds' (9.443). It is his prerogative to know how to represent what he has not experienced directly, what he can foresee better than others (21.122–7). Achilles does not persuade, like Odysseus; he affirms. Without a doubt, without a care: "My speech will come straight through, forgetting tact, just what I think – and I'll see it happen so. No need to sit there muttering each to each" (9.309–11).[23] Achilles does not adapt himself to the world: if he cannot change it, as it happens in his conflict with Agamemnon, he describes it. And he looks at it so as to know what is going to happen.

The defect that may cause the Greeks' defeat is therefore the lack of vision, the lack of foresight of their leader. Whereas *mêtis* ('astute intelligence'), Odysseus' gift, lies in the hands, in the capacity to act upon the world, Achilles' *noûs* ('intellect') is a mental perception; it implies having 'insight and hindsight', showing, in particular 'the ability to plan'.[24] This is a paramount principle for Greek thought, found in Alcmaeon, Xenophanes, Anaxagoras, Herodotus, Thucydides, Sophocles, Euripides,

---

[21]   Marzullo (1986–7), 199.   [22]   Parry (1956).

[23]   See also Parry (1956), but most importantly Friedrich and Redfield (1978), from which I have drawn some examples and Parry's quotation.

[24]   von Fritz (1994 [orig. 1945]).

Gorgias, and finally the so-called 'Hippocratic' medicine, whose main characteristic is the semeiotics of diagnosis and prognosis. The capacity that Achilles claims, as does the philosopher and the scientist, is the capacity to place oneself outside the norm in order to look further ahead.

Generalisation

> Most important: from the origin and the going forth, and from very many accounts and learning little by little, one should gather data and assess whether the things are like one another; again whether the dissimilarities in them are like each other, so that from dissimilarities there arises one similarity. This would be the road (i.e., method; Greek *hodós*). In this way one can develop verification of correct accounts and refutation of erroneous ones.[25]

This statement reveals one essential aspect of fifth-century BC medicine, that is, its incremental character, its being a process of creation of knowledge that unfolds progressively and that requires the subject's active intervention, an intervention based on causal relationships and on the concept of error. This progression must have as its departure point the analysis of the many singularities and their comparison, and as its aim overcoming 'the host of dissimilarities' of the sensible world, the identification of the common element, of the connecting line, of *lógos* in the sense that this concept had in mathematics and in Gorgias (*Encomium of Helen* 14), which is 'establishing a relationship' or ratio. Identifying the common element means to generalise, moving from multiplicity to uniformity, from disarray to system, and thereby to be able to formalise and transmit a knowledge that has become stabilised. This alone can be an art (*téchnē*). The treatment of individual cases requires a general framework of reference. This is the circle of medicine: moving from observing dissimilarities, from the host of singularities, to recognising what they have in common, and therefore to generalise applying the principles thereby identified to ever-changing singularities. The latter can

---

[25] *Epidemics* 6.3,12.

be recognised and classified in general categories, both on the level of knowledge (diagnosis and prognosis) and on the level of therapy.[26] Generalisation has its rules, too, and must be adequate for its object: there is no use in saying that one must know human beings in general, in relation to the universe that surrounds them or to their origin or to the basic elements, but one must be able to say 'what the human being is in relation to foods and drinks, and what it is in relation to other practices, and what will be the effect of each thing on each individual – not simply that "cheese is harmful food, for it causes trouble to one who has eaten too much of it", but rather what trouble, and why, and which of the things in the human being it is inimical to'.[27] This does not mean to go back to the specificity of the individual case, but rather to introduce a different type of generalisation, that which incorporates specific phenomena in to a general framework, explaining them on the basis of something that is not observable (the internal humours). Theory serves to explain differences.[28]

Generalising was not easy, and this difficulty surfaces often; it was nonetheless possible and necessary, as the parallel between *Epidemics* 5.71 and 7.82 shows. The latter text contains general statements that correspond to the description of the individual case that appears in the first text. In fact, in *Epidemics* 5.71, the Hippocratic author describes the case of 'Bias the boxer, a naturally big eater: it happened that he fell into a choleric condition after eating meat; especially after eating rather bloody pork, and fragrant wine and pastry, honey cakes, ripe cucumber, milk, and young barley. In summer choleric problems and remittent fever'; while in *Epidemics* 7.82, the author generalises, looking for the causes while quoting the same elements with no reference to any specific case: 'Choleric conditions, from meat-eating and especially undercooked pork, and from chickpeas and from fragrant old wine'. The author specifies further on in the text that 'choleric conditions are more likely in summer, as also remittent fevers'.[29] There are many

---

[26]   See also Temkin (1953), 219–20.
[27]   *Ancient Medicine* 20.3, trans. Schiefsky (2005), 103.
[28]   See also Schiefsky (2005), 293.   [29]   This example is found in Lloyd (2007).

cases, however, in which statements that are allegedly universally valid have no other foundation but themselves.

Six centuries later, Galen, commenting on the first book of the *Epidemics*, underscores the role of generalisation as opposed to the single cases taken individually. He establishes a hierarchy between reason and experience. According to such hierarchy, the first is necessary for the art (*téchnē*) to be complete, while the second is necessary because the physician operates, in fact, on individual cases.

> There are two ways in which one finds out about something one examines: the first is through reasoning, by which one arrives at knowledge of the general, universal genus of each individual phenomenon, the second is through experience of the individual phenomena until one arrives through it at the general, universal concept. Our claim is that while all concepts that make an art complete are general, the actions that the practitioners of the arts carry out all deal with particular, individual phenomena.[30]

Galen, as his custom, adopts a quasi-ideological posture; indeed his line of thought is but the completion of a route that began in the fifth century BC.

The author of *Sacred Disease* gives an example of this when he proclaims his principles and declares them valid not only for epilepsy, but for all illnesses, which he regards as compound, so that 'this disease styled sacred comes from the same causes as others ... none is hopeless or inescapable of treatment ... For in this disease as in all others it is necessary, not to increase the illness' (*Sacred Disease* 18). The need for generalisation, which the author here reasserts, becomes one of the cardinal characteristics of medicine. This is confirmed in the conclusion of *Prognostic* (25): "One must clearly realise about sure signs and about symptoms *generally* that in every year and in every land bad signs indicate something bad, and good signs something favourable, since the symptoms described above prove to have the

---

[30]   *On Hippocrates' 'Epidemics' I*, Wenkebach (1934), 126, lines 17–24; 17a 251, 18–252, 6 K.; trans. van der Eijk. See also van der Eijk (2012), 42.

same significance in Libya, in Delos, and in Scythia." This is one of the most relevant among the identifying principles of 'Hippocratic' medical art.

Demarcation between Natural and Supernatural

Sacred Disease is regarded as the manifesto of rationality, the first argumentative denial of the role of the divine and of the supernatural in determining an illness. To demonstrate the superiority of naturalistic *téchnē* over the deceitful world of superstition, the Hippocratic author chooses the most extraordinary of illnesses, one that was impossible to cure. The author thus demonstrates that medicine should not be judged based on therapeutic success, but on whether it employs a correct method and sensible procedures. The 'mages (*mágoi*)', whose purification practices are redolent with Mesopotamian[31] therapeutic rituals, are defeated on the level of epistemology, of cognitive control over the world, not on the level of the effectiveness of the cure, which remains in the background. For the first time, what is supranatural is identified and separated from what is not: a hierarchy is established.

The ancient epistemologists of medicine demand a leap of faith: the claims of the author of *Sacred Disease* are as ideological as those of his rivals.[32] He and his colleagues of *Ancient Medicine; Prognostic; Airs, Waters, and Places; Epidemics* 1 and 3; *Regimen in Acute Diseases; Nature of Man; Joints; Fractures;* and the sophists of *Art* and *Breaths* strive to define the boundaries of the domain of rationality. They share the conviction that medicine must be kept within those boundaries. By so doing, they attempt to keep at bay 'purifiers and quacks', unfair competitors. Yet, while the winning side that will dominate the medical canon dictates the enlightened optimism of 'reason', very different visions coexist in the *Hippocratic Corpus*, visions that are often opposed, contemplating even the superstitious practices of amulets of Mesopotamian descent. This is the case, for

---

[31]   Burkert (1992), 55–64; on the relationships between Eastern and Western scientific-philosophic culture, see Gemelli Marciano (in press).

[32]   Lloyd (1979), 148.

example, of *Diseases of Women* 1.77, where the author recommends, to prevent childbirth complications, placing at the woman's side the fruit of a wild cucumber covered in wax and wrapped in red wool.[33] The serious reflection on method did not always (rarely, in fact) correspond to a significant change in practices.

Religion was not considered incompatible with the epistemological principles of the *Hippocratic Corpus*. These reveal a certain degree of reverence towards religious beliefs. As in Pre-Socratic philosophy, the gods and the divine are not the object of a specific theoretical speculation (with the exception of Xenophanes): according to the Greek interpretation of the world, matter has within itself a self-sufficient material principle that determines every form of generation and transformation. In this, namely, a divine that pervades the world of phenomena, nature reveals the often latent pantheism which informs the archaic and classical period. Surprisingly, it is precisely *Sacred Disease* that states this clearly, in the final remarks: illnesses 'are all divine and all human', and 'there is no need to put this disease in a special class and to consider it more divine than the others'.

Some works of the *Hippocratic Corpus*, such as *Regimen*, advise prayer as complementary to therapy, according to a Near Eastern or traditional model.[34] In the beginning of *Prognostic*, the physician is advised to consider carefully whether 'there is something divine in illnesses'. This was an uncomfortable passage for those scholars who upheld an image of Hippocrates as a champion of rationality, to the point that it has been left out from some important editions of the work. It was a difficult battle: even in 1883 the physicist Ernst Mach devoted a paragraph of his *Science of Mechanics* to 'theological, animistic and mystical points of view in mechanics'.[35]

The Notion of Error and Its Epistemological Function

Reading fifth-century BC medical writings, one realises their awareness of procedures, difficulties, successes, and failures. Medicine deals with

[33] See Goltz (1974), 242, 46; Perilli (2009).   [34] See van der Eijk (2004b).
[35] See also Buchdal (1987), 45.

what is visible and what is not, developing the tools that are more fitting to the former case, or to the other. In cases of invisible, internal illnesses, the limit to the success of medicine lies in 'what is possible to achieve' (*Art* 11). For visible illnesses, instead, 'the cures should be infallible' (*Art* 9). The problem of correctness, efficacy, and measurability is recurrent. The author of *Ancient Medicine* writes (9, 3–4): "The doctor's tasks ... require more precision ... It is difficult to acquire knowledge so precise that one errs only slightly in one direction or the other. And I would strongly praise this doctor, the one who makes only small errors; perfect accuracy is rarely to be seen." Bad physicians, whose scarce capacities remain largely uncovered in the most common cases, are liable to the worst mistakes: 'whenever they meet with a great, powerful, and dangerous disease, then their errors and incompetence are evident to all'.

In the conclusion of *Airs, Waters, Places*, the author restates that a correct conjectural procedure allows the avoidance of mistakes: "Take these observations as a standard when drawing all other conclusions, and you will make no mistake." The same happens in nosological treatises: *Diseases* 1.6 distinguishes between mistakes of evaluation and execution. It provides a list of diagnostic mistakes, mistakes about the seriousness of an illness and its outcomes, on the capacity to identify an abscess or a latent illness, or mistakes deriving from not knowing how to discern between curable and incurable patients. Moreover, one can make a mistake in recognising fractures and dislocations, or in discovering the presence of pus in a wound, or bladder stones, or else when inserting a catheter or when making incisions or when cauterising.[36] And that is not all: the conscientious physician knows that he must not disguise his own mistakes, but rather acknowledge and classify them. In them, he has a precious heuristic tool, both for himself and for the others. There emerges a sense of a collectivity, a community that one may define as 'scientific', within which self-examination and the acknowledgement of one's own limits benefit the discipline.

---

[36]   See Schiefsky (2005), 134.

There is no lack of examples.[37] The best known is perhaps the one found at the end of chapter 47 of *Joints*. It not only points out a mistake, but also declares that this can be used as an occasion to gain a better understanding of one's self and to improve, if the mistake is described in detail. Talking about the possibility of intervening on the humps in the spine with a goatskin filled with air, it concludes:

> I once tried to make extension with the patient on his back, and after putting an uninflated wineskin under the hump, then tried to blow air into the skin with a smith's bellows. But my attempt was not a success, for when I got the man well stretched, the skin collapsed, and air could not be forced into it ... I relate this on purpose: for those things also give good instruction which after trial show themselves failures, and show why they failed.[38]

In the fifth book of *Epidemics* (27–30) the physician records, in the first person, a series of failures. He notes: "It escaped my notice that he needed trepanning. The sutures ... deceived my judgement, for afterwards it became apparent"; he observes that when carrying out a drilling he did not remove enough bone, and that two patients died because of a cauterisation that was carried out too late.[39] But recognising and acknowledging one's mistake does not just show awareness of one's limitation: it is the driving force behind a continuous search, that, precisely when confronted with its own limitations, strives incessantly to overcome them.

Argumentative Capacity and Tendency to Apodeictic Statements

Argumentative capacity is one of the strong points of those treatises in the *Hippocratic Corpus* which we define as 'epistemological'. "The style of each work is grave and austere. There is no attempt at 'window-dressing'. Language is used to express thought, not to adorn

---

37   See also Lloyd (1987), 124–31.
38   trans. Withington (1928), 303; with adaptions by Lloyd (1987), 125–6.
39   *Epidemics* 5.28, 5.29, 5.30.

it. Not a word is thrown away …. Thought, and the expression of thought, are evenly balanced. Both are clear, dignified – even majestic."[40] W. H. S. Jones' enthusiasm in describing their prose and language may seem disproportionate: yet the reader cannot but have the impression of a full maturity of expression. Treatises like *Art* share the qualities of Gorgias' most sophisticated rhetoric; it can be compared to the unsurpassed *Encomium of Helen*, with which it shares stylistic and rhetorical choices, consonances, and wordplays; hence, a capacity to manipulate language. Other treatises also display a rare lucidity in argumentation, equal to the likes of Thucydides. The ring composition that binds the first chapter of *Prognostic* to its last is worthy of a professional writer. The style of *Epidemics* 1 and 3 – clear, to the point, free from redundancies – is characteristic of a professional medical writer. The lapidary style of many a passage and the lack of discursive marks in incipits (often present in other authors), confirms this. Suffice it to provide a few examples of opening statements here[41]:

> *Prognostic* 1: "It is the task of the best physician to practise forecasting."
>
> *Ancient Medicine* 1: "All those who have undertaken to speak or write about medicine, having laid down as a hypothesis for their account hot or cold or wet or dry … clearly go wrong in much that they say."
>
> *Air, Waters, Places* 1: "Whoever wishes to pursue properly the science of medicine must proceed thus."
>
> *Sacred Diseases* 1: "I am about to discuss the disease called 'sacred'. It is not, in my opinion, any more divine or more sacred than other diseases, but has a natural cause."
>
> *Art* 1: "Some there are who have made an art of vilifying the arts, though they consider, not that they are accomplishing the object I mention, but that they are making a display of their own knowledge."
>
> *Breaths* 1: "There are some arts which to those that possess them are painful, but to those that use them are helpful, a common good to laymen, but to those that practise them grievous."

---

[40]   Jones (1923a), xv.

[41]   On argumentation in medical and scientific writings see Lloyd (1996); also van der Eijk (1997), Asper (2007).

Wounds in the Head 1: "Men's heads are not alike nor are the sutures of the head disposed the same way in all."

The axiomatic quality of these statements, offered as dogmas – they are, of course, impossible to verify – goes against the awareness of uncertainty, error, limited data, and the difficulties of interpretation. This apodeictic tone probably served the purpose of persuading an audience whose trust the physician had to gain, in order to be 'the more believed to understand the cases, so that men will confidently entrust themselves to him for treatment' (*Prognostic* 1).

Necessity of a Method

The realisation of the necessity of a shared methodology is explicit: "Medicine has long since had everything it needs, both a principle (*archḗ*) and a discovered method (*hodós*, 'the way'), by which many admirable discoveries have been made over a long period of time and those that remain will be discovered ... " (*Ancient Medicine* 2). This method is exclusive, there are no alternatives; it concerns the very identity of medicine, its existence as such:

> Anyone who casts off and rejects all these things, tries to investigate in another way and another manner, and says that he has discovered something, has been deceived and continues to deceive himself: for this is impossible. And I shall try to show why it is necessarily impossible by stating and showing what the art is. From this it will be evident that discoveries cannot be made by any means other than these.

The author here returns upon the central theme of *Art*, that is, demonstrating that medicine is endowed with a specific entity and identity: it exists and it is *something*, it is the distance covered, a journey of progressive growth and enrichment, of discoveries, of method. This self-awareness makes fifth century BC medicine unique in its time. This conceptual upturning did not escape Thucydides: hence historiography, a discipline also committed to the search for exact knowledge, appropriates the principles of lay medicine. He assigns them to the historian, but also to Pericles and Themistocles, and to them only, the latter being 'the ablest of all', 'both a shrewd judge of the immediate present and wise in forecasting what would happen in the most distant future' (I 138, 3). Exact knowledge, once the domain of the gods (Alcmaeon, fr. 1a), is now pursued with the tools of semeiotics.

Naturalistic Causal Explanation

The generalisation process, and with it the idea of being able to find a stable shape in the irregularity of events, to fix a recurring correlation between them, is intimately connected to the conviction that there exist constant categories that lie beneath the ever-changing course of worldly affairs. The scientist's task is to investigate them. Aristotle – building upon Platonic premises – is the champion of this interpretation of the real, in which experience is relegated to a subordinate position, while the search for a stable basis that regulates events takes precedence. This means finding invariants upon which change can be stabilised, with the aim of providing the observer with certainties and to grant that knowledge can be transmitted. Fifth-century BC medicine shares the same premises. It so assigns a causal framework to nature as *phýsis*, which is to say to the world of processes of generation and growth. This mirrors a wider philosophical debate, exemplified in the famous tale of Socrates' disappointment in discovering that even in Anaxagoras' exciting doctrine everything remained bound to purely mechanical causes active in nature, instead of identifying the ultimate and universal cause in the rational element external to matter which Anaxagoras himself had called *noûs* (Plato, *Phaedo* 96 c–d.). Medicine recovers Anaxagoras' aetiological mechanism, which Plato had deemed inadequate and misleading.

The author of *Art* (6) explains that "Medicine consists in the because of (*dià tí*) and in the forecasting," "for everything that occurs will be found to do so through something". Physicians need to know the causes also in order to plan their therapy, as the author of *Breaths* observes in the beginning of the treatise (1): "For knowledge of the cause of a disease will enable one to administer to the body what things are advantageous." It goes on: "Indeed this sort of medicine is quite natural".[42] Therefore, nature itself is seen as structured according to cause and effect relations; it is not man who imposes his own interpretative categories on nature.

There is no need to demonstrate the causal scheme; it is an assumption, a statement of principle. Knowing the concrete causes of illnesses has not only a theoretical value, but also a therapeutic one, because 'the vast majority of illnesses is cured with what causes them' (*Sacred Disease* 18). Nature becomes a uniform field of action. It can be interpreted because it is subject to general, immutable laws that govern the action of each process' ultimate cause (a natural cause), imagining that 'at every moment, in the same external circumstances, the same effect' is produced, as Hermann von Helmholtz (who was a physician and an anatomist before being a physicist) stated in the mid-nineteenth century.[43] A normative system thereby imposes itself since the early beginnings of medicine towards its self-recognition as a discipline: its ideological bent reaches its apex with Galen, partially influencing modern medicine. It is based on that same concept of cause, which, at the end of the nineteenth century, became in Ernst Mach's view 'a primitive and provisional way out of a difficulty',[44] as

> there is no cause nor effect in nature; nature has but an individual existence; nature simply is. Recurrences of like cases in which A is always connected with B, that is, like results under like circumstances, that is again, the essence of the connection of cause and effect, exist but in the abstraction which we perform for the purpose of mentally reproducing the facts.[45]

The concept of cause fits within a vast theoretical apparatus which includes both epistemological reflections and physiological

---

[42] trans. Jones (1923b).   [43]   See von Helmholtz (1873 [orig. 1847]), 2.
[44] Mach (1914 [orig. 1886]), 92.   [45]   Mach (1919 [orig. 1883]), 474.

theories, such as the explanation of epilepsy with life-giving air being stuck in the veins, a process caused by the presence of phlegm coming from the head in the veins; or such as the very idea of *pneûma* or bodily fluids, which respond to the idea, not verified, that all non-bony articulated systems present in the body are containers of fluids.[46] No direct observation and no experimental proof could justify such claims. Theoretical apparatus and experimental observation interact only to a limited degree, and often in a sense opposite to what was expected, the former preceding the latter, so that philosophical hierarchies of human faculties determine the references to experience and demonstrate its being theory-laden, and not vice versa. The notion of *pneûma* – a non-observable entity – for example, confirms this. It is subservient to the completion of a theoretical construction, an image of the functioning of the human body, and this is enough to justify its introduction, as in *Sacred Disease* 16: "When a man draws breath into himself, the air first reaches the brain, and so is dispersed through the rest of the body, though it leaves in the brain its quintessence, and all that it has of intelligence and judgment," or in *Breaths* 3, where *pneûma* becomes the 'great ruler (*dynástēs mégistos*)' of everything and every illness, and receives, sophistically, the epithet of the Great King of Persia (-*dynástēs mégas*) mentioned by Gorgias in the *Encomium of Helen*. The account of the Aristotelian school known as the *Anonymous of London (Anonymus Londiniensis)*, when dealing with Hippocratic medicine and Aristotle's opinion about it, dwells precisely on the theory concerning the cause of illness, which it considered as decisive.

This aetiological pull is not, however, the proof of a sort of modernity of the rationalist physician. It is but the continuation of traditional faith linking each event to the next. The causal explanation played a decisive part in every theological discussion, where the existence of creation demands, if it has to have a cause, the existence

---

[46]   See also Viano (1984).

of a creator. On the contrary, the accidental character of chance (týchē) and spontaneity (autómaton) would lead to an anti-determinism, thus postulating coincidence as a substitute for cause, and thwarting any attempt to control and forecast. This was precisely the aim of Democritus' revolutionary randomness of the vortex of elementary particles, Epicurus' and Lucretius' 'inclination (clinamen)' of the atoms: theories that will be contested and abandoned in favour of a more reassuring and comfortable image of the world.

GEOGRAPHY OF REASON

The epistemologist makes every effort to overcome a confused and static condition and to build a clear framework of reference. The real epistemologists are *geographers of human reason*, to use a definition penned by Immanuel Kant.[47] They are always ready to draw reason's borderlines – which are its raison d'être – delimiting its horizons and possibilities, finding cardinal notions of 'scientific' reasoning and organising them into a system. When they succeed – no matter if that system is well founded – they happen to interpret the content of their discipline according to the terms contemplated by that system, and reject what does not fit within it. When their abidance by the epistemological system reaches this degree, however, it acquires an ideological inclination that does not respect the limits imposed by external conditions, that is, the data acquired from experience, events, *facts*. The epistemologist, then, is not a good *technítēs*, nor a scientist. He fails in his task to build an edifice founded on the constantly changing act of perception, finding at the same time the theoretical connection and the concepts that allow one to establish the relations between the results of experience, thus stabilising them.[48] According to a definition by Einstein, concepts are for the senses 'not like the soup to the beef, but more like the cloakroom number to the coat'.[49] They allow the arrangement and classification, and therefore the knowledge and the possibility of further use.

[47]   Kant (1787), 788.   [48]   See also Einstein (1949), 683–8.
[49]   Schlipp (1949), 133.

The development of every discipline that aspires to the degree of persuasion of what will later be called science is a process of creative innovation, in which the process of detection and selection moves according to a theoretical framework 'a priori' towards the determination of empirical regularities, which can become laws. Through methods of induction, deduction, and proof, on the basis of principles of affinity and variety, continuity and discontinuity, homogeneity, material causality, and teleology sometimes, one obtains the coherence of the totality reduced to unity, whose reliability is possible but not granted.

ORDER IN DISORDER

The Greek world is always fighting against 'the boundless sea of unlikeness', to overcome the era of great disorder, to stop 'the turbulent, irrational mass' which according to Plato is invariably bound to the very origin of cosmos and of the living, to its unregulated movement, to the unstable and abrupt flux that 'the god had already ordered once', and now again 'seeing it in extreme hardships, and concerned that it should not, stormtossed as it is, be broken apart in confusion . . . orders it and sets it straight'.[50] After the pre-Olympian times of Kronos' power, of turmoil and disruption, there follows the time of Zeus, and his bride Metis, who is an incarnation of astute intelligence, Odysseus' first quality.[51] Olympus thereby finds stability in order.

Mêtis, astute intelligence, is also a quality of the physician, as well as the helmsman, the sophist, the general, the politician, that is to say all those who, relying only on their analytic capacities, must be able in only a short time to understand and change the course of events. The physician is equalled to the helmsman both in *Ancient Medicine* 9 as well as in Plato's *Protagoras*, because they both operate in the field of changing, of becoming, of what never stays the same. He is faced, in illnesses, with a force as powerful as that of the sea, an

[50]   *Timaeus* 42b–43d, *Statesman* 271c–273e (trans. after Rowe 1997); see also Zellini (2010), 17.

[51]   Detienne and Vernant (1991 [orig. 1974]), chapter 10.

uncontrollable force that he must strive to dominate. Dominating the sea of the uncertain, introducing the discrete into the continuum: this is the operation that myth ascribes to Proteus, the Old Man of the Sea in the fourth book of the *Odyssey*, who each day at the same time leaves the sea of the uncertain and performs a work of discretisation: he counts. He counts his seals, five by five. He thus performs the most elementary of man's tasks. He arranges, disposes according to ranks, puts entities in relation. After having established that all is in order, that the seals are lying on the beach, he himself lies down among them. He himself, an active subject, enters the realm of objects; he becomes part of it. He lives through his role of object, becoming one with it. He becomes part of experience. He performs an action endowed with a ritual significance that allows events to exist by identifying them and placing them in relation with each other, reducing them to unity. The singularities acquire a meaning in the moment in which they establish relationships with each other: a relationship expressed in *lógos*, which is a bond, a link, a law.[52]

Hence, intelligence and quickness in action, the qualities of Odysseus, are indispensable: he is prudent, astute, proactive, endowed with the computational capacities founded on *measuring* correctly, a concept to which *mêtis* is bound etymologically, as the old Indian *māti-* ('measure') confirms. It is not contemplation, nor general reasoning, but it is the concrete ability to enter a relationship with the world, to gauge, to weigh. It is not wisdom, not generic intelligence, but dexterity of the intellect, of a quick multiplicity of the mind. A mind which 'endows the back with wings', according to a famous image by Giordano Bruno. Like Odysseus, Athena is *polýmētis* (having many kinds of *mêtis*); she therefore needs hands, as the Orphics already predicted and as the disciples of Anaxagoras confirmed.[53] Progress needs hands, time, and events: in Athena, *téchnē* expresses itself. If Odysseus is the hero of *mêtis*, then Achilles, champion of the *Iliad*, is the hero of *noeîn* (of 'using one's intellect'). 'Achilles'

[52]   On Proteus, see Piettre (1993); Zellini (2010), chapter 1.
[53]   See Metrodorus of Lampsacus in DK61A6 (based on a report by Syncellus).

paradigm' is a model of the lightning ability of apperception, of combining and planning, where the different temporal and spatial dimensions interact, moving towards devising a way out.

The 'epistemological' works of the *Hippocratic Corpus* represent the most accomplished and self-aware expression of this essential trait of Greek identity. The prognostic optimism of the Hippocratics, just like Achilles' awareness, relies on the conviction that order exists in the world. The precariousness of the single event, the liability of the single instant, must be overcome by being catalogued. These operations found rationality, and give mankind the security that it may find a meaning in reality, making it an object of knowledge (*epistéme*), grasping it, knowing it, and thereby managing it by following the aggregating capacity of thought.

A verifiable, dynamic trajectory emerges, which takes us back to the very origins of Greek civilisations, since, as Hermann Kleinknecht stated: "For the Greeks, cognition is always the cognition of a law and therefore the fulfilment of this law."[54] This is the essence of the physician's knowledge (*epistéme*) – to know and to know-how: operating on the surgeon's table, measuring like Odysseus, guessing like Achilles.

[54]   Kleinknecht (1942), 78; now also in Perilli (2013), 267.

7   Ethics and Deontology

Karl-Heinz Leven

INTRODUCTION

During the summer of 415 BC, when the Athenians debated the naval expedition to Sicily in the people's assembly, general Nicias urged them to review their decision. He emphasised the dangers and uncertainties of the expedition, and concluded by advising the magistrate presiding over the session to 'become a physician' for the city. He further told him to make sure he performed his function well, as it 'provides the nation the greatest service and at least does not harm it.'[1] This passage clearly echoes the Hippocratic *Epidemics*: "As to diseases, make a habit of two things – to help, or at least to do no harm."[2] Yet the question whether Thucydides has been directly influenced by a Hippocratic treatise has not been answered definitively.[3] More importantly, the maxim of medical treatment, 'to help, or at least to do no harm', was clearly a topos at the end of the fifth century BC, which everyone understood.[4] It is also worth mentioning that the name of Hippocrates or any other famous physician did not play a role in this context.

The *Hippocratic Corpus*, consisting of some sixty texts of different genres and medical disciplines, exposes technical aspects as well as ethical issues. What makes a good doctor? How should he approach the patient? In which manner does he communicate with him and his relatives? When is the right moment to talk about payment? These are a few of the issues that today may be considered as coming under the heading of medical ethics. Hippocratic medicine

---

[1]   Thucydides 6, 14, trans. Smith (1921), 209.
[2]   *Epidemics* 1.11, ed. and trans. Jones (1923a), 164–5.
[3]   Jouanna (1980); Rechenauer (1991), 351–61.
[4]   Anastassiou and Irmer (2006), xviii–xxi.

faced much stronger theoretical and practical limitations than we do today, however. These limitations resulted from restricted diagnostic and therapeutic means on the one hand, and the special, precarious social status of Hippocratic physicians on the other. In the total absence of medical curricula, state examinations, or diplomas, their fame depended on successful medical practice. This included correct prognosis; so even a fatal outcome of a disease, if correctly foretold by the physician, was regarded as evidence of expertise.

The present chapter on ethics in the *Hippocratic Corpus* identifies and describes the different texts dealing with ethical aspects of the physician's art; the basic ethical questions emerging in the whole *Hippocratic Corpus* will be addressed, such as the relation of the physician to his patients, issues of prognostic, limitations of therapy, and questions of salary. The evidence from the *Hippocratic Corpus* has to be checked against the cultural background as it emerges in contemporaneous sources of other literary genres. A special section will be devoted to the Hippocratic Oath, a singular and still 'puzzling document'.[5]

When Hippocrates' name appears in the press today, it is usually mentioned in connection with some medical malpractice or scandal (fraud, deceit, bodily harm, or killing), or controversial issues such as abortion and euthanasia, and here the Hippocratic Oath often features prominently.[6] 'Hippocrates' represents, at least for the lay public, a last resort, a timeless standard for a good physician. This specifically Western view, which combines the continuity of ethical principles from antiquity with a mythically inflated Hippocratic Oath, is itself a historical phenomenon discussed in an article by David Cantor later in this volume.

Thomas Percival (1740–1804) coined the phrase 'medical ethics' in his book of the same title, which according to its subtitle dealt with 'a code of institutes and precepts, adapted to the professional conduct of physicians and surgeons'.[7] For these professions, the concept of

5   Temkin (2002), 21.   6   Nutton (1997); Leven (1998).
7   Baker (1993); Baker and McCullough (2009), 3–15; Percival (1803).

deontology, as a theory of medical duties, was established as well. First used in general philosophy by Jeremy Bentham in 1834, 'deontology' in medicine refers to a theory of the rights and duties of physicians in a professional sense. This related mostly to the physician's conduct towards patients, colleagues, and the general public, and not to any philosophically grounded attitude as such.[8]

Therefore, any discussion about 'medical ethics and deontology' in Hippocratic medicine risks adopting an anachronistic perspective, as the concepts in this title evolved only in the nineteenth century. In the Hippocratic writings, the term *ēthiká*, pointedly coined by Aristotle as a technical term for 'ethics', does not occur. Research on the history of medical ethics from a Western perspective typically and understandably begins with Hippocratic medicine, and the Hippocratic Oath in particular.[9] The editors of the *Cambridge World History of Medical Ethics* (2009) provide an insightful introductory analysis of this tradition; they reflected critically, saying that their monumental work should have been called 'A History of the Discourses at the Intersection of (Bio) Medicine and Morality'.[10] Yet, such a title would be 'too abstruse and academic to be of practical value'. They had to take into account the expectations of their readers, while being faithful to their own intellectual project. The title of the present chapter, 'Medical Ethics and Deontology', can apply in a similar manner to Hippocratic medicine. This can also be justified in practical terms, as the thought, concepts, and texts of antiquity reflect the actions and attitudes of physicians, and allow us to see ethical themes emerge.[11]

---

[8]   The medical historian Julius Pagel (1851–1912) was the first, in 1897, to publish a monograph called *Medicinische Deontologie* (Medical Deontology).

[9]   Norman (1991), 271, introduces the first Renaissance edition of the Hippocratic Oath (1475/83) as the first authoritative text under the title *Medical Ethics*, without further explanation; compare Baker (1993), 853–7.

[10]   Baker and McCullough (2009), 15.

[11]   Similarly, the pragmatic Edelstein (1987 [orig. 1956]), who discusses the "Professional Ethics of the Greek Physician"; compare Flashar (2005) and Nutton (1999b). von Staden (2009), on the other hand, shows greater sensibility for the conceptuality when he addresses the same theme under the title *The Discourses of Practitioners in Ancient Europe*.

This said, we have to find a middle way between three extreme positions. First, we should avoid a traditionalism that tries only to identify universal virtues and values in the Hippocratic writings. Second, we must not project our own modern concerns into past accounts; historians here speak about presentism or a Whiggish approach to the history of science that is to be circumvented. Third, we should not believe that our modern debates and concerns in medical ethics are in essence the same as those in Hippocratic times. This so-called essentialism often rears its ugly head and, encouraged by modern bio-ethical debates, leads to misunderstandings. Hippocratic physicians did not, as this essentialism suggests, deal with the critical and disputed issues of today, such as termination of pregnancy, palliative care, end of life decisions, and euthanasia.

The professional ethics of the Greek physicians differed significantly in content from modern medical ethics. They dealt with questions such as the following: What abilities must a good physician have? What knowledge and skills must he acquire? Was there a fundamental approach to medicine that was forged through professional practice? Did this approach play a role in the private life of the physician? How must the physician behave – at the bedside, in his dealing with patients, relatives, the public, colleagues, and at public events? Finally, when and how should he discuss fees?

To answer these questions, we shall analyse the reports about the comportment and approach of Hippocratic physicians against the background of their medical and social situation and thus reveal the discourses of medicine and morality within the *Hippocratic Corpus*.[12] The boundaries, or rather the possibilities, of Hippocratic medicine were much more narrow than we can imagine today.[13] On the one hand, the diagnostic and therapeutic means were modest. On the other hand, physicians, as professionally active healers and providers

---

[12] Flashar (1997); useful is the collection by Weiss (1910), 248–62, even if the author's interpretative approach is antiquated.

[13] Perhaps a little too pointedly, Nutton (1988 [orig. 1985]), 41, argues that: "Hippocratic medicine ... was little more than good nursing."

operating in a medical marketplace, found themselves in a precarious social setting. As noted earlier, their prestige and reputation depended on their medical successes in the absence of curriculum-based medical education, national exams, or officially recognised certificates.[14] In addition to diagnosis and treatment, prognosis was of crucial importance. As part of a confidence-building strategy, the physician should not just predict future, but also past and present conditions, in order to gain easy access to patients.[15] Even a correct negative prognosis established the professional skills of the physician and could relieve him of the responsibility for the death of a patient. But in the case of a negative prognosis, could he afford to refuse to treat the patient? Questions regarding the treatment of 'incurable' cases and the rejection of treatment indeed played a role within Hippocratic medicine. Yet in Hippocratic medicine these questions were related to something rather different than the modern issue of euthanasia, which involves the ending of life by a physician on request in hopeless cases, help with suicide, or the discontinuation of life support. In the twentieth century, the contemporary debate about euthanasia was at times deliberately projected into Hippocratic texts; for instance, H. E. Sigerist claimed that antiquity was 'a world of healthy and strong people'.[16] Within the Hippocratic corpus, 'incurability' and 'discontinuity of treatment' were indeed discussed, but not in anticipation of a modern dilemma. These concepts should be interpreted in the context of contemporaneous ancient medicine and society, and the specific discourse of the texts.[17]

---

[14]   Kudlien (1988); Nutton (1992).

[15]   *Prognostic* 1, ed. and trans. Jones (1923b), 6–7: "For if he discover and declare unaided by the side of his patients the present, the past and the future, ... he will be the more believed to understand the cases, so that men will confidently entrust themselves to him for treatment."

[16]   "Was the condition of the patient hopeless, his disease incurable, then the doctor would not have anything to do with him": Sigerist (1963), 722. Such seemingly historically based ideologies, even if thoughtlessly expressed by the 'leftist' Sigerist, were radically implemented in crimes against humanity in Nazi Germany; compare Losemann (2001), 728.

[17]   von Staden (1990); Wittern (1979).

Other problematic areas of Hippocratic medicine included the interaction of male physicians with women as patients and female relatives in the household of a male patient. Physicians had to respect the shame that women felt when treated by male practitioners. It was also important for a physician to recognise that with his unique position he could easily break taboos or cross boundaries. He therefore had to compensate by exercising self-control. The treatment of slaves, which from a modern perspective could easily be understood as an ethical problem for Hippocratic physicians, is discussed several times in the *Hippocratic Corpus*. Each of these passages reflects a matter-of-factness towards such practices that shows that in this case there was no ethical problem for Hippocratic physicians.

DEONTOLOGICAL WRITING IN THE HIPPOCRATIC CORPUS

In an attempt to order the heterogeneous *Hippocratic Corpus* in a meaningful way, scholars throughout history have arranged the texts according to criteria such as authenticity, content, literary genre, purpose, or target audience.[18] To answer our question about medical ethics, we need to arrange the writings according to content, the oldest surviving classification. It can be found in Erotian (first century AD), who wrote a glossary of thirty-one Hippocratic works and divides them into five groups: works concerned with signs (of disease, 'semiotic'); works concerned with causation and nature ('aetiological' and 'physical'); therapeutic; mixed; and 'relating to the account of the [medical] art'.[19] The last group of texts 'relating to the account of the [medical] art' largely come from the Hellenistic and Roman periods. In the older writings within the *Hippocratic Corpus*, the actions and attitudes of physicians are also discussed in numerous places, but in an unsystematic way, with remarks scattered throughout. A coherent and systematic presentation of these topics appears only in these later texts.[20]

---

[18] Wittern (1998).   [19] Erotian, ed. Nachmanson (1918), 9.

[20] Fleischer (1939), 46. That the observation that the deontological writings as predominantly ethical Hippocratic texts arose late speaks casually (albeit not conclusively) for a late date of the Hippocratic Oath. With regard to the Hippocratic *Precepts*, see the recent comprehensive treatment by Ecca (2016).

Among the writings 'relating to the account of the [medical] art',
Erotian included the *Oath, Law, Art*, and *Ancient Medicine*, as well as
the *Embassy* and *Speech from the Altar*.[21] Erotian's classification was
adopted by Anuce Foës (1528–95), who further developed it into eight
sections.[22] Foës moved Erotian's fifth category of works related to
'relating to the account of the [medical] art' to the first place.[23] He
moreover added three works to the titles given by Erotian, namely
Physician, Decorum and *Precepts*. For this rearrangement of the sections, Foës partly relied on the tables of contents of the medieval
manuscript tradition of the *Hippocratic Corpus* and on the order of
the texts in the oldest textual witnesses (manuscripts M and V).[24]
Renaissance scholars such as Foës began their printed editions with
the Hippocratic Oath. This preeminent rank in the typographical
arrangement of the Renaissance editions cemented the place of the
Oath as a programmatic treatise allegedly containing the essence of
the whole *Corpus* for the subsequent period.[25]

In order to discuss the 'medical ethics and deontology' of
Hippocratic physicians, one must first identify the texts in the
Corpus that structurally touch on the vaguely defined field of 'medi-
cine as art'. Besides the Oath, Hippocratic scholarship usually recog-
nises the following texts as deontological works: *Law*, the *Art*,
Precepts and *Decorum*.[26]

LAW

Listed by Erotian as one of the Hippocratic writings directly after the
Oath, the short treatise *Law* is probably composed around 400 BC or
later.[27] It deals with 'the deplorable loss' of medicine's reputation in

---

[21]   Erotian, ed. Nachmanson (1918), 1–23; see also Anastassiou and Irmer (2006), 508.
[22]   Hippocratis ... Opera Omnia, ed./Lat. trans. Anutius Foesius, Frankfurt/M. 1595, see
        also Maloney and Savole (1982) 86, Nr. 595; Rütten (1993), 45.
[23]   Unlike Potter (1988a), 14, Foes did not give the individual sections a title, but merely
        numbered them; 'Practice of Medicine', the title of the first section, comes from
        Potter.
[24]   Irigoin (1975); Angeletti (1991); see Jouanna's discussion in Chapter 3 in this volume.
[25]   Rütten (1993), 51–4.   [26]   Rütten (1997), 102–8.
[27]   Craik (2015), 150–5; Jouanna (1999 [orig. 1992]), 396.

the eyes of the public, owing to the lack of effective control mechanisms. Besides the harsh polemic against physicians, who do not deserve to be called this, *Law* creates an ideal image of medical education and concludes with an emotional remark about the 'mysteries of science'.[28]

ART

The *Art* (around the end of the fifth century BC), also listed by Erotian, is an epideictic treatise in the sense of a polemic public speech, supposedly written by a physician, which highlights the precarious situation of physicians.[29] The question of whether the author of this treatise was a physician or a sophist – in other words a rhetorician – and with that a layman, has been eagerly debated since the nineteenth century. Yet, such a dispute is pointless, as it does not reflect the reality of medicine in antiquity, but rather projects modern ideas about professionalisation into the past.[30] Scientific medicine, dominant since the second half of the nineteenth century, also influenced the thoughts and concepts of classical philologists, for whom the ancient physician had to be a scientist after the fashion of their own contemporaries. Yet, the Hippocratic physician depended also on rhetorical and epideictic strategies in exercising his profession. Whether an author of a Hippocratic treatise was a specialist or layman can therefore be hard to determine, especially when a text is apologetic and addresses a larger public.

The main aim of the *Art* is to prove that medicine is an art and to silence those voices degrading it. The work thus fits into the sophistic *téchnē*-discourse of the late fifth and early fourth centuries BC. Sophists, historians, philosophers, and physicians all employed the term *téchnē* for what they did in order to enhance their reputations, and they defended this use against the sceptical public and rivals.

---

28 *Law* 5, ed. and trans. Jones (1923b), 264–5.
29 Craik (2015), 35–40; Jouanna (1999 [orig. 1992]), 377–9; Anastassiou and Irmer (2006), 185.
30 Horstmanshoff (1990).

These arts were teachable and easy to learn, as they contained theoretical and practical elements. Oral instruction was followed by texts. Because these texts were readable, they reached an educated readership beyond what technical treatises could achieve; however, this general interest also rendered them prone to be attacked. It is, therefore, no coincidence that the *Hippocratic Corpus* comprises not only works written for the instruction of colleagues or younger students, but also public (apologetic) medical speeches, as well as other texts that aimed at educating laypeople about medicine. All these genres belonged to medicine as art.

The *Art* is clearly a public speech written to defend medicine. It begins with the simple premise that 'some . . . who have made an art of vilifying the arts' have denied that medicine is an art (*téchnē*).[31] After an epistemological digression, the author defines the purpose of the art of medicine: "In general terms, it is to do away with the sufferings of the sick, to lessen the violence of their diseases, and to refuse to treat those who are overmastered by their diseases, realising that in such cases medicine is powerless."[32]

The *Art* addresses the possibilities and limits of medicine, when treating visible and hidden, curable and incurable diseases; the likelihood of failure; and the responsibilities and defence strategies of physicians in case of unfounded expectations. We shall return to the topic of refusing to treat a patient.

PHYSICIAN

"The dignity [or: *authority*] of a physician requires that he should look healthy . . . ."[33] The treatise *Physician* is especially aimed at beginners, and can be dated to the Hellenistic period or perhaps (much) later on the basis of language and style.[34] It is not mentioned by Erotian. The content shows parallels with *Surgery*; it discusses the

---

[31] *Art* 1, trans. Jones (1923b), 190. [32] *Art* 3, trans. Jones (1923b), 192.
[33] *Physician* 1, trans. Jones (1923b), 310.
[34] Fleischer (1939), 56–7, assumes the third century BC, while Jouanna (1999 [orig. 1992]), 404, considers a later period of formation more likely. See also Craik (2015), 163–5.

performance of the (surgically qualified) physician and his effect on the sick, which depends largely on his character. The treatise explicitly invokes the ideal of nobility,[35] a well-regulated lifestyle, and just character that a physician should possess. The recommendations found in *Physician* correspond to notions in older Hippocratic texts, as well as to certain provisions of the Oath.[36]

DECORUM AND PRECEPTS

Decorum and *Precepts* have both only been transmitted in manuscript M, and are not mentioned by Erotian, Galen, or by anyone else in antiquity. The texts can probably be dated to the first or second century AD.[37] *Decorum* provides an 'instruction in etiquette and bedside manners' for physicians.[38] These respective concepts are only found in *Decorum* and *Precepts*. Despite their similarities, the treatises have different authors.[39] They each, however, discuss the basic principles of the art of medicine as well as more detailed issues such as the physician's fee (although this is discussed only in *Precepts*).[40] The most important goal when exercising the medical art is to gain respect and avoid criticism.

Linguistically, the two texts contain numerous late words from the imperial period. In *Decorum*, some neologisms are found that are not documented in other antique texts. For instance, the term 'lack of superstition (*adeisidaimonía*)' is introduced as one of the virtues of a good physician.[41] The treatise may belong to an imperial context of Stoic and Epicurean popular philosophy, serving as an introduction for a medical audience.[42] The two works share linguistic features, which have caused difficulties for publishers and translators. Already in the medieval tradition, we find indications that the texts were partly

[35] *Physician* 1, ed. and trans. Jones (1923b), 310–12.
[36] Jouanna (1999 [orig. 1992]), 404.
[37] Craik (2015), 57–9; Jouanna (1999 [orig. 1992]), 380, 405; Fleischer (1939); Ecca (2016), 23–5.
[38] Jones (1923b), 271.   [39] Fleischer (1939), 105–6.
[40] *Precepts* 4, ed. and trans. Jones (1923a), 316; see also Ecca (2016), 114–15.
[41] Fleischer (1939), 66, 87.
[42] Fleischer (1939), 103; Jones (1923b), 269–76; Ecca (2016), 2, 16–22.

incomprehensible for copyists.[43] W. H. S. Jones worked as an editor and translator on both texts, yet at times he was unable to restore the corrupt text or provide a translation that makes sense. He concluded that *Precepts* and *Decorum* are 'unnatural and fantastic' in their choice of words and style, and suggested they contained notes of a speech for a medical secret society. Their obscurity would in this case have been intentional.[44]

***

Compared with the mythically inflated Oath, the deontological works just discussed seem trivial, simple, practical, occasionally whimsical, and pretentious; they hardly reflect the ideal of the great Hippocrates. It does not come as a surprise, therefore, that the Oath outshone these deontological works in importance and impact, especially in its modern reception. Just as the other Hippocratic works, these deontological treatises contain numerous examples of discourses of practitioners, the field that Erotian thought related to the discourse of the medical art.

MAIN THEMES OF THE HIPPOCRATIC PROFESSIONAL ETHICS

The doctor–patient relationship is characterised by the maxim 'to help, or at least to do no harm', as we have already seen.[45] Everything else flows from here: to assess which treatments to employ; and for the physicians, patients, and their families to work together. Within this discourse, the perspective of the physician's professional benefit is clear. Gaining the confidence of the patient is key. An accurate prognosis increases the physician's credibility, and the patients 'will confidently entrust themselves to him for treatment'.[46] Empathy with patients and their needs is described as 'kindness'; this includes cleanliness in the preparation of food and

---

[43]   Fleischer (1939), 29; Jones (1923a), 305–11; Jones (1923b), 269–76.
[44]   Jones (1923b), 272; Ecca (2016), 3.
[45]   *Epidemics* 1.11, trans. Jones (1923a), 164.
[46]   *Prognostic* 1, trans. Jones (1923b), 7.

drinks, visitors, conversation, attitude, hair, nails, and smells, that is, how to perfume the doctors.[47] The most important place of a physician's performance remains the patient's bedside. When a physician tends to patients, he gains skills that place him in a position to exercise his profession. At the same time, the intimate doctor–patient relationship is subject to critical reflection from the Hippocratics.[48] It is no exaggeration to attribute to Hippocratic medicine in this respect a unique leading role within the history of (Western) medicine. The physician never forgets that his medical art is a profession. Everything in the contact with patients is geared towards usefulness and purpose; the physician's dignity must be preserved. This is not often stated as clearly as in the later treatise *Decorum*, according to which a physician must demonstrate a certain 'ready wit', but is cautioned 'not to gossip to laymen, but to say only what is absolutely necessary'.[49]

For patients and their families, the outcome of individual illnesses is of crucial importance; however, for the Hippocratic physician, it is only one, albeit important, factor. Immediately following the cited maxim 'to help or at least do no harm' we find the statement: "The art has three factors: the disease, the patient, the physician. The physician is the servant of the art. The patient must co-operate with the physician in combating the disease."[50]

The art of medicine consists of the Hippocratic triangle: disease, patient, physician. The physician is the servant of the art, not of the patient – his thoughts and actions within the therapeutic relationship are geared primarily towards his profession. The relationship of the Hippocratic physician to medicine is closer than to his patients. It is remarkable that the question of fees, presumably of importance for a physician whose living is from his occupation, is addressed only once within the *Hippocratic Corpus*. In the late text *Precepts*, the

---

[47]   *Epidemics* 6.4.7, trans. Smith (1994), 236; see also Deichgräber (1970).
[48]   *Physician* 1, trans. Jones (1923b), 312.
[49]   *Decorum* 7, trans. Jones (1923b), 291.
[50]   *Epidemics* 1.11, trans. Jones (1923a), 164.

author enjoins the physician to raise the topic of payment only with great care and circumspection at a patient's bedside, and under no circumstances during an acute illness, when there would simply not be a right moment to do so.[51] In such situations, the physician should not seek his own benefit, but try to improve his reputation by means of a quick treatment. It is better for a physician to reprimand a patient who is unwilling to pay after he has been cured than to demand fees from a patient in danger of his life. His personal reputation and the esteem in which medicine as a whole is held are of paramount importance. When physicians occasionally forego a (reasonable) payment, they still gain something for the art, as their own prestige and that of their profession increases in the eyes of the public.

Logically, the physician must also take the financial abilities of his patients into account to avoid inhumanity. Occasionally one must therefore provide treatment free of charge in such situations; as *Precepts* 6 puts it: "For where there is love of man (*philanthrōpíē*), there is also love of the art (*philotechníē*)."[52]

The word *philanthrōpíē*, which appears within the Hippocratic Corpus only here, characterises the correct comportment of the physician, and also points to the Stoic and Epicurean background of *Precepts*. The physician's 'love for man' increases the 'love for the art'. This does not just refer to love on the part of patients or laypeople. Rather, the terms *philanthrōpíē* and *philotechníē* belong together: they refer to the qualities of a good physician. A physician's 'love for man' is the expression of his 'love for the art'.[53] His philanthropic actions serve to demonstrate his decorum.[54] The author views any physicians not understanding this connection as 'buried in deep ignorance of the art', and they are virtually set aside as 'non-physicians' or 'unworthy of medicine'. The terms *téchnē*, *philanthrōpíē*, and *philotechníē* belong inseparably together and characterise the profession.

51   *Precepts* 4.6, trans. Jones (1923a), 316–19; see also Ecca (2016), 114–17.
52   *Precepts* 6, trans. Jones (1923a), 318; the textual transmission of this phrase is disputed.
53   Fleischer (1939), 38.
54   *Precepts* 6, trans. Jones (1923a), 318; see also Ecca (2016), 118, 212–16.

Like *Precepts*, the deontological treatise *Decorum* relies on Stoic popular philosophy, which aims to integrate the different arts, including medicine, with philosophy.[55] In this context we also find the wonderful phrase: "For a physician who is a lover of wisdom is equal to God."[56] The conceptual similarities between the statements found in *Decorum* and Galen's implementations are remarkable. Take, for instance, the ideal of the philosopher-physician. Apart from the great Hippocrates, Galen thought that he alone fulfilled this ideal. Another example is the disinterestedness, also advocated by Galen.[57] Yet we should realise that Galen does not mention or comment on the five deontological treatises within the *Hippocratic Corpus* (*Oath, Law, Physician, Decorum, Precepts*), a fact 'which cannot be fully explained', as Jacques Jouanna put it.[58] *Physician, Decorum,* and *Precepts* are also not mentioned by Erotian, and are included in the *Hippocratic Corpus* only in later centuries. Galen evidently did not know the three later texts, or at least did not consider them as Hippocratic. The occasional parallels between these treatises and Galen's works do not result from one author knowing the content of the other, but from views commonly held at that time.[59] The more difficult question that we can only broach here is this: Why did Galen not mention *Oath* and *Law*, although Erotian classified them as 'truly Hippocratic'?[60]

The image of medical ethics in the Hippocratic writings would remain normative and incomplete, if one were to consider only how the ideal physician is described in the *Hippocratic Corpus*. We have to

---

[55]   Ecca (2016), 103.   [56]   *Decorum* 5, trans. Jones (1923b), 286.

[57]   Compare *Decorum* 5, trans. Jones (1923b), 286, with Galen, *The Best Physician Is Also a Philosopher* 2.7 (ed. Boudon-Millot (2007), 288 and also 3.4 (ed. Boudon-Millot [2007], 290), for similar negative assessments of the pursuit of financial gain by physicians.

[58]   Jouanna (2012), 262.

[59]   The 'love of hard work' in Galen (*The Best Physician Is Also a Philosopher* 3.4 (ed. Boudon-Millot [2007], 290) is also found in Hippocrates *Law* 2, trans. Jones (1923b), 262.

[60]   One exception could be a commentary on the Hippocratic Oath, which survives only in a fragmentarily transmitted Arabic translation and may not be authentic. On this commentary see Nutton (2012) and Magdelaine and Mouton (2017).

ask ourselves as well whether and to what extent these ideals were put into practice, and to this end, one needs to consult non-medical sources. Greek literary material of the classical period offers abundant evidence here.[61] Yet the medical texts themselves also provide a corrective to the image of the ideal physician. In addition to the scattered remarks throughout the *Hippocratic Corpus*, the deontological texts explicitly and with singular focus discuss the opposite of the ideal physician, the bad physician, the charlatan. In the agonal Greek culture, even medicine was competitive. Yet this did not imply a straightforward confrontation between 'good and bad' physicians, but rather a more complicated situation. First, physicians appeared as competing experts within medicine while mutually exclusive concepts were sharply criticised. Moreover, good physicians demarcated themselves from bad physicians and healers, whom they considered 'non-physicians'. Finally, medicine as art was fundamentally attacked by a vaguely defined public of laypeople and had to be defended.

These different areas of conflict are also discussed in the Hippocratic texts at various points, and the Hippocratic authors endeavour to find the underlying causes. For example, the complaints about the low public esteem of the art are accompanied with fierce criticism of non-physicians. The short treatise *Law* is exemplary for this line of argument. At the beginning of this speech, the author claims that medicine is the most distinguished of all arts; yet, it has been deeply diminished through the ignorance of its practitioners. As a reason for this decline, the author mentions the fact that medicine is the only art to have no other penalty than dishonour.[62] The positive and negative aspects of Hippocratic medicine are thus aptly characterised in two sentences. As there was no regulation of medical instruction, no curriculum, and no educational or national supervision in the sense of a licence to practise, reputation was the only (symbolic) capital at the disposal of the Hippocratic physician. The Hippocratic treatise *Law* offers an interesting sociological

---

[61]   Cordes (1994).   [62]   *Law* 1, trans. Jones (1923b), 262.

comparison, arguing that the numerous ignorant physicians, who are physicians only in name but not in deed, are like the extras on stage, who are not really actors.

In reaction to this problem, the author of *Law* lists the prerequisite skills that an aspiring physician must possess. "Now first of all natural ability is necessary".[63] He then provides a basic outline of the required training, which could apply to many arts. The overall aim is to learn, so that the knowledge becomes second nature; the author illustrates this in a poignant plant simile, perhaps under Stoic influence.[64] Physicians trained in this way travelled from city to city and were 'recognised as real physicians'.[65] Just as knowledge (Greek *epistémē*) is contrasted here with mere opinion (*dóxa*), so the art (*téchnē*) of the professional physician is contrasted with inexperience (*apeiríē*) and 'lack of art' (*atechníē*). The word *dóxa*, which here clearly means 'mere opinion' and has negative connotations in opposition to knowledge, also has the general meaning of 'reputation', and obviously forging a good reputation is one of the main objectives of medical ethics.

As said earlier, *Law* defends medicine as an art, or rather aims to re-establish it as such in a way that could apply also to other arts. The deontological treatise *Art* addresses problematic areas of medicine, focussing on medicine as a whole and its reputation. In contrast to *Law*, however, *Art* connects the major accusations made against medicine with concrete medical problems. The controversial issue of refusing to treat a patient, which Hippocratic medicine advocates in the case of incurable diseases, is interesting for several reasons.[66] The author of the *Art* defines medicine as a *téchnē* that rejects the incurable. The author argues that the opponents of medicine used this as the ground to level accusations against the art of medicine: it refuses to intervene in desperate cases, when the patients are overpowered by disease. The physicians ought to prove the status of medicine as an art (*téchnē*) in these serious cases, but they rather limit

---

[63] Ibid., 262.   [64] Ibid., 264.   [65] Ibid., 264.
[66] Rosen and Horstmanshoff (2003); von Staden (1990); Wittern (1979).

themselves to easier ones when the patients may just recover by chance.[67] The author of *Art* parried this harsh accusation by saying that it borders on madness to desire from any art what does not belong to it.[68] The curability of diseases depends on the strength of the available remedies: if the strongest remedy fails, the suffering is incurable, and medicine must admit that this is an area that 'it is not supposed to engage with'.[69] The author is thus able to turn the harsh accusations into an apology of medicine as a *téchnē*, a conclusion that he reiterates through different successful arguments.

Incurability and the associated refusal to treat are frequently discussed in the *Hippocratic Corpus*. The last Hippocratic aphorism, *Aphorisms* 7.87, lists the increasing steps of treatment – from medication to the iron (the knife) and fire (cautery), and declares illnesses incurable that are immune to the most extreme remedy, fire.[70] This can be caused by aggravating external circumstances such as incorrect or neglected treatment, lack of the patient's cooperation, or untimely intervention.[71] Contrary to the strong and confident statements in *Art*, Hippocratic physicians did treat incurable cases, including when they were not fatal but instead involved a chronic disability. According to the author of *Joints*, one can learn a great deal from such cases: 'one must study incurable cases so as to avoid doing harm by useless efforts'.[72] Incurability and eventual death of the patient could reveal the failure of medical intervention and thus harm the physician's reputation; he could protect himself against this by foretelling the course of the disease publicly; or, as the author of *Prognostic* put it, 'you will be blameless if you learn and declare beforehand who will die and who will get better.'[73]

One could cite many more instances of incurable cases from the *Hippocratic Corpus*. One may think, for example, of the numerous fatal outcomes in the *Epidemics*. Overall, it appears that the refusal to

---

[67]   *Art* 7, trans. Jones (1923b), 200.   [68]   *Art* 8, trans. Jones (1923b), 202.

[69]   Ibid., 204.   [70]   *Aphorisms* 7.87, trans. Jones (1931), 216.

[71]   For details see literature in n. 66.

[72]   *Joints* 58, Withington (1928), 338; *Diseases* 1.6, trans. Potter (1988b), 112.

[73]   *Prognostic* 1, trans. Jones (1923b), 8.

treat in the case of incurable illnesses so strenuously demanded in the *Art* did not play a large role in practical medicine. Giving an unfavourable prognosis, however, was not as easy in reality as depicted in the literature. This is illustrated by a passage in *Decorum*, in which the physician is urged to 'reveal nothing of the patient's future ... For many patients through this cause have taken a turn to the worse'.[74]

THE HIPPOCRATIC OATH

The ethics of Hippocratic medicine are often described primarily through the lens of the Oath; until now, however, we have approached this topic through the other deontological works and other evidence contained in the *Hippocratic Corpus*. We shall now turn to the Oath, in order to shed light on some important characteristics and concepts of this text.

The text of the Oath in its most common and possibly the oldest version has been transmitted in thirty-eight manuscripts. Of these, two are especially important: M and V.[75] Whether this version can be dated to the late fifth or early fourth century BC cannot be safely established, and we shall leave this question for the time being.[76] Heinrich von Staden has convincingly worked out that the content of the Oath can be reconciled with the statements of other Hippocratic texts.[77] This is not, however, an argument for the dating and contextualising of the Oath, as the author of the Oath could have relied on already existing Hippocratic texts.

Heinrich von Staden has devoted several publications to analyse numerous aspects of the Hippocratic Oath in depth, including its textual form and interpretation.[78] He also provided the following translation of the Oath; it is of necessity an interpretation and relies

---

[74] *Decorum* 16, trans. Jones (1923b), 298.
[75] Diels (1905), 17–18; von Staden (1996), 405; von Staden (2007a), 425, n. 2; see also Jouanna (1996) and the discussion in his Chapter 3 in this volume.
[76] von Staden (2009), 353 calls this widely shared view 'plausible'.
[77] Summarized by von Staden (2009), 353.
[78] von Staden (1996, 1997, 2007a). On the Oath, see also Edelstein (1987 [orig. 1943]); Lichtenthaeler (1984); Nutton (1993a, 1997); Rütten (1997).

on valid hypotheses in the case of controversial phrases. The text is arranged into numbered sections for ease of reference in the following discussion, which will briefly touch on particularly interesting, contentious, or relevant points.

(1) I swear by Apollo the Physician and by Asclepius and by Health and Panacea and by all the gods as well as goddesses, making them judges [witnesses], to bring the following oath and written covenant to fulfilment, in accordance with my power and my judgement;

(2) to regard him who has taught me this *téchnē* as equal to my parents, and to share, in partnership, my livelihood with him and to give him a share when he is in need of necessities, and to judge the offspring [coming] from him equal to [my] male siblings, and to teach them this *téchnē*, should they desire to learn [it], without fee and written covenant, and to give a share both of rules and of lectures, and of all the rest of learning, to my sons and to the [sons] of him who has taught me and to the pupils who have both made a written contract and sworn by a medical convention (*nómos iatrikós*) but by no other.

(3) And I will use regiments for the benefit of the ill in accordance with my ability and my judgement, but from [what is] to their harm or injustice I will keep [them].

(4) And I will not give a drug that is deadly to anyone if asked [for it], nor will I suggest the way to such a counsel. And likewise I will not give a woman a destructive pessary.

(5) And in a pure and holy way I will guard my life and my *téchnē*.

(6) I will not cut, and certainly not those suffering from stone, but I will cede [this] to men [who are] practitioners of this activity.

(7) And as many houses as I may enter, I will go for the benefit of the ill, while being far from all voluntary and destructive injustice, especially from sexual acts both upon women's bodies and upon men's, both of the free and of the slaves.

(8) And about whatever I may see or hear in treatment, or even without treatment, in the life of human beings – things that should not ever be blurted out outside – I will remain silent, holding such things to be unutterable [sacred, not to be divulged].

(9) If I render this oath fulfilled, and if I do not blur and confound it [making it to no effect], may it be [granted] to me to enjoy the

benefits both of life and of *téchnē*, being held in good repute among
all human beings for time eternal. If, however, I transgress and
perjure myself, the opposite of these.

The interpretation of the Oath ought to begin with the text itself
and elucidate difficult passages by considering other texts, mainly
parallels from other Hippocratic works. The Oath begins with a call
upon the two most important Greek gods of healing; first comes
Apollo, followed by his son Asclepius. After them, the author calls
on all other gods and goddesses.[79] The Oath is promissory, meaning
that it guarantees a promise of future action made in all honesty.
In other words, it is not an oath in which the truth of an assertion is
vouchsafed. The Oath promises adherence to the apprenticeship contract formulated in section (1). This whole part is linguistically constructed as a single sentence, in which the predicate verb 'I swear' is
followed by a number of infinitives in the aorist tense.

The main concept in section (2) is 'the medical art', the
'profession'(*téchnē*), which is mentioned in (5) and (9); this term is
also used elsewhere in the *Hippocratic Corpus*. Just as the sophists
offered education for payment (Plato, *Protagoras* 311 b–f), so the pupils
who swore the Oath, but were not related to the physician who taught
them, also had to pay a fee. If, however, they belonged to the family of
a physician, they were educated free of charge. Three generations were
thus connected: the teacher, the pupil who took the Oath, and the sons
of teachers. There appears to have been a historical transition of
medical education from a family context and father–son succession
to a more extensive social structure, where pupils without any relation to their teachers were accepted for a fee. In the apprenticeship
contract (2), some obscurities remain. For instance, what is meant by
'*nómos iatrikós*' at the end of (2)? Does it mean 'by a medical law', 'by
a custom of medicine', or 'by a rule of medical *téchnē*'?[80] Is the Oath
itself a *nómos iatrikós*, or is there any kind of relationship with the
deontological treatise *Law* (*nómos*)? In Erotian's list of Hippocratic

[79]   von Staden (2007a), 434: 'a divine gender balance'.   [80]   Ibid., 442.

works, *Law* immediately follows the Oath. According to the wording of the Oath, those who are not contractually bound by it are not admitted to teaching. Does this mean that there were other candidates who took an oath according to a different *nómos*? The mysteries of science and the essence of medicine should not be accessible to the uninitiated, which is the pompous conclusion at which *Law* arrives.[81]

The Oath's apprenticeship contract (2) is followed by seven sections (3–9) that contain neither a moral code nor prohibitions and commands; rather they consist of warranties and promises formulated in the first-person singular. The pupil taking the oath alternately promises to do, and to refrain from doing, certain things. At the beginning of (3), we find the promise to use regimens for the benefit of the ill. This seems to echo the injunction 'to help, or at least to do no harm', quoted at the beginning of this chapter. But why are regimens mentioned here in particular? Usually, Hippocratic medicine encompasses not just use regimen, but also drugs and surgery. Does this mean that anyone taking this oath will only use regimen, in the sense of regulating diet and lifestyle? Does he not provide resort to pharmacological or surgical treatments as well? This question will be revisited when we come to discuss the alleged ban on surgery contained in section (6). Next, a promise is made to protect the patient from injustice. But where does this injustice originate? From a third party or from the patient himself, in the sense that he may harm himself, for instance, by misconduct or by neglecting the physician's instructions?

What one would nowadays call prohibitions against euthanasia and abortion occupy section (4). There is no doubt that the two injunctions against providing lethal and abortive drugs are linked, as the word 'likewise' shows. Owing to the vague language, however, it is unclear what exactly is meant here. This ambiguity has given rise to ample debate and controversy that still continues today. From a modern point of view, the promise not to provide lethal drugs

<hr>

[81]   *Law* 5, trans. Jones (1923b), 264.

when asked suggests that this is an injunction against so-called physician-assisted suicide or euthanasia. Yet, contrary to popular belief, there are hardly any cases of physician-assisted suicide from antiquity, at least as far as we know.[82] Does it perhaps (also) relate to something else? Who was able to ask a doctor to give a poison? Besides the patient, this could have been a relative, friend, enemy, or ruler. Could murder by poison be the offence that the Oath prohibits? Such an injunction would chime with the suspicions against physicians that were common in antiquity, namely that they gladly help kill their patients. Such a prohibition, however, would hardly fit within the context of the Oath as a solemn pledge.[83]

The ban on abortion is directly linked to the ban on euthanasia. In his translation (1996), Heinrich von Staden understands *pessòs phthórios* literally as 'destructive pessary'. Ludwig Edelstein (1943/1967) and many interpreters of the oath since Christian Late Antiquity have understood this not as a selective, but categorical ban on abortion. The passage would thus mean that one pledges not to give any abortive remedies to women under any circumstances; and 'to give' here means both 'to provide' and 'to administer'.[84] There are no parallel passages in the *Hippocratic Corpus* that directly relate to this phrase. Later interpreters of the Oath, such as Soranus of Ephesus, relied on a different text and cannot therefore provide contextual evidence for the original version of the Oath.[85] The prohibition against lethal and abortive drugs in section (4), which afforded a twofold protection of life, constituted the cornerstone of Ludwig Edelstein's interpretation of the Hippocratic Oath as originating in an esoteric Pythagorean community of physicians. Edelstein's daring suggestion can explain some obscure passages of the Oath, but it is completely out of touch with the reality of medicine in antiquity. It can, therefore, be described only as guesswork, even if his idea was highly original.

In section (5), beginning with the words 'in a pure and holy way', we find the command to strive for integrity; it serves as the structural

[82] Rütten (1997), 78–88. [83] Ibid., 88–91. [84] Ibid., 91–6.
[85] Soranus, *Gynaecology* 1.19, ed. Ilberg (1927), 45.

pivot of the whole Oath.[86] The term 'life' mentioned here should be understood as lifestyle or character. The terms 'pure' and 'holy' express a ritual purity; however, they should not be understood in the sense of pollution in the traditional sense, but rather refer to intellectual and moral transgressions. Von Staden pointed out the 'evident and significant' similarity between the text in section (5) and an inscription at the entrance of the Apollo sanctuary in Epidaurus that survives only as a quotation in a much later literary source; however, whether this enables us to derive a date for the Oath remains disputed.[87]

After the remarks on euthanasia and abortion that are already difficult to comprehend, an even more problematic passage follows, namely the alleged ban of surgery in section (6). For Edelstein, the ban on cutting was another important indication of the Pythagorean origin of the text. Edelstein is to date the only interpreter who has been able to give a satisfactory explanation of this ban, albeit by suggesting the unprovable and unproven existence of a community of Pythagorean physicians. The problem lies in the fact that surgery is part and parcel of the therapeutic arsenal of the Hippocratic physician, and a number of treatises in the *Hippocratic Corpus* deal with it.[88] How can this contradiction be solved? One line of interpretation, strongly advocated by Lichtenthaeler (1984), and recently modified by Witt (2014b), attempts to solve the problem by arguing that the negations 'not ... and certainly not' (*ou ... oudè mèn*) belong to the same prohibition and reinforce each other in the sense that only 'cutting the stone' (or 'lithotomy') is prohibited. This solution does not explain why the Hippocratic physicians did not perform this operation but left it to 'practitioners'. Bladder stones are mentioned within the *Hippocratic*

---

[86]   von Staden (1996), 417; and see also Lichtenthaeler (1984), 153 and Edelstein (1987 [orig. 1943]), 9, but this command referred only to 'euthanasia' and 'abortion ban'.

[87]   von Staden (1996), 431. The inscription is transmitted by Clement of Alexandria, *Patchwork (Stromáteis)*, 5.1.13.3; Porphyry, *On Abstaining from Meat*, 2.19.5. It is unclear whether this inscription from Epidaurus belonged to the fourth century BC; see also Bremmer (2002), 106–8, who dated it much later; 'from the turn of our era'.

[88]   See Chapter 10 by Witt in this volume.

Corpus, but the operation of cutting them is mentioned only in the Oath. The earliest discussion of the operation is found in Celsus (*On Medicine* 7. 26. 2–5), probably going back to Hellenistic sources.[89] The operation was dangerous, but in the case of a large bladder stone the only option. That there would have been specialists for this kind of surgery in the Hippocratic period seems unlikely. Such specialists are not mentioned in any antique sources. This philological solution of the problem in section (6) is also questionable, because the ban on cutting is formulated generally. 'Cutting the stone' is mentioned after the general prohibition to cut; it is as a special case, an operation that should 'also not' be undertaken. Linguistically, a general ban on surgery remains the most probable explanation, but this does not solve the contradiction.[90] This promise not to cut is in clear contradiction to Hippocratic medicine, as documented elsewhere. It should be noted, however, that the argument that surgery is treated in the *Hippocratic Corpus* and that therefore there can be no ban on surgery in the Hippocratic Oath is unfounded. The time and place of origin of the Oath are unknown, and therefore the Oath can contradict the *Corpus*.

Section (7) deals with the physician's visit to the patient's house. Again, the patients' needs are promoted. The physician should keep away from deliberate and harmful misdeeds. The subsequent list of examples for these misdeeds includes sexual acts with women, men, and slaves. The physician's required attitude towards possible transgressions is also described in the Hippocratic treatise *Physician* with the words 'just behaviour' and 'self-control'.[91]

Remarkably, unjust deeds against men, against women, and against slaves are mentioned in the same breath and not differentiated,

---

[89]   Stamatu (2005).

[90]   For an alternative view see Chapter 10 by Witt in this volume.

[91]   *Physician* 1, trans. Jones (1923b), 312: "In every social relation he will be fair, for fairness must be of great service. The intimacy also between physician and patient is close. Patients in fact put themselves into the hands of their physician, and at every moment he meets women, maidens and possessions very precious indeed. So towards all these self-control must be used."

and this betrays again a Stoic influence. Besides, it could simply be the case that women and slaves were merely regarded as possessions of the head of the household, just as *Physician* mentions 'possessions'; therefore, any violations against them are also by implication crimes against their owner.

The pledge of secrecy discussed in section (8) is first formulated negatively: the physician is not to blurt out what he hears during his medical work. This information he should treat as 'unutterable'. One could compare this with the silence in mystic cults.[92] Certainly, this secrecy is not to be equated with modern medical confidentiality, which rather relates to privacy. In the case histories of the *Epidemics*, for example, patients are listed with name and place of residence. The Hippocratic pledge of secrecy falls in the same context of respect for the weak and needy, as does the promise of self-control or self-restraint when entering a patient's house.

The closing formula in section (9) of the Oath forms a ring composition with the opening in section (1). Here, one also finds the underlying motive for taking the oath. It has to do with reward and avoidance of punishment. The desired reward of those who take the oath is 'to enjoy benefits', both in life and in the art. They hope for worldly gratification. At the same time, they want to be praised among all people for all times; the already mentioned 'reputation' is the highest goal for them. They do not try to assuage their conscience and gain rewards in the afterlife; rather, they try to improve their image during the public exercise of their profession. This also shows that Edelstein's attempt to interpret the Oath as originating in an esoteric Pythagorean community of physicians cannot be right. Public esteem was certainly not the goal of the fiercely private Pythagoreans.[93]

Overall, the Oath combines secular elements – the contract between pupil, teacher, and his family; the enhancement of the

---

[92]   von Staden (2007a), 451, mentions parallels from non-medical literature; a possible echo of the Hippocratic text *Law* 5, trans. Jones (1923b), 264, which discusses the 'mysteries of science', seems possible.

[93]   von Staden (1996), 409: "A good reputation is hardly a Pythagorean ideal."

medical art's reputation; remuneration; and medical practice – with religious elements – the call on the gods, the respect for life. The text of the Oath – concise in its expression, yet full of meaning; ambivalent, yet highly relevant – was read in many different ways. It therefore emerged as the most important work on medical ethics in antiquity, and was mentioned repeatedly, beginning in the first century AD: by Erotian, the glossographer; by Scribonius Largus, court physician to the Roman emperor Claudius; and the Methodist physician Soranus of Ephesus.

But what about its suggested period of origin, namely Hippocrates' lifetime? W. H. S. Jones has answered this question in an unintentionally humorous way:

> So some [Greek] physicians did not feel bound by all the clauses, and some may not have felt bound by any. We may suppose, however, that no respectable physician would act contrary to most of the Oath, even if he were ignorant of its existence.[94]

The idea that the Oath dominated antique medical ethics, or that it had a supposedly canonical status, is based on a misconception. To be sure, the Hippocratic Oath is undoubtedly the most powerful antique medical text, yet its impact was felt only in Late Antiquity and it achieved dominance only during the Renaissance. There is a strange gap between the first century AD, when it was first (and repeatedly) mentioned in our sources, and its alleged date during Hippocrates' life. This makes it highly unlikely that the commonly accepted date of its composition, the late fifth or early fourth century BC is right.[95] Moreover, the linguistic features of the Oath suggest a later date within the *Hippocratic Corpus*.[96]

FINAL REMARKS

It is essential to record the reception history of Hippocratic texts in antiquity and to consider ancient witnesses, such as citations and

---

94   Jones (1923a), 296.
95   A proponent of this date is Jouanna (1999 [orig. 1992]), 402.
96   von Staden (2007a).

paraphrases of Hippocratic texts.[97] If the Hippocratic Oath had been
the basis of medical ethics in antiquity, it would have been mentioned
and discussed. Yet this was not the case. The Hippocratic Oath
belongs to the *Hippocratic Corpus*, but it was only in Late Antiquity
that it was perceived as one of its texts. The Oath can hardly be
a source for the general state of medical ethics in from the fifth to
the first centuries BC. Owsei Temkin called it 'a puzzling
document'[98], and yet many consider it as the key document for understanding Hippocratic ethics. Ultimately, it is a document that has
misled many through the sheer power of its impact in later times.
The striking contradictions with other Hippocratic texts should be
recognised and interpreted, and not simply be dismissed.

To sum up, the subject of medical ethics in the context of the
Hippocratic treatises encompasses many different areas, including
obligations (deontology), advice, recommendations, warnings, and
even polemics. Hippocratic physicians acted publicly and in competition with other doctors. Medical training was not regulated, and
there was no state control over either medications or physicians.
Thus, everything depended on the success of the practitioner and
his reputation. The Hippocratic writings emphasise the professional
nature of medicine as an art. The physician who was trained properly
in this art placed the maxim 'not to do harm' at the centre of his
practice. This allowed him to gain the trust of his patients, obtain
a good reputation for both himself and the art, and strengthen the
position of medicine among laypeople. We find these features of
Hippocratic ethics from the fifth century BC onwards. Over time,
they were enriched with philosophical ideas, notably Stoic and
Epicurean, and percolated into the later deontological treatises
within the *Hippocratic Corpus.* Yet the core features remained
valid and continued to exert their influence until modern times.
Especially since the Renaissance, the mysterious language and religious character of the Oath was used to idealise Hippocratic

---

[97]   Anastassiou and Irmer (2006).   [98]   Temkin (2002), 12.

medicine and project a distorted image onto an earlier age. This religious character is in stark contrast to the secular character of Hippocratic medicine as it emerges from the writings contained in the *Hippocratic Corpus*, which project the image of a sophisticated art dealing with natural processes.

8 Nosology

Amneris Roselli

TOWARDS A CLASSIFICATION OF DISEASES

Nosology, from the Greek words *nosos* (disease) and *logos* (discourse), is one of the many neologisms created in the eighteenth century to design the branch of medicine that deals with the classification of diseases. Hippocratic medicine lacks not only such a comprehensive term but also treatises explicitly concerned with criteria for classifying diseases, or at least with a general and systematic classification; nevertheless, it is rich in nosographic descriptions of several diseases, which testify to the efforts made by Greek physicians in the course of the fifth century and the first decades of the fourth BC to write, re-write, organise, and update the traditional lore on the subject. Diseases are, in fact, the core subject of the most ancient treatises among those forming our *Hippocratic Corpus*, which are designed through later titles such as *Diseases*, *Internal Affections*, and *Affections*. A number of modern scholars have regarded them as produced by Cnidian physicians and categorised them as 'Cnidian treatises'.[1] On the other hand, their Cnidian origin has been questioned and we have nowadays a growing consensus that they should be labelled as 'nosological treatises': 'nosological' is a neural term indicating the content of the treatises, rather than their roots or their origin within a certain group of physicians.[2]

---

[1] The most significant modern comprehensive work on these treatises is Jouanna (1974) – updated in 2009 and still unsurpassed in its precise and detailed philological and comparative textual analysis; also see Jouanna (1999 [orig. 1992]), especially chapter 7 (*The Physician and the Disease*), 141–54 (quoting from the 1999 edition).

[2] Goltz (1974), 96, defines them as 'therapeutic treatises', adopting a terminology that underscores the commonalities between the Greek texts and those of the ancient Near East – the latter being, essentially, collections of therapeutic prescriptions introduced by a very brief outline of the symptoms. Di Benedetto (1986), 4 and passim, defines them as 'technical-therapeutic treatises'. See also Chapter 9 by Totelin in this volume.

No definition of disease or affection is provided in those treatises, and we do not observe a substantial difference in the content, so as to justify their different titles.[3] These treatises present a blend of an essentialist and a dynamic vision of the disease: according to the first, each illness is a self-contained entity represented as real; according to the second, it is a temporary conceptualisation, a concretion of symptoms grounded in an idea of the disease predicated on blurry contours and an ephemeral existence. In the second case, symptoms prevail over the disease per se: consequently, the number of possible diseases proliferates – resulting not in further subdivisions, but instead in forms that coexist with equal importance.

Which are the criteria for identifying, naming, and grouping diseases in the nosological treatises?[4]

a) Localisation, or better the localisation of the main symptom or symptoms,[5] is the criterion most regularly used (and never explicitly problematised) to list and group the single nosographical units. Accordingly, we find groups of diseases affecting the head, lungs, thorax, and belly – the canonical order being from head to toe.[6] This criterion was also used in Mesopotamian medicine and, less sophisticatedly, in Egyptian medicine: it is clearly consistent with a consolidated tradition in the whole Mediterranean area, and would remain constant in the Greek and Latin production of the following centuries.

b) Another classification criterion is predicated on how diseases manifest themselves and evolve. The majority of the diseases tackled

---

[3] It may occur that the two terms are used side by side in the same context as in *Diseases* 1.5, 6.146 L. "Opportune moments in medicine, generally speaking, are many and varied, just as are the diseases and affections and their treatments."

[4] For a purview of the classification criteria that have been employed in the Hippocratic treatises without being mutually exclusive and with changing relevance according to the different texts, see Potter (1990, 2014) and Jouanna (1999 [orig. 1992]), 141–76. Jouanna's analysis is extended to the whole *Hippocratic Corpus* and is not limited to the nosologic treatises.

[5] The issue of the identification of affected areas will become important in the medicine of the Imperial Age: both Archigenes of Apamea (first to second century AD) and Galen will eventually write a treatise, *On the Affected Parts* – three books in the case of Archigenes, six in the case of Galen. On the subject see McDonald (2012).

[6] *Diseases* 2.12 begins with the rubric 'Diseases of the Head'.

in the nosological treatises have been labelled in later medical texts as 'acute diseases'; nonetheless, in the Hippocratic treatises they are rarely called this. For instance, the author of *Affections* isolates a group of chapters devoted to four illnesses defined as acute: pleurisy (7), pneumonia (9), phrenitis (10), and *kaûsos*, an ardent fever (11).[7] The author underlines the peculiarity of this name,[8] framing chapters 6–11 between two such sentences: "These diseases are called 'acute', and occur most frequently and violently in winter" (6), and "These diseases, then, are called 'acute', and you must treat them thus" (11, end). Other treatises – such as *Airs, Waters, Places, Prognostic*, and *Aphorisms*, and of course *Regimen in Acute Diseases* – refer to acute diseases, but never provide a (more) complete list.[9] Some treatises identify as 'acute' those diseases characterised by fever[10] and a rapid outcome in the sense of recovery or death. The treatment of acute diseases elicits the highest level of mutual disagreement among physicians as well as the highest level of danger for the patient, but also for the physician if he accepts to treat those patients. The author of *Regimen in Acute Diseases* recognises how difficult they are to treat, saying (chapter 5): "I should most commend a physician who *in acute diseases*, which kill the great majority of patients, distinguishes himself from other physicians for the better." And he emphasises the difference of opinion about how to treat them among practitioners (chapter 8): '*in acute diseases* practitioners have such widely differing opinions that the remedies which one physician gives

---

[7]   These same four diseases are listed together in the final chapters of *Diseases* 1 (26–34), devoted to the causes, course, and treatment of *pleurisy* and *pneumonia, kausos*, and *phrenîtis*. The four diseases can develop complications and possibly lead to a fatal outcome.

[8]   For a comment on the peculiarity of the name, see also *Airs, Waters, Places* 3, trans. Jones (1923a), 75: "Cases of pleurisy, pneumonia, ardent fever and of all the diseases considered acute rarely occur" and chapter 4, trans. Jones (1923a), 77: "Pleurisies are common, likewise those diseases which are considered acute."

[9]   On the other hand, see the general statement in *Aphorisms* 5.30, trans. Jones (1931), 77: "If a woman with child is attacked by *one of the acute diseases*, it is fatal."

[10]   See also *Regimen in Acute Diseases* 5, trans. Jones (1923b), 67: "Now the acute diseases are those to which the ancients have given the names of pleurisy, pneumonia, phrenitis, and ardent fever, and the other diseases which are akin to these, the fever of which is on the whole continuous."

in the belief that they are the best are considered by a second to be bad'. Likewise, the author of *Affections* is concerned that the physician be blamed, although it is not his fault should the patient succumb to the disease (chapter 13):

> Generally speaking, it is the *acute diseases* that cause the most deaths and that are the most painful, and with these the greatest care and the strictest treatment are necessary. Let nothing bad be added by the person treating – rather let the evils resulting from the diseases themselves suffice – but only whatever good he is capable of. If, when the physician treats correctly, the patient is overcome by the magnitude of his disease, this is not the physician's fault. But if, when the physician treats either incorrectly or out of ignorance, the patient is overcome, it is his fault.

Whereas 'acute diseases' were classified early, the opposite class of 'long' or 'chronic diseases' took longer to appear. But once established, the division between 'acute' and 'chronic' diseases was to become the one favoured by physicians who wrote books on diseases and was never to be abandoned in ancient Greek and Latin medical literature.[11]

c) Hippocratic treatises also display the emergence of the two opposite categories of 'individual' and 'common' diseases. In *Airs, Waters, Places* 4 the author maintains that, in towns exposed to northern winds, pleurisy and acute diseases are prevalent;[12] in this treatise, the diseases that most affect individuals in a certain area are also defined through the adjectives 'local' and 'common'.[13] The author

[11] See Aretaeus of Cappadocia's eight books *On the Causes and Symptoms of Acute and Chronic Diseases* and *On Therapy of Acute and Chronic Diseases*, the Anonymous text *On Acute and Chronic Diseases*; (Soranus-)Celius Aurelianus, *On Acute and Chronic Diseases*; and Archigenes, *On Diagnosis of Chronic Diseases*.

[12] The verb *epidēmeîn* occurs nine times in *Epidemics*; see also *Regimen on Acute Diseases* 5 and *Prognostic* 25.

[13] *Airs, Waters, Places* 4: 'he will not, on arrival at a town with which he is unfamiliar, be ignorant of the local diseases, or of the nature of those that commonly prevail'; see also chapters 3 (bis) and 4, and *Humours* chapter 13. Alternatively the author of *Airs, Waters, Places* speaks of 'most common diseases'; see chapter 2 (2.14.8 L.; 189.1 Jouanna): 'the physician will be able to tell what *pánkoina* ['common to all'] diseases will attack the city ... as well as those peculiar to the individual which are likely to

of *Nature of Man* distinguishes a class of diseases presenting themselves as an epidemic (*epidēmíē*; this is the sole testimony of the noun
epidēmíē in the Hippocratic treatises): these are not caused by individual factors – such as nutrition regimen or the prevalence of one
humour – but, instead, by the external air that everyone breathes
in.[14] The notions of '*epidēmíē*' and '*epídēmos*[15] (or *epidēmios*[16]) disease' later refer to diseases that affect a high number of patients (but
are not determined by contagion).[17]

In the nosological treatises, on the other hand, the adjective
epidēmios, to be found only in *Internal Affections*, has a value predicated on a sense of duration. In chapter 37 it refers to a type of
jaundice that occurs *year-round* ("This jaundice is called *epidēmios*
because it occurs in every season"): it is an endemic form of the
disease, different from three other types of jaundice that each manifest
themselves prevalently during a certain season.[18] By contrast, in
chapters 20 and 21, *epidēmios* has a different temporal duration.
The two chapters describe two phlegmatic diseases – one by more
recent   phlegm   (20)   and   another   by   old   phlegm   (21).[19]

---

occur through change in mode of life'; chapter 3 (18.12.16 L.; 192.1 and 6 Jouanna) 'they
are of short duration, unless a *pánkoinon* disease takes place after a violent change' and
'but besides, they are liable to any *pánkoinon* disease that prevails through the change
of the season' (Loeb translation); chapter 4 (22.2; 194.11–12 Jouanna). The term
'*pánkoinos* disease' is present only in this treatise.

[14]   *Nature of Man* chapter 9 (6.54 L.): "But when an epidemic (*epidēmíē*) of one disease is
prevalent, it is plain that the cause is not regimen but what we breathe, and that this is
charged with some unhealthy exhalation."

[15]   In *Epidemics* 3.14.

[16]   Only in *Internal Affections* chapters 20, 21, and 37; *Sight* chapter 9; and
Epidemics 7.59.

[17]   The authors of the Hippocratic treatises do not conceive of contagion. The disease
loimōdes mentioned in *Regimen in Acute Diseases* is also non-contagious.

[18]   The four jaundices are not equally distributed across the four seasons: they prevail
during the summer and winter. The pattern is as follows: the first jaundice (caused by
bile movement) prevails in the summer, the second (caused by external causes such as
drunkenness and cold) in the winter, the third – *epiémios* – in all seasons (because of
excessive filling and cold), and the fourth (caused by phlegm) – opposed to the first – in
the winter. The systematic correspondence between humours and seasons that will in
the future characterise the aetiology of many diseases is absent here: this is a plain list
of jaundices.

[19]   Original distinction by the author, not present elsewhere: cf. Jouanna (2009 [orig.
1974]), 241; Lami (2010), 33.

The presentation of the first disease is framed by the words "The *epidémios* variety is the most recent, and it is easier to treat",[20] and, in the conclusion, 'this is the treatment for the *epidémios* variety of phlegm'.[21] The presentation of the second variety (chapter 21) is opened by a comparison with the first: "If the phlegm happens to be of a longer duration ... he is afflicted more intensely, and has different signs than in the *epidémios* variety of the disease."[22] In all three occurrences, it appears that the *epidémios* variety of the disease manifests itself at a definite moment and has a short course.

d) In the nosological treatises there is no systematic classification of the diseases on a seasonal basis – albeit, as just observed, the diffusion of certain diseases in certain seasons is widely assumed.[23]

e) A classification of diseases predicated on their causes is inconceivable in the nosological treatises, because aetiology is the field characterised by the highest level of disagreement among physicians, and it is too unstable to provide universally accepted criteria. *Diseases 2*, chapter 4 provides a nice example for the problematic nature of disease names that indicate causation. Here, the condition is labelled as an 'overfilling with blood', which would suggest that the cause is an excess of blood. Yet the real cause is an excess of bile or phlegm in the blood, as the author explains in a particularly long parenthetical remark[24]:

> If around the brain, small vessels *overfill with blood* – this name is not a correct one, because no vessel, either one of the lesser ones or one of the greater ones, can actually be overfilled with blood. Still they use this name and say that they overfill with blood. And even if vessels really did overfill with blood, it does not seem probable that a disease would arise because of it, for bad cannot come from good,

---

[20] *Internal Affections* chapter 20, trans. Potter (1988b)– "The common variety is present for only a very short time, and its cure is easiest" – provide a different interpretation from Littré.

[21] *Internal Affections* chapter 20.   [22]   *Internal Affections* chapter 21.

[23] Moreover, the author of *Affections* chapters 14, 15, and 17 describes summer diseases.

[24] trans. Potter (1988b), 172–6.

nor can good be greater than what is fitting, nor would good come from bad. Rather there *appears* to be an overfilling with blood when bile or phlegm enters the vessels—, the vessels are raised up and throb ...

If the vessels in the head *overfill with blood*, they do so on account of the things mentioned before. ... the blood that flows forth is dark, turbid, and diseased; and yet not rightly so according to the name, but the blood should flow red and pure.

While not discarding the 'excess of blood' label for the disease – a label the author finds in his source – in the long and revealing parentheses the author clarifies that an 'excess of blood' actually never occurs, and even if it did, a pathology could not develop from a good thing such as blood.

f) In the nosology of the Hippocratic treatises, references to the solid structures of the body eventually brought to light by Hellenistic anatomy are almost completely absent.[25] Nonetheless, at least in *Nutriment*, a degree of attention towards them as elements of differentiation among diseases can be observed. This rather late text[26] offers in chapter 25 the draft of a classification of pathologies under the title 'Differences in Diseases'; it lists a series of juxtaposed items (anatomical and non-anatomical):

Differences of diseases depend: on nutriment, on breath, on heat; on blood, on phlegm, on bile, on humours; moreover, on flesh, on fat, on vein, on artery, on sinew (*neûron*), muscle, membrane, bone, brain, spinal marrow, on mouth, tongue, oesophagus, stomach, bowels, midriff, peritoneum, liver, spleen, kidneys, bladder, womb, skin.

The list can be divided into three parts. The first part includes respiration, nourishment, and heat, which are the fundamental vital faculties

---

[25]   It should be remarked that this knowledge developed too late to modify the already established classification of diseases and the corresponding terminology.

[26]   Craik (2015) dates it to a post-400 generation, but much more belated dates have also been proposed.

of each individual; the second includes humours; and the third contains – following the Aristotelian classification – first the so-called homeomerous parts of the body (that is, consisting of one part only such as bones); followed by the internal parts listed from top to bottom; and finally the external cover of the body, the skin. This list might constitute the backbone of a general and systematic arrangement of pathology.[27]

g) Finally, the class of women's diseases must be mentioned separately. In the gynaecological treatises, that amount to a significant portion of the *Corpus*, descriptions of the several pathologies affecting the female reproductive organs do not follow an evident criterion; nomenclature is scanty and illness identification is frequently achieved by means of conditional clauses ('if ... then'). The individual gynaecological treaties contain sections ascribable to different chronological layers, and each treatise is formed by a juxtaposition of materials from a broad temporal spectrum.[28] The peculiar issues emerging from a reading of the gynaecological treatises cannot be tackled in the space of this chapter.[29]

THE NOSOLOGICAL TREATISES

The texts most relevant to Hippocratic nosology are those treatises that are entirely or mainly formed by lists of nosographic units. They are synthetically presented in what follows.[30]

Diseases 1–4

Under the title *Diseases*, manuscripts have transmitted four treatises – all very different from each other in terms of structure, content, and

---

[27] Kanhak (2014) has recently interpreted the whole treatise *Nutriment* as an outline for a more comprehensive treatise: see in particular 34.

[28] See Grensemann (1982, 1987, 1989).

[29] On the gynaecological treatises see Chapter 11 by L. Dean-Jones in this volume. On nosology in *Sterility*, see Potter (2014).

[30] A detailed exposition of the content, and a definition of the context and principal issues with regard to each treatise of the *Corpus*, is now to be found in Craik (2015).

dating.[31] The most ancient among them is *Diseases* 2, composed of two textual units, *Diseases* 2 (1) and *Diseases* 2 (2), wrongly reunited in one single treatise since antiquity. The first unit (chapters 1–11), a mere fragment of a longer treatise, is more recent, the second (chapters 12–75), is a complete treatise and is the most ancient.[32] The two units provide a welcome occasion for assessing two different ways of presenting the same material (Table 8.1). Only thirteen records in *Diseases* 2 (1) correspond to the twenty records in the second – and most ancient – part of the treatise (*Diseases* 2 [2]): the author of the first part ignores, and in other cases combines, a number of pathologies listed separately in the second part (chapters 9 and 11); moreover, he is interested in aetiology, while completely omitting therapy. The comparison thus illuminates how each author compiled his text starting from a source but in full autonomy, according to his own objectives. Generally speaking, it is evident that the two authors of *Diseases* 2 – similarly to all the others whose works are preserved in the *Hippocratic Corpus* – never composed their work anew, but instead re-elaborated traditional materials, with different degrees of autonomy and different aims. A common stock of traditional knowledge and traditional formulations is a constitutive feature of Hippocratic nosology.[33]

Diseases 2

Diseases 3 is a short treatise composed of only sixteen nosographic chapters[34] – among which the last (chapter 16) stands out for its unusual length; it is dedicated to various forms of pleurisy and occupies a third of the whole book. Diseases affecting body parts below the lungs are completely missing (Table 8.1 displays the scanty

---

31   The very titles by now established in the modern editions do not always correspond to the titles that identified the materials in the writings of the Hellenistic and early Imperial Age.

32   This twofold composition has been the object of detailed analysis on the part of Jouanna (2009 [orig. 1974]); Jouanna (1983), 7–50.

33   Roselli (1990, 2016).

34   Recent editions Potter (1980, 1988c). On its structure see also Langholf (2004), 233–7.

Table 8.1 *Synoptic Table Illustrating Shared Material in* Diseases *2 and 3*

Diseases 2 (1)	Diseases 2 (2)	Diseases 3
1. <opening is missing>	12 (1). Diseases of the head. Numbness (*narka*) seizes the head.	
2. Another disease. The head becomes covered with ulcers.	13 (2). Another disease. The head becomes covered with ulcers.	
3 Another disease. Intense pain occupies the head.	14 (3). Another disease. Intense pain occupies the head.	2. When the head suffers intense pain
	15 (4). If fluid (*hýdōr*) forms on the brain	
	16 (5). Another disease. Chills, pain, and fever, throughout the head	
4a. If, around the brain, small vessels overfill with blood (ὑπεραιμέσῃ)	17 (6). Another disease. If the small blood vessels around the brain overfill with blood	
4b. If the vessels in the head overfill with blood (ὑπεραιμέσωσι)	18 (7). If the vessels in the head overfill with blood	
	19 (8). If the brain suffers from bile	
5. If the brain becomes sphacelous	20 (9). If the brain becomes sphacelous	4. If the brain becomes sphacelous
6a. Another. Pain suddenly seizes the head.	21 (10). Another disease. Pain suddenly seizes the head.	
6b. If a person suffers this condition subsequent to drunkenness	22 (11). In a person who has lost his speech as the result of drunkenness	
	23 (12). If a sphacelus occurs	

Table 8.1 (*cont.*)

Diseases 2 (1)	Diseases 2 (2)	Diseases 3
7. When a teredo forms in the skull	24 (13). When a teredo forms in the skull	
8. If a person is stricken	25 (14). If a person is stricken	3. The stricken, as they are called
9. Angina arises when ...	26 (15). Angina	
	27 (16). Another angina	
	28 (17). Another angina	
10. Staphylitis occurs when ...	29 (18). If staphylitis arises in the throat	
11. The tonsils, the area beneath the tongue, the gums, the tongue ... become ill as the result of phlegm ...	30 (19). If tonsillitis occurs ...	
	31 (20). If an affection occurs in the area beneath the tongue ...	

coincidences between *Diseases* 3 and *Diseases* 2). The last chapter (17) consists of a list of cooling preparations,[35] preceded by a short introduction.

In *Diseases* 1 the nosological section is limited to chapters 26 through 34. The first part of the treatise (chapters 1–10) deals with broad issues and the general practice of medicine; subsequently, chapters 11–22 offer an almost monographic review of different types of suppuration; chapters 23–25 deal with fever and the origin of shivers and sweat. The nosographic part regards only the aforementioned acute diseases. Structurally speaking, the characteristic format of the nosological treatises consisting in single, autonomous nosographic units (see later) has here been broken.

Despite its title, *Diseases* 4 is not part of the series of nosological treatises, and is usually edited together with the treatises *Generation* and *Nature of the Child* – taken together, these three portions would

---

[35]   As it has been noted, the same happens in the final parts of the two sections of *Nature of Woman*; see Totelin (2009) and also Totelin on therapeutics in this same volume.

constitute one single book. The nosographic section is limited to a few chapters on generation issues.

Internal Affections is the longest among the nosological treatises, although it opens with lung diseases, and head diseases are missing.[36] This text has structural characteristics comparable with those of *Diseases* 2 and 3. It is distinguished from other nosological treatises because of a tendency to group diseases by means of a formula based on their numerical variety ('four jaundices', 'three tetanuses', etc.). It is the only treatise that discusses a group of acute diseases separately, as we have already seen; it is also the only one documenting 'thick diseases' (diseases that make the patient dull); it broadly develops the therapeutic sections, especially at the end of lists of homogeneous diseases. It also displays peculiarities in terms of lexicon and style.

Affections is explicitly composed for non-specialists who are able to understand that 'health is of the utmost value for human beings' – an uncommon choice in this genre of treatises; an address to non-specialists (chapters 1 and 33) frames the nosological chapters (chapters 2–33). The second part of the treatise (chapters 33–61) is an example of what would become the typical content of a treatise on hygiene in the medical literature to come.

Despite the fact that *Regimen in Acute Diseases* does not currently belong to the series of nosological treatises, it is to be regarded as a reference text for a more complete understanding of those treatises. Its *Appendix* – considered as a spurious addition since antiquity – holds a remarkable interest from a nosographic perspective, especially in the first eighteen chapters. Therapeutic concerns prevail in the exposition.

THE FORMAT OF INDIVIDUAL UNITS IN THE NOSOLOGICAL TREATISES

Despite minor structural variations and the presence, or absence, of connecting elements between the single chapters, all the nosological

---

[36] Some believe that this is due to an accidental textual elision; on the other hand, Lami (2002) has convincingly argued that this is actually an authorial choice.

treatises contain a series of nosographic units whose constitutive parts are[37] the following.

(a) A Label Identifying the Disease This label often consists of a single word – a noun such as *pleurîtis, synánchē, kaûsos, thýphos*. The four terms illustrate four different strategies for naming: *pleurîtis* ('pleurisy') is an affection of the lungs, not the pleura, as modern terminology may suggest; in any case, the disease takes its name from a part of the body, in this case the *pleûra. Synánchē* is named after the symptom of suffocation; *kaûsos* is named after the fire caused by an extremely high fever; and *thýphos* (nothing to do with modern typhus) is named after a complex of symptoms clouding the mind 'like smoke'. The label can also consist of a single adjective such as 'black' or 'livid'; in this case, the noun 'disease' is implied, as in 'black (disease)' or 'livid (disease)'; in this way, a symptom or aspect of the disease is directly contained in its name. There are also more complex disease labels such as a pair of words, for instance a noun and an adjective, such as, *'eileòs ikteriódēs'* ('icteric ileus', that is, a painful obstruction of the stomach – *eileós* – resembling jaundice – *íkteros; Internal Affections* 45), and *'eileòs haimatítēs'* ('sanguineous ileus', that is, linked to blood – *haîma; Internal Affections* 46). In some cases, the label is a short phrase mentioning the dominant symptom, such as 'phlegm collected towards the palate' (*Diseases* 2.32), most frequently a conditional sentence introduced by 'if ... '. Some five centuries later, Galen made the following observation about medical nomenclature:[38] '... diseases are named in many different ways: they may take their name from the part affected, from the dominant symptom, from a combination of the two, from the cause of the disease, or from its resemblance to things in the outside world'. Chapters on the same disease, or on diseases affecting the same part of the body, form 'open' lists introduced by 'another'; see also *Diseases* 2: chapter 26: 'quinsy' (*kynánchē*); chapter 27: 'another quinsy' (hetérē *kynánchē*); and chapter 28: 'another quinsy' (*hetérē kynánchē*). The group of ileuses

---

[37]   For the format of nosological descriptions, see Jouanna (1999 [orig. 1992]), 145–6.
[38]   Gal. *On Method of Healing* 2.2 (10.81.18–84.16 K).

(*Internal Affections* chapters 44–46) just mentioned is introduced by the phrase: 'the following diseases are called ileuses', and the series of four 'thick' diseases in *Internal Affections* chapter 47 is introduced by: 'the following diseases are called the thick ones'. Together with 'open' lists, there are also some 'closed lists', which group together a specific number of diseases. For instance, in *Internal Affections* 1, chapters 10–12, we find three 'consumptions (*phthísies*), ... a first ..., a second ..., and a third ... '; in *Internal Affections* chapters 14–17, the author states that 'from the kidneys four diseases arise ... ', and then lists them.

(b) **A List of the Symptoms, or Pathological Conditions** This is the most conservative part of each nosographic unit, resisting substantial change in the course of subsequent redactions. The listing of symptoms[39] in the so-called '*kaì*-style', and the use of nearly fixed formulae, are the main structural and stylistic features. Occasionally, symptoms are qualified by brief comparisons with everyday things (animals, plants, etc.) that illustrate the appearance of secretions or evacuations or of the patient himself: 'sediments on the surface of urine *similar to spider webs*', 'a feeling like ants crawling along the spine', 'lips similar to those of someone who has eaten blackberries' (*Cnidian Sentences*). This visualisation of symptoms provides both precision and vividness. In this section we can appreciate how repeated observation succeeds in isolating the distinctive features of each disease.

(c) **A Section Devoted to Aetiology** In the older treatises, aetiology is concise or absent, but it tends to expand in the more recent ones. Individual constitutions, the patient's age, and the seasons are occasionally recognised as causes of the disease (see later). Diseases are attributed mostly to changes in the quantity, quality, and temperature of humours (mostly phlegm and bile), and only sometimes to a patient's behaviour (e.g., *Diseases* 2 chapter 22, 'if he has lost his speech as a result of drunkenness or to external causes').

---

[39] The term *sēmḗia* as the signs characterising the disease occurs only in *Diseases* 3 chapters 6 (twice), 10, 15, and 16 (twice).

The section on aetiology has stirred great interest among modern scholars because humour-based doctrines have long been regarded as the best touchstone to distinguishing among different authors – who, on this issue, seem to exercise their independence, autonomy, and creativity. Our treatises permit to discern a progress in the process of differentiating several kinds of bile, as well as the amazing evolution of the meaning of *phlégma* from 'inflammation' to '(cold) humour' – a process that took place as physicians 'translated' into the new systematic humour-based physiology something that had been extraneous to it. In the nosological treatises, however, the interpretation of symptoms in terms of the humoral doctrine is only occasionally accompanied by critical comments on previous or traditional doctrines. The broadening of aetiological explanations does not, in fact, involve any expression of the individual physician's personality.

(d) A Section Devoted to Treatment Like the section on aetiology, this may be more or less articulated and developed, even within the same treatise.[40] It is very rarely omitted.[41] This section may contain references to other chapters in the same treatise or to therapies assumed to be known to readers. An extreme treatment for water accumulating in the brain is to 'incise the head at the bregma; bore right through to the brain, and heal the wound *as you would one made by sawing'*; in other words, the author sends the reader to the part about wounds made by sawing.[42] Likewise, in *Diseases* 2 chapter 23, when describing how to deal with *sphákelos* – a sort of corrosion—in the head, he says: 'treat *as you would in the case of a fracture*' and again in *Diseases* 2 chapter 27, for angina, he enjoins: 'if the pus breaks out, treat *as you would in a case of an (internal) suppuration*'. In *Affections* there are references to a book titled *Pharmakîtis* (On Drugs).[43] This section may introduce innovations not only by

---

[40]   On treatment in the nosological treatises see Jouanna (2009 [orig. 1974]), 454–93; Langholf (1990), 68–72.

[41]   As it happens in *Diseases* 2, chapters 1–11; see earlier.

[42]   *Diseases* 2, chapter 15.

[43]   This title returns in the subsequent pharmacological literature and suggests that also in this case we are dealing with a self-contained treatise; on the other hand, Totelin

adding new treatments, but also by allowing physicians to choose the best therapy from various options.[44]

(e) A Section on Prognosis It is very short and often expressed by formulae that differ from author to author. Besides, it is not always present. Prognosis is concerned with healing, improvement, and death, as well as the number of days in which patients are expected to recover or die – the number of days being the only means by which the course of the disease is defined. (The authors of these treatises do not employ the notions of *crisis*[45] of the disease.) The prognosis is seldom introduced by the imperative 'say';[46] in such cases, it is usually unfavourable and accompanied by a mention of what determines the character of incurability.

The order of sections (c), (d), and (e) varies. Aetiology can occupy different positions in the sequence; prognosis is often intermingled with treatment. Each treatise constitutes a clearly recognisable individual entity within the group of texts with which it shares content and, to a certain extent, form.

TWO OPPOSITE TENDENCIES: MULTIPLICATION
AND REDUCTION IN THE NUMBER OF DISEASES

As touched on earlier, the authors of the nosological treatises collect and list together several varieties of the same disease: this can lead to displays of virtuosity in the differentiation, but it implies the risk of an intolerable fragmentation, as lamented by the author of *Regimen on Acute Diseases* (2.226.11–12 L.) – who severely criticizes the manual

---

(2009) and others maintain that we are actually dealing with a handbook of prescription for personal use, or for the use of a group of physicians to whom the book is addressed. See Chapter 9 Totelin in this volume.

[44] See, for instance, *Internal Affections* chapter 12 or *Internal Affections* chapter 20.

[45] There are a few exceptions: one occurrence in *Internal Affections* chapter 27 (on hepatitis) and in *Diseases* 3 chapters 6, 16a (see Jouanna (2009 [orig. 1974]), 432 and note 1 – where he points out the innovations in this treatise, when compared with the other nosological treatises.

[46] For a comparison with an analogous formula introduced by the imperative of the verb 'to say' in ancient Egyptian medical texts see Di Benedetto (1986), 91–3.

(or manuals) he knows by the name of *Cnidian Sentences* (a famous book in antiquity and now lost):

> Yet the many forms and the many subdivisions of each disease were not unknown to some; but though they wished clearly to set forth the number of each kind of illness their account was incorrect. For the number will be almost incalculable if a patient's disease be diagnosed as different whenever there is a difference in the symptoms, while a mere variety of names is supposed to constitute a variety of the illness.

The issue raised by this author is extremely relevant. According to the author, the variety of symptoms warrants a selection of the distinctive, essential symptoms of each disease. This selection can be done only by someone with competence in medicine that must go beyond mere diagnostic observation. Instead of selecting the distinctive symptoms, the compilers of the *Cnidian Sentences*, like the authors of the treatises that have come down to us, multiplied the number of diseases through subdivision – and perhaps someone even thought that the most highly valued manuals were the ones that recorded the highest number of varieties for the same disease; a list was, in fact, a format convenient for adding new items later on. Nonetheless, the risk of multiplication rapidly became evident, and it became necessary to group several items together – as done, for instance, in *Diseases* 2(1), but also in chapter 16 of *Diseases* 3, as Table 8.1 shows.

In his commentary on *Regimen in Acute Diseases*, Galen backs up the Hippocratic author's severe judgement against the multiplication of diseases, and expands on it. In a tirade against this archaic method for organising pathology, he ridicules the lists of 'seven diseases of the bile, twelve of the bladder, four of the kidneys, four kinds of strangury, three of tetanus, four of jaundice and three of tuberculosis'. We do not know whether Galen is here referring to lists he actually found in the *Cnidian Sentences* (or in similar texts), or if he emphatically refers to the existence of long closed lists of various diseases: with its existing closed groups, partially matching Galen's, *On Internal Affections* seems to corroborate the first hypothesis.[47]

Even without reaching the explicit level of criticism evident in *Regimen of Acute Diseases*, nosological treatises display a progressive reduction of disease variety to more manageable sizes: this occurs in *Diseases* 3, *Affections*, and even *Internal Affections* – which combines conservative forms with some innovations (among the archaic 'closed' groups of diseases a synthesis of phlegm-related conditions appears in chapter 20).[48] The reduction process will be complete when each disease corresponds to only one record, and the maximum of distinction will consist in discriminating between the acute and the chronic form of the same disease. Aretaeus of Cappadocia (first or second century AD) – who imitates Hippocrates in syntax, style, and language – compiled a manual so perfect in its one-to-one correspondences that any intrusion would be immediately perceived as a disturbance. Such 'modern' necessity for a strict classification has, over time, disqualified ancient nosology, which nowadays risks appearing as a compilation of materials. Paucity in sources, though, should not persuade one that the ancient method for organising and recording the lore on diseases, criticised by the author of *Regimen in Acute Diseases*, became rapidly degraded to the level of scholarly curiosity. A fragment of a medical text contained in a second-century AD papyrus, but probably dating back much earlier, is very similar to *Internal Affections*.[49] An older papyrus from the third or second century BC preserves a Hellenistic medial text that also testifies for the survival of such forms of writing nosology.[50] This shows that such texts were compiled in the Hellenistic Age and continued to be read until at least the second century AD.

---

[47] See also Galen, *On Hippocrates' 'Regimen in Acute Diseases'*, ed. Mewaldt et al. (1914), 117.11–13; fr. 12 Grensemann.

[48] Lami (2010).   [49] See also Jouanna (2004).

[50] Andorlini (2014); Andorlini and Daniel (2016).

TEXTS ON DISEASES IN MESOPOTAMIAN MEDICAL LITERATURE

In the last few years, a dialogue has emerged between scholars working on Near Eastern medical texts and those working on Greek nosological texts.[51] Both groups have attempted to attain a more complete understanding of their specific texts by means of a comparative reading against the background of a tradition that encompasses East and West.[52] Some scholars have devoted specific attention to the criteria for classifying diseases, pointing out several commonalities[53] – which, on the other hand, cannot be explained as direct influences exercised by more ancient texts on more recent ones. The comparison, on the other hand, can be extended to tackle the issue of rewriting, which is central in both cases. In the Greek nosological treatises, original materials have often been freely reworked – and this has resulted, over time, in a diversified production which displays significant expansions or reductions, as well as substantial transformations, of traditional materials. By contrast, in the Babylonian tradition, the formulation of single and extremely short items is rigid and strongly repetitive and innovation is intentionally stifled, as the case of the *Babylonian Diagnostic Handbook* shows.[54] Like the Greek treatises, the *Babylonian Handbook* is a catalogue of diseases and is composed of more ancient materials. The scribe and physician who compiled it said at the end that the *Handbook* had been commissioned by the king of Babylonia, Adad-apla-idinna (1067–47 BC), as a new assessment

---

[51]   See Horstmanshoff and Stol (2004).

[52]   See Heessel (2004), 100–10, and Geller (2004), who extensively compares some tablets of the *Babylonian Diagnostic Handbook* with *Internal Affections*, focussing his attention on content, the organization of materials, the literary form through which information is transmitted, and similarities in phraseology; also see Geller (2010); Scurlock (2014), 7–13; Asper (2015).

[53]   See Geller (2010), 4 and 25.

[54]   The *Handbook* has been edited and translated into English in its entirety in Scurlock (2014), 7–271. Scurlock identifies this work by the name of *Diagnostic and Prognostic Series* (DPS). The introductory pages stand out because of the originality and subtlety in the analysis of the complex of the Babylonian medical texts. Chapter 3 is of great interest for tackling the issue of rewriting (pp. 295–336 in the Therapeutic Series). I have not been able to look at Scurlock and Andersen (2005).

intended to replace the 'then-current medical knowledge'.[55] The scribe then explained that the new systematisation had become necessary because the *Handbook* had been disfigured by interpolations of non-canonical texts. The scribe physician (or someone on his behalf, or working with him) arranged the materials in order from head to toe: it was put on 40 (largely preserved) tablets and arranged in 6 subseries including more than 3,000 single short entries.[56] The same material is sometimes attested both within the manual itself and in another series – for instance the therapeutic ones.[57] The *Handbook* was an official text, conceived under the impulse and with the seal of royal authority and obviously subjected to continuous – both controlled and uncontrolled – revisions, but, to our knowledge, basically stable. Greek texts, by contrast, were produced in a competitive context, not controlled by a central authority: accordingly, in a short span of time (between the sixth and fifth centuries BC), traditional lore underwent profound revisions. The common basis for the single treatises is discernible at a more profound level, but each of them has an individual character – most evidently manifested in the humour-based theories proposed for motivating the origin and evolution of diseases.[58]

[55] Scurlock (2014), 7.

[56] The content is organised as follows: 1 (tablets 1–2) *omina*; 2 (tablets 3–14) diagnoses organised according to an anatomical principle; 3 (tablets 15–25) diagnoses organised according to time factors and diseases with fever; 4 (tablets 26–30) 'neurology'; 5 (tablets 31–33) 'infectious' diseases (including tetanus); 6 (tablets 34–60) gynaecology and infant diseases.

[57] Bibliography in Scurlock (2014), 8; selected quotations from the *Handbook* in different series of texts, presented and discussed by Scurlock at p. 11, provide interesting prompts for reflecting on the possibility of a transfer of textual segments into a different context, a characteristic that the Babylonian texts share with Greek medical texts (see Geller [2010], 97–108). This phenomenon, especially evident in pharmacological texts, can be compared with the presence of short textual passages in similar Hippocratic texts – as it occurs in *Epidemics* 2 and 6.

[58] See Roselli (2016).

9 Therapeutics

Laurence M. V. Totelin

INTRODUCTION: THE DIVISION OF THERAPEUTICS

There is probably no better introduction to a chapter on Hippocratic therapeutics than a concrete example. I have chosen a treatment for a red flux from the womb recorded in the gynaecological treatise *Diseases of Women* 2. After a brief description of the symptoms, the compiler describes the following long treatment:

> Red flux ... If you take on her care from the beginning, you must treat her in the following way. If she is not feverish but is strong, purge with hellebore. Once this has happened, leave an interval of three or four days, then give a drug to purge downwards. After the purgation, administer the following regimen, so that the flux becomes watery and smooth. In the morning, while fasting, give to drink some of the drugs, which I will list against the flux, sprinkling them in wine. After the drug, treat with a general regimen, and in particular treat the womb as follows. If it is swollen and closed up, there is need for an emollient fomentation until the mouth of the womb becomes soft. After the fomentations, administer the clysters that seem appropriate, either those that purge or those that soften. After the clysters, apply softening pessaries. If the mouth does not become soft, foment and apply emollient pessaries, which I will list, until it opens up. If after these measures the flux does not stop, cleanse the head, and administer the following regimen. If she has difficulties passing urine, let her drink ass's milk. Let her [eat] boiled, garden vegetables and wild ones, with the exception of garlic, leek, cabbage, and long radish. She should eat, among the sea products, the skate, the scorpion fish, conger-eel, ray, eel, turbot,

and gudgeon; boil them with onions and coriander in a sweet and
oily brine. Among the meats, she should eat first pork, then lamb or
mutton, boiled rather than roasted, and soups. White wine, honey-
sweetened and watery. Baths, without [immersing] the head, not
too hot and not too frequent. If after this regimen, the ulceration and
inflammation have ceased, and the womb becomes moist, suppress
the baths; instead of tawny wines, use red ones, and pure instead of
watery; instead of barleygroats, breads; instead of fish, roasted
meats, and all drying foods, as we recommend in cases of diarrhoea.
Get rid of all clysters, except those made of wine and water.
Fumigate with astringents. It is excellent for the patient to become
pregnant. If she is young, prescribe vomiting while fasting, repeat
frequently, and after that give a little breakfast. This is the regimen
that is appropriate to these fluxes.[1]

The compiler refers to this long process both as 'treatment' (using the
verb therapeúein) and 'regimen' (díaita). He mentions various drugs
(phármaka), foods (both to eat and to avoid), drinks, clysters, pessaries,
fomentations, fumigations, and baths. In this paragraph, the word
'phármakon' refers to purgative drugs, drugs that cleanse
(kátharsis) – the meaning of the word is rather limited; the pessaries,
clysters, fomentations, and fumigations mentioned are not here classified as phármaka.[2] The meaning of 'díaita', on the other hand, is
very broad, almost synonymous with that of 'therapeúein'; it appears
to encompass aspects of pharmacological administration. The principle of the therapy is relatively simple. The mouth of the womb is
closed and hard, preventing the healthy evacuation of menstrual
blood, and causing an unhealthy flux. The physician must soften the
mouth of the womb, using emollient foods, drinks, baths, and treatments. Sea products are believed to be emollient by virtue of living in

---

[1]   Diseases of Women 2.115 (8.248–50 L.).
[2]   On the meaning of the Greek word 'phármakon' see Artelt (1968); Touwaide (1996);
Totelin (2015). On Hippocratic pharmacology, see Stannard (1961); Goltz (1974);
Scarborough (1983); Hanson (1991, 1992b, 1998, 1999); King (1995a, 1995b, 1998);
Laskaris (1999); Totelin (2009).

water; watery wine is more emollient than pure wine; boiled or braised meats are more emollient than roasted ones. Vegetables such as garlic must be avoided because they are 'windy' and astringent. Once the womb has become moist, the physician must then use more astringent and drying treatments to counteract the effects of the previous, lengthy treatment. The best solution, however, if possible, is for the woman to become pregnant. Pregnancy will 'weigh down' the womb and settle any dangerous flux.[3]

In the centuries that followed the writing down of *Diseases of Women* (which dates to the end of the fifth or to the beginning of the fourth century BC), physicians would come to distinguish clearly three branches of therapeutics: dietetics, pharmacology, and surgery. These branches are clearly outlined in the preface to Celsus' *On Medicine* (first century AD).[4] I would argue that, in the fifth and fourth centuries BC, the boundaries between the two first branches of therapeutics, those that will concern us here, were far more blurred. Scholars have tended to see dietetics as the most prestigious branch of ancient Greek therapeutics, with surgery and pharmacology being somewhat less advanced. For instance, Michel Foucault wrote, "Whereas medications and operations acted upon the body, and the body submitted to that action, regimen addressed itself to the soul, and inculcated principles in the soul."[5] Maria M. Sassi, for her part, argued that in the classical period, with the exception of dietetics, medicine experienced a 'therapeutical stasis'.[6] Iain Lonie, finally, suggested that "If we exclude diet, therapy in Hippocratic texts reduces to a few simple formulae for purges and emetics. The one exception to this generalisation is offered by the gynaecological texts."[7] In some ways, these scholarly views are correct: dietetics

---

[3]   On the principles of ancient gynaecological therapy, see Hanson (1991, 1992b, 1998, 1999); Demand (1994); Dean-Jones (1994); King (1995a, 1995b, 1998); Totelin (2009).

[4]   Celsus, *On Medicine*, prooemium 12.   [5]   Foucault (1985), 107.

[6]   Sassi (2001), 142.

[7]   Lonie (1983), 153–4. There is a large literature on Hippocratic dietetics; see, e.g., Ackerknecht (1973); Scarborough (1978); Edelstein (1987 [orig. 1931]); Lonie (1977); Smith (1980); Scarborough (1982); Mazzini (1989); Sigerist (1989); Jori (1993); Craik (1995a, 1995b); King (1995a); Longrigg (1999); and Steger (2004).

was the most dynamic branch of medicine at the time of the Hippocratic physicians. In other ways, this view is misplaced: dietetics was not so sharply differentiated from pharmacology; or rather pharmacology was subsumed under the heading of dietetics by the Hippocratics. In this chapter I shall argue that this was a deliberate strategy, and that it does by no means signify that pharmacology was stagnant in the classical period. I start by introducing the treatises of the *Hippocratic Corpus* that are therapeutic in nature. I then review the forms of treatments available to the Hippocratic physicians, as well as the principles behind their application. Following this, I introduce the 'actors' in the therapeutic 'market' in the Greek classical period and their representation (or lack thereof) in the *Corpus*. I conclude with some thoughts on possible ways to further research in the field of Hippocratic therapeutics.

THE TREATISES

In the first century AD, the lexicographer Erotian classified what he considered to be Hippocratic treatises in four categories: semeiotics, aetiology and physiology, therapeutics, and 'mixed'. He described the therapeutic treatises, as follows:

> Therapeutics: on the one hand, those that pertain to surgery: *Fractures; Joints; Wounds; Wounds and Missiles; Wounds in the Head; Surgery; Mochlicon; Haemorrhoids; and Fistulas.* On the other hand, those that pertain to regimen: *Diseases* 1 and 2; *Ptisánē* [sc. *Regimen in Acute Diseases*]; *Places in Man; Diseases of Women* 1 and 2; *Nutriment Sterility; and Waters* [sc. *Use of Liquids?*].[8]

It is quite telling that Erotian does not have a 'pharmacology' category here. It is true that the *Hippocratic Corpus* does not contain any pharmacological treatises strictly speaking, that is, nothing that resembles treatises on simples (substances used pharmacologically) such as Dioscorides' *On Medicinal Substances* or Galen's *On the*

---

[8]   Erotian, *Lexicon* 9.15–17 ed. Nachmanson (1918).

Mixtures and Properties of Simple Remedies, or treatises on compound remedies such as Galen's *On Remedies according to Types*,
On Remedies According to Places, and *On Antidotes*.[9] The treatise
Affections, however, refers on various occasions to a *Pharmakîtis*
book (*Pharmacological Book*), or rather, following the interpretation
of Elizabeth Craik, to several such treatises.[10] Craik suggests that the
author of *Affections* enjoins his readers to consult their own 'files on
drugs'.[11] From the little we know of these pharmacological works, it
appears that they contained recipes for *phármaka*, as well as information that we would classify as 'dietetic', information on food and
drink, as in the following example: "If he suffers from dysentery ...
administer draughts and drinks, gruels and foods as prescribed in your
Pharmakîtis."[12] It is not surprising that these works are lost: recipe
books, as a genre, tend not to survive the vicissitudes of transmission
particularly well. Each practitioner would have made his own selection of recipes, reorganising them into a system that worked for him.[13]

In addition to references to the lost pharmacological works, the
Hippocratic Corpus contains many recipes, the majority of which we
would class as pharmacological. Most of these are concentrated in the
gynaecological treatises of the *Corpus*, but not exclusively so.[14]
It would therefore be wrong to argue that pharmacology is not represented in the *Hippocratic Corpus*; it is simply not as conspicuously
present as in later Corpora.

---

9   See Vogt (2008) for a general introduction to Galen's pharmacology. See also the papers
     in Debru (1997). See Riddle (1985) for a general introduction to Dioscorides' *Materia
     Medica*. A recent translation into English of Dioscorides is available: Beck (2005).
10   On the *Pharmakitis*, see also Schöne (1920–24); Monfort (2002); and Totelin (2009),
     98–102. References to a *Pharmakîtis* are found at *Affections* 15 (Potter [1988b], 28, line
     5; 6.224.8 L.); 18 (Potter [1988b], 32, line 13; 6.228.4–5 L.); 23 (Potter [1988b], 42, line
     20; 6.234.23 L.); 28 (Potter [1988b], 50, line 7; 6.240.9 L.); 40 (Potter [1988b], 64, line 4;
     6.250.12 L.). The work is also called '*Tà Phármaka*': *Affections* 4 (Potter [1988b], 12,
     line 4; 6.212.10 L.); 29 (Potter [1988b], 50, line 25; 6.240.22 L.).
11   Craik (2006), 17.
12   *Affections* 23 (Potter [1988b], 42, lines 9 and 18–20; 6.234.15 and 21–23 L.).
13   On the transmission of recipes and catalogues of pharmacological recipes in antiquity,
     see Youtie (1996); Hanson (1997); Totelin (2009). Wilkins and Hill (1996), 147 make
     this point for the cookery books of antiquity.
14   See Totelin (2009).

With these remarks in mind, let us introduce the Hippocratic texts that deal with therapeutics. Various treatises that may have started their life as discourses in front of audiences discuss therapies and therapeutics in a general manner. The author of *Ancient Medicine* presents various forms of diet, ancient and modern, foreign and Greek, and their effect on the body. *Sacred Disease* claims that usual traditional treatments for the so-called sacred disease, purifications and incantations, are ineffective, and that one must look for natural causes and treatment of the disease (see later for more detail). *Art* defends the status of medicine as a professional art (*téchnē*) and claims that no healing is spontaneous, but is rather caused by the administration of regimen and medicines. *Breaths* is another sophistic treatise, the author of which argues that bad regimen is the cause of diseases and makes the famous statement whereby 'opposites are cures for opposites' (see later). *Nature of Man* is the treatise best known for expounding the theories of the four humours (blood, yellow bile, black bile, and phlegm). It also states the principle of allopathy, and offers treatments for various diseases. It ends with a section on regimen to preserve health (sometimes called *Regimen in Health*), which is addressed to laypeople.

Other treatises focussed more specifically on diet, on the medicinal use of foods and drinks. Perhaps the best-known Hippocratic therapeutic treatise is *Regimen* (in four books), Book 2 of which contains a catalogue of foods and dietetics practices (walking, running, etc.), and Book 3 of which explains how to achieve the perfect balance between foods and exercise in order to avoid drugs (chapter 67). *Regimen in Acute Diseases* is principally a treatise on the use of *ptisánē*, a sort of thin barley porridge, in the treatment of acute diseases. It is polemical in tone, directing its polemic mostly at the author of the treatise (now lost) *Cnidian Sentences*. An appendix to this treatise is found in some manuscripts; it includes a short catalogue of foods (chapters 45–50). A short treatise *Use of Liquids* deals, not with liquids to be consumed by mouth, but applied externally in the treatment of a vast array of afflictions. It lists drink-water, sea-water, vinegar, and wine. *Nutriment* is a difficult, enigmatic short treatise that deals with nutrition in the broadest meaning of the term (air, for instance, is nutrition).

Five of the nosological treatises are also therapeutic in outlook: *Diseases* 2, *Diseases* 3, *Affections*, *Internal Affections*, and *Places in Man*. As indicated by numerous parallel passages, these treatises shared common sources. The first part of *Diseases* 2 (chapters 1–11) deals with fourteen diseases (and treatments) of the head and throat, which are described again in the second part (chapters 12–75), with the addition of diseases of the nose, chest, and back. *Diseases* 3 deals with sixteen diseases classified in a rough head-to-toe order, and ends with a catalogue of cooling remedies (chapter 17).[15] *Internal Affections* describes fifty-four diseases, again ordered from head to toe, but starting with the chest rather than the head. *Affections* is, according to its author, a treatise addressed to laypeople (see later). It starts with a nosological section (1–38) organised from head to toe, followed by a dietetic section (chapters 39–61), which recommends various foods and drinks according to their power, for example, drying, strengthening, laxative, and so forth. After describing various parts of the body, the author of *Places in Man* presents treatments for various diseases, makes interesting comments on therapeutic principles (see later), and closes his treatises with a chapter on gynaecological ailments (chapter 47).

Six of the Hippocratic gynaecological treatises are therapeutic in outlook, and contain numerous recipes as well as prescriptions relating to food: *Diseases of Women* 1 and 2, *Sterility*, *Nature of Women*, *Superfetation*, and *Excision of the Foetus*. As is the case with the nosological treatises, numerous parallel passages in these treatises indicate that they had common sources. *Diseases of Women* 1 describes afflictions relating to women's reproductive life, from

---

15   See Chapter 8 by Roselli, who discusses the interrelation in detail.

menstruation to the aftermath of childbirth. It ends with catalogues of recipes (chapters 74–92) for diseases and a collection of 'spurious' recipes in the manuscripts (chapters 92–109). *Diseases of Women 2* deals with the treatment of specific gynaecological diseases, in particular fluxes and movements of the womb. It also ends with catalogues of recipes for these diseases (chapters 192–212), as well as some cosmetic recipes (chapters 185–191). *Sterility* is concerned with diseases that affect women's abilities to conceive. It too closes with catalogues of recipes (chapters 232–248) and a description of how to excise dead foetuses (chapter 249). *Nature of Women* is composed of two subtreatises on women's affections, each ending with catalogues of recipes (chapters 2–35 and 35–109). *Superfetation* opens with consideration on the rare phenomenon of superfetation, but then deals with diseases relating to women's reproductive life, starting with pregnancy, and ending with menstruation. As all the gynaecological treatises presented so far, it ends with catalogues of recipes (chapters 33–43). The short treatise *Excision of the Foetus* (which only deals with this procedure in the first chapter) also contains information on the treatment of gynaecological ailments.

Recipes and therapeutic indications are also found in the three short surgical treatises *Fistulas*, *Haemorrhoids*, and *Sores*; in *Sight*, in the *Aphorisms*, and in Books 5 and 7 of the *Epidemics*. The deontological treatises *Precepts* (perhaps Hellenistic in date) and *Decorum* (which is late in date) include considerations on drugs, how to prepare and administer them, and on the correct use of regimens. Finally, the Oath famously forbids the use of abortive pessaries and lethal drugs.

THE MODES OF TREATMENT AND PRINCIPLES OF TREATMENT

Excluding surgery, which is covered in Chapter 10 by Mathias Witt in this volume, there were numerous forms of treatment available to the Hippocratic physicians. They can be classified in two main ways: their mode of application and consumption, and their effect on the body.

Before I present these, I must say a few words on the meaning of the word *phármakon* in the *Hippocratic Corpus*. In the introductory example (therapy for a female flux), we saw that the word *phármakon* was applied to purgative remedies, remedies that cause a *kátharsis*. This was the common usage in the *Corpus*. For other forms of therapy, which we could call 'pharmacological', the Hippocratics used specific technical words such as 'pessary', 'clyster', 'fumigation', and so on. I have argued elsewhere that the Hippocratics avoided giving too broad a meaning to the word *phármakon*, because they knew that various substances could fall both in the 'drug' and in the 'food' category, as well as in other categories beside.[16] For instance, the Hippocratics made use of garlic as a food (see example at the beginning of the chapter), as a means to test whether women could become pregnant or not, and as a remedy for the eyes. The fact that so many substances can be used both as medicine and as food has led anthropologists to develop the concept of the food–medicine continuum, whereby medicine is a prolongation of cooking.[17] Here to account for the polyvalence of natural substances, I will use the category 'medicinal substances' to encompass both foods and drugs.[18]

The mouth was perhaps the most common point of entry for medicinal substances in Hippocratic medicine. We saw that the *Corpus* contains several lists of foods. Often ancient physicians forbid their patients to take solid food until their disease had reached a turning point – fasting had an important role to play in ancient medicine. As a transition between fasting and foods, semi-solid soups and gruels also received special attention from the Hippocratics. In particular, they debated on the use of *ptisánē*, a barley gruel that, according to the author of *Regimen in Acute Diseases*, was

---

[16]   See also Goltz (1974), 297–302; Lonie (1977), 245; von Staden (1999a), 257–8; Thivel (1999), 35–7; and Holmes (2010b), 79 n. 161.

[17]   Etkins and Ross (1982, 1991); Johns (1990); Etkins (2008); and Leonti (2012).

[18]   The different types of medications for which we have recipes in the Hippocratic Corpus are listed and well described by Goltz (1974), 197–237.

especially well suited to the treatment of acute diseases. Other semi-solid aliments included the *kykeṓn* (a thick drink made of barley flour to which were added various ingredients, which also played an important role in the initiation to the Mysteries of Demeter), gruels, and soups. Among the drinks, wine, honey-wine, water, and vinegar get most attention. Numerous recipes for draughts are to be found in the *Corpus*; many of these would have had a purging effect on the body. Also administered by mouth were the electuary, pill, and gargle.

The second most important point of entry for medicinal substances in Hippocratic medicine was the skin, to which were applied ointments, plasters, cataplasms, and medical powders. Some fomentations (see later) were made by means of a sponge or cloth to the skin. Baths had an effect on the skin. The third and fourth points of entry for medicinal substances were the anus and vagina, to which were applied pessaries or suppositories and enemas or clysters.

Other medicinal substances 'enveloped' the body rather than penetrated it. These were vaporous medicines destined to be inhaled through the mouth and nose or fumigated or fomented. Technically, there is a difference between a fumigation and a fomentation: the fomentation involves hot and wet vapour, whereas the fumigation involves dry smoke. In actual fact, however, the Hippocratic authors often used the words we translate as 'fumigation' and 'fomentation' interchangeably.[19] Finally, the *Corpus* contains a handful of references to medicaments to be bound to the body as amulets.[20] Other treatments took the form of actions rather than substances. Such actions included exercise, walking, running, sleeping, resting, sexual activity or abstinence, vomiting, and so on.[21]

The effects these various medicinal substances and treatments had on the body are perhaps too numerous to enumerate. Most commonly listed are heating, cooling, moistening, emollient, drying,

[19]   See Gourevitch (1999), esp. p. 208.
[20]   On amulets in the *Hippocratic Corpus*, see Hanson (1995); Hanson (1998), 82–4; Hanson (2004). Amulets are criticised by Theophrastus at *Enquiry into Plants* 9.19.2.
[21]   On surgical actions such as venesection and cauterisation, see Chapter 10 by Witt in this volume.

astringent, purgative, and strengthening. The principle that under-lines most Hippocratic therapies is that of 'opposites are cures for opposites', which is given by the author of *Breaths*:

> For instance, hunger is a disease, for anything that grieves man is
> called a disease. What then is a remedy for hunger? That which
> checks hunger. This is eating. Then by means of eating, hunger
> must be cured. Again, a drink checks thirst; and again depletion
> cures satiety; and satiety cures depletion; rest cures fatigue.
> In short, opposites are cures for opposites. For the medical art is
> subtraction and addition: subtraction of what is in excess, and
> addition of what is lacking.[22]

In the case of our introductory example, an emollient regimen was used to cure a hardened mouth of the womb. This principle of oppo-sites being cured by opposites, known as 'allopathy', is mechanical, simple, and rational. However, though allopathy is the healing prin-ciple most commonly underlining treatments in the *Hippocratic Corpus*, not every ailment could be treated in that way. Therapeutics was complicated, as the author of *Places in Man* ascertains:

> It is not possible to learn the medical art quickly because it is
> impossible to find in it any established principle ... Medicine
> [unlike the art of writing] now does one thing, and the next moment
> the opposite; and it does one thing and its opposite to the same
> person; and it even does things that are contradictory to each
> other.[23]

He goes on to say that, in some cases allopathy works; in others, depending on the person, either allopathy or homeopathy. The reason for such complexity, according to our author, is the weak-ness of the body. Another reason for such complexity was perhaps the

---

[22]   *Breaths* 1, Jouanna (1988), 104; 6.92 L. See also *Nature of Man* 9, Jones (1931), 24;
       6.52 L.
[23]   *Places in Man* 41, Potter (1995), 80; 6.330–332 L.

highly competitive nature of ancient medicine in general, and therapeutics in particular. We turn to this subject.

PEOPLE INVOLVED AND THE STATUS OF DIETETICS

Treatment was a contentious area, one where debates were frequent, and one where physicians had to compete against each other and against other healers, in what Vivian Nutton has called 'the medical marketplace'.[24] The compiler of *Ancient Medicine*, for his part, calls most physicians bad in relation to the treatments they prescribe.[25]

According to the author of *Regimen in Acute Diseases*, physicians often disagreed on what to prescribe in cases of acute illnesses, giving a very bad name to medicine among patients:

> Indeed if, with regard to the most acute diseases, experts differ from each other to the point that [the remedies] prescribed by one, because he believes them to be the best, are considered by another to be bad; then one may indeed argue that the art resembles divination, for seers consider the same bird to be a good sign if it is on the left, and a bad one if it is on the right, while other seers argue the opposite.[26]

The author's polemic is directed against the authors of the *Cnidian Sentences* (lost), who are unable to prescribe *ptisánē* correctly and who rely on a very limited amount of treatments (purges, whey, and milk). Such ignorant physicians are dangerous because they can trick gullible laypeople.[27]

While the author of *Regimen in Acute Diseases* conceived of laypeople as ignorant, other Hippocratic compilers thought of them as important actors in therapeutics. For instance, the compiler of *Affections* tells us that laypeople can play a role in discovering new therapies:

---

[24] Nutton (1992).   [25]   *Ancient Medicine* 9.

[26] *Regimen in Acute Diseases* 8, Joly (1972), 39, lines 8–20; 2.240–242 L.; Roselli discusses this further in Chapter 8 in this volume.

[27] *Regimen in Acute Diseases* (chapter 6 in ed. and trans. Jones [1923b, 66], chapter 2 in Littré, 2.234–6).

It is worth learning from everyone about medications that are drunk
or applied to wounds. Indeed people do not discover these by
reasoning, but rather by chance, and not more by experts than by
laypeople. But whatever is discovered in the art of medicine by
reasoning, whether about foods or about drugs, must be learnt from
those who have discernment in the art [of medicine], if you want to
learn anything.[28]

This author, like several others, also claimed to write for an audience
of laymen, thus indicating that normal people may have read medical
treatises and applied the therapies described therein.

The form of certain verbs in recipes of the *Corpus* shows that the
patients themselves were involved in the preparation of their remedies. Literature has examples of 'laypeople' preparing drugs for family
members or themselves.[29] In Greek societies, as in most societies,
people who cooked and tended gardens were aware of the health
benefits of plants and other substances. By writing down such knowledge, the Hippocratics appropriated it for themselves, and perhaps
transformed it in the process.

In addition to competing with other physicians and laypeople,
the Hippocratics had to deal with magicians, purifiers, charlatans, and
quacks. According to the author of *Sacred Disease*, these people treated that malady through purifications and incantations, proscribing
the use of baths and foods.[30] Unlike these healers, the Hippocratic
physicians argued that diseases had natural causes and should be
treated by natural means, making use of the mechanical, rational
principles of allopathy or homeopathy.[31] Certainly, the Hippocratic
authors do not recommend chants or prayers to accompany their
therapies, but the actual treatments they recommend are not really

---

[28]   *Affections* 45, Potter (1988b), 68, lines 14–22; 6.254.9–14 L.
[29]   In Aristophanes' *Thesmophoria*, 483–6, a husband prepares a remedy for his wife's
alleged stomachache (in reality an excuse to go out to meet her lover).
[30]   *Sacred Disease*, 1 Jones (1923b), 138; 6.352 L.
[31]   For two contrasting views of the 'rationality' of Hippocratic therapeutics, see Lloyd
(1983), 131–2 and Laskaris (2002), 1–2.

different from contemporary treatments known from other sources. Indeed, scholars have uncovered much overlap between Hippocratic medicine, on the one hand, and the healing practised by root-cutters (rhizotómoi), drug sellers (pharmakopôlai), and religious healers, on the other hand. Similarities are to be found in the forms of treatments (e.g., purgation, fumigation, amulets), activities surrounding treatment (e.g., fasting, sleeping, and dreaming), and substances (e.g., hellebore). Again, the Hippocratics may have borrowed from these sources, adapting their material in the process. They also conspicuously did not mention many of these healers. To learn about the root-cutters and root-sellers, one must turn principally to book nine of Theophrastus' *Enquiry into Plants*;[32] and to learn about the therapies carried out in the temples of Asclepius and other healing gods, one must turn to comedies and epigraphic material.[33]

It seems highly unlikely to me that patients did not perceive the similarities between Hippocratic therapies and other therapies available. A purge is a purge is a purge. Yet I would argue that Hippocratic medicine was indeed different from these other types of healing. It differed not so much at the level of individual recipes or forms of therapies, but rather in its attempts at regulating all aspects of the patient's life, in its attempts at being all encompassing. Encounters with root-sellers, priests, and purifiers were probably punctual, specific events. Hippocratic physicians, on the other hand, followed their patients for long periods, prescribing treatments that stretched over several days, as in our introductory example. All-encompassing dietetics was what distinguished the Hippocratic from other healers. This perhaps explains why pharmacology is not as prominent in the *Hippocratic Corpus* as in later Corpora. The Hippocratic physicians

---

[32]   See Lloyd (1983), 122ff; Scarborough (1978); Scarborough (1991), 146. Theophrastus even gives the name of some of the *rhizotómoi* – they are all men. See Scarborough (1991), 166, n. 38. The *Corpus* includes some reference to *pharmakopôlai*, but they are to be found in the *Letters*, but they are late in date.

[33]   See for instance Edelstein (1937); Kudlien (1967, 1968a); Lloyd (1983); Laskaris (1999); Lloyd (2003), chapter 3; and von Staden (1992).

knew that there were many other experts who knew about *phármaka* – pharmacology had a history that stretched back to the mythological past, to Apollo and the Centaur Chiron. They could not claim superior knowledge in this field, so they subsumed it to their dietetics.

Sources suggest that dietetic medicine was an invention of classical Greece. It did not exist at the time of Homer, but had been devised by the philosopher Pythagoras of Samos, Herodicus of Selymbria, or Hippocrates of Cos himself.[34] That new type of medicine was, however, not to everyone's taste. In the *Republic*, Plato lambasted it for being affordable only to the wealthy, and not to those, who like a carpenter, must work for a living. [35] The comedian Aristophanes, for his part, put the following words in the mouth of the tragedian Euripides (whom he despised), addressing his predecessor Aeschylus:

> But immediately as I took over the art from you,
> Swollen by boasts and ponderous fluxes of words
> First of all I stayed her and diminished her weight
> By means of versicles, digressive walks and white beets,
> And I gave her nonsense juice extracted from books. [36]

Aristophanes is clearly parodying dietetic methods here: tragedy is treated with a combination of literary devices, foods (beet), weight loss, medicinal juices, and walks or digressions. Aristophanes wittily plays on words: the Greek *peripátois* (here translated as 'digressive walks') means both 'digressions' and 'walks'; and the word *rhemátōn*, which refers to ponderous words (here translated as 'fluxes of words') is similar in sound to '*rheumátōn*', fluxes.

---

[34]   The sources are conveniently collected in Longrigg (1998), 146–7. Smith (1980) and Thivel (1999) both argue that Hippocrates himself played an important role in the 'invention' of dietetics.

[35]   Plato, *R.* 3.15 (406d–e). In the *Timaeus* (89b–d) Plato has a more positive attitude towards dietetics.

[36]   Aristophanes, *Frogs* 939–43. On the imagery of this recipe, see Jouanna (2000b), 191–3.

CONCLUSIONS

I have argued that, far from experiencing a period of stagnation in the classical period, therapeutics was a field of immense development. The Hippocratics built upon pre-existing knowledge of medicinal substances, both foods and drugs – many substances could play a dual function – to create a new, all-encompassing dietetic medicine. This dietetic medicine was linked to literacy, and considered bookish by some. The Hippocratics did not invent new treatments; they borrowed them from laypeople (who knew the properties of common plants through cooking) and from experts (who may have specialised in dangerous substances). In borrowing these treatments, they also transformed them and stripped away references to prayers and incantations. The Hippocratic physicians and their patients were aware that this type of medicine was new. As a result, they often felt the need to defend its status as a professional art (*téchnē*). Pharmacology, on the other hand, was a very old practice – it needed little justification. The Hippocratic authors therefore developed a cunning strategy: they subsumed pharmacology to dietetics, leading many scholars to believe that pharmacology was underdeveloped in the classical period. I have suggested the reverse was the case: it was dietetics that was a work in progress.

Much work remains to be done on ancient therapeutics. One possible avenue of research would be to look further at the boundary between 'internal' and 'external' medicine.[37] I have so far – deliberately – avoided using these terms, talking instead about 'points of entry to the body'. My reason for doing so is the claim, made by Brooke Holmes in her magisterial *The Symptom and the Subject*, whereby the notion of body was still in the process of being established in the fifth century BC.[38] The ancients did not conceive of the boundaries of the body in the same way as we do today. The distinction between 'internal' and 'external' medicine

[37]   Lonie (1983), 153–4.   [38]   See also Chapter 4 by Holmes in this volume.

may therefore not be valid. Was the skin the ultimate boundary of the body? When in medicinal fumigations vapours surrounded the body and created a space in which the patient occupied the centre, did that space become a sort of 'second skin'? These are some questions, among many, that deserve further research in the future.

10 Surgery

Mathias Witt

INTRODUCTION

The Roman encyclopaedist Celsus (first century AD) says about surgery that 'its effect is the most obvious of all [three] branches of [therapeutic] medicine ... '.[1] By this Celsus means that the results of surgery are generally evident, whereas in the other two therapeutic disciplines (dietetics, pharmacy) it often remained doubtful whether healing was due to chance or to a medical intervention. "Although this branch [i.e. surgery] is most ancient,' he continues, 'it was elaborated more by Hippocrates, the father of all medicine, than by his predecessors." Indeed, the *Hippocratic Corpus* is our oldest written source on Western surgery and the second oldest source on surgery in general (after the Edwin Smith Papyrus from seventeenth-century BC Egypt).[2] Nevertheless, the Hippocratic surgical lore is considerably older than the composition date of the surviving treatises of the *Corpus* and almost certainly goes back to Mycenean times (second millennium BC).[3] Already in the *Iliad* (eighth century BC), military surgery and wound care are described.[4] When studying ancient surgery, modern researchers can draw on four strata of written medical sources:

1. The surgical writings and passages of the *Hippocratic Corpus* (fifth and fourth centuries BC)
2. The surgery outlined in Celsus' *On Medicine* (first century AD)

---

[1]   *On Medicine*, 7 pr. 1.
[2]   See M. Hanson (1999), 52; Grmek (1983a), 288–90; Westendorf (1999), 16–21.
[3]   See Grmek (1983a), 285–8; M. Hanson (1999), 52; Gurlt (1898), Vol. I, 280.
[4]   See Grmek (1983a), 288.

3. Galen's commentaries and accounts on Hippocratic and other ancient surgery (second century AD)
4. The surgical sections of the Byzantine epitomes by Oribasius (fourth century AD), Aëtius (sixth century AD), and Paul of Aegina (seventh century AD)

Celsus, Galen, and the Byzantine compilers still had access to Alexandrian surgical treatises (from the third century BC onwards), which are all lost today.

FORMS OF SURGERY IN ANTIQUITY

Before turning to Hippocratic surgery in detail, one question has to be raised first: What does 'surgery' in antiquity actually refer to and what does it mean in the context of the *Hippocratic Corpus*? A closer look at the terminology is absolutely essential, as modern interpreters have varying ideas of ancient surgery which are often biased by their own concepts of the term 'surgery'.[5] There is a widespread misconception that Hippocratic surgery was almost exclusively limited to orthopaedics, whereas wound care of the soft tissues is deemed to have been rather primitive and is often reduced to 'burning and cutting'.[6] The fragments of the lost Hippocratic surgical treatise *Wounds and Missiles*, however, disprove the allegedly primitive state of soft tissue surgery.[7] For the evaluation of the achievements of Hippocratic surgery its fragments were not taken into account until quite recently.

The well-known sentence in the Hippocratic Oath, 'I will indeed not cut sufferers from stone' has been interpreted in two

---

[5] Edelstein (1987 [orig. 1943]), 30 uses, for example, the plain terms 'surgery' and 'operating' when referring to burning and cutting and reaches the result that Pythagorean doctors did not practise 'operative surgery' or 'bloody operations'. These vague terms are also used by others (see, e.g., Lichtenthaeler [1984], 168 or Michler [1962], 1). None of the authors ever defines surgery (or 'operative' or 'bloody surgery'), nor is there any attempt to get intrinsic evidence from the *Hippocratic Corpus* as to what kinds of surgery are mentioned in the *Corpus* and whether the Hippocratics practised all or only some kinds of surgery.

[6] See, e.g., Michler (1962), 1. For 'burning and cutting' as a means to cure internal diseases, whenever pharmacotherapy failed, see n. 29.

[7] Witt (2009), and see further discussion later.

ways by modern scholars[8]: it is taken either as a rejection of lithotomy or, more generally, as 'a ban on all forms of surgery' (Vivian Nutton).[9] That the latter understanding cannot be true becomes apparent on examining the ancient use of the term as well as the surgical lore transmitted in the *Corpus*. Celsus distinguishes two branches of surgery: one in which the physician 'makes the wound' and one where he 'finds it'.[10] In modern terms, this is the distinction between non-trauma surgery and trauma surgery. Operations such as couching cataracts, lithotomy, and so on belong to the first category, as opposed to trauma surgery, which deals with fractures, dislocations and wounds due to injury. A series of important writings on trauma surgery is preserved in the *Corpus*. One should therefore conclude that the passage of the Oath in question could, at best, have been a 'general ban' on non-trauma surgery, the only form of surgery that is appropriately described with the verb 'to cut' (where the physician 'makes the wound').

THE AFTERLIFE OF HIPPOCRATIC SURGERY IN ANTIQUITY

This being said, the question, "What does surgery in the context of the *Hippocratic Corpus* mean?" can be taken up again. It can best be answered by examining the afterlife of Hippocratic surgery in antiquity in order to get an idea how Hippocratic surgery was used or adapted by later authors. Whereas Celsus devotes a whole book to non-trauma surgery of the soft tissues (*On Medicine*, Book 7), we have only very few and rather simple interventions of this kind mentioned or described in the *Hippocratic Corpus*. Since we lack evidence of lost Hippocratic treatises on this subject, it is clear that Celsus drew mainly from Alexandrian sources when elaborating the seventh book *On Medicine*. In contrast, his eighth book on orthopaedics and

[8]   The grammatical structure allows for the readings (1) "I will not cut, indeed not even sufferers from stone" or (2) "I will indeed not cut sufferers from stone." See also Chapter 7 by Leven, who discusses this passage in greater detail and offers a different perspective.

[9]   Nutton (1995), 519. This is the view of Ludwig Edelstein and his followers; see below.

[10]   *On Medicine*, 7 pr. 5.

'bone surgery' (see later for this term) shows several parallels to Hippocratic surgery of the same kind. When examining the Byzantine epitomes, the results are the same: the sections on 'bone surgery' are either direct re-elaborations of Hippocratic passages or (more frequently) excerpted from Galen's accounts of these passages.[11] The sections on non-trauma surgery of the soft tissues, however, are excerpts from the books on surgery (cheirourgóumena) by late Alexandrian surgeons.[12] Among their fragments are not only descriptions of procedures we would call surgical operations today, but also advice how to remove fishbones stuck in the throat, rings stuck on a finger, how to perform urinary catheterisation, and so on. Considering these chapters we learn that in antiquity the notion of surgery was used for all sorts of manipulations with hands and instruments on a patient, in the very literal sense of the word cheirourgía or 'the part [of medicine] that cures with the hand', as Celsus translates it.[13] It is therefore a modern anachronism to think that ancient surgery merely consisted in 'cutting'. For in many areas of ancient surgery such as orthopaedics, cutting was not used for treatment.

HIPPOCRATIC SURGICAL TREATISES AND ANCIENT COMMENTARY

For the surgical writings of the *Hippocratic Corpus* the same applies as for the gynaecological ones: they represent a kind of thematically specialised sub-corpus within the *Corpus*. Erotian, who compiled a Hippocratic glossary in the first century AD, includes, in the preface to his work, an index of those treatises that he judges 'definitely

---

[11] There is no systematic study on this subject. However, the extensive apparatus of sources in the critical edition of Oribasius' *Medical Collections* by Raeder (1928–1933) allows verifying this thesis for the surgical sections of Oribasius' *Collections*, from which Aëtius of Amida's and Paul of Aegina's epitomes are, at least partly, derived.

[12] These treatises seem to have almost uniquely dealt with that non-trauma surgery of the soft tissues, judging by the preserved fragments. Oribasius drew from four Hellenistic 'surgical manuals (cheirourgoúmena)', the ones by Leonides (approx. first century AD), Archigenes (first to second century AD), Heliodorus (second century AD), and Antyllus (second century AD). For further details see my forthcoming edition of these works.

[13] *On Medicine* 7.1. See also the Pseudo-Soranian *Medical Definition* 38 (Cod. Carnotensis).

authentic works by Hippocrates'. In the index, eight surgical treatises constitute the category 'therapeutic writings, pertaining to surgery'.[14] With the exception of the one lost treatise *Wounds and Missiles*, all are preserved. The following surgical treatises are found in Erotian's list:

1. Trauma surgery
   a. Bone surgery
      i. Independent treatises: *Fractures, Joints*
      ii. Drafts/epitomes: *Surgery, Mochlicon*
   b. Partly bone, partly soft tissue surgery: *Wounds in the Head*
   c. Soft tissue surgery: *Sores, Wounds and Missiles*

2. Non-trauma surgery; soft tissue surgery:[15] *Haemorrhoids and Fistulas*

The treatises are not presented in Erotian's order here,[16] but according to the classifications trauma versus non-trauma surgery and bone versus soft tissue surgery. These classifications help to assess the peculiarities of Hippocratic surgery. Above all, the aforementioned lack of treatises on non-trauma surgery becomes clear. This branch of surgery is taught only in the minor treatises *Haemorrhoids and Fistulas* that deal with anal surgery.

Whereas modern critical editions of all surviving treatises are available (as well as a collection of fragments of the lost treatise mentioned), Littré's edition; Adam's commented translation; and, above all, Pétrequin's edition (with a translation and thorough commentary) remain standard reference works for

---

[14] In contrast, Erotian mentions only three of the eight Hippocratic gynaecological treatises that have come down to us. These three are, moreover, not presented as a group, but are assigned to different categories by him (aetiologic/physiological/dietetic writings). See also Chapter 11 by Dean-Jones on the medical treatment of women in this volume.

[15] In the *Hippocratic Corpus* there is no mention of non-trauma surgery of the bones, save for advice on the therapy of certain congenital disorders (clubfeet, etc.) that is included in the treatises *Fractures* and *Joints*.

[16] Erotian's order is: *Fractures, Joints, Sores, Wounds and Missiles, Wounds in the Head, Surgery, Mochlicon,* and *Haemorrhoids/Fistulas*. See also Chapter 9 by Totelin on therapeutics in this volume.

commentary on the surgical treatises, even if some of their views have been disproved by modern scholarship. When perusing the foregoing list, it is noteworthy that some headings are abbreviated and are therefore not immediately comprehensible. *Joints*, for example, is short for *Setting of Dislocated Joints*, and the title *Wounds and Missiles* is an abbreviation of *Deadly Wounds and the Extraction of Missiles*.[17] The compound work *Haemorrhoids and Fistulas*, as it appears in Erotian's index, is divided into two separate treatises in our manuscript tradition. Likewise *Wounds and Missiles*, which also occurs as one treatise in Erotian's index, is split up into two parts in later work lists.[18] The process of dividing such 'double treatises' seems to have occurred at different periods of time.

Commentary on all major Hippocratic writings is attested since Alexandrian times. However, for the surgical writings only the illustrated 'commentary' on *Joints* by Apollonius of Citium (first century BC) survives, as well as three of Galen's surgical commentaries.[19] Galen deals with the Hippocratic surgical treatises *Sores, Wounds and Missiles, Fractures*, and *Wounds in the Head* in the first section of his main therapeutic work, the *Method of Healing*, which is partly a 'synthetic' commentary on the respective Hippocratic writings. There he discusses and explains elementary matters of therapy that beginners need to know before embarking on the original Hippocratic works.[20] As a guide for advanced learners, Galen later composed lemmatic commentaries for *Fractures, Joints, Surgery, Wounds in the Head*, and *Sores* which were intended to assist readers of the Hippocratic treatises. The first three of the five Galenic commentaries mentioned survive, whereas the ones on *Wounds in the*

---

[17]   For both full title versions we have manuscript evidence, e.g., in the index in manuscript *V* (see Chapter 3 by Jouanna in this volume, on *Textual History*), see also Witt (2009), 65–6.

[18]   For example, again in the index of manuscript *V*, see also Witt (2009), 61–71.

[19]   See Ihm (2002), 6–7 on the special nature of Apollonius' commentary.

[20]   For a comprehensive study on the relation between the sections of commentary in Galen's *Method of Healing* and his lemmatic surgical commentaries see Witt (2012).

Head and *Sores* are lost and only few excerpts survive in Oribasius' huge medical compilation *Medical Collections*.[21] In Byzantine times, commentaries on *Fractures* have been written by Palladius and Stephanus of Athens (both from Late Antique Alexandria).

THE DOCTOR, HIS SURGERY, AND HIS PATIENTS

Generally speaking, the surgical treatises of the *Hippocratic Corpus* are very technical in that they focus on describing the different steps on diagnosis and therapy. In contrast, we gain very little information about the social circumstances of the persons involved. Assistants (*hypērétai*, literally 'servants') are repeatedly mentioned,[22] but nothing is known about their training or position, or whether they were spontaneously recruited or permanent assistants to the physician. We also know very little about a surgeon's professional training. Owing to cultural taboos, no human dissections were performed in antiquity, save for a very short period in Alexandria (third century BC). The Hippocratics could, therefore, gain anatomical knowledge only through random observations of injured patients or by dissecting animals. Of course their anatomical knowledge is markedly inferior to that of physicians of the post-Alexandrian period or even of Aristotle's time. It has been shown, however, that the authors of *Fractures* and *Joints* and *Wounds in the Head* surpass Aristotle regarding the knowledge of the anatomy of the musculoskeletal system and of the head.[23] Some information concerning the preparations and circumstances of operations can be found in the treatise *Surgery* that gives advice on general topics such as how to equip a surgery, how to position as an operator, how to use natural and artificial light, and so on. Also the clothing, manicure, and skills of a surgeon are addressed here. The more extensive second part of *Surgery* is devoted to bandaging. The style of this treatise is very concise to the point of obscurity

---

[21]   For a collection of fragments of these two lost commentaries see Witt (2014a).

[22]   In the writings *Surgery, Fractures*, and *Joints*. An assistant is mostly just addressed as *tís* (someone), *állos* or *héterós tis* (someone else), or by definite articles with particles (*hoi mèn ... hoi dè ...* – the ones ... the others ...).

[23]   Oser-Grote (2004), 315.

and, as a whole, the work has a more draft-like character than that of an elaborated treatise. There are passages that presuppose the knowledge of passages in *Fractures* and vice versa. Therefore both treatises might have a common origin or might have been composed from the same source material.[24] Further information on general surgical matters is available in the treatise *Physician*, which was intended for beginners and focuses mainly on surgery. It outlines the deontology of the physician and surgeon and gives some advice on how to equip a surgery. Furthermore, it is recommended that someone wishing to practice military surgery should gain experience by joining foreign army expeditions. This is the only hint concerning a surgeon's professional training in the *Hippocratic Corpus*. The treatise *Physician*, however, is mentioned neither by Erotian nor by Galen. It is included in Pétrequin's edition of the surgical Hippocratic writings, but is generally not counted among the surgical treatises of the *Corpus*. It supposedly dates to the late Hellenistic or even early Christian era, but its code of ethics corresponds to the oldest surgical writings of the *Corpus* and there are resemblances and parallels to the other Hippocratic surgical treatises.[25] This might be due either to the conservative attitude of the writer or to the fact that older material was incorporated in this treatise.

Although narcotic drugs such as mandrake and opium were known since Homeric times, all surgical operations during antiquity were obviously performed without anaesthesia. The fact that Hippocratic surgeons did not administer narcotic drugs prior to operations is evident from the following passages from *Physician*, *Haemorrhoids*, and *Joints*:

> In cases where the surgery is performed by a single incision, you must make a quick one; for since the person being cut generally suffers pain, this suffering should last for the least time possible, and that will be achieved if the incision is made quickly. However, when many incisions are necessary, you must employ a slow

[24]   See Littré's remarks at 3.266 L.   [25]   9.198–202 L.

surgery, for a surgeon that was fast would make the pain sustained and great, whereas intervals provide a break in its intensity for the patient.

(Physician 5)

Let assistants hold the patient down ... while he is being cauterised so that he does not move – but let him shout during the cautery, ...

(Haemorrhoids 2)

... if the patient suffers pain during the amputation, and the limb happens to be not yet dead at the place where it is cut away, there is great risk of collapse from pain; and collapses of this kind have brought sudden death to many.

(Joints 69, similar to Fractures 43)

In a similar vein, Celsus admonishes the physician not to get distracted by the patient's cries during the operation.[26] That narcotics were used neither in Hippocratic nor in Alexandrian or later antique surgery is explained mostly by the fact it was difficult to achieve the right dosage in ancient preparations of such drugs, making the risk of killing a patient too high. It therefore seems to have been preferable in surgery to not administer narcotics at all.[27] Bleedings were treated mostly by administering styptic drugs locally. If a severe bleeding in one part of the body could not be stopped this way, bloodletting was performed in other parts – until the patient fainted.[28] This method was applied because of a very rudimental knowledge of human anatomy and a poor understanding of the vascular system. Venesection was used not only for treating bleeding, but also widely as an evacuating measure in the context of humoral pathology. It is this way that the famous last Hippocratic aphorism 7.87 has to be understood: "Those diseases that medicines [i.e. evacuating remedies] do not cure are cured by the knife. Those that the knife does not cure are

---

[26] *On Medicine* 7, prooem., 4: 'the surgeon should be ... filled with pity, so that he wishes to cure his patient, yet is not moved by his cries, to go too fast or cut less than is necessary; but he does everything just as if the cries of pain cause him no emotion.'

[27] See Cavenaille (2001), 36.   [28] Lichtenthaeler (1984), 172.

cured by fire. Those that fire does not cure must be considered incurable." Cauterisation was regarded as the last resort to prevent the spread of disease in the body. Such uses of venesection and cauterisation are, however, not subject to the specifically surgical writings of the *Corpus*, but are rather instances in which surgery is used as a last resort to cure 'internal' diseases.[29]

As we learn from the surgical treatises, the Hippocratic surgeon was faced with both acquired and congenital disorders in equal measure, with curable and incurable ones as well as defect healing and impaired body function following surgery. Frequently several alternatives of treatment are described, ranging from soft to violent. This way the surgeon was able to avail himself of a broad repertory of alternative treatment methods if one proved to be unsuccessful. Furthermore, the author of *Fractures* and *Joints* regards it as a sign of expertise that all possible methods of reduction are known to the physician.[30] The requirements of 'the [medical] art', in an abstract sense, as well as the need to appear skilful both to colleagues and laymen are frequently addressed in these two writings.[31] It needs to be pointed out that an ancient physician practised to a higher degree in public than his modern colleagues; he was constantly being judged by colleagues and laymen, so that there was a strong need of publicly displaying surgical expertise. As a means for public demonstrations of surgical skills, complicated bandages and spectacular orthopaedic treatments were used, for example.

Bone Surgery (Fractures *and* Joints)

Fractures and *Joints* constitute the main Hippocratic work on bone surgery. The type of 'bone surgery' is not to be understood in a modern sense because invasive bone surgery was not practised in antiquity. The treatments taught belong instead to a category that today would

---

[29]   For pharmaceutical evacuation, burning and cutting as three subsequent steps of therapy see Jouanna (1999 [orig. 1992]), 155–61.

[30]   See *Joints* 1: 'expertness includes knowledge of all the methods by which physicians effect reduction, and the best way of using these methods'.

[31]   See Witt (2014b), 102, 12.

be referred to as conservative traumatology and orthopaedics. Basically, most of the treatments described belong to trauma surgery. However, electively treated orthopaedic disorders such as malpositioned joints, chronic joint diseases, and congenital malformations (clubfeet etc.) are addressed as well. The titles of *Fractures* and *Joints* are somewhat elusive in that each treatise deals with the therapy of fractures and dislocated joints. There are cross-references in both works relating to each other in a complex way. These references indicate that both treatises once constituted one single work and that at some point in time the order of the chapters was disrupted. The material was then inaptly rearranged. Both Erotian and Galen knew *Fractures* and *Joints* as separate treatises. Galen speculates that the original compound treatise was split up into two parts soon after it had been written and informs us that also other commentators before him were aware that *Fractures* and *Joints* originally formed one single work.[32] There is evidence that Ctesias of Cnidus (late fifth and early fourth century BC) and Diocles of Carystus (fourth century BC), who were almost Hippocrates' contemporaries, knew the treatise *Joints*, whereas the name of the author they thought wrote this treatise remains unknown.[33]

Galen considered both works part of the 'most genuine' Hippocratic writings.[34] He nevertheless informs us that some thought that these treatises were not written by the great Hippocrates, but rather by his grandfather, Hippocrates, son of Gnosidicus.[35]

[32] See Galen's *Commentary on Hippocrates' Fractures*, Book 1 18b,324 K. Thus, in the Alexandrian literature still available to him, there was obviously no trace of a compound treatise *Fractures* and *Joints*, and this theory was already in antiquity based only on a textual relationship.

[33] Ctesias is reported by Galen to have criticised Hippocrates for his method of reducing a dislocated hip (see Galen's *Commentary on Hippocrates' Joints* 18a.731.6–9 K.), a method that is comprehensively described in *Joints* 70. Galen furthermore lets us know (see *Galen's Commentary on Hippocrates' Joints* 18a.519.11–15 K.) that Diocles paraphrased one sentence from *Joints* (4.186.3–4 L.) in his treatise *On Bandages*. See Anastassiou and Irmer (1997), 145.

[34] Galen's *Commentary on Hippocrates' Epidemics*, Book 3 17a.484.12, 577.12 and 625.30 K.

[35] Galen's *Commentary on Hippocrates' Regimen in Acute Diseases*, Book 1 (15.456.2–4 K.), Galen's *Commentary on Hippocrates' Fractures*, Book 1 (18b.324.1–2 K.).

Commentators in antiquity tended to ascribe Hippocratic writings to several members of Hippocrates' family in order to explain divergencies in style and content and to preserve the coherence of the *Hippocratic Corpus* at the same time. According to Galen, those who attributed *Fractures* and *Joints* to Hippocrates' grandfather were aware of the inapt titles and thought that the original title of the compound work had originally been *Surgery* (as the title of another small surgical treatise of the *Corpus*; see earlier).[36]

Hermann Grensemann carefully analysed the aforementioned cross-references in *Fractures* and *Joints*, and thus was able to reconstruct the original order of the chapters, as intended by the author. The original order is not in head-to-toe format, which became popular later on not only for surgical treatises, but for other medical writings as well. Grensemann came to the conclusion that the original work had two parts, the first of which dealt with injuries of the extremities and the second with injuries of the facial skull (except for the neurocranium) and the trunk. The first part was subdivided into the treatment of (1) simple injuries and (2) injuries with accompanying soft tissue damage.[37] The second part did not have any further subdivisions.

In *Fractures* and *Joints* reduction techniques for dislocated joints are described that modern medicine still associates with Hippocrates, such as the so-called 'Hippocrates manoeuvre', a method for reducing a shoulder dislocation described in *Joints* 3. Another well-known passage is the classical distinction of four types of hip joint dislocations (*Joints* 51). Interestingly, the author already uses finger traps for the repositioning of finger dislocations (*Joints* 80), which are still in use for surgical purposes today. In another well-known chapter of *Joints*, 42, the Hippocratic bench is described, an ancestor of orthopaedic traction devices, both ancient and modern – and the medieval rack. Such a use is foreshadowed by the Hippocratic author who almost gives a 'hidden recommendation' to employ this

---

[36] Galen's *Commentary on Hippocrates' Fractures*, Book 1 (18b, 324,16 K.).
[37] See Grensemann's reconstructed reading order (Grensemann [1970], 235).

device in a detrimental way: "This reduction apparatus ... has such power that, if one wanted to use such forcible manoeuvres for harm and not for healing, it is able to act strongly in this way also" (*Joints* 47).[38]

With the exception of the bench and some other simple devices, the author is otherwise reluctant to use apparatuses for extensions of fractures and reductions of dislocated joints. He criticises other physicians for the unnecessary use of some devices just to give their audience a spectacle:

> ... succussion (shaking) on a ladder never straightened any case [of hump-back], so far as I know, and the physicians who use this method are chiefly those who want to make the vulgar herd gape, for to such it seems marvellous to see a man suspended or shaken or treated in such ways; and they always applaud these performances, never troubling themselves about the result of the intervention, whether bad or good. As to the physicians who devote themselves to this kind of thing, those at least whom I have known are incompetent. ... I felt ashamed to treat all such cases in this way, and that because such methods appertain rather to charlatans.
>
> (*Joints 42*)

Nevertheless, the desire to entertain an audience is not altogether rejected, just in cases in which entertainment is regarded as an end in itself without providing the patient with a medical benefit. When a procedure is medically useful, however, it is not judged negatively if there also happens to be an entertaining component: "It is a good and correct method [for reducing a dislocated thighbone], and in accordance with nature, and one, too, that has something striking about it, which pleases a dilettante in such matters" (*Joints* 70).

As mentioned earlier, another means of publicly displaying surgical skills was the use of elaborate and complicated bandages, often without exhibiting a beneficial use for the patient. This is also criticised by the author:

---

[38] A similar remark can be found in Celsus' *On Medicine* 8.20.5.

> If the nose is broken ... those who delight in fine bandaging without judgement do more damage than usual. ... those who devote themselves to a foolish parade of manual skill are especially delighted to find a fractured nose to bandage. The result is that the practitioner rejoices, and the patient is pleased for one or two days; afterwards the patient soon has enough of it, for the burden is tiresome.
>
> *(Joints 35)*

THE HIPPOCRATIC AUTHOR

From antiquity to recent times, when the 'Hippocratic question' finally was abandoned, the author of the treatises *Fractures* and *Joints* often used to be identified with the historical Hippocrates. For the lack of external evidence this ascription was based on vague criteria like a pre-eminence in style and scientific approach over other treatises of the *Corpus*. Owing to the influence this concept of "Hippocrates" had on medical history it seems desirable to examine how the author of *Fractures* and *Joints* characterises himself. First of all, we are faced with an experienced author, who is able to evaluate different methods of treatment from his own longstanding practice and knows which methods are to be recommended and which ones are not. The author is very present throughout the treatises, in that he speaks of himself and his experience, and he criticises colleagues and the sensationalism of people, using polemics as well as irony. He has been described as having an 'aristocratic attitude' that is 'hostile to laymen'.[39] He is nevertheless very candid with his own errors, failures, and problems:

> ... my attempt was not a success ... I relate this on purpose; for those things also give good instruction which after trial show themselves failures, and show why they failed.
>
> *(Joints 47)*

---

[39] Knutzen (1964), 70.

> I myself once got into disrepute both with doctors and the public by
> denying that this appearance [the head of a humerus projecting
> forwards in a patient] was a dislocation. I seemed to them the only
> person ignorant of what the others recognised, and found it hardly
> possible to make them understand that the case was as follows:
> suppose one laid bare the point of the shoulder of the fleshy parts ...
>
> *(Joints 1)*

What follows is a kind of anatomic dissection of the human shoulder, portrayed through thoughts. As mentioned earlier, human dissections were taboo during this period of time in ancient Greece, so that even a fictitious dissection seems rather unusual.[40] Similar thought experiments can also be found elsewhere (*Joints* 46). To demonstrate the impossibility of reducing a certain vertebral dislocation in the spine, the author imagines a fictitious operation in which the patient would have to be cut open to perform this type of reduction. The author proves to be spontaneous and inventive not only in thought but also in practice. In the case of a nasal fracture he describes having improvised once by using a piece of sheep lung, which happened to be at hand, as an intranasal splint (*Joints* 38). He also proves to be a very keen and scrupulous observer. In several chapters, especially the chapters on hip dislocations (chapters 51–60), he carefully describes what happens if dislocations are not treated, how the patient develops afterwards, what the patient is still able to do with the mutilated limb, and whether the function of the limb can be improved through use and exercise. He likewise stresses the need to study incurable disorders: 'one must study incurable cases so as to avoid doing harm by useless efforts' (*Joints* 58). In another context, the author drastically illustrates how the right treatment can influence a patient's life:

> The proper treatment of those whose shoulders are often being
> dislocated is a thing worth learning. For many have been debarred

---

40   Brockmann (2008), 127.

from gymnastic contests, though well fitted in all other respects, and many have become worthless in warfare and have perished through this misfortune.

(Joints 11)

The author is not only an expert in medical matters, but also educated in a general sense. It has been pointed out that stylistically the treatises *Fractures* and *Joints* are influenced by the rhetoric of the Greek sophist Gorgias (ca. 485–380) and that they reflect aesthetic and literary criteria from the fifth century BC.[41] Furthermore, parallels between the Hippocratic author's body concept and that of the sculptor Polycleitus have tried to be established.[42] Remarkably, the Hippocratic author also quotes Homer and refers to the myth of the Amazons (*Joints* 53), which seems to be quite unusual for even an ancient medical textbook.

BONE SURGERY (MOCHLICON, WOUNDS IN THE HEAD)

In contrast to the sophisticated treatises *Fractures* and *Joints*, *Mochlicon* is a succinct and stylistically sober summary of bone surgery, mainly the reduction of dislocated joints. Contrary to *Mochlicon's* title, which literally means 'relating to leverage', or 'treatments through leverage', this treatise also deals with methods of reducing dislocations without using levers, and the therapy of fractured bones and cartilage. It is arranged from head to toe and was either compiled from *Joints* (to a lesser extent, from *Fractures*), or from a precursor work that served as a source for both treatises.[43] In the wake of the textual transmission, two longer passages from *Mochlicon* were later inserted into *Joints* to fill gaps, so that in modern editions *Mochlicon* 7–19 and 26–31 are identical with *Joints* 17–29 and 82–87.

Wounds in the Head is – along with *Fractures* and *Joints* – the third main treatise on bone surgery in the *Hippocratic Corpus*. Soft tissue surgery of the head is also addressed here, as the nature of head wounds comprises both types of surgery. Compared with *Fractures*

[41]   Brockmann (2008), 126.   [42]   Ibid., (2008), 133–7.   [43]   Craik (2015), 168.

and *Joints*, the treatise *Wounds in the Head* is much more matter-of-fact and descriptive, without any kind of special rhetorical stylisation. The author remains in the background and hardly uses first-person narration, nor does he use polemics or irony. As mentioned earlier, the treatment of fractures and dislocations of the facial skull are described in *Fractures* and *Joints*; however, injuries of the neurocranium are not discussed. Such injuries are separately outlined in *Wounds in the Head*. This treatise begins with a description of the bones and sutures of the skull. The account of the anatomy of the cranial sutures, which comprises four types of suture patterns, is highly inaccurate from a modern viewpoint and has been commented upon at length by Pétrequin.[44] In a later chapter (12), the author of *Wounds in the Head* addresses the difficulty of differentiating between cranial sutures and fractures of the skull. Celsus' well-known praise of Hippocrates for admitting to having mistaken a cranial suture for a fracture (*On Medicine* 8.4) does not refer to this passage, but to *Epidemics* 5.25, a treatise whose author seems to have known *Wounds in the Head*.[45] Following the anatomical introduction, the author of *Wounds in the Head* distinguishes five types of head injuries, the pathomechanism of these lesions, the examination of patients, and both conservative and operative treatment. The main treatment for head injuries is trepanation, performed with both rasps and (apparently bow-driven) crown trephines. It might strike modern readers that the need for trepanation is indicated fairly often, even in cases of minor injuries. Once the observation had been made that trepanation prevented neurological damage and allowed patients with severe head injuries causing intracranial pressure to survive, it was likely to have been applied to all kinds of head injuries, even in uncomplicated cases in which trepanation appears highly questionable from a modern viewpoint.

As mentioned earlier, Galen already supposed that the treatises *Fractures* and *Joints* once formed one single treatise. When

---

[44] Pétrequin (1877–78), 1.552–8.   [45] Craik (2015), 168.

considering all the Hippocratic writings on bone surgery, in his introduction to *Surgery*, Littré (III, 270) goes further in assuming that at one
point there was an even bigger Hippocratic work on this topic that was
never edited the way that the author originally intended. Indeed,
multiple parallels and textual interdependencies[46] between the single
surgical treatises of the *Corpus* suggest such a theory. Littré regards
the five Hippocratic treatises on bone surgery as fragments of this
large surgical work: *Fractures*, *Joints* and *Wounds in the Head* are
seen as parts that can be put into a certain order; *Surgery* is seen as
either an excerpt or a sketch for the big surgical work and its position
(before or after *Fractures*) is impossible to determine. *Mochlicon* is, in
contrast, not a separate part, but rather an abridgement of *Joints*.
Given the elaborate stylisation of *Fractures* and *Joints* and the characteristic and unique tone of the author, it seems implausible that this
very person also wrote the other surgical treatises. Littré's hypothesis
can hardly be advocated with regards to *Fractures* and *Joints* in their
present state: it does, however, make sense with regards to an older
precursor treatise of *Fractures* and *Joints*, perhaps being stylistically
more sober than the present treatises and of which *Mochlicon* might
be an abridgement, if not directly derived from *Fractures* and *Joints*.

SURGERY OF THE SOFT TISSUES (SORES, WOUNDS, AND MISSILES)

Unlike bone surgery, which is well represented in the *Hippocratic
Corpus*, only one minor work on trauma surgery of the soft tissues has
come down to us, namely *Sores*. Because other writings on this subject
are lacking, Hippocratic surgery was basically understood as bone
surgery by modern scholars. Yet, a treatise with the title *Wounds
and Missiles* existed, which is likely to have been the main
Hippocratic work on trauma surgery of the soft tissues. Before turning
to this treatise, *Sores* will first briefly be characterised. Treatments for
traumatic lesions (for example from injuries, burns, etc.) as well as for

---

46   These mutual interdependencies are comprehensively discussed by Pétrequin in his
     prefaces to the respective treatises.

different kinds of chronic ulcers are presented in this work; both types of injury are designated with the Greek term *hélkos*. Thus, *Sores* does not focus exclusively on trauma surgery, but also on non-trauma surgery of the soft tissues. A peculiarity of the therapy taught is the administration of evacuating measures and laxatives to promote wound healing. Intertextual examinations have indicated numerous parallels between *Sores* and other surgical writings of the *Hippocratic Corpus*, especially with *Wounds in the Head*.[47]

Whereas *Sores* only deals with smaller lesions, *Wounds and Missiles* was devoted to severe injuries. The first part of this double treatise was entitled *Deadly Wounds*. Fragments of this work can be found in the writings by Galen as well as the Byzantine writers Paul of Aegina, Eustathius, and Theophilus Protospatharius. An analysis of the fragmentary material permits an approximate insight into the contents of this lost work. According to the fragments, the Hippocratics already knew how to suture penetrating abdominal wounds. A suture of the abdominal wall was called "gastrorrhaphíē" (lit. "suture of the abdomen") in antiquity. This term was already used in the lost Hippocratic writing *Deadly Wounds*, as one fragment transmitted by Theophilus Protospatharius clearly indicates.[48] According to further fragments of *Wounds and Missiles*, treating injured inner organs apparently consisted mainly of drug therapy. Hereby the advice was given to administer drugs as directly and as close to the site of injury as possible, lest their effect be attenuated or diluted. Thus, upper gastrointestinal lesions were treated by administering oral drugs, while lower ones were cured using clysters.[49] Erasistratus of Alexandria (third century BC) seems to have been heir to this ancient Hippocratic doctrine of pharmacotherapy. He opened the (intact!) abdomen of a patient suffering from liver disease in order to apply the drugs directly to the organ.[50] The intention seems to have

---

[47]   Pétrequin (1877–78), 1. 260–70; M. Hanson (1999), 53. A common authorship of the two treatises has, however, recently been disproved by computer-assisted stylometric analysis (Labiano [2014], 123).

[48]   Witt (2009), 212–23.   [49]   Ibid., 231–2.

[50]   Caelius Aurelianus *Chronic Diseases* 3 4.65, ed. Bendz (1990–3), 2.716.

been, again, to place the drugs as near to the site of disease as possible. As in *Sores*, also evacuating measures and laxatives were used to treat deadly wounds in *Wounds and Missiles*. The second part of the lost treatise dealt with the extraction of spears, arrows, and similar weapons from injured patients. In the treatise *Wounds in the Head*, war surgery is briefly mentioned, which may be seen as an allusion or cross reference to this part. According to the fragments, several special extracting instruments were mentioned here. Various sophisticated methods of extraction were described depending on the type of weapon (e.g., with or without barbs); for example, some barbs were covered with pieces of reed prior to extraction. If the weapon was not visible, probes were used. If it was hidden within the soft tissues, methods were taught on how to cut the adjacent tissues and enlarge the entry channel of the weapon in order to remove it without causing too much damage.

The Hippocratic writings on emergency surgery when taken together, including the lost treatise *Wounds and Missiles*, form a harmonious ensemble in which bone and soft tissue surgery are almost equally well represented. *Wounds in the Head* fills the gap that was left by *Fractures* and *Joints*, in which the treatment of injuries of the neurocranium was not outlined. *Wounds and Missiles*, in turn, fills the gap that was left by *Sores* and *Wounds in the Head*, in which there is no discussion of severe injuries and war wounds, even though this subject matter is internally suggested in Hippocratic surgery by (1) allusions to war surgery given in *Wounds in the Head* and (2) the lack of a discussion of severe wounds in *Sores*. Given this apparent unity of the Hippocratic treatises (judging solely by the fragmentary material of the lost work) it seems possible that there was not only a big treatise on bone surgery that was later split up into several smaller ones, as Littré suggested for the writings on bone surgery, *Surgery*, *Fractures*, *Joints* and *Wounds in the Head*. The original treatise may have been even bigger and could have encompassed both bone and soft tissue surgery. Thus, the four treatises mentioned as well as *Sores* and *Wounds and Missiles* could all be descendants of one large work or, rather, an archive on emergency surgery that was never published as originally intended, but instead divided into several treatises by somebody else, treatises that were in turn re-elaborated by several different authors.

NON-TRAUMA SURGERY OF THE SOFT TISSUES

One paradox of Hippocratic surgery remains, as already noted earlier: the almost complete absence of purely elective non-trauma surgery. It has been mentioned that in writings that otherwise focus on emergency surgery some elective forms of treatment are included, such as treatments for congenital malformations, non-traumatic ulcers, and so on. There are, however, no works transmitted in the Hippocratic collection that exclusively deal with the elective branch of soft tissue surgery, except for *Haemorrhoids* and *Fistulas*. In these treatises, which are somewhat thematically detached from the other surgical writings of the *Corpus*, treatments for haemorrhoids, anal prolapse, and fistulas are outlined. In *Fistulas* 4 a method for treatment of fistulas by gradually cutting them with a tied thread is described. This technique was later called *apolínōsis* – literally 'constricting with a linen thread' – and is today still known by the name of 'cutting seton technique'. We hear of only one further Hippocratic treatise on elective surgery, a work on the surgery of tumours (or rather cysts) filled with liquid or mucous substances. In *Joints* 40, the author announces that he plans to write this work, but no traces of it survive, if it was written at all. In other treatises of the *Corpus* further elective operations are referred to, such as the removal of nasal polyps, the puncturing of pleura empyema, of liver abscesses, and of the peritoneal cavity (in order to drain ascites).[51] These procedures are mentioned only in passing without any clear description.

Fridolf Kudlien suggested dating Hippocratic treatises dealing with non-trauma surgery to the period of the third century BC or later, as it was only 'around 300 BC that the reluctance to cut was

---

[51]   Nasal polyps: *Affections* 5, pleura empyema: *Aphorisms* 6.27, *Diseases* 2.47, 3.16, draining of ascites *Aphorisms* 6.27, *Affections* 22, liver abscesses: *Aphorisms* 7.45.

overcome.'[52] This hypothesis, however, cannot explain that the author of *Joints* announces a treatise on 'tumour' surgery and that *Haemorrhoids* and *Fistulas*, treatises on non-trauma surgery that are commonly dated to the same period as *Fractures* and *Joints*, have come down to us as part of the *Corpus*. It is therefore evident that, besides emergency surgery, the Hippocratics of the classical period must already have practised some non-trauma surgery of the soft tissues as well. At one time, several treatises on this subject were probably available to the Hippocratics, of which *Haemorrhoids* and *Fistulas* are the only surviving examples. It has even been speculated that *Haemorrhoids* and *Fistulas* were once parts of a more comprehensive surgical manual (it must have been a work of elective soft tissue surgery then),[53] but there is otherwise no evidence for this assumption.

THE REJECTION OF LITHOTOMY

The best-known passage in the *Corpus* that concerns non-trauma surgery is the rejection of lithotomy as expressed in the Hippocratic Oath, which is a work that is, like the surgical treatises, listed in Erotian's index of the most authentic Hippocratic writings. Yet, the prohibition in the Oath to cut stones is striking, because since Alexandrian times, this procedure seems to have been a standard operation: it is described by Celsus in the first century AD, Antyllus in the second, and Paul of Aegina in the seventh. There have been various attempts to explain this paradox, as Leven outlined in Chapter 7 on medical ethics in this volume. Very recently parts of an ancient commentary on the Oath surfaced in Arabic translation, including this particular passage on surgery. The commentary is ascribed to Galen in the Arabic tradition (a fact that is commonly accepted) and is, without any doubt, the translation of a Greek original.[54] Interestingly, the commentator, our only source for an antique interpretation of this passage, understands it as being a ban

---

[52] See Kudlien (1961), 331–2.   [53]   See Craik (2015), 94.
[54]   See Magdelaine and Mouton (2017, in press); see also Overwien (2012a), 82.

on lithotomy, not on surgery in general. The reason for this ban was due to the fact – he explains – that especially lithotomy tended to attract charlatans. This operation, he states, was often unnecessarily and incompetently performed and quack doctors fraudulently presented fake stones to their patients in order to simulate a successful surgery. To distance oneself from these quacks this operation was banned in the Oath, as the commentator informs us.[55] This explanation appears fairly plausible, also with reference to *Fractures* and *Joints*, treatises in which charlatanry is constantly fought. It must, however, be kept in mind that there was hardly a direct exegetical tradition of this passage going back to Hippocratic times. The reason given must rather be considered an explanation from the Roman Imperial period, although it certainly reflects older Alexandrian exegesis. The original reason for the rejection of lithotomy may therefore have been completely different.

Elsewhere, I have tried to explain this paradox based on the 'intrinsic' evidence that we can derive from the *Hippocratic Corpus*: the role of non-trauma surgery in this collection, the very nature of lithotomy and the social standing of the Hippocratics.[56] Non-trauma surgery is explicitly advocated only in such cases in which it does no harm. For instance, the author of *Haemorrhoids* 2 states that 'these [surgical procedures] seem to be dangerous, but in fact will do no harm.' Likewise, in *Joints* 40, the author stressed that puncturing ganglion-like tumours does not cause any harm to the patient, as we have seen earlier. Lithotomy, in contrast, was one of the most risky and audacious procedures of elective non-trauma surgery in antiquity, almost certainly causing complications in patients.[57] Elective non-trauma surgery was apparently avoided by the Hippocratics and practised only in cases in which the risk of endangering the patient could practically be ruled out. This may also be a plausible explanation as to

---

[55] I owe this information to Jean-Michel Mouton and Caroline Magdelaine, Paris, who are currently preparing an annotated critical edition of the hitherto unknown Arabic fragments of this commentary that were discovered by Jean-Michel Mouton.

[56] Witt (2014b).   [57] Lichtenthaeler (1984), 172–3.

why this branch of surgery is so poorly attested in the *Corpus*. The apparent tendency of the Hippocratics to avoid riskier forms of non-trauma surgery may be due to their social standing, above all their aristocratic background; the Hippocratics traced their origin to Asclepius, they had privileges in the temple at Delphi, and so on.[58] With reference to this aristocratic code of ethics scholars usually explain why the Hippocratic doctors were driven by a strive for wealth, glory (*tímē*), and a good reputation (*dóxa*) as opposed to altruistic motives, which becomes clear throughout the surgical treatises.[59] In hopeless cases, for example, in which the doctor's reputation was likely to suffer and the patient would not have any benefit from receiving treatment, it was recommended to abandon the patient rather than to treat him.[60] But even in cases of bladder stones, which can in principle be treated successfully through surgery, comparable thoughts might have compelled Hippocratic physicians to not perform an operation. Lithotomy is a risky intervention that could be detrimental to a physician's reputation, either because of the complications involved or because people associated this operation with charlatanry. The Oath left it to those 'who are craftsmen in this kind of work'.[61] This might be interpreted in a similar way as the refusal to treat hopeless cases: refusing this kind of treatment was intended to save the Hippocratics' reputation, which was judged as being more important than providing help under all circumstances.

STONECUTTERS?

The wording 'craftsmen in this kind of work' in the Oath allegedly referred to stonecutters, semi-professional healers, as they are known from the Middle Ages and early modern times; or to surgeons

---

58   Witt (2014b), 109–10.   59   Ibid.,2014b 106–8.

60   See especially *Fractures* 36 and *Joints* 63. For the Hippocratic refusal of treatment see von Staden (1990); Wittern (1979); and Chapter 7 by Leven in this volume.

61   Although this statement resembles *Joints* 63 at first sight, it has been pointed out by Kudlien (1978), 259, that the vocabulary is clearly distinct: in *Joints* physicians (*iētroí*) are addressed as opposed to craftsmen (*ergáteis ándres*) in the Oath.

'specialising' in stonecutting, to whom patients are referred.[62] Then the passage would indicate that general medicine and surgery were already separated at that time.[63] Both assumptions, however, seem to be anachronistic: (1) stonecutter craftsmen are not attested in antiquity. In this period of time there was no distinction between 'academic physicians' and 'surgical craftsmen' as was the case in medieval and early modern Europe. There was no academic formation for physicians who were, apart from that, generalists and practised surgery as well as other aspects of medicine.[64] (2) According to Celsus it was only in Alexandrian times (from the third century BC onwards) that therapeutic medicine split into the three different branches of dietetics, pharmacy, and surgery.[65] Thus, it hardly seems plausible to assume that a sub-specialisation of the surgical branch resulting in the specialty profession of lithotomy surgeons could have existed, given that in the fifth century BC there was no proof that different subject areas of medicine even existed. A possible clue for interpreting this passage might be seen in the decisively pejorative ring to it, which was already noted by Charles Lichtenthaeler. Hippocratic doctors would never speak of their 'work' or 'job' (*prêxis*), but always of their 'art' (*téchnē*).[66] Nor are the Hippocratics 'craftsmen' (*ergáteis*), but rather prestigious doctors with an aristocratic family tradition. The phrase "I will leave [stonecutting] to those who are craftsmen in this kind of work" can thus be understood to mean that risky types of surgery were not undertaken by aristocratic Hippocratic physicians, but instead left for ordinary doctors who did not practise medicine and surgery as a 'noble' art, but rather as a craft, which seems to apply to most physicians outside of the Hippocratic circle.

The interpretation here attempted of the ban on lithotomy can explain several peculiarities of Hippocratic surgery simultaneously: the fact that only a few, rather simple forms of non-trauma surgery are

---

[62]   See Lichtenthaeler (1984), 167–9, for a refutation of these theses.
[63]   Such an assumption is refuted by both Edelstein (1987 [orig. 1943]), 30 and Lichtenthaeler (1984), 171–2.
[64]   See Lichtenthaeler (1984), 169.   [65]   Celsus *On Medicine*, prooem. 9.
[66]   Lichtenthaeler (1984), 172.

attested for in the *Hippocratic Corpus* and that it is stressed that the few interventions described 'Do no harm.' Furthermore, this explanation takes into account that 'cutting' can refer to nothing but non-trauma surgery; it thus does not establish a contradiction to the preserved surgical writings of the *Corpus* (writings mainly on trauma surgery), even when interpreting 'cutting' in a broader sense and not just with reference to lithotomy. The fact that lithotomy was rejected is explained here in a way that is somehow similar to Edelstein, namely with reference to a code of ethics that are common to a particular, limited group. But there is no need to detach the Oath from the *Corpus* and speculate on possible Pythagorean or other influences, as Edelstein has done. It is sufficient to refer to the aristocratic code of ethics of the Hippocratics, in which treatment is refused in the case that the image and repute of the physician is likely to suffer. The refusal of lithotomy can probably best be interpreted in this way.

GYNAECOLOGICAL SURGERY

For historical reasons, it is arguable whether a chapter on Hippocratic surgery should include references to gynaecological surgery, as well. In antiquity, such operations are generally outlined in separate gynaecological writings and scarcely in treatises on general surgery: Celsus' surgical section includes only two gynaecological chapters, Paul of Aegina's includes four; both authors give a chapter on the excision of a dead foetus as well as one on imperforate hymen surgery.[67] Among the remnants of the Alexandrian *cheirourgoúmena* there is not one single fragment devoted to gynaecological interventions. Accordingly, modern historians of medicine tend to refer to gynaecological surgery only when studying Hippocratic gynaecology, but omit these interventions when focussing on 'Hippocratic surgery' in general.[68] Despite the historical separation of general and gynaecological

---

[67] Celsus, *On Medicine* 7.28–9 and Paul of Aegina 6.72–5.

[68] In Gurlt's and Pétrequin's studies, for example, there is no mention of gynaecological surgery. This subject is, however, treated in the gynaecological studies by Wulfsohn (1889) and Fasbender (1897).

surgery, the latter will be discussed here briefly, not only for the sake of completeness, but also because these interventions are clearly classifiable as *cheirourgía* in the ancient sense of the word. Surgical interventions in Hippocratic gynaecological writings are performed in two different contexts: in the context of obstetrics and with regards to general pathologies of the female genitalia. Several techniques on how to change foetal malpositions are mentioned in the form of a shaking of the mother and special version manoeuvres. Whether these latter versions were external (by manipulating the abdomen from the outside) or internal (by intravaginal and intrauterine manipulations) is not entirely clear from the rather vague descriptions. If the infant's limbs prolapsed during delivery and thus presented an obstacle for childbirth, then the limbs were repositioned into the uterus. If the embryo had died, the cervix was manipulated using probes in order to promote the expulsion of the dead foetus. If it could not be extracted manually, it was cut out. This operation is described in the treatise *On the Excision of the Foetus*, in which only the first chapter deals with this subject. There are two further descriptions of this operation in *Diseases of Women* 1 (chapter 70) and *Diseases of Women* 3 (chapter 37). As mentioned previously, both Celsus and Paul discuss this operation within the surgical sections of their respective works.

Beyond obstetrics, manipulations were used in order to remove excrescences from the outer genitalia and the cervix. To cure infertility, the removal of 'a membrane at the mouth of the uterus'[69] is recommended; this was evidently a case of imperforate hymen. A cause for infertility that is frequently mentioned in the gynaecological writings of the *Corpus* is 'stenosis of the cervix'. There were surgical attempts to cure this condition by dilating the cervix with probes and introducing pessaries. Several methods to cure vaginal and uterine prolapse were available at the time, also surgical ones. There was a manoeuvre that attempted to reposition prolapsed genitalia by tying the woman upside down to a ladder and then manually

---

[69]   *Nature of Women* 67 (7.402 L.).

repositioning the prolapsed genitalia while shaking the ladder.[70] This procedure somehow parallels the orthopaedic succussions with a ladder that are described in *Joints* 42 (see earlier). Another method to cure genital prolapse consisted of making multiple incisions on the surface of the prolapsed uterus followed by pharmaceutically inducing an inflammation, so that the uterus stays in place after repositioning and scar contraction. All in all, Hippocratic gynaecological surgery techniques seem similar in nature to the interventions of Hippocratic non-trauma surgery: they are rather simple and not very audacious, ensuring that there is no particular danger for the patient as in, for example, lithotomy. Finally, it can also be observed that female healers or rather doctors (*akestrídes, iētreúousai*) are mentioned in the gynaecological writings.[71] There is almost no information available on whether women were treated differently than men in surgery and what role female doctors played during a patient's treatment. In the surgical treatise *Haemorrhoids*, it is mentioned, in the context of treating haemorrhoids in women (chapter 9), that a certain medication was 'given to be anointed'. This might indicate that either the woman herself or possibly another woman applied the drugs.[72] There was a certain tactfulness when treating women's intimate parts; however, further details on social respect towards women in surgery are unavailable in the transmitted writings of the *Corpus*.

CONCLUSION

Hippocratic surgery can be evaluated best if it is divided into trauma and non-trauma surgery, and further divided into bone and soft tissue surgery. In the case of trauma surgery, the major writings on bone surgery have been preserved, whereas the main work on soft tissue surgery, *Wounds and Missiles*, is lost today and can be assessed only through the surviving fragments. Internal cross-references and allusions within the traumatological writings suggest that there might once have been a very comprehensive precursor work or, rather,

---

[70]   Diseases of Women 2.144 (8.316–318 L.).   [71]   See Fasbender (1897), 137–8.
[72]   See Craik (2015), 95.

a Hippocratic archive of emergency surgery from which the treatises *Surgery, Joints, Fractures, Wounds in the Head, Sores,* and probably also the lost *Wounds and Missiles* are fragments. Despite marked coherence in content and more or less overt cross-references there are stylistic differences among these writings suggesting that material that was originally related was later rewritten by different authors. Whereas the Hippocratics practised all types of emergency surgery, including therapies of injured organs and abdominal wall sutures, elective non-trauma surgery seems to have been performed only if it was not particularly risky or detrimental to the Hippocratic doctors' reputation. Today, the only surviving traces of Hippocratic elective surgery are the treatises *Haemorrhoids* and *Fistulas*. Further treatises on minor elective surgery may have existed, of which, however, no traces remain.

11 Female Patients

Lesley Dean-Jones

INTRODUCTION

In the first century AD, the doctor Soranus argued against the position that women needed a branch of medicine particular to themselves outside of conditions of the reproductive system. In a sense the Hippocratics are in accord with Soranus: women need a different medicine from men only when their reproductive system is compromised. But for the Hippocratic authors a woman's reproductive system comprised most of her body. A Hippocratic doctor need not take sex into account when reducing a fractured humerus, but many, if not most, would consider sex important in determining the treatment of, say, *phthísis* ('wasting') or gout.[1] This did not lead to any ancient Greek doctor becoming anything like an obstetrician or gynaecology specialist. Indeed many Hippocratic authors evince appreciation for input from their female patients in a way that has no parallel with their male patients. This is at least in part due to a belief in a cognitive break between what they perceive as a subjective experience of the male body and the experience of being female, which they can access only at second-hand.[2] I will begin by summarising the nature of the gynaecological texts in the *Corpus* and then outline the access that Hippocratic doctors had to female patients. I will move on to describe the model of the female body which emerges from the gynaecological texts and the wide range of conditions accounted for by specifically female anatomy and physiology. The final section will

[1]   *Phthísis* is probably to be identified with pulmonary tuberculosis; see Grmek (1983b), 183–8.
[2]   See Dean-Jones (1995).

show how the same model underlies women's treatment and differentiates their diseases from those of men in the rest of the *Corpus*.

THE GYNAECOLOGICAL TREATISES

The gynaecological works of the *Hippocratic Corpus* comprise eight treatises: (1) *Diseases of Women* 1 and 2 contain the bulk of material dealing with female anatomy, physiology, and pathology as well as many issues of reproduction. (2) *Sterility* is a continuation of *Diseases of Women* 2, but focuses primarily on causes and treatment for infertility. Some of the material in these books may date from the first half of the fifth century BC, but the ancient editor who compiled them also inserted later material, including an independent treatise on women's diseases written by the author of *Generation* and *Nature of the Child*. It has become standard to refer to three layers – A, B, and C – within *Diseases of Women* 1 and 2 and *Sterility*. (3) *Nature of Women* contains descriptions of female diseases and remedies which correspond to what are considered the earlier sections of *Diseases of Women* 1 and 2 and *Sterility*. (4) *Superfetation* also includes some material found in *Diseases of Women* 1 and 2 and *Sterility*. The first part of the treatise focuses on the problems of pregnancy and childbirth and the second part on sterility. The treatise takes its name from the topic of the first chapter: the rare occurrence of a second conception in an already pregnant woman. (5) *Excision of the Foetus* is a very short treatise on childbirth and its attendant problems, which also takes its title from the topic of the first chapter. (6) *Seven Month Infant* and *Eight Month Infant*, which deal with embryology and the problems of premature births, are a single treatise most often referred to as *Eight Month Infant*, though the title *Seven Month Infant* is sometimes retained when referring to the chapters that formed what was traditionally thought to be a self-contained work. Similarly, (7) *Generation* and *Nature of the Child* form one continuous treatise on conception, gestation, and parturition, with *Generation* being used to refer to the first eleven chapters. There is in addition a very short treatise, maybe a fragment of a treatise on epilepsy, (8) *Diseases of Girls*.[3]

Generation and *Nature of the Child*, and therefore the latest sections of *Diseases of Women* 1 and 2 and *Sterility*, are the most reliably datable of the treatises. *Diseases* 4, which is by the same author, is concerned to reduce the humours into a tetrad schema similar to that of *Nature of Man*, with the watery humour *hýdrops* taking the place of black bile. It should therefore be dated to the end of the fifth or the beginning of the fourth century BC.[4] The other gynaecological treatises, too, are thought to have taken their present shape around this time, although they probably enshrine much older material.

FEMALE CLIENTELE OF THE HIPPOCRATICS

The evidence of the *Epidemics* suggests that Hippocratic physicians did not have as many women patients as men. There are twice as many male case histories as female. Many of these female patients are suffering from a condition attributed to a malfunction of the reproductive system. There might have been fewer female case histories, because the authors bothered recording them only if it was a gynaecological complaint, as Japp Mansfeld suggested in a personal communication, but this seems unlikely. A more probable explanation is that many women preferred to turn to traditional female healers when they fell ill, and availed themselves of Hippocratic medicine only at the insistence of their husbands or fathers, who might be more inclined to intervene, if the birth of a healthy heir was at stake.[5]

Women's preference for a traditional healer is also a possible explanation for the far wider range of medicinal substances in the

---

[3] All of these, apart from *Diseases of Women* 1 and 2, are now available in translation in the Loeb Classical Library. I will cite Loeb references by edition as well as Littré (L.) references. Translations of sections of *Diseases of Women* 1 and 2 can be found in Hanson (1975) and Lefkowitz and Fant (2005), 233–7, 38–9.

[4] Lonie (1981), 54–62, 71.

[5] Lloyd (1983), 69–70; Dean-Jones (1994), 33–5, 136. There are also far fewer female case histories in the so-called Epidaurian *iámata*, inscriptions in the temple that record various cures.

gynaecological treatises than in the rest of the Corpus. *Diseases of Women* 1 and 2 and *Nature of Women* alone account for more than half of all named medicinal substances in the *Corpus*, the majority of them found in long lists of substances designed to cast out material from the womb and cleanse it.[6] The drug preparations mentioned in the gynaecology are often much more elaborate than those in the rest of the *Corpus*, too, occasionally including animal excreta, which does not appear outside the gynaecology.[7] The cure for bad breath mentioned below (p. 257) involves a concoction of the head of a hare, three mice or rats (two of them having had all their innards removed apart from their brains and liver) burnt up and mixed together in a mortar of marble or white stone, greasy wool, water, honey, anise, dill, myrrh, and white wine. The author remarks that this recipe is called an Indian medicine. Apart from the myrrh, most of these ingredients would be readily available to any doctor in Greece. Exotic elements were probably added to more common ingredients because of associations with traditional sacred rituals which could give the appearance of enhanced efficacy.[8] It has been suggested that the Hippocratics adopted traditional therapies for women more often than men to attract their custom away from traditional healers.[9] Female healers working alongside the Hippocratic physician have a shadowy presence in the gynaecology, in a way they do not in the rest of the *Corpus*. On the other hand, some Hippocratic authors make mention of a *Pharmakîtis*, presumably a handbook of sorts on medicinal substances.[10] It has also been suggested that each doctor kept a record of his own preferred treatments and used them

---

[6]   Riddle (1987), 39 n. 32; von Staden (2008); Totelin (2009), 111–39.

[7]   See von Staden (1992).

[8]   See Lloyd (1983), 82 and Laskaris (1999). Totelin (2009), 125–31, argues that the exotic and expensive ingredients in Hippocratic recipes were aimed at a clientele who wished to be considered elite. She terms this *Haute Médecine*.

[9]   Hanson (1991), 78–9; Totelin (2009), 138–9, suggests that 'gynaecology may have been a privileged area for experimentation with recipe writing', because the womb could be treated both externally and internally.

[10]   See Chapter 9 by Totelin on therapeutics in this volume.

on men as often as on women.[11] Even if this were so, it is noteworthy that pharmacology is integrated into the gynaecological texts in a way it is not in other treatises in the *Corpus*.

It is possible that the Hippocratics were more ready to learn from women and the methods of traditional healers of women, because they had only objective knowledge of the female body. They refer to 'experienced' women patients in a way they do not for men,[12] and they record the information they receive from their female patients more punctiliously than from their male ones. In the *Epidemics*, the authors three times report that women informed them of their subjective sensations: "It seemed to the wife of Polemarchos that something was collecting round the heart"; "The wife of Agasios seemed to hear cracking in her chest"; "The wife of Hermoptolemos claims her heart 'went lame' on her."[13] There are no comparable reports of male subjective bodily experiences.

But knowledge about the female body did not come from women's accounts alone. If a woman was considered 'experienced' she might perform necessary examinations of her own genitalia, and if not the examination could be performed by an intermediary, either for reasons of modesty or because the male doctor felt a woman would have a better understanding of female genitalia than he would. But surprisingly, given that Greek women in different communities seem to have lived in greater or lesser seclusion, it is clear that male doctors often performed intimate examinations themselves.[14] They also often performed the therapy on the genitalia themselves, such as inserting pessaries in the vagina. Sometimes the therapeutic procedure went as far as the male doctor manipulating the cervix and artificially dilating it by inserting probes of incrementally greater diameter in order to

---

[11]   Craik (2006), 17; Totelin (2009), 98–102.
[12]   *Diseases of Women* 1.62 (8.126.4–19 L.). See Dean-Jones (1995), 53.
[13]   *Epidemics* 5.63 (Smith [1994], 196.9; 5.242.10 L.), 6.4.4 (Smith [1994], 248.1–2; 5.306.14 L.) and 7.11 (Smith [1994], 314.7; 5.382.15 L.). See Dean-Jones (1995), 56–7.
[14]   See Dean-Jones (1995), 42–3.

insert medications directly into the womb.[15] These procedures would have been highly dangerous.

Normal childbirth is not often referred to in the gynaecology of the *Corpus*. It would seem that a Hippocratic doctor would be called only to attend a problematic parturition. *Diseases of Women* 1.34 (8.80.4–5 L.), however, mentions that throughout labour the woman has pains at intervals because the intestines, and especially the womb, contract around the embryo. Most other accounts of parturition describe the foetus as fighting its way out of the womb.[16]

Visits of Hippocratic doctors with their female patients probably took place within the woman's home. The Oath mentions meeting women and children on entering homes, and the *arýballos* (a small ceramic vase used for perfumes and medicines) painted by the 'Clinic-painter' around 470 BC, shows no woman patient.[17]

THE SCOPE OF HIPPOCRATIC GYNAECOLOGICAL MEDICINE

The discussion of the treatment of women in the *Hippocratic Corpus* normally takes as its starting point a passage in *Diseases of Women* 1.62 (8.126.15–20 L.), where the author asserts:

> Doctors make mistakes when they do not learn the cause of the [woman's] illness accurately but proceed to treat as if they were dealing with men's diseases. I have in my time seen many women die from these types of diseases. But from the beginning you have to question her minutely about the cause. For there is a great difference between treating women's diseases and men's diseases.[18]

---

[15]   *Diseases of Women* 2.133 (8.288.12–290.6 L.).

[16]   See Hanson (1991), 87–95 and Dean-Jones (1994), 211–15. Hanson (1990), 324–30, argues for the Hippocratic conception of the womb as an inverted jar from which the foetus has to be shaken out and can sometimes get caught athwart the mouth, as an olive stone across the mouth of a jar. However, given its powers of expansion a better image would seem to be that of the wine skin. It is referred to as such at *Diseases of Women* 1.61 and 2.170 (8.124.15–21 and 350.16–17 L.) and is described as soft at *Nature of the Child* 19 (Potter [2012], 82.12; 7.532.6 L.). See Dean-Jones (1994), 65.

[17]   Denoyelle (1994), 136 n. 63.   [18]   All translations are my own.

One might imagine that this could also be the end point of the debate about whether the Hippocratics practised gender-neutral medicine, but besides the fact that the author could be in a minority of one in his point of view, we have also to consider the scope of the term 'women's diseases' (tà gynaikễia nosễmata); perhaps it simply refers to diseases of the female reproductive system. The argument against this is that the author's statement draws a parallel with 'men's dis-eases' (tà andrikà nosễmata), and in the Corpus there is no identifiable group of conditions that centres on the male reproductive system.[19] Another possibility is to take the term 'men's' (tà andriká) as a rhetorical flourish meant simply to show the inability of some doctors to differentiate diseases in female patients which arise from their reproductive system from those with some other origin which they share with men. In this case the term 'men's diseases'(tà andrikà nosễmata) would encompass all the non-reproductive diseases to which both men and women were susceptible. The strong interpreta-tion, and the one for which I will argue, is that to many a Hippocratic mind there is a dichotomy between the way women fall ill and the way men do, the way women should be treated and the way men should, and that the term 'men's' (tà andriká) is deployed to blame doctors who do not differentiate therapies according to sex even for the same symptoms.

I will describe the model of the female body that we find in the gynaecological treatises to illustrate why a Hippocratic doctor might be led to think that whatever ailment a woman suffered from should be treated with specific reference to her female anatomy and physiol-ogy. I will then adduce references from other works in the Corpus to demonstrate that the model is not restricted to the gynaecological treatises. The Hippocratics had a very strong two-body system.[20]

---

[19]   In fact there is a marked absence of references to such ailments as erectile dysfunction, which we might expect to have affected at least some men in classical Greece; see Berrey (2014).

[20]   See King (2013) for a full argument against Laqueur (1990) that the ancients had a 'one-body' system.

FEMALE ANATOMY, PHYSIOLOGY, AND PATHOLOGY IN THE GYNAECOLOGICAL TREATISES

Menstruation was fundamental to Hippocratic theories of female health and disease. *Diseases of Women* explains the process by appealing to the nature of a woman's very flesh and its difference from that of a man:[21]

> So then a woman, insofar as she is spongier, draws more of the moisture from her belly into her body than a man, and she does so more quickly. And insofar as the woman is of softer flesh, when the body is full of blood, if it does not flow out affliction ensues because the flesh has become full and heated. For a woman has hotter blood, and on account of this she is hotter than a man.[22] But if the accumulated excess flows away the affliction and the heat from the blood does not occur. Because a man has denser flesh than a woman, he does not fill up with blood to such an extent that if some part of the blood does not flow away each month an affliction supervenes; rather he draws as much as his body needs for nourishment, and his body, because it is not soft, does not become over-distended and overheated by the excess like a woman. The fact that a man works harder than a woman is a big factor in this, because hard work draws off moisture.[23]

A woman produces excess moisture in her body because she is more idle than a man and so cannot use up all her nourishment.[24] Reducing food intake or increasing exercise could perhaps eliminate this excess, but there is a teleological need for its production, the nourishment of

---

[21]   Though the Hippocratics also noted that the *phýseis* (natures) of individual women could differ according to age, humoural constitution, and so on; see Dean-Jones (1994), 121–3 and Bourbon (2008).

[22]   This view is not shared by all Hippocratic authors. Some think of a woman as colder than a man, e.g., *Sterility* 4 (Potter [2012], 342.1–2; 8.416.20–23 L.) and *Regimen* 1.34 (Jones [1931], 280.8–17; 6.512.13–19 L.). All authors, however, agree she is moister than a man.

[23]   *Diseases of Women* 1.1 (8.12–14.17–7 L.).

[24]   *Generation* and *Nature of the Child* have a slightly different account for the production of menstrual blood; see Dean-Jones (1994), 49–50, 59–60.

the embryo. This more or less disqualifies women from availing themselves of the battery of advice given by the Hippocratics on maintaining health by regimen. Most ancient Greek communities would not countenance their wives, daughters, and mothers engaging in regular running, boxing, or wrestling. Exercise is recommended for women, but always in very general terms and always with the caveat that it be gentle or light.[25] The knowledge that athletic pursuits were not available to the physician in addressing underlying conditions in his female patients would lead to a fundamental difference in approach in recommendations for keeping men and women healthy.

So, a woman's digestive system metabolises the food she eats into blood and this is drawn from her stomach by her spongy flesh. If a critical mass of blood in the flesh is reached without the woman becoming pregnant it is evacuated by the womb drawing the blood into itself through its two internal mouths (the stumps of the fallopian tubes which the Greeks would be aware of from animal butchery).[26] The critical mass normally takes about a month to accumulate, hence the term *kataménia*, 'the monthly things', for the menses. If the passages through a woman's body leading to the womb have not been widened through pregnancy (*Diseases of Women* 1.1 [8.10.1–15 L.]), this monthly drawing of the blood all at once through the body can cause a woman problems such as coldness, tiredness, headaches, sore throats, and mist in front of the eyes.[27] If she is pregnant, on the other hand, the embryo utilises the blood as it is produced and the quantity passing through the passages does not put a strain on the body. After a woman has given birth, the profuse lochial flow was thought to open up the passages and thereby to relieve the pain and discomfort of subsequent menstruation.

---

[25]   Dean-Jones (1994), 115–16.   [26]   Ibid., 4, 63–7.

[27]   *Nature of the Child* 4 (Potter [2012], 38.25–26; 7.492.21–494.2 L.); *Coan Prenotions* 537 and 541 (Potter [2010], 240. 9–11; 5.706.15–17 L.; and Potter (2010) 240.19–20; 708. 2–3 L.), see Dean-Jones (1994), 125–6. It is noteworthy that there is no mention of stomach pains caused by menstrual cramps, the most commonly reported problem in menstruation today.

The hazards of menstruation are greater if, once the blood reaches the womb, it is unable to leave the body through the cervix. Once a woman begins and continues to have sexual intercourse her cervix opens and remains open to receive the seed of the man, closing only when conception has taken place and remaining closed for the duration of pregnancy.[28] If the descent of the menses to the womb takes place while a girl is still a virgin, or if the cervix had closed over, owing to the woman ceasing to have intercourse for any reason, the blood is trapped and either festers in the womb, eats its way out through the flesh, or is drawn off to another part of the body. In the case of young girls, in particular, this can cause cognitive and affective problems leading to suicidal thoughts. The condition can be resolved naturally through a nosebleed or vomiting, but if there is no natural evacuation of the material a doctor has to intervene.[29] The most common form of intervention is to give the woman a drug that induces menstruation, an emmenagogue, either as a drink or as a pessary, aimed at opening the cervix. Of course, the Hippocratics recommend defloration by, and regular intercourse with, a husband as preventative measures preferable to treatment.[30] This contrasts with the advice that they give men on sexual intercourse, which tends more towards restraint.[31]

Another threat a woman faces if she does not have intercourse is that her womb will become too dry. In ancient Greece, it was believed that the womb could not only become displaced from a loosening of the ligaments, causing some retroversion, anteversion, or prolapse,

---

[28]   Dean-Jones (1994), 62.

[29]   The only young girl who is recorded as dying after a nosebleed is the daughter of Leonidas, *Epidemics* 7.123 (Smith (1994), 414.1–3; 5.468.5–7 L.). The Greek states that 'after she bled from the nose there was a change (*diēllagē*). The doctor did not understand. The girl died.' I believe that the order of these statements indicates that the doctor caused the girl's death by intervening after the nosebleed, which would have been sufficient to cure her had he left well alone (*diēllagē* usually signifies a change for the better); but see King (1989), who believes that the girl died because she was not old enough to benefit from a nosebleed.

[30]   See Dean-Jones (1992) for an argument that this theory may have originated with women, or at least been readily acceded to by them.

[31]   Foucault (1985, 1986).

but also that it could roam freely about the body; this is the so-called 'wandering womb' syndrome.[32] Hanson has suggested that this belief began because the male body was taken as paradigmatic of the human body, and because it contained no proper place for the womb it was thought there could not be one in the female body either.[33] I would expand upon this observation to note that the womb was in a sense considered a shared organ of reproduction into which both male and female placed their seed. It was located in the woman's body but was not entirely hers, and in fact could be better controlled by her male partner than by herself. The Hippocratics do not give the womb an animal consciousness as Plato did, who claimed that it issued from the vagina looking for intercourse, when deprived for too long.[34] Instead they believe that if the womb were not irrigated by regular infusions of male semen, it would be drawn to alternative sources of moisture within the body. The areas of the body to which the womb was attracted were the brain, heart, liver, and diaphragm, each of which could be thought to house the consciousness at the time that the Hippocratics were writing.[35] Treatment for this condition could involve hanging the woman upside down overnight for a prolapsed womb[36] or pushing down on her diaphragm and binding her tightly below the breasts.[37] The most common treatment, however, was 'odour therapy', which involved sitting a woman over one strong-smelling substance, or inserting it in her vagina, and wafting another beneath her nose.[38] A pleasant smell attracted the womb; a fetid smell

---

[32]   I believe that the vocabulary used in the *Hippocratic Corpus* and the methods used to treat the condition imply that the Hippocratics believed the womb could physically relocate in the body, see Dean-Jones (1995), 69–77. Hanson (1991), 81–7, argues that the symptoms ascribed to womb movements resulted from the uterus pushing against bodily structures next to it causing a feeling of 'overcrowding'. See Faraone (2011) for an argument that the concept developed because the womb was viewed as a source of disease in other parts of the body.

[33]   Hanson (1991), 82.   [34]   *Timaeus* 91b–d.   [35]   Manuli (1983), 149–204.

[36]   *Diseases of Women* 2.144 (8.318.21–322.2 L.); *Sterility* 3 (Potter [2012], 392.15–18; 8.462.3–5 L.); *Nature of Women* 5 (Potter [2012], 198.20–24; 7.318.11–14 L.).

[37]   *Diseases of Women* 2.127 and 149 (8.272.16–17 L. and 8.324.17 L.).

[38]   For example, *Diseases of Women* 1.13, 2.126 and 142 (8.50.19–52.8, 270.20–272.1, 314. 22–4 L.); *Nature of Women* 3 and 14 (Potter [2012], 196.3–5 and 212.16–18; 7.314.21 and 332.6–7 L.).

repelled it. If a woman seemed to be having trouble conceiving, a variant of this therapy was used as a diagnostic test. A strong-smelling pessary would be inserted into her vagina, or she would sit over a strong-smelling substance, and after an interval of a day or so the doctor would test to see if he could smell the substance on her breath or hair.[39] If he could not, it meant there was a blockage in her passages, which was preventing her seed from reaching her womb.[40] It is in situations of this sort that the Hippocratics would deploy their assortment of emmenagogues, both orally and vaginally. To loosen the menstrual fluid they also advised warm baths, poultices, and so on.

But errant menses and wombs could be held responsible for much more than blocking the seed. As previously mentioned, they could cause affective and cognitive problems in young girls, problems that were aligned with epilepsy in males, an affliction associated with phlegm in *Sacred Disease*. So some Hippocratics at least, when presented with the exact same symptoms in a boy and a girl, would take their sex into consideration when treating them. In the gynaecology trapped menses cause, and released menses cure a wide variety of diseases that we would not consider gynaecological, for example, headaches, consumption, gout, and haemorrhoids.[41]

There is even a specific cure for bad breath in women nestled between descriptions of treatment for a phlegmatic womb and inflamed breasts. The section begins, 'When a woman gives off a bad smell from her mouth and the gums are black and painful ... ' (*Diseases of Women* 2.185 [8.366.6–20 L.]). This is probably to be

---

39 For example, *Diseases of Women* 2.146 (8.322.10–14 L.); *Nature of Women* 96 (Potter [2012], 302.14–15; 7.412.19–414.3 L.); and *Sterility* 7 (Potter [2012], 349.11–350.2; 8.422.23–424.13 L.).

40 These procedures imply that women were commonly thought to contribute seed to the conception of a child, as is stated explicitly in *Generation* and *Regimen* 1; see Dean-Jones (1994), 153–60.

41 On headaches: *Nature of Women* 18 (Potter [2012], 218.23; 7.338.7 L.); consumption: *Diseases of Women* 1.2 (8.18.16–18 L.). Gout and haemorrhoids are attributed to suppressed menses in non-gynaecological treatises, *Aphorisms* 6.29 (Jones [1931], 186, lines. 3–4; 4.570.6 L.) and *Epidemics* 4.24 (Smith [1994], 116, line 7; 5.164.9–10 L.) respectively.

explained along the same lines as the odour therapies, a connection between mouth and vagina. There is no corresponding cure for bad breath in men in the *Corpus*, but the *Philogélōs* (a collection of jokes put together in the second century AD, though containing some jokes dating from much earlier) has a section of twelve jokes on 'smelly mouths', in one of which (235) the patient complains to his doctor that his uvula has decayed (*'katébē'*, which can also mean 'has gone down'). The doctor recoils from his examination and says "No, your anus has come up." Whether or not the Hippocratics associated halitosis with emanations from the bottom of the body, *Diseases of Women* 2.185 presents the suggested cure as specifically suited to women.

One of the best ways to secure the health of a woman was to have her conceive, a course of action clearly not viable for male patients. The foetus anchored the womb in place and used up the excess blood in a woman's body. It also drew the blood to itself in the womb at a steady pace throughout the month, thereby avoiding the pain and discomfort caused by the menses being drawn through the narrow passages to the womb all at once. Once a woman had given birth the abundant lochial flow broke down her body, opening up the passages and making her menstrual mechanism less likely to malfunction in the future, another reason why it was considered healthy for a pubescent girl to marry.

WOMEN'S ILLNESSES OUTSIDE THE GYNAECOLOGICAL TREATISES

To this point, I have been discussing only complaints detailed in the gynaecological works. Clearly emmenagogues and uterine odour therapies would not be applicable to male patients. The question remains to what extent these therapies were practised on women when they presented with the same symptoms as men. To what extent did the Hippocratic physician think of the medicine outside of the gynaecological treatises as a male-centred or gender-neutral medicine?

The basic assumptions of many Hippocratic treatises have been outlined in previous chapters. To recap, health was generally thought to be a matter of balancing various fluids either held in reservoirs or flowing round the body. Most men could achieve this by monitoring the quality and quantity of the food intake and exercise; they did not need a monthly evacuation as a matter of course to keep their bodies from building up an excess, though the more watery their constitution the more artificial purging by vomiting and hellebore is recommended for men in *Regimen* 1.35.[42] When a man did fall ill, the Hippocratics hoped for an *apóstasis*, a pooling of whatever bodily fluid was causing problems into one location in the body, so that the excess material could drain off naturally. *Diseases* 4.10 mentions the four natural outlets for these purges: mouth, nose, anus, and urethra.[43] The omission of a reference to the vagina here is striking. Of course, it could mean that this particular doctor saw menstruation as a useful purge only for specifically reproductive disorders, but if so this is not a view shared by every Hippocratic author. *Epidemics* 1.16 in describing a dysentery epidemic in Thasos states:[44]

> Although many women fell ill, there were fewer of them than men and they died less often . . . . In most cases menstruation appeared during the fevers, and for many unmarried girls, this was the first time it happened. Some of them bled from the nose, and there were occasions when nosebleeds and menstruation appeared in the same patients . . . . I do not know of anybody who died among those for whom any of these things occurred sufficiently.

Helen King has noted that there were two possible results for a Hippocratic physician when treating a patient: health or death.[45] Of the approximately 130 female case histories in the *Epidemics*, no woman is recorded as having menstruated and subsequently died.[46]

---

[42]   Ed. Jones (1931), 284.14–286.17; 6.516.2–518.2 L.; *Regimen in Health* 5 (Jones [1931], 50.1–52.21; 6.78.3–80.17 L.) details the use of emetics and enemas in a man's health maintenance regimen.

[43]   Corresponding to chapter 41 in Littré (Potter [2012], 124.9–15; 7.562.8–10 L.).

[44]   Ed. Jones (1923), 170.4–16; 2.646.9–648.5 L.   [45]   King (2005), 156.

[46]   Dean-Jones (1994), 144–6.

And not all of the female patients in the *Epidemics* were suffering from what we might consider reproductive ailments. Two women, for example, were said to be suffering from depression. One menstruated and one did not; the former survived and the latter did not.[47]

Yet, despite the importance of menstruation as a prognosticator in women's illnesses, *Prognostic* and *Regimen in Acute Diseases* make no reference to menstruation as an indicator of a patient's health. Sometimes, Hippocratic physicians mention women as an afterthought. This indicates that they did not think of female patients when writing 'general' medicine. For instance, *Epidemics* 3.14 describes the physical characteristics of consumptives with no indication of gender at all.[48] Among other characteristics they are said to have smooth skin, bright eyes, and projecting shoulder blades. After the list the author remarks 'and women likewise'. *Airs, Waters, Places* 10 lists ailments during childbirth following a mild winter and cold spring. He concludes with the remark that 'these things happened to women, but to the rest dysentery and dry eyes'.[49]

I have argued elsewhere that differences in the nature of flesh account for the comparative scarcity of child patients in Hippocratic treatises, only in this case children's flesh is seen as more compact than male flesh as well as women's flesh.[50] The repercussions of this compactness are seen most clearly in *Places in Man* 24 which recommends the following treatment for dropsy:[51]

> Cauterise in a circle around the navel, but not right into the navel, as lightly and as superficially as possible so that it will be able to retain the water, and draw the water off each day.

The following chapter details how to treat a child suffering from the same ailment:[52]

---

[47]   *Epidemics* 3.17 cases 11 and 15 (ed. Jones [1923a], 276.1–18 and 282.7–284.2 = 3.134. 1–14 and 142.6–146.6 L.).
[48]   Ed. Jones (1923a), 10–17; 3.96.4–98.5 L.   [49]   Ibid., 100.12–14; 2.46.3–4 L.
[50]   Dean-Jones (2013).   [51]   Potter (1995), 64. 13–16; 6.316.5–7 L.
[52]   Potter (1995), 64, lines. 20–24; 6.316.11–14 L.

Make lots of small incisions with a scalpel in the parts that are
swollen and full of water; make the incisions in every part of the
body, and administer vapour-baths, and apply a warming
medication to each of the incisions.

If *apostáseis* do not form readily in a pre-pubescent child, a single
incision at the navel would not effectively drain the water from
throughout its body. Many incisions are needed all over the body
because the fluid is slow to seep through the dense flesh.[53] In the
case of women, on the other hand, the hydroptic fluid, like other
peccant humours, is drawn from the flesh along with the menstrual
blood. The author of *Diseases* 4.26 says:[54] "Women also suffer from
dropsy – on the uterus, on the stomach and on the legs: the symptoms,
too, are all the same. I have described the disease in *Diseases of
Women*." This is in all probability a reference to the many chapters
dealing with dropsy in *Diseases of Women* 1 and 2, where dropsy is
indeed usually associated with a particular organ, most often the
womb, but also the liver. In either case, women swell up just like
men suffering from dropsy, but the therapy always involves
a purgation of the womb rather than surgery.[55]

Now we cannot, of course, be sure that the author of *Places in
Man* shares this belief. It may be that he would incise his female
patients. There is nothing in the text to say that he is thinking only
of male patients and that he assumes that if a student wanted to know
how to treat a woman suffering from dropsy he would know to consult
the gynaecology.[56] The same is true of the discussion of dropsy at
Affections 22 which likewise recommends incisions by the navel
and does not explicitly exclude women from this therapy.[57] But it is
a fact that there are relatively few references to surgical intervention

[53] For further discussion of the treatment of children in the *Hippocratic Corpus*, see
      Dean-Jones (2013).
[54] Corresponding to chapter 57 in Littré (*Potter* [2012], 184.8–12; 7.612.19–22 L.).
[55] For example, *Diseases of Women* 1.59–61 (8.116.20–126.3 L.).
[56] von Staden (2008) argues that unless the sex of the patient is explicitly mentioned we
      should assume the medicine of the *Hippocratic Corpus* is gender neutral.
[57] Ed. Potter (1988b), 42.6; 6.232.13–234.14 L.

on women in the form of venesection, cupping or cauterisation in the *Hippocratic Corpus*. Of the fourteen patients who are bled in the *Epidemics*, twelve are male. In the gynaecology, venesection is occasionally recommended as a last resort if it has proved impossible to stimulate the menses or lochia in any other way.[58] The conclusion is inescapable that maybe not all, but very many Hippocratic physicians offered a different type of medicine to their male and female patients.

CONCLUSION

The model of the female body that emerges from these diverse treatises is in general consistent and coheres with female physiology and pathology in the general works of the *Corpus*, when it is differentiated from that of the male. It is a body characterised by spongy flesh, which absorbs the blood derived from nourishment that a man uses to build a bigger, stronger body and for greater physical exertion. If the woman becomes pregnant, the blood serves the function of nourishment for the foetus. If, however, it is not so used, or it is not evacuated at regular intervals, it can be trapped in the woman's body and cause a multitude of ailments, frequently leading to death. The other side of this coin is that if the regular evacuations do occur, a woman benefits from a periodic natural purgation that can prevent her succumbing to illnesses that attack men. However, because the word that the ancient medical writers used for 'patient' is an unmarked term, it is possible that some Hippocratics assimilated women's bodies to men's to a greater extent than the gynaecological authors.[59]

---

[58]   Dean-Jones (1994), 142–4.

[59]   The extent of the effect of sexual difference on disease *and* response to treatment is becoming more and more widely appreciated today (King [2005], 150–1). A recent scientific study showed that the same diet and manipulations of diet affected males and females differently because of sexual differences in the composition of microbiota in the gut (Bolnick et al. [2014]). Their concept of spongy flesh in women may have been way off base, but the Hippocratics were perhaps not as erroneous in their understanding of the extent of women's medicine as has been thought.

12 Doctors and Patients

Chiara Thumiger

INTRODUCTION

The expectations and emotions arising from medical encounters (modern or ancient) are universally among the strongest human experiences, involving danger, worries, and deep-seated feelings such as trust and fear. As a consequence, the risk of anachronistic superimpositions is especially high when we try to reconstruct the relationship of power, dependence, and assistance between doctor and patient that is preserved to us through ancient texts.[1] If the dynamics of power and submission, the manipulations, the emotions, and the negotiations that shape our own relationship to the practitioners we choose to care for our health invite a connection with the experiences of ancient patients, in fact, these relationships in Hippocratic medicine were also radically different in important ways, both in practice and ideology, and defy simplistic identifications.

A first central point is the fact that in the Hippocratic texts the doctor–patient relationship the way we intend it – a two-way exchange between the source of the therapeutic act and its receiver – is mostly not seen as a problem in need of special attention, or a topic of discussion; indeed, awareness of such a thing is hard to find in these texts. Yes, communication with the patient is valued by the Hippocratic doctor as important and even necessary, and manifestly so, as a source of precious information; the reverse, however, the personal reactions of the ill and the mutual nature of the contract

---

[1] Contributions about the topic are the fundamental, and broader discussions are provided in Gourevitch (1984); Leven (2007); Steger (2007); and Holmes (2013) for a discussion of the construction of the authority of the doctor vis-à-vis the patient; and Petridou and Thumiger (2015) on ancient patients in general, with individual studies about the Hippocratic texts (esp. chapters by Wee and Thumiger).

between healing authority and patient, rarely emerge as relevant, nor is there a direct acknowledgement of the point of view of the patient as scientifically or deontologically essential.

Several other peculiarities of our sources follow this central point. First, there is no such thing as a 'doctor figure' established as a permanent presence in the life of individual patients, groups, or communities; there is no 'family doctor', although patient cases bear witness to long-lasting visit patterns, sometimes with follow-up encounters after long pauses. Secondly, and accordingly, there is no sense of the medical duty of coaching a patient through a chronic illness, diagnosing it, and caring for him or her from crisis to recovery or death: the suggestion is rather that the recognition of a definitively hopeless case should mark the end of medical intervention. Thirdly, notwithstanding the rich and detailed accounts preserved by the patient cases of the *Epidemics*, with their many named patients and itemised illnesses, there is no appreciation of each individual in his or her psychological reactions to the illness. Named patients are representative of natural courses and as such presented as natural phenomena, not idiosyncratic experiences. This determines a form of detached reporting that is largely the product of a rhetorical strategy, the erasure from our access of the emotionality of the doctor–patient exchange that must have been there. This impersonal posture may be read as one of the distinctive ways in which the Hippocratic physician builds his own professional and scientific credibility, delimiting his own territory against the sphere of action of other healing figures, both competing to preserve the trust of current clients and win new audiences and aimed at defining his own profession as grounded on a fundamentally scientific methodology.[2]

To give concreteness to this general picture, I will begin the chapter with a survey of the factual information about the exchange between doctor and patient in Hippocratic medicine that can be gathered from the texts, the practical aspects of their relationship. These

---

[2]   On this aspect, see Holmes (2013); Thumiger (2016), 198–200.

include the nature of visitations; their frequency and duration; and the communication established between the two parties. In the second part I will concentrate on aspects of our texts that help us reconstruct the viewpoint of the professional physician as authoritative force in the exchange, on the one hand; and the elements that may guide us in a search for the point of view of the patient, on the other. Finally, I will consider the emotions associated to medicine in our texts, the emotional experience of medicalised suffering as well as medical attendance.

I will concentrate on those texts of the *Corpus* that can be considered part of the original nucleus of Hippocratic medicine, such as *Epidemics* 1 and 3, but also on treatises that can shed light on this milieu although considered by scholars of a later date (*Epidemics* 5 and 7). The gynaecological texts will also be important for our reconstruction, as well as key passages from *Affections, Regimen* and *Art* in which the supremacy of the doctor as authority figure and the possibility of informed patienthood are placed at the centre of the discussion. I shall exclude, instead, the thematically relevant information that is brought to us by the deontological treatises, which all belong to a later period (at times, as late as the imperial age) and as such would not be a relevant testimony for our cultural-historical reconstruction.[3]

SOME FACTS

The Epidemics as Source

It is from the patient case reports preserved to us by the books of the *Epidemics* that we gather the majority of the practical information we have about the nature of medical exchanges in classical Greece.[4] A figure of an itinerant physician emerges through these texts from the so-called constitutions, assessments of the locations visited in the different seasons and their effects on health, found mostly in

---

[3]   On the deontological texts see Chapter 7 by Leven in this volume.

[4]   For a general introduction to Hippocratic therapeutic practices see Jouanna (1999 [orig. 1992]), 112–40, lines 25–36; Nutton (2013 [orig. 2004]), 87–102; and Chapters 8 and 9 in this volume.

Epidemics 1 and 3, and most of all from the patient reports. The latter is rather diverse material: the patient cases include carefully crafted narratives as much as quick mentions of individual cases. This variety reflects not only the different kinds of encounter and care provided by the Hippocratic doctors, but also the textual vicissitudes that converged to form the seven books of the *Epidemics*: there is thus a wide gap between the patient reports of *Epidemics* 1 and 3, which show signs of revision and narrative awareness and are organised as diaries,[5] the numerous extended narratives of *Epidemics* 5 and 7 and the miscellaneous *Epidemics* 2, 4, and 6, where structured passages alternate with scattered notes and the use of lists of patients in an exemplary, 'statistic' spirit, to illustrate the prevalence of a pathology, for instance.[6] As one might expect, this translates into different degrees of development of individual cases, so that we can propose various typologies (without strict categorisation): (a) cases proper, with the patients' account of their medical history, description of the illness, prognosis, outcome, and daily reports; (b) long narratives, but missing some of the elements listed in (a); (c) short cases, organised around an element of relevance, constituting a segment of the illness; (d) mention of names to substantiate a general point, or add 'statistically' to an event described.

Reading these texts, in short, we deal simultaneously with possible variations in medical practices and with textual differences (in terms of style, transmission of record takings, editorial elaboration, and so on).

Itinerant Medicine

Hippocrates and his entourage of colleagues, students, and helpers, as well as other doctors of the classical period, travelled around the Aegean, visiting various locations in mainland Greece and Asia Minor. The understanding of the activity of the doctor as itinerant is traditional in Greek culture[7]; the very title *Epidemics*, which was

---

[5]   See Hellweg (1985) on these (and other) stylistic aspects of *Epidemics* 1 and 3.
[6]   See Graumann (2000) for a survey of the patients of the Hippocratic *Epidemics*.
[7]   See the famous passage in *Odyssey* 17, 383–6, where a doctor is summoned from a faraway land, mentioned by Nutton (2013 [orig. 2004]), 40–1. See also Langholf

perhaps assigned to the texts at a later stage (although before the second century AD, since Galen knew this title), should be interpreted as indicating the 'visits to the city', 'visits to the people' that are paid by the physician and his staff.[8] The most important Hippocratic clinical source that we have is thus organised following the geographical and seasonal context of the encounters, giving us precious information about the practical variables in the experience of medical meetings.

Timeframe

In terms of the chronology and topography of the physician's visits, the precision and level of detail of our information varies greatly in the *Epidemics*. The physician's timetable is written down clearly and in detail only for the patient reports of *Epidemics* 1 and 3; in the other books, duration and locations are often left uncertain.[9] From those reports we infer that the doctor's visits to one place could last from weeks to months. Although many of these appear to be one-off cases, a physician might return to the same patient time and again, as is sometimes made explicit: for example, in the case of Androthales in *Epidemics* 5.80. This patient has 'voicelessness, delirium', and then 'survived for various years' before suffering a relapse, on which occasion he is visited by the same doctor, or entourage after an interval of many years. Consider also the consumptive patient at *Epidemics* 7.122, who 'died in the seventh year'; this indication implies a lasting relationship between patient and physician, although the frequency of contacts in between is not known. The majority of patients recorded, however, appear to be those visited on a one-off basis (that is, for one illness-event).

As far as frequency of visits within each case is concerned, these might occur every day, even more than once in the same day, and this

(1990), 36, 135–231; Horstmanshoff (1990), 177–9, 88; and Nutton (2013 [orig. 2004]), 87.

8   On the meaning of the name *Epidemics* as 'visits to the people/to the communities,' see Langholf (1990), 78–9.

9   See Potter (1989) and Smith (1989) for a survey of these data.

for a longer time than a week; or following larger intervals. The repertoire of cases in *Epidemics* 1 and 3 has wider range, from patients seen once (e.g., Criton, in *Epidemics* 1.9) to patients visited 15 times over 80 days, like the wife of Epicrates (*Epidemics* 1.5), or followed for a longer period of time, such as the man in Thasos of *Epidemics* 3.17.1, who dies on the 120th day. In the looser reports offered by *Epidemics* 2, 4, and 6, patients are discussed outside the diary-like format that we find in *Epidemics* 1 and 3. Here we find lesser detail about each individual, but a larger timeframe, especially when it comes to female patients whose illnesses associate with the longer cycles of pregnancy or gynaecological changes: at *Epidemics* 2.1 the wife of Stymarges is said to enjoy a four-month period of quiet,[10] for instance; and at *Epidemics* 4.23, the illness of the 'daughter who lived with the wife of Comes' is followed over a period as long as two years. Male patients, too, may receive longer therapeutical attention, although it is rarer – as with Apellaeus at *Epidemics* 5.22 or Hecason at *Epidemics* 5.31. Moreover, we should always bear in mind that time patterns reflect not only the actuality of visits, but also the authorial and scientific project behind the drafting and preserving of certain patient cases, and possibly not others: what appears to be predominant in the selection of reports that reached us, therefore, should be taken as indicative of a specific didactic or intellectual agenda, rather than illustrative of a prevalence in actual medical practice. There is, however, enough variety in our material to give us an idea of the range of visiting possibilities these encounters entailed.

Familiarity

Especially in the longer cases, the reports suggest on occasions familiarity and even intimacy between the two parties. First of all, information about the patients can be meaningful. Important variations are found in this respect: at one end of the spectrum great precision in reporting personal names and family connections, the address or

[10]   See also *Epidemics* 2.2.10, or *Epidemics* 2.3.13, where Hippostratus' wife is also discussed over a longer period of time.

position in which the patient was found and the time of the year (such accuracy characterises especially *Epidemics* 1 and 3); at the other extreme, we find a more vague labelling through anonymous indications, in *Epidemics* 2 and 4 especially. Here not names but periphrastic expressions are used which seem aimed merely at distinguishing one individual from the next or offer a mnemonic token for future recollection[11]: for instance, 'the wife of the leatherworker who made my shoes', the 'woman with pain in the hips'[12]; 'the men whose head I opened', 'the man whose calf was cut';[13] 'the ropemaker', 'the branded slave'[14]; 'the Chalcedonian carried from the gates to the agora ... '[15]; 'the wool carder'[16]; 'the newly purchased servant girl whom I saw'.[17] In *Epidemics* 6 we find a similar mechanism at work: names and addresses are specified, as in the *Epidemics* 1 and 3, but periphrases may also be adopted: 'the man stretching while twisting the vine pole'[18]; 'the one who was corroding on the head'[19]; 'the man to whom Cyniscus brought me'[20]; and so on.[21]

In addition to these formulas, which may suggest acquaintance with a variety of personal details, there are comments about the patient, his or her condition and life, his or her appearances – and so on: when the author of *Epidemics* 5 labels a patient 'the pretty virgin of Nerios',[22] it is legitimate to wonder about the gratuitous remark: a mnemonic purpose, or just a spontaneous engagement with the young patient as individual, or both. At the other end of the spectrum there are the quicker mentions that show no deep acquaintance, referring simply to the occasion for the contact with the physician, or to the doctrinal usefulness of the case.

---

[11] For an exploration of this topic see Thumiger (2018).
[12] *Epidemics* 2.2.17 and 18 (5.90.7 and 13 L.). [13] *Epidemics* 4.1 (5.144.3 L.).
[14] *Epidemics* 4.2 (5.144.9; 12 L.). [15] *Epidemics* 4.3 (5.144.17–8 L.).
[16] *Epidemics* 4.36 (5.178.10 L.). [17] *Epidemics* 4.38 (5.180.5 L.).
[18] *Epidemics* 6.3.8 (5.296.5–6 L.). [19] *Epidemics* 6.4.5 (5.308 L.).
[20] *Epidemics* 6.7.10 (5.342.8–9 L.).
[21] Here and throughout, translations from the Hippocratic texts based on the Loeb translations. See the appendix for details.
[22] *Epidemics* 5.50 (5.236.11 L.).

THE PRAGMATICS OF HIPPOCRATIC MEDICAL SCIENCE

The next question concerns what a medical visit would have been like at the time of Hippocrates, in a concrete sense: the contact between physician and patient as a fundamental part of the therapeutical process and instrument of scientific knowledge.

The Senses

First and foremost, the actions of the physician inspecting the ill and seeking to understand his or her predicament consisted in a direct observation (through vision and other senses) of the patient's body. This programme returns in the *Epidemics* and elsewhere. A good physician must use all five senses to inspect the ill,[23] as stated at *Surgery* 1.1: "It's the business of the physician to know ... [things] which are to be seen, touched, and heard; which are to be perceived in the sight, and the touch, and the hearing, and the nose, and the tongue, and the understanding." Most succinctly, at *Epidemics* 6.8.17 we read that 'it is a laborious task to employ the whole body in the inquiry: vision, hearing, nose, touch, tongue, reasoning arrive at knowledge'.[24] The sensorial appraisal of the patient's physical state (body temperature, wetness and dryness; sweating or tremors; sensitivity of individual parts) and of the quality of his or her discharges (urine, faeces, and other bodily fluids) to be observed, touched, smelled, and even tasted by the physician are the initial and fundamental forms of contact. Once the senses fail to shed light on the ailment, other faculties would come into play – namely reasoning and competence. Most clearly in the words of the author of the *Art* (chapter 11), the physician must resort to the 'eye of the mind' to understand what lies beneath the surface (of the skin, or of the explorable parts of the body and its fluids more generally) once the sensorial examination is proven to be

---

[23]   See Jouanna (1999 [orig. 1992]), 54, on Hippocratic observation and Totelin (2014) for a recent discussion on the senses of the physician.

[24]   See also *Art* 13 on the role played by other explorations when vision is unable to explore the hidden disease – in particular, the voice of the patient is mentioned as useful to understand his or her state.

insufficient. The dialectic and cooperation of reason and senses is foundational to the self-definition of Greek medicine, from the start through to its later developments.[25]

Extracting Information from the Patient

The next step in the examination is the gathering of additional information about the patient's present state and past condition, either by direct conversation with him or her or through exchange with family and friends. If the sensorial exploration of the body is mostly entrusted to the active role of the physician, with the patient turned into an inert object of observation, the 'voice of the patient' gains an irreducible independence in this second component of the visit.[26] It would be misleading to think that the Hippocratic doctor had any rigorous sense of the importance to note down faithfully the patient's words, or that he would acknowledge their subjective experience as clinically relevant, seeing it as an ally in the healing process: the information offered by the patient, in fact, remains functional to the agenda of the physician and is informed by his own checklist. Nonetheless, it is in this phase of the visitation that we can find traces of the perspective of the ill men and women of the time, their perceptions of their own suffering and their expectations from the medical encounter.

A passage at *Epidemics* 1.23 allows us to see in which way the doctors were aware of communication as relevant. We find the following instructions about the 'things to be observed':

> ... the following were the circumstances attending the disease, from which I framed my judgements, learning from the common nature of all and the particular nature of the individual, from the disease, the patient, the regimen prescribed and the prescriber – for based on these things may become more favourable or less so; ... from the custom, mode of life, practices and ages of each patient;

[25] See Langholf (1990), 37–72, on the interaction of theory, vision, and the senses in the Hippocratic texts; Jouanna (1999 [orig. 1992]), 248–9, for a concise summary.
[26] See Jouanna (1999 [orig. 1992]), 134–6.

> *from talk, manners, silence, thoughts,* sleep or absence of sleep, the
> nature and times of dreams, plucking, scratching, tears ....

We cannot know whether this list – and other similar lists of 'things to observe' found in the Hippocratic texts, for instance in the treatise *Humours* – form a proper checklist, a set of questions for the physician to ask, or should rather be read more loosely as 'themes' for interrogation. It is, however, apparent that communication with the patient is considered to be one of the key sources of knowledge. The importance assigned to talk in the symptomatology of patient cases can also be brought into association with this: the Hippocratic doctors report with attention and detail about the attitudes towards communication, the quality of voice, the diction and type of speech of their patients.[27] Silences, talking modes, and even the patient's voice are commented on and seen as important signs, both as pathological indicators and as disruptions in the flow of information from the patient the physician needs. There are the common expressions 'he or she says many things' and 'she or he experiences delirium', 'he or she talks nonsense'; at the other end of the spectrum, silences and refusal to talk but also refusal to reply and so on.[28]

Not only do the physicians take notice of the patients' ability to communicate; they also pose questions and prescribe interrogation on specific topics. We do not have in our corpus any articulate, systematic theorisation of clinical questioning, of the kind illustrated by the *Medical Questions* by the first-century physician Rufus of Ephesus[29]; still, in some cases our physicians explicitly recommend to inquire directly with the patient about individual circumstances. For instance, the author of *Nature of Women* 10.2 enjoins to 'ask her then if the flux is inflammating or ulcerating'; in the *Prorrhetic 2*, a text that has much to say about clinical matters, the author

[27] See Gourevitch (1983); Ciani (1987); Montiglio (2000); Webster (2015); and Thumiger (2017) 115–43.

[28] For instance, at *Epidemics* 3.1 case 2.

[29] Letts (2015) goes as far as to emphasise the absence of a culture of 'questioning the patient' in the Hippocratics by comparison with Rufus of Ephesus' *Medical Questions*.

repeatedly advises to ask the patient, saying, for instance, 'but ask about the blood' (chapter 42). At *Diseases* 2.51, the patient's viewpoint is predicted as part of the disease description, 'if you ask him, he will tell you that he ... '. Instances in which the patients are represented as speaking directly about their state, with explicit expressions of saying, often have to do with the feeling of pain, and, therefore, with the subjective experience of the patient. So, at *Epidemics* 7, 11: 'after the first days, when asked, she said that no longer only the head, but now also her entire body ached'[30]; likewise in *Prorrhetic* 2.42, 'she said that she was often in pain ... in her temples' and later 'ask also if their head hurts; for they will confirm it'; or in chapter 24, 'these women say that their head aches'.

Not only are the specific answers given by the patients on individual matters important, but also the manners in which the patient speaks – from details about voice, articulation, clarity, and even consistency of speech and style. A passage in *Epidemics* 6.8.7 goes so far as to recommend a kind of critical approach to the utterances of the patient, whereby the doctor should observe 'speech, silence, saying what he wishes. The *words with which he speaks: loudly or many, unerring or moulded*'. The last two terms in particular suggest a stylistic appreciation of what the patient says: whether the words are 'precise, strict' or instead 'built up, involute', rather than an evaluation in terms of veracity; the way in which a patient chooses to describe the illness seems thus to have relevance in itself. In his commentary to this passage, Galen interprets the phrase as a concern with the veracity of the narrative offered by the patient; the point here, however, seems to be a richer appreciation of the style and intensity of communication.[31]

---

[30] Pain is an experience where the patient's (and the physician's) choice of words become important; see Roby (2015).

[31] Galen, *On Hippocrates' 'Epidemics 6'*, Wenkebach (1956), 448, lines 1–19; see Manetti and Roselli (1982), 172.

Taking the Patient's History

Still today, by 'taking history' medical practitioners indicate that phase of the medical examination in which the physician gathers information about the past of the patient, his or her previous illnesses, regime, and life habits; his or her familial situation, occupations, and so on as far as recent pathological events. Nowadays, as at the time of Hippocrates, this part of clinical activity naturally necessitates dialogue with the patient and his or her family, and is fundamental for designing a therapy, even if what marks the excellence of the profession is precisely the ability of the physician to fill in the gaps in the patients' stories, guessing 'those things which the patients left out in their account about their present and past' (in *Prognostic* 1.1).

Consider some examples of such narratives, and the kind of exchange between patient and physician that they reveal. Inquiry into the past is central in the psychic suffering of Parmeniscus at *Epidemics* 7.89, one of the few explicitly mental cases in our collection:

> Parmeniscus previously had been visited by dejection and desire to end his life, but sometimes again with positive mood. One time in Olynthus in the autumn he took to his bed, voiceless. He kept still, hardly attempting to begin speaking. At times he said something, and again voiceless. Sleep came on, and periodically wakefulness, and tossing silently, and delirium, and his hand went to his midriff as though he was in pain. And at times he turned away and lay still. His fever was continuous and he was breathing easily. He later said that he recognised people who came in. At times for a whole day and night when they offered water to drink he did not want it, but at times he would suddenly seize the water cooler and drink it down. His urine thick like a mule's. He was cured about the fourteenth day.

In this passage various features of interaction between patient and physician can be recognized: the implicit dialogue with members of the family; an attention to the ongoing emotions of the patient, his desire to die and his return to positive mood; some vivid details, which reveal the presence of the doctor at times (he would say something; he would toss around); the communication with the patient, who narrates about his illness over a long period ('previously' he had already suffered); the discussion with him after the recovery ('he said afterwards ... '). Especially the data about Parmeniscus' past record of mental disorder, and his suicidal thoughts can only be understood, if we think of a close exchange between the physician, the ill, and perhaps his family.

Consider also Apollonius in *Epidemics* 3.17, case 13, a longer case report whose first section reads as follows:

> Apollonius, in Abdera, was suffering for a long time, without betaking himself to bed. He had a swollen abdomen, and for a considerable time there was a constant pain around the liver, and then he became affected with jaundice, flatulent, and of a whitish complexion. Having eaten beef, and drunk cow milk unseasonably, he became a little heated at first, and put himself to bed. Having used large quantities of milk, that of goats and sheep, both boiled and raw, and a bad diet otherwise, great damage out of all these things. For the fever was exacerbated.

This passage tells us about a chronic condition that afflicts the patient for a long time (as it is repeated twice), and in this broad timeframe it offers details about the patient's everyday habits, including features of life style and regimen. How can we imagine the physician getting hold of this information? Some of it might have been inferred; most, however, bear the sign of the fundamental role played by communication with the patient and his family, careful questioning and writing down, perhaps over a longer period of time, or stretching the questioning to explore remote antecedents to the present disease.

History-taking appears thus to be the place in which the voice of the patient remains unchallenged by the dominance of the physician's competence or intuition. Several shorter examples could be given – for example, the patient at *Epidemics* 4.42, about whom we read that 'as time passed', 'there were many recurrences' of his pains in the loins and legs. Or Gorgias' wife at *Epidemics* 5.11, whose period 'stopped for four years, save for very small amounts'; then 'she became pregnant and pregnant again', before managing a successful pregnancy. Such information might be a sign of trust and confidence on the part of the patient or of a relationship with the woman, and with her family lasting for some time, as the aftermath of the births are also monitored; or both. In fact, the line between the story narrated by the patient and the actual observation of the physician is sometimes difficult to trace: in the case of Posidonius (*Epidemics* 7.16), for instance, we read that he 'suffers for many years in the chest', and that 'many years early he had become empyemic'. Had he been visited by the same doctor many years before, or is this physician offering a retrospective diagnosis based on the patient's history? The voice of the patient is intertwined with the data the doctor presents objectively in ways impossible to disentangle; we know the speaking and feeling individual is there, but his original message is impossible to retrieve away from the main clinical narrative.[32]

A Special Case: Female Patients

An interesting special case to understand the gathering of information from the patient or his or her family through dialogue (as opposed to observation) is that of female patients in the specific case of gynaecological complaints, such as Gorgias' wife we mentioned earlier. It is true, as it has been pointed out, that sensitivity to sexual themes is often much more in the eyes of the modern reader than in the ancient medical text we read, where female sexuality appears to be depicted as physiological fact, hardly categorised as an emotional or social event by the Hippocratic sources.[33] On the other hand, it is difficult to imagine an exchange between a male doctor and a woman not only involving

[32]   See also Dean-Jones (1995), 42, 45.

[33]   King (1998), 220–1, makes important points about the gap between modern sensibility and Hippocratic gynaecology.

genital complaints, but also topics such as pain during intercourse and sexual activity, as entirely devoid of delicacy, as Dean-Jones asks.[34] Communication and history-taking must have been subject to special norms, at least in part, in the case of female patients and gynaecological issues.[35] Consider in this light the case in *Epidemics* 5.25:

> In Larissa, the servant of Dyseris, when she was young, whenever she had sexual intercourse suffered much pain, but otherwise was without distress. And she never conceived. When she was sixty she had pain from midday, like strong labour. Before midday she had eaten many leeks. When pain seized her, the strongest ever, she stood up and felt something rough at the mouth of her womb. Then, when she had already fainted, another woman, inserting her hand, pressed out a stone like a spindle top, rough. She was immediately and henceforth healthy.

This passage poses a number of interesting questions: how was this information about sexual intercourse to reach a male physician? Both the delicate nature of the topic, and the comparison with labour pain (in a patient who never had children) suggest a middle-figure, in this case a female; additionally, should we consider the servile status of the woman also to be a factor, allowing greater freedom to speak about such topics? Who is the 'other woman' giving aid to the ill woman, and assisting her in the extraction of the stone?

Social status seems to be one element of the answer in another episode, the recollection of an anecdote by the author of *Nature of the Child* 13 also concerning a low-status female patient, a dancer. Here the desire to avoid pregnancy in a non-married woman who has many partners is discussed, as well as the efficacy of a contraceptive procedure, and the kind of things 'women say to each other':

> In fact, I myself have seen seed that remained in the mother for six days and then fell out, and it is from how it appeared when it was revealed to my understanding on that occasion that I make my

---

[34] Dean-Jones (1995), 48–9.   [35] See Chapter 11 by Dean-Jones in this volume.

further case. How I came to see this seed at six days I will now tell you. A female relative of mine once owned a very valuable singing girl who had relations with men, but who was not to become pregnant, lest she lose her value. The singing girl had heard what women say to one another, that when a woman is about to conceive, the seed does not run out of her, but remains inside. She understood what she heard and always paid attention, and when she one time noticed that the seed did not run out of her, she told her mistress, and the case came to me. When I heard, I told her to spring up and down so as to kick her heels against her buttocks, and when she had sprung for the seventh time, the seed ran out onto the ground with a noise, and the girl on seeing it gazed at it and was amazed.

This passage allows us to make important observations: first of all, the amount of information shared by the female patient about her sexual relations, which can be explained with her status as slave, as well as the 'things heard' from other women; the variations in levels of knowledge acquired from other women, here tacitly endorsed, and yet the patient's amazement at the following successful abortion[36]; finally, the fact that the episode enabled the doctor to acquire a specific knowledge about the qualities of the seed, as he then goes on to describe. The conversation between physician, slave-owner at first, and then patient in first person illustrates the centrality of communication and exchange in the construction of knowledge, and in the devising of a cure; at the same time, the practice of the tentative remedy is what allows the scientist, through a quasi-experiment, to observe what happened to the retained seed – what he takes to be the product of conception.

A similar exchange underlies the explanation given by the author of *Flesh* 18. The passage comes after the statement that in the uterus the foetus forms itself in all its parts in seven days. The medical author explains his knowledge of this as follows:

---

[36]   See Dean-Jones (1995), 45–6; King (1998), 136 on this passage, and also King (1995b) on women's self-knowledge in Hippocratic gynaecology.

You might wonder how I know this: well, I have learned much in the following way. The common prostitutes, who have frequent experiences in these matters, after having been with a man know when they have become pregnant, and they destroy the child. When it has been destroyed, it drops out like a piece of flesh. If you put this flesh into water and examine it in the water, you will see that it has all the parts ... it is also very obvious to women who have knowledge of these things when a woman becomes pregnant: at once [she feels] a chill: heat, shivering and tension set in, and [she feels a] contraction in her joints, whole body and uterus.

Here too, the physician relies on information exchanged with patients who are experienced in the matter discussed; they tell him that they 'know' when they become pregnant – as they are 'experienced' and 'knowledgeable' in such things – and describe the sensorial feelings that accompany conception, such as temperature, spasms and a kind of shrinking sensation. The physician acknowledges these symptoms as acquired facts using the language of objectivity, but their knowledge obviously depends entirely on the perceptions of the patient, and their communication with the doctor.

PHYSICIAN'S VIEWPOINT AND PATIENT'S VIEWPOINT?

To shed further light onto the relationship between physician and patient we shall now look at the Hippocratic testimony not only as storage of factual information about the medical encounter, as we have done so far, but also as texts that can illumine aspects of this relationship in terms of the perspectives they encapsulate. This kind of reading applied to an ancient document is to an important extent a move of literary criticism independent of historical analysis. Any attempt to highlight a 'point of view' within a text, in fact, is necessarily a literary exercise: our sources are nominally authored by physicians for their own use and reflecting their agenda (the *Epidemics*), and even when seemingly addressing patients (*Regimen*), they still do it from a strongly set authoritative standpoint.

We shall begin by exploring the features of Hippocratic medicine that best highlight the positioning of the physician within the relationship with the patient, illustrating how the doctor fashioned his own status before the eyes of the patient, rather than, or as well as to the service of the community of doctors. Indeed, the figure of the medical practitioner in Hippocratic medicine appears to initiate the long Western tradition that continues until today of the doctor as dominating presence—therapist and main agent of operations, scientific authority, and finally key narrator of the illness story. The first part of our analysis of viewpoints will thus concentrate on the top-down modality of communication and self-fashioning of this figure before the patients. Secondly, we shall try to probe the possibility of accessing the point of view of the patient from the records we have.

The Doctor's Viewpoint

The best case to illustrate the perspective of the physician, and his mode of action in Hippocratic medicine towards the receiving patient, is offered by prognosis, notoriously one of the defining features of Hippocratic medicine. The physician dealing with patients is obliged to clarify to them or their families the possibility of recovery and the likely outcome, more than he is expected to give a name to the disease at stake. As often stated, Hippocratic medicine is fundamentally not concerned with diagnosis – to assign a particular disease label to the patient's illness – but with the foresight of the outcome of the illness; whether recovery or death should be expected, but also details about the development of the disease, its crises and resolutions, or the transmutation into other diseases.[37] The *Hippocratic Corpus* contains several treatises devoted to prognosis – *Prognostic, Prorrhetic* 1 and *Prorrhetic* 2, and *Coan Prognoses* as well as sections in several other texts, notably the *Aphorisms*. In this central aspect of Hippocratic medical thought and practice, the complex entanglement of scientific

---

[37] The classic discussions of prognosis are Edelstein (1987 [orig. 1967]); Robert (1975), 262–5; Marzullo (1986–7); von Staden (1990); see also Nutton (2013 [orig. 2004]); Lloyd (2003), 56–8; and Jouanna (2013).

enterprise and negotiation between doctor and patient is especially evident.

The way prognostic verdicts appear to be prepared and delivered is striking for a modern audience in two senses: first, for the somehow 'dry' approach to the forecasting of the outcome of an illness, even if grim or fatal, in open disregard for the patient's emotional reception of a negative verdict. Intense reactions must often have been the case; the general lack of consideration for the psychology of the communication process, or even for the ill as its primary audience, for whom the information is existentially crucial is surprising for us as modern readers; second, for the primary importance given to what one might describe as a public relations programme of protection of the physician's reputation against blame for having caused the death of a patient by applying the wrong treatment.

Regarding the first point, we should observe that Hippocratic prognosis, unlike our own use of the modern English corresponding term, appears to indicate a knowledge of the future, but also control over what is hidden in the present and past: 'the present, and what happened before, and what will foreseeably happen' as famously expressed in *Prognostic* 1.[38] This formula foregrounds the physician's control of hard facts[39]; it is a pragmatic assessment that bears no consideration for the patient's perception of well-being. In the Hippocratic sources the term *elpís* – in other contexts translated as 'hope' (subjective and irrational longing for a positive outcome) – is used by and large as part of an 'intellectual vocabulary', as Perilli (1994) put it, to indicate the calculation of chances of improvement or survival. Thus at *Prognostic* 7.7, *elpís* is used to express the '*expectation* of madness', whereas at *Epidemics* 6.8.32 it refers to 'chance': 'there was only one *chance* ... '.

The objective of Hippocratic prognosis is thus to design a course of action, such as cures and diets, and in the first place to deliberate whether or not to attempt to cure the patient. Later deontological

---

[38] 2.110, 3–4 L. [39] See Jouanna (2013), 82–3.

literature will pay attention to the dangers of explicitly informing a patient about the imminent death[40]: in the classical world, where acute disease, incurability, and painful death must have been an experience just as common, we would also expect a prognosis of death to be handled with care in its psychological impact.[41] In our texts, however, nothing of this kind is found. The way in which prognosis, the backbone of Hippocratic medicine, is conceived is entirely scientific and the relationship with the patient is mentioned solely in terms of professional reputation.

This takes us to the second aspect, the management of the impressions these predictions might produce on the broader audience of the medical encounter – family, bystanders, colleagues, and a general 'public'. The expectations of recovery, that might fail to be met resulting in great damage for the reputation of the art, and of the individual physician is a risky business to be handled with caution. Consider *Prognostic* 1: 'you will be blameless if you foresee and indicate in advance those who will die and those who will get better'. Incurability should be recognised and made known beyond doubt, mainly to the purpose of protecting the reputation of the doctor against criticism after the death of a patient.[42] The complement to this is the prescription not to cure patients considered to be hopeless: in *Art* it is clearly said that doctors should 'not treat those who have been defeated by the disease', referring to hopeless cases; and at *Art* 3.6 the definition of medicine returns to the same topic: '... in general terms, it is to do away with the sufferings of the sick, to lessen the violence of their diseases, and to refuse to treat those who are

---

[40] On these, see Chapter 7 by Leven in this volume. See Horstmanshoff (1999), 1 and 22–3, on hope and fear as important agents in the experience of disease and therapy (and relevant to the interpretation of historical information); Edelstein (1987 [orig. 1967]), 76, on the psychology of death prognosis.

[41] See Edelstein (1987 [orig. 1967]), 76; von Staden (1990), 109–11; Thumiger (2016), 209–13 (on the language of hope, hopelessness, and despair); and Martzavou (2012) (on popular medicine).

[42] See Edelstein (1987 [orig. 1967]); Wittern (1979); Jouanna (1999 [orig. 1992]) 100–11; and Rosen and Horstmanshoff (2003). Von Staden (1990) has illustrated better than anyone else how these borders between curability and incurability were more shaded and conditional than it might appear at first sight.

overcome by their diseases, realising that in such cases medicine is hopeless'.

The importance of never giving positive predictions that are later disproven by reality and to admit the limitations of the art are key to gaining the trust of patients insofar as they advertise a competent doctor. At the opening of *Prorrhetic* 2 we find an illustration of this as an important concern, as the author ridicules and criticises the ultra-precise, ludicrously esoteric predictions offered by show-off physicians who, for instance, predict 'survival but blindness' in openly desperate patients, or surprise their audience by 'predicting madness in travellers and merchants'.[43] Our author recommends instead that only predictions in line with human possibilities should be made.

So, in short, prognosis fashions the role of the doctor as detached, unemotional, and rational, not intercepting the subjectivity of the patient per se. We can thus understand why scholarship has often emphasised this aspect of Hippocratic medicine as disproportionately siding with the authoritative physician. It is in this spirit, for example, that Steger looked at the seven books of the *Epidemics* to conclude that in their primary focus on 'descriptions of signs of disease' they do not reveal 'how the patient lived his (or her) disease, how he viewed the way it had been dealt with', and offer 'no insight into the experience of the doctor in exchange with the patient, leaving the experience of the patient entirely precluded to us'.[44]

There are, however, corrections and qualifications to be made to these strong claims. Allowing for a distinction within Hippocratic genres, Jori shows that the information coming from the patient in first person was indeed recognised already by the physicians of the fifth and fourth centuries.[45] Yet the other model, the one based on theoretical knowledge totally dismissive of the patient's view, effectively 'laid the groundwork for a practice of medicine in which the

---

[43]   Potter (1995), 218–21 (9.6.5–6 and 11–12 L.).
[44]   Steger (2007), 234 and 237 (my translation).   [45]   Jori (1997).

physician does not talk to the patient' from the start.[46] If we accept Jori's observation, we should still within the Hippocratic material distinguish two outlooks: what he calls the 'Hippocratic model', open to the view of the patient, and a 'doctor-centred model', exemplified for him by *Art*[47]; the first is alive in the several instances in which the patient is called upon through questioning, or reports that appeal directly to his or her viewpoint. We should try to look at corrections to this view next.

The Patient's Viewpoint

To look at our texts trying to identify the perspective of the sufferer and receiver of care is a much harder task, and one that can be tackled only indirectly: hardly ever, in fact, is the subjectivity of the patient engaged with explicitly, nor is the patient's perception of wellbeing framed as the final end of the therapeutic process, which is generally sketched as a struggle of the physician against a disease.[48]

Giving Voice to the Patient

A first area of inquiry is the extent to which, in the evidence from the texts we have, we can retrieve a dialogic, relational nature to Hippocratic medicine giving voice to the patient. We have shown that in some cases the information required by the physician originates from the patient. Historians have been reflecting on the question whether it is possible to write the history of medicine 'from below', from the patient's perspective. This patient-centred approach has inspired an interest in Hippocratic medicine beyond its apparent clear demarcation of vertical relationships of power between patient and doctor, in search for more nuanced perspectives.[49] On some occasions the patients' words are engaged with beyond the mechanical gathering of information, letting the patient's perception and

---

[46] Cassell (1976), 56 in Brody (2003), 8; see also Webster (2015); Entralgo (1970) 158–70; and Letts (2015).
[47] Jori (1997), 191.
[48] See Rosen and Horstmanshoff (2003), 99–104 and von Staden (1990), 97–9.
[49] See Thumiger (2015) and discussions in Petridou and Thumiger (2015), esp. 1–20.

subjectivity filter through; in addition, there is the information whose origin we can realistically locate in the patient.

The first vehicle for the point of view of the patients as conscious, sentient beings are their words, their own communications about their state. Of course the conveying of someone's words by a third party is always a double-edged matter: indeed they embed the point of view of the speaker, but they can also represent a subtler form of manipulation, as the author and authority appropriates both sides of the portrayal of an individual, the external observation and the internalised experience. The Hippocratic authors themselves were aware of incompetence and bad faith as possible forces behind the manipulation of medical narrative. The author of *Prorrhetic* 2.3, in his attack against those physicians who try to make an impression boasting the amazing exactness of their prognosis, writes explicitly that '(even) if some of these cases ... have been accurately reported ... the *reporters have narrated* the tale *more portentously* than it really happened', in order to result more praiseworthy.

Notwithstanding the irreducible unreliability of the authorial figure, with its self-styled posture of objectivity and promise of veracity, it still pays to consider the occasions in which the physicians appear to deem a patient's words worthy of attention. In some cases this is made explicit through formulas such as 'he said ... ', 'she felt that ... ', and so on. Verbs of saying can hardly be seen as channels of the literal words used by the patient (no sense of the value of being loyal to the patient's exact wording is mentioned, as we have said); still, some cases are better candidates than others. For instance, the incidental formula '(as) he or she says' is used for received information on which doubt is cast: at *Epidemics* 4.6, 'she said that she had lost another (baby), a male, towards the twentieth day. Whether it was true, I don't know'; here, the statement of the patient is met by the unreliability the physician attributes to it. Elsewhere, it is instead a subjective experience which attracts interest: at *Epidemics* 5.74, (and 7.36) we read: 'problems with the tongue: *he said* he could not articulate everything'; here, the patient reportedly spoke about his own inability to speak properly. This passage at first sight seems to expose its own fictionality, but reveals in fact the complex intertwining of patient's words, their interpretation, and final synthesis in the written text. Nicanor, at *Epidemics* 5.81, qualifies by himself his own phobia as more severe in the night: 'he could hardly bear it, when it happened in the night' (see also *Epidemics* 7.86 with a very close wording). Democles, at *Epidemics* 7.87 (and *Epidemics* 5.82), is quoted on his own vertigo: 'he said he could not go along a cliff . . . '. In these instances of indirect speech, we may take the words to be close (if not identical) to those of the patient—especially given the psychological disturbance discussed.

A much more problematic instance is that of the expression 'it seems' (*dokeî*), a case that exposes the dialogue between subjectivity and objectivity implicit in these texts.[50] The verb can be constructed personally or impersonally, often with no clear grammatical marker to help us in the interpretation if the subject is a third person. The translation of these phrases, therefore, often remains unresolved between 'it seemed to the patient' and 'it seemed *that* the patient . . . '. Take the example of *Epidemics* 5.82, describing Democles' phobias of height: 'Democles *edókei* ('appeared' or 'felt') to be blurred in vision and slacken in the body'. What follows is the report on a subjective fear, so that this *edókei* (the past tense of *dokeî*) seems to be subjective in kind, although Smith (1994) translates with 'he seemed blind . . . '. Another example is *Epidemics* 5.83: 'Phoenix. (To him) it seemed to see flashes like lightning in his eyes'. Again, this appears to be a subjective report, but in fact the interpretation of the physician could be at stake as much as the patient's impression. What emerges from these and other similar cases is that the patients participated in making these texts subjective.

In some cases the voice of the patient behind the written data can be reasonably inferred, even when the indirect speech is not reported. First of all, this is the case with sensorial experiences:

---

[50]   See Thumiger (2015), 118–20 and Thumiger (2016) on these problems.

these necessitate a close hearing of the patient's words of suffering or self-perception. For instance, at *Ancient Medicine* 10, where a certain type of patient has

> the mouth bitter; he feels as if his bowels were hanging; there come dizziness, low mood, and listlessness. Besides all this, when he puts himself to dine, food brings no pleasure, and he cannot digest what formerly he used to dine on when he had lunch. The food, descending into the bowels with colic and noise, burns them, and disturbed sleep follows, accompanied by wild and troubled dreams.

All of this information, although delivered as factual, channel the point of view of the patient – unless we wish to imply a malignant intention to distort reality and fabricate facts on the part of the physician: the taste in the mouth, the feeling about the bowels, the response to appetite and food, as well as dreams, must all be voluntarily offered by the patient. Likewise, the feeling of being pricked by a sting experienced by the patient of *Diseases* 2.73, for whom 'when he eats something, there is a heaviness in his inwards parts, and his chest and back seem to be being pricked by styluses.' This perception is too precise and idiosyncratic not to come from a suffering individual, and is one example of a patient's participating in the formation of the text that reached us.[51]

A comparable area of subjectivity is that of the emotions as an important feature of the patient-doctor relationship; not the medicalised emotions that emerge as pathological experiences (most prominently anger) but those that are implicit in the status of patient and doctor. Finally, emotions are experienced by the physician in his relation with the patient, or, most to the point, shared by both parts. Pain or grief, despair, fear, reluctance, or disproportionate sadness in the patient cases might be interpreted as the feelings that accompany the state of the ill patients as suffering from illness, in their relationship with the disease and the medical authority, and as they

---

[51]   See Jori (1997), 195, on this point.

contemplate the possibility of a cure. The fact that patient reports incorporate these aspects also implies closeness, dialogue, and voicing the testimony of the feeling patient, although, as we have said, they are not engaged with or addressed therapeutically. For instance, the woman at *Epidemics* 3.1, case 6, at the end 'felt hopeless about herself'. A dialogue with the physician is implied by this anecdote, in which the prognosis is discussed and engaged with emotionally by the patient. The same is true for the fears that often accompany illness.[52] Fear can even cause disease under certain circumstances. Likewise, at *Epidemics* 7.45, the patient, Mnesianax, shows traits of what in English are called 'hypochondriac' anxieties. During the course of his illness 'when he was in control of himself, he did not want to go out, but said that he was afraid; and if someone mentioned to him about serious illnesses, he was taken by fear'. What the patient 'said' is mentioned as is the attack of fear that he experiences.

These patients' fears and hopes surface, but are not directly treated by the physicians as iatrogenic emotions: the difference in this respect from the deontological treatises is evident. The only case in which a hint of a medicalisation of hopelessness emerges can be found is *Prorrhetic* 1.8, where we read that 'forms of derangement in those who *are letting themselves* (or, *giving up on themselves*; *proapaudáō*) are most harmful, like in those who are too passionate (*thrasýnō*)'.[53] The Greek verb *proapaudáō* can be interpreted as a form of 'fainting', 'languishing' *in advance*, in anticipation for the outcome of the disease; it is opposed to the Greek verb *thrasýnō*, 'to be bold' or 'to be excited', thus associated with the projection of one's wearing off and loss of strength. Our texts notice these feelings as manifestation of the patient's state, but do not unpack them as part of the medical encounter – nor do they mention any medical action directed at soothing them.

This fact may leave the impression of a lack of empathy in our medical writings, a specific choice to refrain from aspects of

---

52   For example, *Epidemics* 1.9; *Epidemics* 3.1, case 11; *Epidemics* 3.17, case 11.
53   Smith (1994), 267; see Manetti and Roselli (1982), 174–5.

identification and compassion as part of the profession. Several readers have noticed such absence of pity[54] or lack of 'identification' with the patient.[55] It is, however, important to separate the strategy of self-presentation, which in these authors privileges pragmatic efficiency over empathy, and the actuality of the exchange, that must have involved emotional communication and sympathetic feelings, too. A famous passage at *Breaths* 1 offers us a unique, but telling commentary in this sense, reflecting on the shared suffering between patient and physician: '[the physician] sees terrible sights, touches unpleasant things, and the misfortunes of others bring a harvest of sorrows that are peculiarly his'. [56]

Matters of efficiency and practical implications remain, however, paramount: in relation to to these emotional aspects, more attention is paid to the patients' trust and their obedience to the indications given by the doctor, or their manipulation by the physician in turn. At *Prorrhetic* 2.3–4 we have a testimony that the acceptance of therapeutic indications was not straightforward, as disobedience is discussed together with the possible ways to uncover it. One can easily detect patients' noncompliance, we read, in the case of someone who is lying ill in a fixed place and had been prescribed a strict regimen, because his or her deviance will produce evident signs for the experienced physician to detect (*Prorrhetic* 2.4). The slighter 'faults' of patients, he remarks, are instead not detectable (and it is absurd to think that physicians could individuate them: 'confessions' of petty infractions are preposterous and of no consequence, worthy of laugh). This discussion, and its irony about excessive subtlety in the investigation of patients' discipline and compliance testify to a general awareness of the possibility of a breach in the cooperation between patient and physician. This breach could also work all the way around, and be a manipulation

---

[54]   Kosak (2005).

[55]   Holmes (2013). See also Kazantzidis (2016), 60–2; on the 'friend-doctor' (*medicus amicus*), see Mudry (1980) and Stok (2009).

[56]   See Thumiger (2016) on hope and empathy in the Hippocratic texts.

operated by the doctor to provide psychological soothing, a placebo effect. This is possibly the case at *Epidemics* 6.5.7.4, where we find the following recommendation:

> If the ear aches, wrap wool around your fingers, pour on arm oil, then put the wool in the palm of the hand and put it over the ear so that something *will seem* [to the patient] to come out. Then throw it in the fire ... a deception ....

The text is corrupt in its last part.[57] Several ancient readers, however, have interpreted this passage as a scene in which the doctor performs a therapeutic procedure in order to offer a suggestion of cure – and in fact a psychological healing – that is recognised as a form of deceit. Whether this meaning was original or not to the Hippocratic text, the interpretation in terms of placebo by the ancient commentators testifies to the awareness of this effect, and of the therapeutic potential of persuasion and manipulation. A clearer example is found in *Regimen in Acute Diseases* 23, where purging and emetic drugs such as hellebore are discussed. The physician suggests that these drugs can also be given in gruel, 'if they are not too unpleasant owing to bitterness or other unpleasant taste, or owing to quantity, colour, or some other quality that *arouses the patient's suspicion*'.

CONCLUSIONS

Many readers have found the relationship between physician and patient established in the *Hippocratic Corpus* as one-way traffic, a pragmatic application of doctrine disenfranchised from the perceptions and will of the patient, and programmatically detached from his or her emotions and existential states. This reading is generally supported by a significant amount of evidence. On the other hand, it is important to follow Leven's (2007) advice not to evaluate the attitudes of these physicians by the modern standards, and shift the paradigm by which we evaluate patient–doctor exchange. In many ways the

---

[57]   See Manetti and Roselli (1982), 111–13.

Hippocratic doctors relied on communication with their patients, although this was often filtered through a pragmatic agenda. They were aware of the complexities of this relationship of trust and service.[58] They were also used to the emotional intensity the experience of pain and illness must bring, although they choose not to engage with these as part of the profession. It is thus important to draw the distinction between what physicians and patients experienced in their actual exchanges, and what the former chose to preserve in their records. On the one hand, the doctors depict (in its extreme formulation) the patients as those who (*Art* 7)

> know neither what they are suffering from, nor the cause thereof; neither what will be the outcome of their present state, nor the usual results of similar conditions. They receive orders, suffering in the present and fearful of what is to come; ... they desire treatment rather to enjoy immediate alleviation of his sickness than to recover their health through their powerlessness in the face of pain to endure ....

On the other hand, this patronising representation is eroded by the many instances in which the patient's voice appears to be of essential use, his or her competence evaluated as an important part of one's ability to heal and preserve health, his feelings and emotions considered as caused by the physician, and his or her knowledge of one's own experience a precious source of clinical training and scientific advancement. In this light we can better understand the sense of texts openly addressed to discerning and intellectually competent patients, such as the audience of *Regimen*, or the intelligent men addressed in *Affections* 1, who can understand and judge what the physician says, and help himself to preserve his own health. In this way, the authoritative discourse crafted by the Hippocratic writings often reveals lively aspects of the exchange with patients, and the active contribution of the latter to the creation of Hippocratic doctrines.

---

[58] See van Shaik (2015) for a discussion of trust in Hippocratic and contemporary medicine.

13 Galen's Hippocrates

Véronique Boudon-Millot

... ἐν γὰρ ταῖς οὕτως ἀσαφέσι λέξεσι μαντείας μᾶλλον ἢ σοφίας εἰς τὴν ἐξήγησιν χρήζομεν ...

... in the case of such obscure utterances [sc. by Hippocrates], we need divination rather than knowledge to explain them ...

Galen of Pergamum, *Commentary on Hippocrates' 'Surgery'*[1]

Galien au I. commentaire du livre d'Hippocrate De l'officine du médecin, dict que le-dit Hippocrate a escrit aucunefois si obscurément que pour l'interpréter il requeroit plustost une divination qu'une science.

In his first *Commentary on Hippocrates' 'Surgery'*, Galen said that Hippocrates had once written so obscurely that to explain him, one needs divination rather than a science.

Ambroise Paré (1510–90)[2]

Quae sacer Hippocrates oracula protulit olim
Plana facis puro, docte Galene, stylo.
The obscure words that the divine Hippocrates once uttered
you made plain, learned Galen, through your pure style.
Anonymous annotator of Galen's Complete Works, *Basle 1538*[3]

Galen claimed that Hippocrates' writings are at times so obscure that they require divine inspiration rather than sober reasoning to understand and interpret them. Two Renaissance figures, Ambroise Paré,

---

[1]   18B.715.9 K.   [2]   Paré (1585), 1191.
[3]   A handwritten note in the fifth volume of Galen's *Collected* Works (*Galeni opera omnia*, Basle 1538) in the copy preserved in the Convent of the Carmelites in Krakow under the shelf mark 7261.

the famous Parisian barber surgeon, and the anonymous annotator, who both lived nearly 2,000 years after Hippocrates, agree with Galen, as the opening quotations show. Moreover, they regarded Galen's commentaries as the best possible guide and introduction to Hippocrates' works. Indeed, the Hippocratic writings are compact and concise, and often require explanation to be understood correctly by the lay reader or beginner. As a result, a secondary literary tradition developed early in antiquity which aimed to explain and interpret the Hippocratic text. Well before Galen in the second century AD, commentators such as Bacchius of Tanagra (c. 275–200 BC), Artemidorus Capito (first century BC), Aretaeus of Cappadocia, and Erotian (both first century AD) were already involved in debating and interpreting the Hippocratic text.[4] The initial exegetical literature consisted both of glossaries and of commentaries. It developed in the circle of the anatomist Herophilus, one of whose disciples, Bacchius of Tanagra, was the first great glossator of Hippocrates; his glossary reflects knowledge of about twenty treatises attributed to Hippocrates within the circle of Herophilus. He also commented on some of Hippocratic's works, such as *Aphorisms* and *Epidemics* 3 and 6, although these commentaries are now lost.[5] These scholarly activities primarily took place in the library of Alexandria, where the works of Hippocrates were gathered during the Hellenistic period. In addition, there was a centre of medical studies in Pergamum, where Eumenes II (195–157 BC) founded a great library that competed with the library of Alexandria from the second century BC onwards. The physician Apollonius of Citium (first century BC) wrote a commentary on Hippocrates' *Joints*, which he dedicated to one of the Ptolemies, and, in the first century AD, Erotian dedicated his glossary to Emperor Nero's physician, Andromachus. The first editions of Hippocrates with known authorship, one by Artemidorus Capito, and one by his contemporary Dioscorides, date from this period as well. A century

---

[4]   Jouanna (1999), 94.   [5]   von Staden (1989).

later, Galen used and critiqued these editions, lost today, blaming them for not conserving ancient teachings.[6]

From the Hellenistic and Roman periods onwards, referencing Hippocrates became a necessity within the various new medical schools (such as the dogmatic, empirical, Methodist, and pneumatic schools). Some physicians even began to refer to themselves as 'Hippocratics'.[7] The empirical school in particular became a hotbed of Hippocratism; its adherents rejected the theoretical medicine that they viewed as too focussed on searching for hidden causes. For them, Hippocrates embodied the ideal of the clinician and man of practical experience. Therefore, they devoted much scholarly effort to Hippocrates' works and the subsequent tradition. For instance, in the early third century BC, the founder of the empirical school, Philinus of Cos, wrote a Hippocratic glossary in which he criticised the interpretations proposed by Bacchius. Other empirical physicians included Apollonius of Citium (already mentioned earlier), Glaucias and Zeuxis (both second century BC), and Heraclitus of Tarentum (first century BC), all of whom were used by Erotian. The dogmatic school, the main rival of the empiricists, equally claimed Hippocrates as their master. In turn, the Methodists criticised Hippocrates openly, as did, for instance, the Methodists Thessalus and Soranus of Ephesus (first century AD). Their criticism subsequently provoked Galen's wrath.

Among the rivalling schools of medicine, engaged in a war of ideas about the best medical method, the Hippocratic works became a key battleground. They used Hippocrates to defeat their adversaries by praising him (even if he sometimes got contested) and reinterpreting him in their own image. Onto this highly competitive scene emerged Galen, the most talented commentator and most effective defender of Hippocrates; in his extant works, Galen refers to Hippocrates more than 2,500 times.[8] The following three sections

---

[6]   See, e.g., Galen, *On Hippocrates' 'Nature of Man'* 1.2, ed. Mewaldt et al. (1914), 13–16.
[7]   On the fact that the term 'Hippocratic' is found in Galen, see Boudon–Millot (2015).
[8]   Boudon-Millot (2014); see also Daremberg (1854), i.

first discuss the method that Galen used to edit and comment on the Hippocratic texts. I shall then turn to the three pillars that form the basis of Galen's Hippocratism: the primary importance of anatomy, the doctrine of innate and external heat, and the theory of the four humours. Finally, I shall describe the image of Hippocrates that emerges from the Galenic writings: that of an excellent physician and extraordinary teacher.

THE METHOD OF GALEN, GLOSSATOR, EDITOR, AND COMMENTATOR OF HIPPOCRATES

Galen lists the works that he wrote and that are devoted to Hippocrates in his two bibliographical writings, *On My Own Books* and *The Order of My Own Books*.[9] In addition to his *Glossary* and his numerous commentaries, he also deals with Hippocrates in his *Elements According to Hippocrates* and *On the Doctrines of Hippocrates and Plato*, and, in particular with philological questions in his *On the Genuine Works of Hippocrates*. Therefore, throughout his life, Galen practised more than just one exegetical method, ranging from glossaries and commentaries to books devoted to a particular aspect of Hippocrates' works. The image of his exegetical activities that Galen presents in *On My Own Books*, however, is no doubt a reconstruction produced towards the end of his life and he wrote this bibliographical account.

At the beginning of his career, Galen commented on Hippocrates just for himself in private. He donated some of his commentaries to his friends without anticipating that they would subsequently disclose them to a much larger public. A first series of commentaries was thus edited for private usage, at a time when Galen recently moved to Rome and had not yet brought his library from Pergamum. These commentaries therefore lack any polemic with other authors. A second wave of commentaries was subsequently prepared for the public. According to Galen's account in his *On My*

---

[9]   Ed. Boudon-Millot (2007).

Own Books, the catalyst of this second wave of commentaries was his encounter with a man called Lycus, who explained one of Hippocrates' aphorisms in the wrong way:

> As with my other works written for friends, so especially with the works of Hippocratic commentary, I had no expectation that they would reach a wider audience. Their origin, in fact, was my writing notes on those works purely as an exercise for myself. Going over the whole of the science of medicine by subject, I made myself a set of works containing all Hippocrates' statements of relevance to the art, but put into clear terms and with all the conclusions drawn out. So, for example, I wrote specifically on Hippocrates' views on critical days; on his views on difficulty in breathing; and so on. The whole method of healing was thus covered in fourteen books. Word-by-word commentaries had already been written by many of my predecessors, and I knew their work pretty well; and if I found what I considered errors in those writings, I thought it superfluous to refute them; for I would already have made those points in the works I had given to people on request, where, however, I seldom made direct reference to commentators. To begin with I did not have their commentaries with me in Rome, as all the books in my possession remained in Asia. If, then, I remembered some particularly gross error on the part of one of them, such that anyone who followed it would suffer a severe setback in his medical practice, I would indicate this; otherwise, I would confine myself to my own interpretation, without reference to the conflicting interpretations of others. The *Commentary on the 'Aphorisms'* was composed in this way, as were those on *Fractures* and on *Joints*; also those on *Prognosis*, on *Regimen in acute diseases*, on *Wounds*, on *Injuries to the head*, and on Book 1 of the *Epidemics*.

> After I had composed the above works, I heard someone praising a false interpretation of one of the *Aphorisms*. From that point on, whenever I gave one of these works to anybody, it was composed with an eye to general publication, not just to the attainments of

that individual. In this category are: the commentaries on Books 2, 3, and 6 of the *Epidemics*; then also those on *Humours*, on *Nutrition*, on *Prediction*, on *The Nature of Man*, and on *Surgery*, as well as that on *Airs, Waters, Places* . . . .. The *Commentary on the 'Aphorisms'* is in seven volumes; on *Fractures*, in three; four on *Joints*; three on *Prognosis*; three on the genuine part of *Regimen in Acute Diseases* and two on the parts that were added to that text subsequently. *Wounds* and *Injuries to the Head* were each covered in one book, while the first and third books of *Epidemics* were each covered in three. The second book of *Epidemics* has six volumes of commentary, and the sixth eight. On *Humours* I wrote three commentaries, and the same number on *Prediction*, on *Surgery*, as well as that on *Airs, Waters, Places*; four on *Nutrition*, two on *The Nature of Man*. After the composition of this last commentary, I heard certain individuals attack that particular work as not being an authentic work of Hippocrates; and so I wrote three more volumes, entitled *The Manifest Consistency of Hippocrates' Views between 'The nature of man' and His Other Writings*. Other works belonging in this Hippocratic category are: *Hippocrates' Views on Regimen in Acute Diseases*; a handbook explaining Hippocrates' use of words; the work addressed *To Lycus*, concerning the Aphorism which begins: 'Things growing have the most innate heat'; the *To Julian*, the Methodist, on his criticisms of the Hippocratic *Aphorisms*. There is one other very short work which also belongs in this category as relevant to Hippocrates, in which I demonstrate that *The Best Physician in Every Way is Also a Philosopher*. (The work appears also with a shorter title, Galen's *Hippocrates*, suggesting that Hippocrates was subsequently considered as the physician-philosopher par excellence).[10]

We should add that throughout his life Galen continued to modify his writings, inserting references to later works within earlier texts, a phenomenon of cross-referencing which obviously makes the

---

[10] Galen, *On My Own Books* 9.1–14; ed. Boudon-Millot (2007), 159–62; trans. Singer (1997), 15–16 (with modifications).

precise dating of his commentaries difficult. With over twenty-five works devoted to Hippocrates, and adding to that *On the Elements according to Hippocrates* and *On the Doctrines of Hippocrates and Plato* not mentioned in this list, the total amount of works that Galen devoted to explaining the thought of Hippocrates is impressive. In *On My Own Books*, Galen provides an annotated list of all his works, and this allows us to recognise his main areas of interest: the debate on the authenticity of Hippocrates' writings; the central role of the *Aphorisms*; the polemic against the Methodists; the importance of the theory of innate heat; and the figure of Hippocrates as a philosophical physician.

Just like his predecessors, Galen recognised the difficulties involved in Hippocrates' writings. Their style is characterised by coming straight to the point without any preambles and they often only hint at general principles without spelling out the details. Galen justified this style, which is excessively concise in some treatises, with Hippocrates' desire only to address a specialist audience and not laypeople. An example of this is the *Aphorisms*, the most widely read, cited, and commented on work in the *Hippocratic Corpus*. In a passage from *Difficulties in Breathing*, Galen compares two descriptions of the famous Athenian plague of the fifth century BC: that given by Hippocrates and that by his contemporary, the historian Thucydides:

> The ancients believe that he [Hippocrates] has described all the symptoms of the ill, just like Thucydides. Yet, this is not the case; the writings of Hippocrates are rather the exact opposite of those of Thucydides. For Thucydides describes everything that is known even by non-specialists, leaving nothing of this unmentioned, whereas Hippocrates only writes that which matters for the overall condition which endangers the patient. He mentions many other things which escape the non-specialist and contribute to a professional and exact diagnosis.[11]

---

[11]   Galen, *Difficulties in Breathing* 2.7, 7.850, 11–851, 3 K.

Galen concludes his comparison with the following bold statement in which he contrasts the technique of both authors: "Thucydides has given an account of what happens to the ill as a non-specialist to non-specialists, Hippocrates however has written as a professional to professionals."[12] Jacques Jouanna summarises it perfectly: "The difference is therefore that Thucydides describes all the symptoms visible to non-specialists, whereas Hippocrates only selects some of these, those which are significant for the overall condition; while Hippocrates reports symptoms which escape non-specialists but are vital for formulating a diagnosis in line with the art [of medicine]."[13]

In his commentaries, Galen does not strive to disentangle the true from the false in the *Hippocratic Corpus*, because for him Hippocrates is infallible. Rather, he leaves it to his reader to recognise which commentaries are correct and which are not. The preface of *On Hippocrates' 'Fractures'* forms a clear example of his method:

> Before proceeding with a more detailed explanation, one should be generally informed about every explanation to what extent it is able to make clear what is obscure in the writings. Demonstrating that what is written is true, rejecting what is false, mounting a skilful defence, if someone has criticised it – [all this] has nothing to do with explaining it. It is, nevertheless, what one tends to observe in all commentators, so to speak. By Zeus, nothing prevents the commentator from adopting this in a measured way. To debate the author's doctrines in depth, however, exceeds the limits of explanation. I do not aim at this, but at what I have said [sc. to make clear what is obscure]. This said, I am going to add a few words to the explanations themselves, in order to confirm what I am going to say. This genre of explanation can be divided in two types, because there are two types of obscurity. Therefore, it seems best to me to address this before I begin. I shall do so only briefly, however, in summary fashion as it were, because I have already set this out separately at

---

12 Galen, *Difficulties in Breathing* 2.7, 7.854, 6–8 K.   13   Jouanna (2014), 223.

great length in my treatise *On Exegesis*. I show there that there are
things that are obscure in themselves, and others that are not
rendered obscure through themselves. For instance, many
differences in understanding arise because of the educational
background, whether one is familiar with the sort of prose or not; or
whether one is clever or obtuse. . . . Therefore it seems preferable to
me to explain all these sorts of things, because most of the book's
readers do not have knowledge of anatomy . . .. When I myself read
a book together with someone, I am able to adapt the level of
explanation, as I understand the background of the student. When
I write for everyone, however, I do not specifically aim at the best
prepared or the least prepared. Indeed, for the majority it will be
obscure, whilst lingering on clear passages will be tedious.
Therefore, in my opinion the best thing is to aim at those who have
an average education.[14]

When commenting on Hippocrates, Galen is aware that he is part of
a long line of commentators whose names he cites in a passage of
On the Order of My Own Books. Among them we find his two main
teachers: Satyrus, who has remained loyal to the doctrine of his teacher Quintus, although he has not explained Hippocrates' thought
precisely; and Pelops, who has understood him better. Besides these
two we also find Numisianus, whose writings were already lost to
Galen; despite his prolonged efforts to find them, he never succeeded.
There are also Sabinus (second century AD) and Rufus of Ephesus (c.
100 AD). According to Galen, these last two interpreted Hippocrates'
doctrines more correctly. Finally, Galen also mentions Aephicianus,
who interpreted the Hippocratic writings through a Stoic lens. The
worst among them, according to Galen, is Lycus, a contemporary of
Galen mentioned earlier. This Lycus ventured to criticise Hippocrates
'because he did not understand his doctrines', and gave a wrong interpretation of one of the aphorisms, something Galen denounced in his
treatise *Against Lycus*:

---

14   Galen, *On Hippocrates' 'Fractures'*, prologue (18B.318–321 K.).

It will be easy to judge whether an exposition is correct or not, if one has been previously schooled in our writings. On some of Hippocrates' works there are even commentaries by me. These are the ones I have written so far; I shall attempt to complete what remains, if only I live. If I die before commenting on the most important treatises of Hippocrates, those who wish to know his views may consult my major works, as has been stated above, as well as those commentaries so far completed; and also, among previous Hippocratic commentators, the works of my teacher Pelops, and if possible those of Numisianus (very few have survived); in addition, the works of Sabinus and of Rufus of Ephesus. Quintus and his followers have not understood Hippocrates correctly, and therefore make many mistakes in exposition; Lycus, meanwhile, often criticises Hippocrates and accuses the man of errors without understanding his views; but the works of Lycus have been exposed. My teacher Satyrus, with whom I studied before moving on to Pelops, did not give the same expositions of Hippocratic texts as Lycus; and it is generally agreed that Satyrus preserves the doctrine of Quintus most accurately, without adding to or removing from them. Aephicianus, on the other hand, gave them a somewhat Stoic slant. I had the two different experiences of, first, hearing Quintus' interpretations from Satyrus and then some time later, read some of Lycus' works; and I convicted both of having misinterpreted Hippocrates' views. The followers of Sabinus and Rufus had understood it better, but anyone schooled in my writings will be able to judge their works too, and find out their correct statements as well as any mistakes they may have made.[15]

This catalogue of Hippocratic commentaries written by Galen's contemporaries or his immediate predecessors testifies to an engaged exegetical literature almost all of which is lost today – apart from

---

[15]   Galen, *On the Order of My Own Books* 3.4–12, ed. Boudon-Millot (2007), 97–9; trans. Singer (2007), 26–7 (with modifications).

Galen's commentaries, many of which survive. The vagaries of transmission alone cannot explain why Galen's commentaries survived when others did not. Their success depended for a large part on Galen's exegetical method. He first aims to confirm the authenticity of the Hippocratic text, and then continues to verify that the text in front of him has been properly prepared. If this is not the case, he prepares the texts himself by comparing the different versions in circulation and debating each of the problematic readings. Subsequently, he cites Hippocrates' words, the so-called lemmas, and adds a commentary in which he discusses different previous explanations of the passage in question and, where necessary, adds his own interpretation. Thus, Galen does not only work as a commentator; he is also an editor of Hippocrates' works.

The first stage of Galen's method thus consists of establishing whether the work in question really is by Hippocrates. Galen devoted a long treatise to this question, entitled *On the Authentic and Inauthentic Treatises of Hippocrates*, which unfortunately is now lost. He cites this treatise in his *Commentary on The Nature of Man*. There, Galen reports on the bitter disputes among his contemporaries about whether or not this commentary is authentic[16]:

> So also, someone might marvel at those who think that the book
> *On the Nature of Man* is not one of the legitimate works of
> Hippocrates, but rather, as they are accustomed to say, a bastard
> work (*nóthon*): they have been fooled by its arrangement, and by the
> interpolations in it; I will explain these things fully in this treatise.
> But for now it suffices to repeat what has been said in the treatise
> *On the Authentic and Inauthentic Treatises of Hippocrates*, in the
> passage which reads thus.[17]

---

[16]   See also Jouanna (2000a), 290.

[17]   Galen, *On Hippocrates' 'Nature of Man'*, ed. Mewaldt et al. (1914), 7; trans. Lewis-Beach (n.d), www.ucl.ac.uk/~ucgajpd/medicina%20antiqua/tr_GNatHom.html (accessed 26 July 2017) (with modifications).

The following argumentation in favour of the treatise's authenticity is too extensive to be fully cited here, although it is exemplary. It suffices to remark that after having delivered a close analysis of the content, in which he distinguishes the different sections which make up the treatise, Galen concludes that:

> It contains a first account, where it expounds concerning the elements and humours, in accordance with the system of Hippocrates, as well as a second account, where it expounds on the differences between epidemic and sporadic diseases. It also contains an appended work concerning the anatomy of blood vessels, which is completely spurious. For this appended work is not consistent with actual observation, and is at odds with what is said in the second book of the *Epidemics*. Although after this it sets down those topics that were investigated in the book which I have already written about, still these things are noteworthy, well-expressed and concise, and adhere to the system of Hippocrates, as do also those things that are said concerning the healthy regimen.[18]

The first principle of Galen's exegetic method can thus be summarised as follows: everything in accordance with Hippocrates' doctrines is authentic, and everything that is not is inauthentic. Thus, Galen rejects the authenticity of Book One of *Regimen* and especially *Epidemics* 5, which, in his opinion, deviates from Hippocrates' doctrine, as does *Epidemics* 7, which he believes is made up of bits and pieces of a rather recent origin:

> There are seven books in the *Epidemics*. Of these, the seventh, as has been agreed unanimously, is obviously a bastard work, more recent and modified. The fifth book is not by the great Hippocrates, the son of Heraclides, but by the young Hippocrates, the son of

---

18   Galen, *On Hippocrates' 'Nature of Man'*, ed. Mewaldt et al. (1914) 8. Trans. Lewis-Beach (n.d), www.ucl.ac.uk/~ucgajpd/medicina%20antiqua/tr_GNatHom.html (accessed 26 July 2017).

Draco. The second, fourth and sixth books are, for certain, by the sons of Hippocrates, while the others are by Hippocrates himself.[19]

At this point, one can perceive a great weakness in Galen's argument. He make himself the final arbiter of Hippocratic orthodoxy, and as Hippocrates is infallible, Galen risks having to condemn all the passages in the *Hippocratic Corpus* that he considers wrong as non-Hippocratic.

A second method that Galen uses to elucidate the Hippocratic text consists of making the implicit explicit. For instance, Galen mentions a certain Theon, a fitness instructor and master masseur, in his *Therapeutic Method*.[20] Theon distinguishes six types of massage or rubbing. Therefore, Theon thought that Hippocrates must have been wrong, because in his *Physician*, he described only four types: massage relaxing the body parts, tightening them, increasing the flesh, and slimming.[21] Yet Theon, as cultured as he was, and having treated his subject better than others, had not correctly understood Hippocrates.[22] He had not managed to interpret the compact and brief form, nor managed to supply that what was evident in the eyes of Galen and thus implied by Hippocrates: the two intermediate forms of massage: moderately strong and moderately long.

Finally, a third method consists in explaining the words the meaning of which has changed over time, as he did in his *Glossary of Hippocratic Terms*; or in elucidating notions that have been completely transformed since the time of Hippocrates. Certain Greek terms can simply not have been used by Hippocrates.[23]

In doing so, Galen introduces, be it consciously or not, certain concepts that are completely foreign to Hippocrates and reflect contemporaneous debates. Galen's exegetic activity thus consists of

---

[19]   Galen, *Difficulties in Breathing*, 2.8, 7.854 K.

[20]   Galen, *On the Preservation of Health*, 2.3, 6.93 K. On this passage, see Debru (1987).

[21]   Hippocrates, *Surgery* 17 (3.322 L.), ed. Withington (1928), 76: "Friction can produce relaxation, constriction, increase of flesh, attenuation. Hard friction constricts, soft relaxes: if long continued it attenuates, when moderate it increases flesh."

[22]   Galen, *On the Preservation of Health*, 2.4 (6.119 K.).

[23]   Littré (1839–61), 1.239 n. 3, provides a number of examples.

trying to demonstrate that Hippocrates had already discovered and understood everything before everyone else and to present him as the ideal physician.

THE THREE PILLARS OF GALEN'S HIPPOCRATISM

Three fundamental principles (*archaí*), or indisputable doctrines (*dógmata*), emerge from the abundance of Galenic commentaries that form the pillars of Galen's Hippocratism: the primary importance of anatomy, the doctrine of innate and acquired heat, and the theory of the four humours.

The Primary Importance of Anatomy

Galen takes every opportunity to praise Hippocrates' anatomical knowledge, and he insists that this subject ought to be at the forefront of one's own teaching. He even wrote a (lost) treatise called *On Hippocrates' Anatomy*, dedicated to the consul Boethius. In this treatise Galen responds to a contemporary named Martialius, a follower of Erasistratus, who attacked Hippocrates and argued that his anatomical ideas ought not to be studied.[24] The progress of Alexandrian medicine and the discoveries of the two illustrious anatomists Herophilus and Erasistratus in the third century BC must have led some physicians to revise the Hippocratic work in this area. Galen refused to join their ranks and continued to proclaim the superiority of Hippocratic anatomy. The way in which he presents this anatomy is largely a fabrication. For instance, he praises the medical teaching formerly provided in the closely knit family of the Asclepiad. There, according to Galen, 'children learned from their parents to practise dissection, just as they learned to read and write.'[25] In this golden age of medicine, written teachings based on a small number of anatomical manuals replaced an anatomy which depended mostly on

---

[24] Galen, *On My Own Books* 1.7, 9 (19.13–14 K.); ed. Boudon-Millot (2007), 138.
[25] Galen, *On Anatomical Procedures* 2.1 (2.280 K.); ed. Garofalo (1986), 1.71, 3–4; trans. Singer (1956), 32 (with modifications).

oral instruction. Yet, according to Galen, just as a captain cannot learn to navigate from books, a physician cannot give up practical instruction.[26]

In parallel with this historical reconstruction, Galen strives to defend a 'Hippocratic anatomy' designed to correspond as much as possible to his own views on the topic.[27] Did Hippocrates have a clearly wrong opinion? Not a problem. Galen, as we have seen, declares that the passage or theory in question is apocryphal; it cannot be by the great Hippocrates. For instance, in *Nature of Man* (chapter 11, mentioned earlier), Hippocrates maintains that four pairs of veins come down from the head through the whole body, yet he pays no attention to the role of the heart.[28] For Galen, this false theory could not have been the work of Hippocrates. After he lists all the great anatomists and confirms that 'of all these man, and many others who have written anatomical books, nobody believed that four pairs of veins come from the head',[29] he concludes that the said passage has been written in the Hellenistic period. He claimed that it was the work of one or more forgers who aimed to group together two smaller parts, and thus create a treatise large enough to be published.

Contrary to what Galen thought, however, the composite nature of the Hippocratic treatise cannot be accounted for by the intervention of one or more forgers. A passage from Aristotle's *History of Animals* actually proves that in the fourth century BC Aristotle had already read the new theory of the four pairs of veins and attributed it not to Hippocrates himself, but to one of his pupils, his son-in-law Polybus.[30] In this case, Galen was carried away by his admiration for Hippocrates: unable to imagine that the master, or one of his most loyal pupils, could have made such an anatomical error, Galen simply preferred to consider this part of the treatise as apocryphal.

---

[26]   On this theme, see Roselli (2002).   [27]   See Vegetti (1999), 351.

[28]   On this anatomical 'problem', see Chapter 3 by Jouanna in this volume.

[29]   Galen, *On Hippocrates' 'Nature of Man'* 2.6, ed. Mewaldt et al. (1914), 70.16.

[30]   Aristotle, *History of Animals* 3.3 (512a12–513a7).

The Doctrine of the Two Heats: Innate Heat and Acquired Heat

The theory of the two kinds of heat belongs to what Galen, in his *Commentary on the Epidemics 6*, calls 'the principal doctrines of Hippocrates' method'.[31] While commenting on the meaning of the Greek term for 'having a hot belly' (*thermokoílios*), Galen sets out to prove that Hippocrates had demonstrated in many of his works that living beings had not one single, but two types of heat. One of these is an innate, natural heat, imperceivable to the senses, which draws its existence from the liver, that is from blood and from organs filled with blood. The other type of heat can be perceived by the senses, is sharp, biting, and burning, and comes from the heart. Fever belongs to the second type of heat.[32] Galen took this distinction seriously and even devoted a complete treatise to it, entitled *There Is No Mistake in the Aphorism that Begins with 'Growing Creatures Have Most Innate Heat'*, directed against the famous Lycus, whom we already encountered earlier.[33] At the time, there raged a debate, in which some physicians maintained that there was only one type of heat. Lycus adhered to this view, which according to Galen is clearly a mistake. Lycus could make such an error of judgement, because of 'his ignorance of the best doctrines' of Hippocrates, and his unawareness of the essential difference between fever and innate heat, which Hippocrates had already identified, at least in Galen's view.

To compete with his adversaries, Galen ignores that this distinction between innate heat and acquired heat which he attributes to Hippocrates is in fact a later medical development. The question of

---

[31]   Galen, *On Hippocrates' 'Epidemics 6'*, 4.26; ed. Wenkebach (1956), 242.17–18.

[32]   With regard to this distinction, see Galen, *On Hippocrates' 'Epidemics 6'*, 4.26, ed. Wenkebach (1956), 239.1–5; and also Galen, *On His Own Opinions*, 4 and 13, ed. Boudon-Millot and Pietrobelli (2005), 194 and 208. Vivian Nutton (1999c) has previously edited and translated this text, based on a Latin translation of a lost Arabic translation of the Greek text, which Pietrobelli found in a manuscript in Greece.

[33]   The aphorism in question is *Aphorisms* 1.14 (4.466 L.); ed. and trans. Jones (1931), 104–5, in which Hippocrates declares that "Growing creatures have most innate heat, and it is for this reason that they need most food, deprived of which their body pines away." On Galen's treatise, also known as *Against Lycus*, see Wenkebach (1951).

innate heat only occupies a modest place in the *Hippocratic Corpus*. It is unrelated to the debates and disputes in Galen's days, when he and his adversaries discussed the nature of fever. Some viewed it as an illness in itself, whereas others regarded it as a mere symptom. Galen has clearly chosen a side in this debate. He distinguishes between innate heat (which cannot develop into a fever, even if it is obstructed by perspiration), and acquired, non-natural heat (which can develop into a fever).[34] In this debate, Galen wanted to have Hippocrates on his side.

From the Doctrine of the Four Humours to the Four Elements and Qualities

No treatise discusses the four humours (blood, phlegm, black bile, and yellow bile) so extensively as *Nature of Man*, and none has proposed such a systematic presentation of nature itself with each humour aligned to one of the four seasons. In general terms, Galen views Hippocrates as the ultimate 'philosopher of nature'. A large part of the introduction of his commentary on this Hippocratic work is devoted to the question of what must be understood by the term *phýsis* ('nature').[35] Galen even goes so far as to attribute the concept of the 'sympathy of the parts' to Hippocrates, a theory he has drawn from the treatise *Nutriment* and even Leibnitz still believed that there is an exchange and mutual affection between the body parts.[36] Galen has extensively commented on *Nature of Man*, devoting five books to it, yet he thought that Hippocrates' medical system is based more on the theory of the four elements and the four qualities than on that of the four humours, even though the work is strongly related to this latter theory. In fact, the four elements and qualities take a larger place in Galen's writings than the humours, which are mentioned considerably less often. Galen specifically discusses these issues in his treatise

---

34   On this distinction, see especially, Ps.-Galen, *Introduction* 13 (14.729 K.), ed. Petit (2009b), 48.

35   See Jouanna (2000a), n. 19.

36   On the importance of this theory of the 'sympathy of parts' and its legacy, see Holmes (2012, 2014).

On the Elements according to Hippocrates, and the four humours in his *Commentary on Hippocrates' 'Nature of Man'*. Moreover, when he had just finished this commentary, he penned another treatise entitled *On the Fact that Hippocrates Seems to Share the Same Opinion in Other Writings as the One Expressed in 'On the Nature of Man'*.[37] In *On the Elements according to Hippocrates*, Galen criticises his opponents, and especially Lycus, for having given an erroneous explanation of the well-known aphorism on the two types of heat and for completely ignoring the complex relations between the elements (fire, air, water, and earth), the qualities (warm and cold, and dry and wet) and the body, which itself consists of elements.[38] Moreover, in *Against Lycus*, he tries to demonstrate that living bodies are made up from a mix of qualities and elements rather than from the humours themselves:

> If I were the first or only one to say that Hippocrates considers that the body of living beings consists of warm, cold, dry, and humid, then I might have shown more restraint when criticising Lycus for writing commentaries on Hippocrates' works before knowing the basic principles of Hippocrates' art. [. . .]. For, I swear to all the Gods, Lycus is so ignorant of Hippocrates' art that after having read the first explanations in his commentary on the *Aphorisms*, I could not continue to take in the rest of a book, which seemed far off the mark from the thought of the ancient physician.[39]

At the beginning of his *Against Lycus*, Galen also advises those who want to learn scientifically about the principles of Hippocrates' thought to read his book *On the Elements according to Hippocrates*, in which the warm, cold, dry, and wet underpin the generation for all living beings.[40] The reader can then, Galen urges, continue reading his

---

[37] See Galen, *On My Own Books* 9.12 (19.36 K.), ed. Boudon-Millot (2007), 161.15.

[38] See especially the beginning of *Against Lycus* 1, ed. Wenkebach (1951), 3.15; Galen repeats accusations against Lycus already made in his *On Hippocrates' 'Epidemics 3'* 1.4, ed. Wenkebach (1936), 16.11–17.8.

[39] Galen, *Against Lycus* 1, Wenkebach (1951), 3.17–4.13.

[40] Galen, *Against Lycus* 2, Wenkebach (1951), 5, lines 3–7.

treatise *On Mixtures*. The essential part of this teaching lies therefore in the first elements, which are the foundation of both the body and of Hippocrates' thought, of which they form the basic principles. Indeed, in Galen's writings, the term 'elements' (*stocheîa*) simultaneously refers to the constitutive elements of the body and the constitutive elements of Hippocrates' medical philosophy, which is the foundations of the Hippocratic doctrine.

At the end of this demonstration, Galen has thus worked out a subtle shift from the theory of the four humours to that of the four qualities and four elements, which constitute an inevitable methodological assumption on the basis of his own medical philosophy:

> On the question of method, unless it is agreed that the causes of genesis and destruction are the four qualities, it is not possible to start the method, nor to advance it, nor to bring it to completion.[41]

One may appreciate the subtlety of Galen's Hippocratism, built on a few grand principles raised to the rank of dogma and regularly employed by Galen against his most dreaded rivals, who claimed the same authority as he, Hippocrates.

Hippocrates, the Excellent Physician and Ideal Teacher

Galen thus portrays Hippocrates as infallible and endowed with a sort of foresight. This is not merely an idealised image, but is constructed from accurate references to Hippocratic treatises. This is illustrated by=the treatise *The Best Doctor Is Also a Philosopher*, in which Galen emphasises the utter contrast between Hippocratic medicine and the medicine practised by his contemporaries. In this treatise, Hippocrates embodies the figure of the philosopher physician in response to a Methodist physician called Thessalus (never mentioned as such but continuously alluded to), who attempts to teach his disciples medicine within only six months. Galen sees Hippocrates first and foremost as a model to be imitated for his pedagogical qualities

---

[41]   Galen, *On the Therapeutic Method* 3.3 (10.186 K.), trans. Johnston-Horsley (2011), 285.

and the content of his teaching. Galen laments the sorrowful state of medical teaching in his own time and says that it is due to the fact that although his contemporaries 'pay lip-service to Hippocrates, to be sure, and look up to him as to a man without peer; but when it comes to taking the necessary steps to reach the same rank themselves – well, they do quite the opposite.'[42] What does Hippocrates recommend in his teachings?

> Now, the opinion of Hippocrates was that astronomy (and therefore clearly the study which is prior to astronomy, too, that is, geometry) is of central relevance to the study of medicine; *these* people [sc. contemporaneous physicians] are not only personally ignorant of both disciplines, they actually censure those who practise them.[43]

Galen adds that Hippocrates said the following about the nature of the body:

> Furthermore, Hippocrates set great store by accurate knowledge of the body, as the starting point of the whole science of medicine; these doctors fail, in their studies, to learn any of the following matters: the substance, formation, construction, size, and relationship to its neighbours of each part of the body – and indeed its position too.[44]

Galen also writes the following about prognostic, the main field of dispute between rational physicians and charlatans of second-century Rome[45]:

> Again, Hippocrates says that one should employ great forethought in the construction of a 'prognosis' of the present, past, and future state of the patient; today's doctors are so perfectly studied in this

---

42   Galen, *The Best Doctor Is Also a Philosopher* 1.1 (1.53–4 K.); ed. Boudon-Millot (2007) 284; trans. Singer (1997), 30.

43   Ibid. 1.2 (1.54 K.); ed. Boudon-Millot (2007), 284–5; trans. Singer (1997), 30.

44   Ibid. 1.3 (1.54–5 K.); ed. Boudon-Millot (2007) 285; trans. Singer (1997), 30.

45   See on this point Boudon-Millot (2003).

branch of the art that if someone predicts a haemorrhage or a sweat they denounce him as a magician or a speaker of riddles.[46]

Moreover, the Hippocratic physician should follow Hippocrates' example in the area of ethics in his refusal to let the treatment of the rich take precedence to that of the poor[47]:

If such a person exists, he will scorn Artaxerxes and Perdiccas.[48] He will wish never to come into the sight of the former; as for the latter, he will heal him of the disease he suffers, regarding him as a man in need of the Hippocratic art. He will not, however, spend all his time with Perdiccas, but will treat the poor people of Cranon, Thasos, and the small towns.[49]

Furthermore, it is truly remarkable to note how the image that Galen constructs of Thessalus at the beginning of his work *On the Therapeutic Method* differs in all aspects from that of Hippocrates in *The Best Doctor is Also a Philosopher*.[50] Thessalus embodies everything a true teacher should not be and combines in his person a sum of defects largely shared by other teachers criticised by Galen. Worse still, this ultimate anti-Hippocrates has dared to critique the great Hippocrates: Thessalus reviles him and the other Asclepiads, as Galen writes in *On the Therapeutic Method*.[51] Worse, Thessalus claims that 'Hippocrates stands at the beginning of a harmful

---

[46]   Galen, *The Best Doctor Is Also a Philosopher* 1.5 (1.54–5 K.); ed. Boudon-Millot (2007) 285; trans. Singer (1997), 30. This alludes to a mishap that Galen himself suffered and that he evokes in the *On Prognosis*.

[47]   On the Hippocratic ethics given to a long posterity, see Jouanna (2012 [orig. 1997]).

[48]   An illusion to the king of the Persians, Artaxerxes the first, who is believed to have searched Hippocrates' services to fight the pest among his army, and to the Macedonian king, Perdiccas II, who received Hippocrates' care in the treatment of consumption, which in reality turned out to be lovesickness. See Chapters 14 by Manetti and 15 by Pormann on the afterlife of these episodes.

[49]   Galen, *The Best Doctor is Also a Philosopher* 3.1 (1.58 K.); ed. Boudon-Millot (2007) 288–9; trans. Singer (1997), 32.

[50]   On this opposition between the good master embodied by Hippocrates and the bad master embodied by the methodological physician Thessalus, see Boudon-Millot (2006).

[51]   Galen, *On the Therapeutic Method* 1.2 (10.10–12 K.), ed. and trans. Johnston-Horsley (2011), 16–17.

tradition!' and even 'dared to criticise the *Aphorisms.*'[52] In short, for Galen, Thessalus is delusional.[53]

When Thessalus rejects the Hippocratic doctrine of the nature of man, about which Galen said in *That the Best Physician is Also a Philosopher* that "Hippocrates deems it important to know the nature of the body in detail, arguing that it is the basis of all medical reasoning", it is because he has not understood it:

> None of these men, most audacious Thessalus, condemned the teachings of Hippocrates on the nature of man which, to begin with, you do not seem to me either to have read or, if you have read them, to have understood. And if you did understand them it would, at the very least, be impossible for you to judge them since you are someone brought up in women's quarters with a father who, in his sorry plight, carded wool.[54]

Galen provides an argument that would convince future generations and thus reaches a conclusion that cannot be challenged: as the only one who has rightly understood Hippocrates, he is the only one worthy of commenting on his works and teaching them. And indeed, for several centuries after Galen and his commentaries, Hippocratic science continued to spread.

CONCLUSION

In a polemic context in which Hippocrates' heritage had become a source of intense debate between rival medical schools, Galen did not hesitate to portray Hippocrates both as a weapon and a shield. Aptly placing himself above the schools, he did not hesitate to openly argue with those who identified themselves most directly as Hippocratic, namely the Hippocratics of Rome, in order to impose his own vision of Hippocrates as an excellent physician and ideal teacher. Galen's flawless determination to impose his own vision of

---

[52]   Ibid., 1.2 (10.8.5–7 K.), ed. and trans.Johnston-Horsley (2011), 12–13.
[53]   Ibid., 1.2 (10.7.10 K.), ed. and trans.Johnston-Horsley (2011), 12–13.
[54]   Ibid., 1.2 (10.10.1–5 K), ed. and trans.Johnston-Horsley (2011), 16–17.

Hippocrates clearly proves that he must already have had to confront other competing visions in his time, but that his finally won, making an impression that lasted for centuries. Galen aims to differentiate himself from his adversaries, whom he reproaches for not having rightly understood Hippocrates' teachings because of their ignorance of his doctrines, carefully positioning himself as the only and genuine heir to the Hippocratic tradition. He skilfully redefined the essential dogmas of this tradition in order to respond to the new issues of Graeco-Roman medicine, namely the claim of the primary importance of anatomy, the doctrine of innate and external heat, and of course the theory of the four elements and four qualities derived from the theory of the four humours.

Owing to the influence of Galen's commentaries on the Byzantine encyclopaedias, Galen quickly became a classic reference alongside Hippocrates, sometimes even exceeding the reputation of his illustrious predecessor. Thus, at the beginning of the sixth century AD, the commentator Palladius remarks with no hesitation that 'Hippocrates has sown, Galen has grown.'[55] The Arabic translators who, in the ninth century AD, prepared their translations of Hippocrates while arranging the Hippocratic lemmas parallel to extracts from Galen's commentaries contributed definitively to the fact that the Hippocratic text was henceforth mostly read and interpreted according to a Galenic interpretation. In other words, Galen has said everything; everything was in Galen. With the risk that the main elements of this Hippocratism, or Hippocrates' original thought, can no longer be seen except through a distorting prism imposed by the great contemporary debates between ancient rival physicians, one should remember that the image of Hippocrates drawn in the Galenic corpus must not be confused with that of the historical Hippocrates. Still, Galen's testimony plays an indisputably major role, even today, in understanding Hippocrates and his legacy.

---

[55]   Palladius, *Commentary on Hippocrates' Epidemics* 6, 6.3.

14 Late Antiquity

Daniela Manetti

INTRODUCTION

Indisputably, after Galen a standard version of the Hippocratic doctrines became widespread. It drew together the theory of the four
humours, the concepts of *krâsis* (blend of humours) and *dyskrasía*
(morbid unbalance in the blend of humours) that form the basis of
the theory of temperaments (or mixtures), the concept of therapy by
opposites, as well as the need to adapt the treatment to the patient, to
the season, and so on.[1] All these features thereafter became the standard basis of the so-called rational medicine. Among the physicians
who shared this common doctrinal basis, simplified and mediated by
Galen, it is worth citing Philagrius (third to fourth century AD) and
Alexander of Tralles (sixth century AD) in the Greek world, Cassius
Felix (fourth century AD) and Theodore Priscian (fifth century AD) in
the Latin world.

To trace this heritage in the post-Galenic period would mean
largely to write the history of Late Antique medicine. In particular,
I shall consider how the 'man' Hippocrates is invoked, remembered,
and quoted, and how the episodes from his life and his utterances
gained relevance for later readers. I shall then turn to the
Hippocratic Corpus, and explore how it was read by different audiences and what role the various Hippocratic treatises played, whether
direct or indirect, in the professional training of physicians. I will
restrict my analysis to the period from the second to the sixth
century AD, although I am fully aware that this is merely
a conventional division, as there was effectively full continuity in

---

[1]   See Chapter 13 by Boudon-Millot in this volume.

the reception of Hippocrates in the sixth and seventh centuries and beyond, both in the Byzantine and the Arabo-Islamic world.[2]

It is my intention to track the different streams of Hippocrates' reception in later medicine, the different 'Hippocratisms' so to speak, and also look beyond purely medical texts. I shall focus on two aspects:

(a) The man Hippocrates as a 'character': it involves naturally his biography, not as a source for the historical Hippocrates (on which, see Chapter 2 by Craik in this volume), but to understand what purposes and audiences the later accounts of his life serve. Here the 'sayings of Hippocrates', often transmitted in the biographies, will also come under scrutiny.

(b) What role the texts within the *Hippocratic Corpus* played in the professional training of physicians; here one has to distinguish the different levels of medical education. Already in Galen's time, physicians had a varied training according to their social status; a high level of education, including the complete course of the traditional education called *paideía*, was restricted to very few physicians. The majority had to rely on practical handbooks and apprenticeships with more experienced physicians.

I do not aim at being exhaustive, but only hope to give some idea of the complexity of Hippocrates' reception.

THE BIOGRAPHY BETWEEN HISTORY AND LEGEND

The nucleus of the biography of Hippocrates dates back to the distant fourth century BC in Cos, and by the third century BC a biography of Hippocrates was already circulating in Egypt at Alexandria.[3] Over the following three centuries it was enriched by additional material about places, such as Crannon and Thasos,

---

[2]   One need only think of *Aphorisms* in the so-called *Hippocratic Problems* studied by Jouanna (1997); Guardasole (2003, 2007); and Anastassiou (2010); see now also Guardasole (2014). On Hippocratism at Byzantium, see Ieraci Bio (2014); or the *Aphorisms* in the Arabo-Islamic tradition, see Pormann and Karimullah (2017).

[3]   Manetti (2014).

where he had been active.[4] Much later texts from the fourth and third centuries BC such as *Embassy* and the *Speech from the Altar* celebrated various achievements of Hippocrates.[5] Hippocrates descended from Asclepius; lived on the island of Cos; studied under his father Heracleides and others such as Prodicus or Gorgias, and Democritus; travelled to Thessaly and Macedonia; was connected with Athens; died in Thessaly; and left offspring in the form of sons and pupils.[6]

Materials of diverse origin clustered around two core narratives, Hippocrates and the king of Persia Artaxerxes, and Hippocrates and the philosopher Democritus. These led to a small corpus of 'Letters of Hippocrates' (*Letters* 2–9 and *Letters* 10–18). It was later expanded with two introductory letters that built up the genealogy and an 'encomium', praising Hippocrates. Several later letters (19–24) extended the history of the relation between Democritus and Hippocrates.[7] The *Letters* were not yet included in the list of the works of Hippocrates compiled by the grammarian Erotian in the first century AD, but they were familiar and known as Hippocratic works by the Neoplatonic commentators of the fifth and sixth centuries AD in the philosophical schools of Athens and Alexandria. Other anecdotes about the plague from the North or about Prince Perdiccas of Macedonia did not find their way into the *Letters*, but were included in a biography attributed to Soranus and datable to the first to second century AD.[8]

Hippocrates was invited by the Persian king Artaxerxes to move to his court, with the promise of rich rewards and honours, but he

[4] Crannon and Thasos are mentioned in the *Epidemics* as a place where a group of travelling physicians operated.

[5] Erotian (first century AD) includes *Embassy* and *Speech from the Altar* at the end of the list of Hippocrates' works and distinguishes them from the other, saying that 'they show that Hippocrates was more a patriot than a physician'. About dating and comments on these works, see also Smith (1990), 2–18.

[6] Pinault (1992), 5–34.

[7] Smith (1990), text and English translation: dating between first century BC and first century AD.

[8] See Pinault (1992).

refused to serve an enemy of Greece.[9] When he was invited to treat Prince Perdiccas of Macedonia, Hippocrates soon realised that the actual ailment was the prince's love for one of his father's concubines; Hippocrates restored the prince to health and extricated himself from a delicate situation, but then declined to extend his stay as court physician.[10] Furthermore, he was invited by the kings of the Illyrians and the Paeonians to come to their aid in quelling a plague. Hippocrates refrained, however, from travelling to their land, preferring instead to send his pupils to ensure protection of the Greek cities against the disease.[11] Hippocrates thus emerges as a true patriot, who scorns the wealth offered by kings, but is generous towards the people, as well as being skilled in diagnosing disease.

Celsus (first century AD) and the *Lives* of Hippocrates report that Hippocrates was a pupil of Democritus.[12] In the *Letters* (10–21), however, he is merely invited by the inhabitants of Abdera, where Democritus lives, to restore his health, as they believe that he has gone mad. When Hippocrates meets the great philosopher, who suffers from continuous outbursts of laughter for unknown reasons, he realises that Democritus does not suffer from madness, but laughs at human vanity as a truly wise man. Here the real protagonist of the episode is Democritus, and the *Letters* give in this point the impression of being based on material derived from philosophical rather than medical sources. Hippocrates may effectively be seen as little more than the sidekick of Democritus, who is the true philosopher. This episode is not so much about medicine as about an argument about mere opinion and truth, and has Cynic overtones.[13] Diogenes Laertius (third century AD) provides a brief account of a meeting between

---

[9]   *Letters* 1–9, Smith (1990), 48–54.   [10]   *Life* by Soranus 5, Pinault (1992), 7–8.

[11]   *Embassy* 7 (Smith [1990], 116–18) is the most ancient testimony, but the episode underwent many alterations, and confusion arose between the plague of the Illyrians and the more famous plague of Athens: see Pinault (1992), 35–60.

[12]   Celsus, proem to *On Medicine* 8, and then *Life* by Soranus, *Suda* and Tzetzes, but not the so-called *Life of Brussels* (Pinault [1992], 7–8, 18–19, 21–2, 25–7).

[13]   See Rütten (1992), 8–35 and 116–34; Smith (1990), 21–3; and Roselli (1998b), 14–16.

Hippocrates and Democritus, where the latter displays his own diagnostic ability to the former[14]:

> Athenodorus in the eighth book of his *Walks* relates that, when Hippocrates came to see [Democritus], he ordered milk to be brought, and, having inspected it, pronounced it to be the milk of a black she-goat which had produced her first kid; which made Hippocrates marvel at the accuracy of his observation. Moreover, Hippocrates being accompanied by a maidservant, on the first day Democritus greeted her with 'Good morning, maiden', but the next day with 'Good morning, woman'. As a matter of fact the girl had been seduced in the night.

Additional anecdotes circulated, which likewise did not find their way into the overall pool of biographies. On the whole, the vast array of biographical material exemplified Hippocrates' remarkable ability to observe symptoms and formulate a diagnosis. The philosopher Posidonius (mid-second to mid-first century BC) may perhaps be credited with the anecdote of Hippocrates and the two twins, known to us from Augustine: Hippocrates suspected two brothers who fell ill simultaneously to be twins, and he was right.[15] All these episodes demonstrate the moral and scientific superiority of Hippocrates and are clearly directed at a general audience.

HIPPOCRATES THE WISE MAN

Hippocrates resembled more and more one of the great sages of Greece. He is 'divine', 'great', 'the wise old man', 'the most holy', and so on.[16] In the later versions of the anecdotes, he appears as a learned man. For instance, in the late *Life of Bruxelles* (known to

---

[14]   Diogenes Laertius, *Lives of the Eminent Philosophers* 9.49. Diogenes alluded to the episode also in 9.24, speaking of Melissus, who had met Heraclitus upon the invitation of the Ephesians, just as Hippocrates had met Democritus upon the invitation of the Abderites.

[15]   Witt (2011): the anecdote is cited in Augustine, *The City of God* 5.2, who quotes Cicero, who quotes Posidonius.

[16]   Inscription 334 of Samama (2003); see Roselli (1998a), 14–15.

us in a fifth century AD Latin translation), Hippocrates brought back many books from Persia and Egypt, as did other wise men such as Thales, Solon, or Plato.[17] Occasionally, the anecdotes circulate on their own, as did, for instance, that of the lovesick prince Perdiccas, mentioned earlier. This topical tale, retold repeatedly, became popular and left traces in many Greek and Latin authors of the Imperial age[18]; it even reappeared in a fairly radically reworked form in a poem attributed to the Latin African poet Dracontius of the fifth century AD, called *Perdiccas' Illness* (*Aegritudo Perdicae*). Moreover, a mosaic in Algiers decorating the tomb of Cornelia Urbanilla (third century AD) depicts the scene in which Hippocrates tests the pulse of the emaciated young Perdiccas.[19] It thus spread both East and West, all the way to North Africa.

HIPPOCRATES' 'SAYINGS'

A wise man is also revered for his words. Accordingly, just as there exist the sayings of the Seven Wise Men, so the Hippocratic biography became linked to 'sayings'. For instance, Stobaeus (fifth century AD) refers to the episode of Hippocrates with the Persian king in his *Anthology* simply with the following witty exchange[20]: "Someone wanted to persuade Hippocrates to go up to Xerxes by saying 'he is a good king', but Hippocrates answered 'I have no need of a good master".' The sentence does not derive from the *Letters* or from any other known source. The inclusion of Hippocrates in the collections of sayings of the wise men of Greece is poorly attested in the Greek tradition, but is prominent in Arabic *Collections of Sayings*

---

[17]   Pinault (1992), 88.

[18]   An analogous episode is that of Antiochus, Seleucus' son, who was in love with his young step-mother Stratonice: the affliction was solved by the famous physician Erasistratus, cited by a number of Greek and Latin sources. An allusion to Perdiccas in Lucian, *How One Must Write History* 35 and in Latin authors such as Claudianus (*Minor Poems* 8.69), Fulgentius (*Myth.* 3.2), *Latin Anthology*, 220. See also Pinault (1992), 61–77; Amundsen (1974).

[19]   According to Chamoux (1962), 386–96.

[20]   *Anthology* 3.464 (Wachsmuth and Hense [1912]), 10–13.

(*gnomologia*).[21] Numerous sayings from *Aphorisms*, the most widely read Hippocratic text, appear among Hippocrates' sayings, even if to the modern mind there is a great deal of 'technical' material contained in them. To the ancients, however, the *Aphorisms* 'are adapted not only to medicine, but to life in general. For they are universal laws foretelling and regulating events'.[22]

Many memorable phrases appear in the *Hippocratic Corpus*, which were later extracted and became catch-phrases of Hippocratic medicine among a general public. *Breaths*, for instance, is a text on which Galen did not write a commentary, and yet some expressions from this work were often cited by non-medical authors, especially Christian.[23] It lent itself to becoming proverbial; for example, in *Breaths* 1 we find the famous statement that 'opposites are the cure by opposites'. Other examples of pithy saying that enjoyed great popularity include 'conflux one, conspiration one, all things in sympathy',[24] 'moisture [is] the vehicle of nutriment'[25] and 'to refuse to treat those who are overmastered by their diseases'.[26] Other phrases attributed to Hippocrates do not appear in the *Corpus* as it survives today, such as 'coitus is a slight epileptic attack',[27] and 'cure for the foot is rest'.[28]

HIPPOCRATES FOR A LARGE MEDICAL AUDIENCE

We have focussed so far on what one could call the 'exterior' aspect of Hippocrates' afterlife. We shall now turn to the reception in medical circles and the development of 'Hippocratism', for which Galen was

[21]   See Gutas (1975), 1–3, 459–63; Gutas (1981); Overwien (2017); Alessi (in press); and Chapter 15 by Pormann in this volume.

[22]   Flashar (1962), 405; English translation by Kapetanaki and Sharples (2006), 88, lines 23–5; see also Overwien (2017); on this text see also Sluiter (1994) and Roselli (1998a). On the reception of *Aphorisms* in ancient literature, see also Nachmanson (1933).

[23]   Especially *Breaths* 1, 6.90, 5–6 L.: the physician sees and touches horrible things.

[24]   *Nutriment* 23 (9.106.6 L.).   [25]   *Nutriment* 55 (9.120.3 L.).

[26]   *Art* 3 (6.4, 18–6, 1 L.).

[27]   Gellius *Attic Nights* 19.2.8, see also Macrobius, *Saturnalia* 2.8.16 (Willis [1963]).

[28]   Pseudo-Alexander of Aphrodisias, *Problems* 3.4 (1.4 in Kapetanaki-Sharples [2006], 97), Sextus Empiricus, *Outlines of Pyrrhonism* 1.71 (1.20.22–24), Stephen of Alexandria, *Commentary on Hippocrates' Fractures*, ed. Irmer (1977), 55.10–11.

highly influential.[29] Owsei Temkin laid the bases for the history of Hippocratism in a seminal article published in 1932, identifying a moment of crisis or a 'gap'[30] in the third century AD, after Galen, and the advent of a division between Greek and Latin medicine. It cannot be denied that in the third century AD, there was a considerable decline in the availability of the sources of culture and background on which physicians drew to enhance their professional knowledge. Furthermore, the political and administrative situation in the two parts of the Roman empire, the West and the East, became markedly differentiated. In medical practice, a tendency arose towards simplification, and a practical approach to diagnosis and therapy tended to be adopted, with the resulting abandonment of any kind of theoretical speculation. Some Latin authors, such as Gargilius Martialis, turned to the Latin authorities (Pliny, Celsus) rather than Greek ones, such as Dioscorides, Galen, or Oribasius. Temkin therefore denied the existence of Hippocratism in the Latin authors – and of Galenism as well.[31] It was the encyclopaedic work of Oribasius (fourth century AD) that marked the true beginning of Hippocratic Galenism – the reception of Hippocrates mediated through Galen's interpretation – in the eastern part of the Empire.[32] The fifth and sixth centuries AD then saw a revival of studies in Alexandria in Egypt, which led to the canonisation of a group of works both by Hippocrates and by Galen (with a parallel in Ravenna, in Italy, during the same period), thereby crystallising and establishing order in the doctrines, which then passed into the Arab world and the Middle Ages in the West.

Temkin's account of these developments is still regarded as an effective portrait today, but it needs to be corrected in certain aspects. The third century AD can hardly be called a blank spot any longer, and the relations between the Greek and Latin areas of the Mediterranean

---

[29]   See Chapter 13 by Boudon-Millot in this volume.

[30]   See, e.g., 'blank spot', Kudlien (1968b), or 'black hole', Nutton (2004), 292. Kudlien followed the strands of a (simplified and systematized) 'university medicine' which may have had its origins in the third century.

[31]   Temkin (1973), 59–60.   [32]   Temkin (1932), 32–4.

were closer than Temkin thought. We must make allowances for the cultural and social differences among the authors: for example, Gargilius was *not* a physician. The differences between urban and provincial environments, between the centre and the periphery, also played a role. High-level professional and cultural training was reserved to a select few, whereas the ordinary practitioners had only limited training.

For instance, in Egypt, where medicine had always flourished, strikingly different texts purportedly of Hippocrates and Galen were in circulation between the third and the fourth centuries AD. There were careful copies of erudite works such as Galen's *On the Doctrines of Hippocrates and Plato*; a highly erudite commentary on Hippocrates' *Nutriment*; a good number of copies of Hippocratic texts of varying degrees of accuracy. But all of these coexisted with a copy of *Aphorisms*, in which the text was intermingled with a commentary and paraphrase of disarming simplicity that was completely independent of Galen. Such a text clearly represents a very low level of Hippocratic exegesis.[33] Moreover, it can be presumed that the Hippocratic text was in some sense rewritten, because it appears to have lost any trace of original ionic dialect forms. In an environment far away from Egypt, in a provincial area – albeit not culturally devoid of interest – such as Bordeaux in the late fourth century AD, Marcellus, known as 'Empiricus', composed a drug handbook (*On medicaments*) designed for a non-professional public, and added as an introduction a series of *Letters* to his work. Out of a total of no fewer than seven *Letters*, two are attributed to Hippocrates (*Letter to the King Antiochus* and *Letter to the King Maecenas*), which Marcellus transcribed directly from the work of a certain Largius Designatianus, who is said to have translated them from Greek. The two letters are actually late apocryphal texts, with parallel

---

[33]   All these texts are reedited and commented in Adorno et al. CPF 1.2 (2008); see also Manetti (1995) (the commentary on *Nutriment*); for the 'popular' commentary on *Aphorisms*, see Manetti and Luiselli (2008).

content, based on a common Greek model.[34] They display a very basic knowledge of anatomy and physiology (including the humours and their working) and this is probably the very aim of their presence in Marcellus' work: all the introductory letters seem to portray different aspects of medicine but, taken as a whole, they form a summary of the principles of anatomy and physiology, ethics, therapy, pharmacology, and drug knowledge.[35] This picture suggests that even though the name of Hippocrates was a forgery and was merged with the names of Latin authorities, its symbolic value was still very high and guaranteed legitimacy even for a text that distinctly reflected popular medicine, such as that of Marcellus. It also reveals that contacts between the Greek and the Latin world were still active in the medical professional environment, because Greek standardised medical texts were translated into Latin.

Other text typologies should also be taken into consideration and could help to broaden our knowledge of Hippocratism in the Imperial age. The recent edition of the Pseudo-Galenic treatise *The Physician* or *Introduction* by Caroline Petit (2009b) has led to renewed focus on Galen's apocryphal texts, which tend to be neglected in the critical literature. The text is a general introduction to medicine. Hippocrates enjoys a pre-eminence of quasi-divine aspect, but the author often distorts or rewrites Hippocrates' words or attributes to him opinions that cannot be located in the *Hippocratic Corpus*. In many cases he simplifies Hippocrates in order to give to the passage as general a meaning as possible. No title is ever given to the Hippocratic treatise, even when it is explicitly quoted. Petit emphasises the brevity of most of the quotations, which is consistent with the general style of a concise introduction. The end result is a 'Hippocrates boiled down to a series of propositions, ... a basic Hippocrates to be learned by heart, a simplified, second-hand Hippocrates'.[36]

---

[34]   It is the text preserved by Paul of Aegina and attributed to Diocles of Carystus; see also Opsomer and Halleux (1985) and Zurli (1990).
[35]   Cilliers (2010).   [36]   Petit (2010) 357; see also Petit (2009a).

In the fourth century AD Oribasius composed a voluminous medical encyclopaedia called *Medical Collections*. A native of Pergamon, he completed at least part of his studies in Alexandria under the guidance of Zenon of Cyprus (between 364 and 388 AD) and soon became the personal physician of the future emperor Julian, whom he followed throughout his life, also accompanying him on his military campaigns.[37] He wrote his encyclopaedia at Julian's behest, after presenting to the emperor an epitome of the works of Galen. He aimed at gathering the writings of the best physicians. Such a composition, he asserted, would be extremely useful for readers. He selected authors and organised the work by themes, thus avoiding repetition; however, he did not omit any material contained in his epitome of Galen, as he himself says: "I will omit nothing of this arrangement seeing that this author [sc. Galen] surpasses all the other writers in the same suggestions, since he makes use of the most exact methods and definitions following Hippocratic principles and opinions."[38] Here Oribasius pays tribute to Hippocrates, yet as interpreted by Galen.[39] Therefore, the extracts from Galen's works form the backbone of the *Medical Collections*, and although the range of Hippocratic texts genuinely cited in Oribasius' works is extensive, they are always taken indirectly, from other sources, mostly Galen, and Oribasius rearranges his material in all cases.

THE STUDY OF HIPPOCRATES BETWEEN THE GREEK AND LATIN WORLD

Hippocratic texts formed the core of high-level medical training, although not many aspiring physicians could gain familiarity with the whole *Hippocratic Corpus*. At least from the fifth century onwards, a Hippocratic curriculum emerged in the Greek environment of Alexandria. Moreover, there is some evidence such as the *Aphorism* commentary mentioned earlier that already in third- and

---

[37]   Oribasius' birthplace and origins are controversial; see Grant (1997), 1.

[38]   Orib. *Introd.* 1, 3, English translation by Grant (1997), 25.

[39]   See Chapter 13 by Boudon-Millot in this volume.

fourth-century AD Egypt, Hippocrates was systematically studied, even if at a rather lower level. We know of two physicians who taught Hippocrates at this time, Philagrius and Magnus of Nisibe.[40]

In the first half of the fourth century AD, Philagrius[41] worked in Thessalonica, where he composed a commentary on Hippocrates, although unfortunately little of it is known. At the same time as Oribasius, Magnus of Nisibe studied with Zenon of Cyprus, and he later became an *iatrosophist* (professor of medicine) in Alexandria.[42] He composed at least one commentary on the *Aphorisms*, which is cited several times by Cassius Felix, a physician and translator from Numidia. In 447 he wrote a Latin work inspired by Greek dogmatic medicine, thus testifying to the close relations between the learned environments of Greek-speaking Alexandria and Latin North Africa. Although Cassius Felix favoured practical medicine, he intended his work for well-educated physicians. He based it mostly on Galen, in particular on *To Glauco on the Method of Healing*, although he quotes Hippocrates (mainly the *Aphorisms*) on a number of occasions. He may have taken some of his quotations from Galen; yet because Cassius admits that he quoted the *Aphorisms* with the interpretation of Magnus, he probably also drew on other sources.[43] This is further confirmed by the work of the Methodist physician Caelius Aurelianus, active in North Africa in the fifth century AD: he could draw on an extremely rich array of Greek sources. In the same milieu, St Augustine (354–430) referred to debates on Hippocratic writings in a polemic about the authenticity of the Apostolic works; St Augustine summarised Galen's arguments, and his source may have been the physician Avianus Vindicianus.[44] These examples show that in fifth century AD North Africa Hippocratic exegetical texts must have circulated.

---

40   On all these authors, see also Overwien (2012b).

41   Suidas φ 295; Temkin (1932) 30 (who dates it to the first half of the fourth century AD), Nutton (2000), 779; as to the Arab sources, Sezgin (1970), 154–6 and also Masullo (1999).

42   Temkin (1932) 30; Nutton (1999a) 698.   43   Palmieri (2007).

44   See Speyer (1976), 126 and 89–90.

Since the third century BC, Alexandria had always been an important centre for training physicians, and later also for philosophical and grammatical studies; after the death of Proclus (485 AD), the school of Athens was plunged into a severe crisis and was continued in Alexandria. In this period the teaching of higher education in philosophy, grammar, rhetoric, and medicine became progressively more and more homogeneous.[45] For every discipline teaching became systematised, with a course of studies based on an approach modelled on the philosophical teaching of the Neoplatonic school of Ammonius; the exegetic method adapted to general teaching practice was profoundly influenced by Aristotelian logic.[46]

Students of medicine were instructed to read and comment on the 'classics' in a certain order, and the phenomenon concerned both Hippocrates and Galen. This resulted in the formation of a precise curriculum of readings, although it should not be taken as a fixed and exclusive 'canon': it was a process that took shape from at least the fifth century AD, developing further up to the seventh century AD and beyond in the Arab context. Among the works of Hippocrates and Galen, a choice was made with a selection of writings intended (by the Alexandrians, not always by Galen) for beginners. The works in question were organised into groups according to the educational level and were read in the appropriate order, under the guidance of the teacher during class. Works that were not encompassed in the so-called 'Canon' were by no means excluded, but were left for individual in-depth study.

According to information from later Arabic sources, the Alexandrians decided that one should read Galen before Hippocrates, selecting first and foremost four Hippocratic treatises, namely *Prognostic*; *Aphorisms*; *Regimen in Acute Diseases*; *and Airs, Waters, Places*.[47] Galen thus came first and was regarded by the

---

[45]   For medicine studied on the higher levels together with grammar, rhetoric, logic, philosophy, immediately after Galen: Marasco (2010). See also Lamberz (1987), 1–20.

[46]   For example, Westerink (1964); Duffy (1984); Wolska-Conus (1992); Roueché (1999); and Ieraci Bio (2003).

[47]   Lieber (1981), 172–4.

Alexandrians – as by Oribasius before them – as key to understanding the Hippocratic tradition.

The image of Hippocrates as a writer, however, changed over time. Galen had defended the Hippocratic writings against their detractors, emphasising the clarity and brevity of the Hippocratic texts and adopting exegetic strategies to justify their manner of presentation. In contrast, students in Late Antique Alexandria faced severe difficulties in understanding the texts. Hippocrates had an obscure – nearly oracular – writing style. Galen was the only sure guide for a correct interpretation of the meaning of his words. Galen, therefore, offered the only access to Hippocrates, so that his legacy could be preserved.[48] One can perceive both the difficulty of understanding Hippocrates and the quasi-religious reverence for him from the following two quotations:

> Hippocrates did indeed belong to an earlier age, whereas Galen was writing at a later date, but Hippocrates has transmitted to us the 'seeds'. Galen cultivated those seeds, he propagated and perfected them; therefore Hippocrates should be introduced (*sc.* to beginners), though not for his position in the ranking but as a figure rich in glory. But because, in order to proceed to this introduction there is a need for persuasion (indeed, the ears of those who are to be introduced would be unable to grasp such profundity), thus let us take Galen and award a central position to his book on the introduction (that is *On the Sects for Beginners*), so that with the aid of his rich explanations and sweetness we find what we are looking for.[49]
>
> Having instructed (you) in the preliminaries of the Hippocratic mysteries, let us now proceed from the sacred rites themselves to the inner sanctuary of the teaching of Hippocrates.[50]

---

[48]   Roselli (1999).

[49]   John of Alexandria, Comm. on Galen's *On the sects*, 2ra, 48–49 Pritchet (1983).

[50]   John of Alexandria, Comm. on Hippocrates' *Epidemics* 6, ed. Duffy (1997), 28.7–9.

One approaches the Hippocratic text under the guidance of the master, as if one were initiated to the mysteries of a cult. In the Neoplatonic milieu, we find similar metaphors, although such language had already been used earlier in Hippocratic texts such as *Law*, or in an anonymous papyrus from the second century AD, which mentions the *Oath* as a prerequisite to be introduced into the 'mysteries' of Hippocrates.[51] The Alexandria curriculum is attested in many Greek and Arabic sources, and one can reconstruct the following version from Palladius and Stephen of Athens: *Aphorisms, Nature of Man, Nature of Child, Use of Liquids, Nutriment, Prognostic, Regimen in Acute Diseases, Joints, Fractures, Airs, Waters, Places, Epidemics,* and *Diseases of Women*, although there are many variations in the Greek and Arabic sources.[52]

Recently, a commentary on *Epidemics* 6 (preserved in a Syriac translation) has been attributed to Gesius of Petra, a pagan physician who enjoyed great fame, and who, at the end of the fifth century AD, studied at Alexandria under a master of considerable repute, Domnus, about whom very little is known.[53] The commentary on *Epidemics* 6 first quotes the source text to be explained – and this quotation is known as the 'lemma' – and then comments on it. Galen appears to be the main source, or, as Kessel put it, this Syriac commentary is 'in a certain sense a supercommentary, a commentary on Galen's commentary'.[54] The exegetic approach typical of Late Antique Alexandrian commentaries can clearly be perceived, for example the division of teaching activities into lessons (*práxeis*), each composed of a general part (*theoría*) and text analysis (*léxis*).

---

[51]   *Law* 5 (4.642, 3–5 L.); P.Oxy. 4970, 5–6 (Leith et al. [2009]).

[52]   Iskandar (1976), 235–8; Duffy (1997), 9–11; Irmer (1987), esp. 170–72; Garofalo (2000), 144–6; Overwien (2012b); see also Anastassiou and Irmer (2012), 439–40 and 441–57 and Bräutigam (1908), 43–4.

[53]   Kessel (2012a), in particular 98–9. On Gesius, see also Temkin (1932), 73–4; Nutton (1984), 6–7; Duffy (1983), 23; Wolska-Conus (1989), 50–5; Nutton (1998); and Watts (2009). On Domnus, see Ihm (2002), 85–6.

[54]   Kessel (2012a), 98. For Gesius as the possible source of an Arabic commentary on *Prognostic*, see Joosse and Pormann (2012).

Other commentaries survive: by Palladius on *Epidemics* 6, *Fractures*, and *Aphorisms* (partially preserved in Arabic)[55]; by Stephen of Athens[56] on *Aphorisms, Fractures*, and *Prognostic*.[57] In addition there remains a commentary by John of Alexandria on *Epidemics* 6, partially transmitted in Greek and completely in Latin, and on *Nature of Child*, again in the Latin version.[58] Both Palladius and John of Alexandria wrote a commentary on *Regimen in Acute Diseases*; Palladius probably composed a commentary on *Prognostic*, as perhaps did Gesius.[59] Furthermore, over the last few decades fragments of anonymous commentaries on Hippocrates have been identified in various Greek manuscripts, all traceable to the same cultural milieu.[60]

Although the texts are mostly independent of one another, they display a marked basic homogeneity: they are all influenced by the exegetic approach of the school of Ammonius.[61] They reveal awareness of the philosophical issues involved, albeit varying from a passing acquaintance to a high degree of familiarity, and all the texts reflect the same teaching and learning practices. These texts consistently presuppose that the works, whether Hippocratic or Galenic, will be read in a specific order, which generally corresponds to that of 'curriculum'. The basic content is derived from Galen, who remains a constant reference, although this is not always stated explicitly.

---

[55]   Dietz (1834), Vol. 2, 1–204; Irmer (1977), see also Irmer (1975); Pormann et al. (2017); pace Magdelaine (2003); Duffy (1997), 9 n. 4; Biesterfeldt (2007); see also Wolska-Conus (1996).

[56]   He has been identified by Wolska-Conus (1989) with the philosopher Stephanus of Alexandria; but see also Westerink (1985), Vol. 1, 19–23.

[57]   Westerink (1985–1995); Irmer (1977); Duffy (1983); see also Wolska-Conus (1989); Roueché (1990).

[58]   Duffy (1997), 13; Pritchet (1975); see also Bräutigam (1908), 51.

[59]   Overwien (2011); Joosse and Pormann (2012), 254–5.

[60]   Fragments of anonymous commentaries on *Epidemics* 6 in Duffy (1997), 119–25; Roselli (1999); Ieraci Bio (2012). In the work of ʿAli ibn Riḍwān, segments of two commentaries on *Diseases of Women* 1–11 have been identified, one falsely attributed to Galen, the other attributed to an Asclepius, Ullmann (1977); the fragment of a commentary on *Precepts* was analysed by Bräutigam (1908), 54–6.

[61]   It should be underlined that all the texts reveal a strong link with oral teaching, and even their title often makes it clear that they derive from notes prepared for an oral lesson (for the formula that appears in the titles 'from the voice of', see also Richard [1950], 204–5).

As was typical in Alexandrian medical scholasticism, the material is divided into lessons (*práxeis*). The traditional eight points according to which the text analysis is organised are presented in the first lesson, and there is a strong tendency towards constant use of division (*dihaíresis*).[62]

Most of the commentators mentioned above remain shrouded in mystery.[63] Palladius and Stephen certainly taught in Alexandria, as did John. Palladius probably preceded John, and both preceded Stephen.[64] Stephen of Athens has been identified by Wolska-Conus as being the same as Stephen of Alexandria, the commentator of two works by Aristotle who reportedly arrived in Alexandria between 567 and 572.[65] John of Alexandria and Stephen summarise the essence of exegesis in three or four points: (1) the text should be made clear; (2) the ancient author's thought should be well defined and stand out clearly; (3) the advantage or utility deriving from the text should be highlighted (only in Stephen); and (4) there should be clear distinction between true and false.[66] At the root of this approach there lies, as always, the work of Galen, who, however, tended to view the last point as extraneous to the commentary itself.[67] The basis for their interpretation of Hippocrates always resided in the work of Galen, although they did not consistently follow the model of the Galenic commentary concerning the particular work with which they happened to be dealing. Rather, they often opted in favour of cross-references when using works by Galen, of which they had a profound knowledge, just as they also had in-depth knowledge of the Hippocratic texts above and beyond the 'curriculum'. In his

---

[62] Duffy (1984); Mansfeld (1992), 326–31; Ieraci Bio (2003), 11–13; and Ieraci Bio (2007).

[63] Bräutigam (1908), 35–46, dates them all to the period 550–650 AD. For the dating of John to the first half of the sixth century, see Duffy (1997), 12 and Kessel (2012b).

[64] Wolska-Conus (1989), 82–4; Irmer (1977).

[65] Wolska-Conus (1989): her opinion is shared by Roueché (1990) 108–28, but is refuted by Lautner (1992), 519–22.

[66] John of Alexandria, *Commentary on Hippocrates' 'Epidemics'* 6, ed. Duffy (1997), 28. 14–18; Stephanus, *Commentary on Hippocrates' 'Aphorisms'*, ed. Westerink (1985/1998), 32.20–25.

[67] See also Duffy (1984), 22–3; Wolska-Conus (1996), 42–7, but also the previous articles: Wolska-Conus (1992), 77–86; Wolska-Conus (1994), 33–42.

commentary on *Prognostic*, Stephen exhorts his students to read *Nature of Man*, which was not part of the 'curriculum'.[68] Similarly, in his commentary on *Aphorisms* 1.1, he introduces new material not mentioned by Galen in his commentary, namely a passage from *Epidemics* 6.4.7:

> Kindnesses to those who are ill. For example to do in a clean way his food or drink or whatever he sees, softly what he touches. Things that do no great harm and are easily got, such as a cool drink where it is needed. Entrance, conversation. Position and clothing for the sick person, hair, nails, scents.

He then embarks on a lengthy digression about medical etiquette when examining the patients, and alludes to several Hippocratic deontological treatises.[69] This shows that although there was a common pool of material largely derived from Galen on which the commentators drew, they also displayed originality and innovation.

The same concern with high-level medical education is also found in Latin texts originating in Ravenna, an important centre for political reasons, which also boasted a medical school about which little else is known. This said, a Latin manuscript originating in the school environment of Ravenna has different Latin translations of *Prognostic; Sevens;* and *Airs, Waters, Places*.[70] It also contains Late Antique Latin commentaries on Galen's *On Sects for Beginners, Art of Medicine, On Pulses for Beginners, To Glauco on the Method of Healing,* that are basically notes taken by students who attend courses on these texts: the *iatrosophist* Agnellus explained the texts in Ravenna, his pupil Simplicius copied his lectures.[71] There are many similarities with the teaching in Late Antique Alexandria. The commentary on *On the Sects for Beginners,* for instance, reveals

---

[68] *On Hippocrates' 'Prognostic'*, ed. Duffy (1983), 32.

[69] Stephanus, *Commentary on Hippocrates' 'Aphorisms'*, ed. Westerink (1985/1998), 42; Galen, *On Hippocrates' 'Epidemics 6'*, who mentions the aphorism (ed. Wenkebach (1956), 204.17–19); on the general behaviour of the physician ibid., 206.12–207.21.

[70] Palmieri (1981), 204–11; Palmieri (1989), 27–46.   [71] Palmieri (2001), 237–46.

many close parallels with the text attributed to John of Alexandria.[72] On the basis of the Latin Hippocratic translations, Augusto Beccaria argued that an autonomous Latin medical school existed in Ravenna where the translations originated.[73]

In total, we have Latin translations of *Aphorisms, Airs, Waters, Places, Prognostic, Regimen, Diseases of Women, Sevens*, as well as a fragmentary Latin version of *Nature of Man*. Most of these works form part of the Alexandrian curriculum. Adopting an approach similar to that of Beccaria, Mazzini and Palmieri locate all the Latin translations of Hippocrates in Ravenna.[74] Mazzini, in particular, analyses a series of affinities among all the translations, examining vocabulary, morphology, and syntax but also assessing the translation technique. He notes that some translations are extremely faithful to the original, whereas others are relatively free re-workings of the source text. In contrast, Anna Maria Ieraci Bio insisted on the distinction between production and circulation: just because a translation circulated in Ravenna does not necessarily mean that it was produced there.[75] There may, therefore, have been more than one centre of translation in Italy; Hippocratic works were certainly translated in northern Italy, but also in southern Italy.[76]

The surviving Latin translations confirm that Greek medical texts circulated widely in Italy. Early twentieth-century philologists have repeatedly labelled these Latin translations as barbaric in character, yet translating Hippocratic texts was a highly specialised task to facilitate study and scholarly engagement. The earliest translation of *Aphorisms*, Hippocrates' most widely read work, is a case in point.[77] It is rarely found on its own, but rather in the context of a commentary.[78] Two such commentaries from the sixth century AD

---

[72]   Nutton (1991), 511–13.
[73]   Mørland (1932), 190–94; Beccaria (1959, 1961, 1971); and Palmieri (1991, 1993, 1994, 2002).
[74]   Mazzini (1977, 1983, 1984, 1989, 1991); Mazzini and Flammini (1983); and Palmieri (1981) and her works cited in the previous footnote.
[75]   Ieraci Bio (1994).   [76]   See Vázquez Buján (1982, 1984, 1992) and Manetti (1992).
[77]   Beccaria (1961), 5–6; Müller-Rohlfsen (1980), xxii–xxiii; Fischer (2002).
[78]   Vázquez Buján (2010).

have come down to us in a great number of manuscripts.[79] One offers
a general prologue on the parts of medicine that shows an affinity with
the *Introduction to Philosophy* of the Neoplatonic school.[80] It then
discusses the traditional eight points of text analysis, displaying
a number of correspondences with Stephen's commentary. This erudite
commentary aims at helping beginners by offering explanations different from those given by Galen; in this, it reflects an Alexandrian Greek
tradition.[81] The second commentary from a much later date contains
a prologue and an abbreviated and much simpler commentary.[82] In its
plainness, it resembles the Greek commentary on the *Aphorisms* surviving on papyrus mentioned earlier. We can thus discern a long-term
continuity in the reception of Hippocrates.

THE OTHER HIPPOCRATES OR THE REWRITTEN
HIPPOCRATES

Jacques Jouanna has been studying the continuous influence of
humoral pathology, and in this context brought to light a series of
poorly known or unpublished texts, often attributed to Hippocrates,
but also to other authors (John of Damascus or Galen), or in some cases
anonymous. These texts transmit a Galenic version of Hippocrates'
theory of the four humours that is expanded to include the so-called
'temperaments'. These texts show that humoral pathology continued
to be discussed and developed in both Greek and Latin.[83] The material
includes Latin texts such as *Letter of Vindicianus to Penthadius*;[84]
and *Introduction to Good Health (Isagoge saluberrima)* by Pseudo-
Soranus.[85] The latter's Greek sources share material with the Latin
treatise *Hippocrates' Book on Pulses and Mixtures to his Pupil Galen*,
from which there derives another text with the title *What Is Man?*

---

[79]   Beccaria (1961), 22.
[80]   See Fischer (2002), 93–5, 212, 287–9; Beccaria (1961) 30–1; see also Haverling (1995).
[81]   Fischer (2002), 291–3.   [82]   Ibid., 279–80.
[83]   Jouanna (2005a, 2005b, 2005c, 2006a, 2006b, 2007, 2008, 2009) and Jouanna and
       Fischer (2007).
[84]   Rose (1894), 485–92.   [85]   Fischer (2000).

attributed to John of Damascus. Other Greek texts sharing the same material are *On Man's Constitution* (*De formatione hominis*), also surviving in Armenian and Hebrew[86]; *On the Composition of Universe and Man*; *Letter to King Ptolemy about Man's Constitution*;[87] Pseudo-Galen, *On humours*; Meletius' *On the Nature of Man*, and so on. Essentially, then, we have a text on the doctrine of the four humours that is at one and the same time both systematic and mobile (malleable in its formulation, but stable as regards the essence of its contents) – a sort of hypertext. There is an implicit awareness that the Hippocratic doctrine ought not only to be interpreted through Galen, but also 'translated' and 'rewritten' in a language suited to a different age. The actual reference to the Hippocratic authorship of the doctrines expounded in the texts has become a residual element, no longer strictly necessary; in fact the texts are attributed to a variety of authors. What counts is above all the continuity of the doctrines. The most striking collateral effect of Jouanna's studies is that it sheds new light on the relations of the Latin witnesses with the Greek sources, and this in turn prompts deeper reflection on the network of connections that continued to exist between the two parts of the empire, even at a fairly late date.

The greatest difficulty in reconstructing the process by which such texts took shape resides in the fact that only a very rough approximation can be given as to the date when they were originally created, because most of them have come down to us in manuscripts from a much later date. Jouanna believes they may have originated within the cultural milieu of Alexandria, which remained remarkably stable from the fifth to the seventh century AD. There may also have been some contact with Ravenna, as far as Latin translation is concerned, and other versions were recast in Byzantium.[88] Jouanna points out that Hippocrates' *Nature of Man*, from which the theory of the four humours derives, was *not* included in the Alexandrian curriculum,

---

[86]   Jouanna and Mahé (2004) and Jouanna (2006a), 130 n. 41.
[87]   Ideler (1841), 1.303.   [88]   Jouanna (2006b), 292–6.

even though it was well known and widely appreciated. The most obvious explanation for this omission could be, quite simply, that *Nature of Man* actually had already been superseded by Galen's *On the Elements according to Hippocrates* and *On Mixtures*. It was therefore not studied within the medical school, where students were soon introduced to the more complete texts of Galen. Already at a very early date, the theory of the four humours found in *Nature of Man* was reformulated and expanded to include new aspects such as the cosmic elements. The Pseudo-Galenic *Introduction* already testifies to this process of reformulation, although the author remained still close to the original texts, as the following quotation shows[89]:

> Of what elements is man composed? Man is composed, as scholars of physical phenomena who follow Hippocrates[90] also agree, of the prime cosmic elements: fire, air and earth .... And as man dissolves, he dissolves in the prime elements, as Hippocrates himself states ...
>
> (Man is also composed) of the secondary elements – which are close to human nature – blood, phlegm yellow bile and black bile.

Introduction marks the first stage of this process of reformulation. Later, Oribasius constructs his own description by explicitly conflating several different passages from Galen[91]:

> From Galen, *On the Elements according to Hippocrates*. Of earth, of fire, of water, of air, thus it has been shown, are composed all the bodies that are born and die, and the only real truth is the statement by Hippocrates, who says that as the elements become blended with one another and undergo exchanges with one another, thereby experiencing numerous alterations, what comes about is the generation of animals and plants ... Hippocrates, after demonstrating that hot and cold, moist and dry are common to all beings, then goes on to deal with another genre, not the first but the

---

[89] *Introduction*, 9.1, 9.2, (Petit [2009b]), 19, 20.

[90] I follow the translation of Roselli (2011) 184: 'selon la physique d'Hippocrate'; cf. Petit (2009b), 19.

[91] Oribasius *Collectionum medicarum reliquae*, ed. Raeder (1933), 75.

one that is proper to warm-blooded animals, blood and phlegm, yellow bile and black bile.

Thus direct citation from *Nature of Man* is synthesised in light of Galen's ideas. The presentation of the arguments starts out from a consideration of the cosmic elements, explicitly attributed to Hippocrates, subsequently continuing on the subject of the humours, but drawing almost exclusively on Galen's *On Elements*.

It is therefore evident that the manipulation and rearrangement of the Hippocratic theory of the four humours began long before the fifth century AD. Jouanna himself corrected his first hypothesis on when the complete theory of the four humours and four temperaments was first formulated by studying a passage preserved by Stobaeus' *Anthology* (fifth century) containing the 'opinion' of Galen on Hippocrates, which represents another redaction of the theory of the four humours.[92] The text preserved by Stobaeus can be dated: more specifically, it must be dated to before the beginning of the fifth century. This is not actually by Galen, but it still acknowledges a relation between the theory of the four humours and the text of *Nature of Man*, and it does not contain the theory of the temperaments. It therefore represents an intermediate stage in the evolution of the texts on the four humours. But the initial part of the passage reveals further elements[93]:

> He (*sc.* Hippocrates) says that man and all of the animals are composed of solid, liquid and aerial elements, and one cannot even exclude the nature of plants from this threefold generation.

Thus Hippocrates is credited with a classification of the elements of the body into solids, liquids, and aerial parts, yet this is not attested in Hippocratic texts, but it derives from Galen's commentary on *Epidemics* 6.8.7 : 'the things they contain, which are contained and which move').[94]

---

[92] Jouanna (2010); the passage had been already discussed by Kudlien (1968b).
[93] *Anthology* 4.37.14.
[94] Trans. Smith (1994); see also Galen, *On Hippocrates' 'Epidemics 6'*, ed. Wenkebach and Pfaff (1956), 446.

The Pseudo-Galenic *Introduction* presents a similar text[95]:

> He (sc. Hippocrates) says also that man once he has been born is composed of three connected elements, as follows, liquids, dry matter and the airs: he calls them 'the things they contain, which are contained and which move'.[96]

This effectively offers the same interpretation as that attested in Stobaeus, but the author of the *Introduction* is very clearly aware of the original Hippocratic passage, which he cites explicitly, whereas Stobaeus omits any reference to the passage from *Epidemics*. Stobaeus subsequently also devotes attention to determining in which works Hippocrates had made a special study of solids, liquids, and aerial elements. Stobaeus thus represents a more advanced phase of the process of systematisation, reinterpretation, and rewriting of the theory of *Nature of Man*, which had begun long before the fifth century, a gradual process which probably had its origins already in the third century immediately after Galen.

It is likely that the expected audience of these kinds of texts, indifferent to the history of the discipline or the paternity of the doctrine, was composed of practitioners rather than of students who were following the lessons of the iatrosophists. In conclusion it is probable, as Jouanna suggests, that the Late Antique Alexandrian milieu rearranged the materials and imposed a proper order on a fluid body of writings that had long been in circulation, in order to form a solid basis for professional and practical purposes, parallel with those of the higher medical education imparted by the iatrosophists. Both ways have been important for the transmission of the Hippocratic doctrine to the Middle Ages.

CONCLUSION

Like other Greek wise men, Hippocrates himself and his life have over the centuries become a symbol for good science, the good life, and

---

[95]   *Introduction* 9 (Petit [2009b]), 20.
[96]   See also *Epidemics* 6.8.7 (5.346.5–6 L.; ed. Manetti and Roselli (1982), 170–2.

wisdom for a much wider public than just physicians. His words were selected, extracted, and recorded, often together with the philosophers' sayings. His name alone commanded prestige: its symbolic value increased as less and less was known about his life and when it became increasingly difficult to determine which of the works attributed to him were genuine.

The reinterpretation and revision of his doctrines started very early – Galen himself testifies to it. For beginners in medicine, it produced a summarised, sometimes distorted and simplified version 'a basic Hippocrates to be learned by heart'. Otherwise Hippocrates' wording was filtered through Galen's texts that in a way substituted the original author. Later on, in opposition to the direct reading of the texts, other texts transmitted an enriched version of the four-humour theory in a remarkable variety of texts in Greek and Latin, referring all to the same 'model'. The Hippocratic doctrine is adapted, also deformed with the addition of Galenic or later elements and summarised in order to simplify, systematise, and popularise Hippocratic doctrine among practitioners who needed only its substance. In highly cultured contexts, both Latin and Greek, a common kind of exegesis was practised, largely based on Galen, but responding to the different strategies of the physicians: the circulation of exegetical texts was larger than it appears from the preserved texts.

One feature of this complex story is in my opinion particularly interesting: whatever the level of Hippocrates' reception, be it his life and anecdotes for a non-professional public or his popular medical reception or the most refined activity of commenting the texts, there appear many clues of a remarkable continuity and contiguity over time of the Greek and Latin medical environments. The geography of Hippocrates' reception shows strong connections between the Greek-speaking learned Alexandria and Latin Africa of the fourth-fifth century; however, even in Gallia there was an echo of the Greek popularised Hippocrates. Italy too has revealed its deep relationship with the learned environment of the Alexandrian medical school.

15 Arabo-Islamic Tradition

Peter E. Pormann

In the Arabo-Islamic medical tradition, Hippocrates became the most famous Greek doctor, arguably even more famous than Galen of Pergamum. Although Galen's influence on this tradition far outstrips that of Hippocrates, the latter exercised greater power over the imagination of generations of Arab and Muslim physicians and became something of a household name. Therefore, to give an overview of how physicians and philosophers engaged with Hippocrates' legacy, it is necessary not only to look at the *Hippocratic Corpus* and ask how it was transmitted into Arabic, and how various authors, intellectuals, and thinkers adapted, adopted, and altered it. We also have to consider how the historical (and often elusive) figure of Hippocrates inspired legendary accounts of the father of medicine's life and deeds. In other words, we shall look both at how Hippocrates, the man, and the works attributed to him, impacted on the Arabo-Islamic tradition.

This chapter is divided into three unequal parts. The first deals with the information about Hippocrates as a historical and legendary figure that appears in the Arabic sources. The second investigates the transmission of the *Hippocratic Corpus* from Greek into Syriac and Arabic, for which the Alexandrian tradition in Late Antiquity is of crucial importance. In Late Antiquity, a select number of Hippocratic texts featured prominently in the amphitheatres of the so-called iatrosophists, professors of medicine steeped also in philosophical learning. Three texts in particular were central among them: the *Aphorisms*, the *Prognostic*, and the *Epidemics*. The third section of this chapter will offer case studies on how physicians engaged with these three texts. Galen's commentaries on various Hippocratic works will remain a focus throughout this chapter, as Galen often served as the prism through which Hippocratic works were read, translated, and interpreted in the Arabo-Islamic tradition.

HIPPOCRATES

Ibn Abī Uṣaybiʿa (d. 1270), author of a medical history entitled *Essential Information about the Classes of Physicians* (*ʿUyūn al-anbāʾ fī ṭabaqāt al-aṭibbāʾ*), divides the history of Greek medicine roughly into four periods: a mystical prehistory in which descendants of Asclepius gained only partial access to medicine; the period of the physicians 'among whom Hippocrates propagated the art of medicine'; the period of Galen, his contemporaries, and his successors; and the Late Antique Alexandrian tradition. In other words, Ibn Abī Uṣaybiʿa recognised that Hippocrates and Galen were the most important Greek physicians, around whom he organises two of his 'classes' (Arabic '*ṭabaqāt*'), groups of physicians somehow united in time and space. He often provides rich details about both these physicians' lives and works.

Ibn Abī Uṣaybiʿa represents a tradition called 'bio-bibliographical', because the works belonging to it provide a vita and bibliography for the various personalities that they discuss. Apart from Ibn Abī Uṣaybiʿa, the main authors who provide bio-bibliographical information about Hippocrates are the following: Ibn al-Nadīm in his *Catalogue* (*Kitāb al-Fihrist*, fl. 980s); Ibn Ǧulǧul in his *Classes of Physicians and Learned Men* (*Ṭabaqāt al-aṭibbāʾ wa-l-ḥukamāʾ*, d. c. 994); and al-Zawzānī, who abridged the *History of Learned Men* (*Taʾrīḫ al-ḥukamāʾ*) by al-Qifṭī (d. 1270).[1] Yet, we also find accounts about Hippocrates in the so-called Wisdom Literature or works on gnomology; here two prominent examples are the *Cabinet of Wisdom* (*Ṣiwān al-Ḥikma*) by the Baghdad intellectual and philosopher Abū Sulaymān al-Siǧistānī (d. c. 985), and the *Choicest Maxims and Best Sayings* (*Muḫtār al-ḥikam wa-maḥāsin al-kalim*) by the

---

[1]   See Weisser (1989), 399 n. 2.

eleventh-century Egyptian historian and scholar al-Mubaššir ibn Fātik.

Both the bio-bibliographical and the gnomological literature in Arabic contain numerous legends about Hippocrates, many of which go back to Late Antique material. By way of example, I shall briefly discuss the following two apocryphal stories from Hippocrates' life, which we find in a number of Arabic sources. In the first, Hippocrates cures a love-sick prince, and in the second, he refuses to help the king of Persia. I shall then turn to an apocryphal exchange of letters between Hippocrates and some eminent contemporaries, and finally discuss the sayings (or apophthegms) attributed to him in the Arabic tradition.

Al-Siǧistānī relates the story of a lovesick prince cured by Hippocrates in his *Cabinet of Wisdom*.[2] It goes something like this. A prince became ill and was wasting away. Hippocrates was called, and he saw that the prince was in love. He ordered all the women in the harem of the king to be brought before the prince, one by one, while he was palpitating his pulse. It never changed, and Hippocrates concluded that the prince must have fallen in love with someone else in the palace (for he had lived all his life there and never ventured out). Hippocrates then had the king's concubine brought before the prince, and his pulse began to race. Through a rhetorical stratagem, Hippocrates then got the father to agree to part with his concubine, so that his son could be cured.

A version of this story already appears in the Greek *Life of Hippocrates*, falsely attributed to Soranus (fl. AD 100).[3] It goes back to an account about King Seleucus of Antioch's son falling in love with his stepmother and being cured by the great Alexandrian anatomist Erasistratus (fl. third century BC).[4] Galen himself also knew it, and tells of how he diagnosed lovesickness in similar circumstances.[5]

---

[2]   Pinault (1992) discussed this episode in chapter 6, and prints a translation of it on pp. 136–7.

[3]   Ed. Ilberg (1927), 176.

[4]   See Lightfoot (2003), 373–9 for a discussion of this story and further literature.

[5]   Ed. Nutton (1979), 100–105.

Moreover, Avicenna (d. 1037) states that he used this process of feeling the pulse while members of the opposite sex are brought in 'a number of times' to diagnose lovesickness, and we also have accounts of him curing members of the ruling elite in a similar way.[6] Owing to the popularity of this story, it is therefore not surprising to see it associated with Hippocrates both in the Greek and in the Arabic tradition.

Like the episode of Hippocrates' diagnosing lovesickness, the story of how he refused to treat the Persian king goes back to Greek sources, but proved popular in Arabic as well. King Artaxerxes (called Bahman Ardašīr in the Arabic versions) writes to Paitus, king of Cos (called Fīlāṭūs in the Arabic), to send him Hippocrates. As Persia and Greece are at war, out of patriotism Hippocrates refuses to go. Both al-Siğistānī and Ibn Fātik relate this episode, although they tell it with slight variations.[7] This episode is interesting also for a different reason, as one Greek version of it includes an exchange of letters among the two kings, Hippocrates, and other interested parties. We find reflections of this short epistulary novella (if one can call it that) also in Arabic sources.

One version of this exchange is preserved in a curious Arabic manuscript kept in the British Library, the authenticity of which is much debated.[8] This manuscript also contains an Arabic version of letters between Hippocrates and Democritus, an exchange that again goes back to Greek sources.[9] However one judges the authenticity of this particular manuscript, it is clear that versions of epistolary exchanges came down into the Arabic tradition, and in particular the so-called wisdom literature.

In this wisdom literature, which includes collections of pithy sayings (or 'gnômai', hence gnomology), we also find Hippocrates again. We already mentioned the *Cabinet of Wisdom* and the *Choicest Maxims*, which include sayings attributed to Hippocrates. Many of these actually go back to the Hippocratic *Aphorisms*.

---

[6]   Pormann (2013a), 96–7.

[7]   See Pinault (1992), chapter 7, for an in-depth discussion.   [8]   Cottrell (2016).

[9]   Rütten (1992).

The first and most famous one is of course a prime example: "Life is short, the art is long, opportunity fleeting, experience dangerous, and decision difficult. ... "; yet, others also make it into this collection, such as aphorism i.3, which warns athletes that once they have achieved their peak, they can only go down from there.[10] These gnomological collections often go back to similar Late Antique Greek sources, and the fact that they proved popular in Arabic illustrates the important influence of Late Antiquity on the nascent Arabic tradition.

The so-called Hippocratic question was already debated in antiquity and continues to occupy the minds of scholars of the Arabo-Islamic tradition. Galen constituted the main authority when considering which of the works in the *Hippocratic Corpus* were genuine and which were not. In other words, although the Arabs had some notion that certain works were not by the historical Hippocrates (such as *Ancient Medicine*), they were still confident that many others were. This said, Ṯābit ibn Qurra (d. 901) reportedly distinguished among four different 'Hippocrateses (*Buqrāṭūn*)': the first is the 'famous and well known one'; the second (Hippocrates, son of Heracleides) lived nine generations later; the third (Hippocrates, son of Draco) lived another eleven generations later, and the fourth is the third's nephew. Ṯābit probably gets this information from a Late Antique source: Stephen of Alexandria, for instance, distinguished among four different Hippocrateses.[11] Ṯābit then goes on to say[12]:

> When the translators obtained their books [sc., of these four Hippocrateses], they mixed them up, explained them and commented upon them, without distinguishing between individual authors, because their theories are so close together. They took later authors to be earlier ones. It is said that the first to write about medicine was the first Hippocrates, namely the son of Gnosidicus.

---

10   Pormann (2013b).
11   Ed. Duffy (1983), 30, lines 16–17: "For there are four Hippocrates: the son of Gnosidicus, the son of Heracleides, the son of Draco, and the son of Thessalus."
12   al-Qifṭī, ed. Lippert (1903), 100, lines 12–15.

As the commentaries by Galen on various Hippocratic works were translated into Arabic (a topic to which we shall return later), Arab authors also became familiar with Galen's discussions about the authenticity and spuriousness of various writings. Take his *Commentary on Hippocrates' 'Epidemics'* as an example. Galen considered as genuine Books 1, 2, 3, and 6 of the *Epidemics*, while regarding Books 4, 5, and 7 as pseudepigraphic, as he explains in the opening section of Book ii.4 of his commentary[13]:

> In this lemma we find a summary of the anatomy of the blood vessels described succinctly. This is one of the things that bears witness to the truth of the assertion that Hippocrates' son Thessalus compiled the second book from what he found recorded by Hippocrates on leaves, sheets and scattered pieces. ... [some claimed correctly] that the first and third books are the only two books by Hippocrates written to be distributed as books. One of their strongest pieces of evidence for this is Hippocrates' style in these two [books].

Therefore, Arab authors assumed – like Galen before them – that some books attributed to Hippocrates were genuine, whereas others were forgeries, and on occasion they distinguished between them. Before we can address the question of how the 'genuine' works were rendered into Arabic, we need to stop briefly, so to speak, in Late Antiquity and investigate how the medical curriculum there impacted on the reception of Hippocrates in Arabic.

LATE ANTIQUE ALEXANDRIAN CURRICULUM

The debt to Alexandria in Late Antiquity, in particular, is felt strongly in the Arabic tradition. The main translator of medical works from Greek into Arabic, Ḥunayn ibn Isḥāq (d. ca. 873), had studied in Alexandria and compared medical teaching in Baghdad to that

---

[13]   Vagelpohl (2014, 2016); see also ed. Pfaff (1934), 310; the Greek original of this book is largely lost; see Duffy (1983) and, more generally, Pormann (2008, 2012b).

undertaken there.[14] Hippocrates' and Galen's prominent positions in the Alexandrian medical curriculum influenced later medical education. For instance, Riḍwān (d. 1068) wrote a *Useful Book on How to Teach the Art of Medicine* (*Al-Kitāb al-Nāfiʿ fī kayfīyat taʿlīm ṣināʿat al-ṭibb*), in which he devoted one chapter (i. 4) to 'The purposes of Hippocrates' books and the [right] way to teach them (*Aġrāḍ kutub Buqrāṭ wa-naḥw taʿlīmihā*)'. There he makes the point that many of Hippocrates' works are written in an enigmatic fashion (*ʿalā ṭarīq al-luġz*) and consequently require explanation. He continues[15]:

> Anybody who wants to study the art of medicine ought first to understand the purpose of each of [Hippocrates'] books according to the explanation given by Galen. I am going to provide to you here my understanding of Hippocrates' books. Therefore, I have copied some of them [myself] and have bought others, and I corrected all of them which came into my possession. I read them, learning from individual examples through the rules of logic [*muʿtabiran bi-šayʾin minhā bi-qawānīni l-manṭiqi*], and I extracted from them the most relevant passages and compiled them as an aide-memoire.

Ibn Riḍwān then lists individual Hippocratic titles, namely *Nature of the Child; Nature of Man; Airs, Water, Places; Aphorisms; Prognostic; Diseases of Women; Regimen in Acute Diseases; Epidemics; Humours; Nutriment; Joints;* and *Wounds in the Head.* He concludes the chapter by stating that one ought to use only drugs that are tried and tested.

This list of Hippocratic works gives a taste of how the Late Antique curriculum remained relevant in the medieval Islamic world. Ibn Riḍwān also lists a canon of four Hippocratic and sixteen Galenic works that were read in the amphitheatres of Alexandria, saying about the former[16]:

---

14   Lamoraux (2016).   15   Ed. Sāmarrāʾī (1986), 79.
16   Trans. Iskandar (1976), 249.

The most eminent physicians of Alexandria confined [medical courses] to four of the books of Hippocrates: *Aphorisms, Prognostic, Regimen in Acute Diseases*, and *Airs, Waters, and Places*. If the naturally gifted and resolved students, those eager for learning, were to consult these [four] books, they would desire to read the remaining books of Hippocrates, on account of his great wisdom.

These four core Hippocratic texts were all commented on repeatedly[17]: Galen, for instance, wrote commentaries on all four works, as did many earlier and later authors.

Some of the Late Antique commentaries of these works survive, either in Greek or in Arabic. They reflect the teaching methods employed by the iatrosophists in the amphitheatres of Alexandria. Many of them claim to be literally 'from the voice (or mouth)' of the teacher; that is, they are lecture notes. In these notes, the basic notions of Aristotelian philosophy are used to explain the text. The principle of division is also often at work: topics are divided and subdivided, or arranged into categories that are numbered. In the preface to the various commentaries, we also find eight subject headings discussed in a systematic fashion: (1) the intention, (2) usefulness, (3) authenticity, (4) title, (5) place in the curriculum, (6) how it is divided, (7) to what branch of medicine it belongs, and (8) the form of presentation.[18] These different elements also recur in the Arabic tradition, where Aristotelian philosophy plays some role in medicine. For example, division is present in such seminal works as the *Canon of Medicine* by Avicenna (Ibn Sīnā, d. 1037).[19] Likewise, we find the eight headings also in Hippocratic commentaries such as that on the *Prognostic* by ʿAbd al-Laṭīf al-Baġdādī (d. 1231).[20] It was on the basis of this Late Antique tradition that translators such as Ḥunayn ibn Isḥāq, who himself spent some time in Alexandria,

---

[17]   Anastassiou and Irmer (1997–2012).

[18]   For instance, in Stephen of Alexandria's *Commentary on Hippocrates' Aphorisms*, ed. Westerink (1985/1998), 28–33.

[19]   Pormann (2010b).   [20]   Joosse and Pormann (2012).

rendered most of the available medical literature from Greek into Syriac and Arabic.

TRANSLATING HIPPOCRATES

The *Hippocratic Corpus* was rendered from Greek into Arabic in the wake of the Graeco-Arabic translation movement, which has been the subject of a number of general studies.[21] This movement is a complex phenomenon that spans the period from the mid-eighth to the mid-tenth centuries. Generally speaking, one can distinguish a first period in the second half of the eighth century; the heyday of the movement in the mid-ninth century when translators in the circle of al-Kindī (d. after 870) and Ḥunayn ibn Isḥāq's workshop were active; and a later period, in the early tenth century, when members of the so-called Baghdad Peripatetic School translated certain works of Aristotle such as the *Poetics*.[22] For our purposes, we need not concern ourselves here with al-Kindī's circle and the Baghdad Peripatetic School around al-Fārābī (d. ca. 950), as they were engaged mostly in rendering philosophical texts.[23]

It is clear that by the late ninth century, the vast majority of Greek medical texts available in Late Antique Alexandria had been rendered into Arabic. We are particularly well informed about the Graeco-Arabic translations of Galen, because the most important translator, Ḥunayn ibn Isḥāq, left us an *Epistle* (*Risāla*) about 'the books of Galen that, according to his knowledge, were translated [into Arabic] and some of those that were not translated'.[24]

---

[21]   Gutas (1998) remains authoritative, as does the earlier overview by Endress (1987, 1992); for case studies, see, for instance, Joosse and Pormann (2012) and Vagelpohl (2008), and, on Greek textual criticism, the excursus in Gutas (2010), 93–101. Saliba (2007) gives an account of the translation movement, which ought to be used with caution; see Pormann (2010a) for a detailed discussion.

[22]   On the last, see now Gutas (2012), with Pormann (2015a).

[23]   On al-Kindī and his circle, see Adamson (2002, 2007) and Adamson and Pormann (2012); on al-Farabī, see now Pormann (2015b).

[24]   Lamoraux (2016).

Over the last decade or so, Manfred Ullmann has produced crucial work that helps us understand much better the development of how medical texts were rendered from Greek into Arabic.[25] In earlier scholarly accounts, one sometimes encounters the idea that one can distinguish between an older and a newer translation technique.[26] The older is allegedly characterised by a more literal (word-by-word) approach, whereas the newer, that of Ḥunayn ibn Isḥāq, aims at rendering the overall sense of the sentence. It is clear, however, that this description does not reflect the linguistic reality on the ground, which is rather different.[27]

The studies of Endress, Gutas, Ullmann, and others that defy this description can best be summarised as follows. For medicine, the early translations of the second half of the eighth century are characterised by their paraphrastic nature, their tendency to prefer simple sentence structures (e.g., coordination) to more complex ones (e.g., subordination), and the lack of an established technical vocabulary. By contrast, Ḥunayn's translations are more idiomatic, could draw on a large range of technical terms that had already been established, and display much greater sophistication in rendering the nuances of the Greek text. The opposition is therefore not one of word-for-word versus sentence-by-sentence, but one of greater mastery of both source and target text.

We can illustrate these two periods of translation with the example of the *Aphorisms*. The Hippocratic text was rendered into both Syriac and Arabic at least twice, and three of the four versions have come down to us, at least partially. The Syriac version that survives is by Ḥunayn ibn Isḥāq, although this attribution is not entirely certain.[28] Moreover, we have some quotations from the Aphorisms in a text called *Syriac Epidemics*, presumably

---

25   Ullmann (2002, 2006–7, 2009); his main points are summarised in English in Pormann (2011).

26   For example, Salama-Carr (1990).   27   Pormann (2012a).

28   Mimura (2017); Barry (2018), pace Overwien (2015).

translated by Sergius of Rēš ʿAynā (d. 536).[29] This allows us to compare a sixth-century Syriac translation with a ninth-century one.[30] The two Arabic versions are by al-Biṭrīq (fl. mid-eighth century) and Ḥunayn ibn Isḥāq, although, again, the identity of al-Biṭrīq is disputed. My preliminary conclusions for the Syriac match those of Manfred Ullmann's for the Arabic: the older trans-lations are more paraphrastic and less detailed and exact than the newer ones.[31] This older translation also reappears in an anon-ymous commentary attributed to Palladius, although recent research has shown that it cannot be by this Late Antique iatrosophist.[32]

The example of the *Aphorisms* also illustrates that Hippocrates was translated into Arabic mostly in the wake of the commentary tradition. The newer translation of the Hippocratic text by Ḥunayn ibn Isḥāq is extracted from his translation of Galen's *Commentary on Hippocrates' 'Aphorisms'*. In other words, the medieval and early modern manuscripts that survive and contain the Arabic translations of the Hippocratic *Aphorisms* are taken from the lemmas (or quota-tions) containing the Hippocratic text that are found in the commen-taries. The same situation applies to other Hippocratic texts on which Galen commented: where they survive independently, that is, with-out the Galenic commentary, they clearly come from the lemmas of Galen's commentary.

Ḥunayn's version of the *Aphorisms* (*Kitāb al-Fuṣūl*) was the first Graeco-Arabic text to be edited in modern times.[33] Towards the end of the nineteenth century, a German orientalist produced an edition of the Arabic version of the *Prognostic*.[34] Two Cambridge academics edited and translated the two other Hippocratic texts that were taught in Late Antique Alexandria, as well as additional Hippocratic texts that were core curriculum in the medieval Islamic world; they are *Regimen in Acute*

---

[29]   Kessel (2012a).   [30]   Pormann (2016).   [31]   Ibid.
[32]   Pormann et al. (2017), pace Biesterfeldt (2007).   [33]   Tytler (1832).
[34]   Klamroth (1886).

Diseases (*Fī Tadbīr al-amrāḍ al-ḥādda*)[35]; *Nature of Man* (*Fī ṭabī'at al-Insān*)[36]; *Airs, Waters, Places* (lit. 'On endemic diseases' *Fī l-amrāḍ al-bilādīya*)[37]; *Humours* (*Fī l-Aḫlāṭ*) and *Nutriment* (*Fī l-ġiḏā'*)[38]; and *Generation* and *Nature of the Child* (lit. 'Book on Embryos' *Kitāb al-Aǧinna*).[39] All these Arabic translations were extracted from the lemmas of commentaries by Galen. We also have the case of the famous Hippocratic Oath, on which Galen wrote a commentary, which survives only in Arabic fragments.[40] Likewise, the Arabic version of the *Epidemics* circulated in Arabic as extracted from the lemmas of Ḥunayn's Arabic translation of Galen's commentary.[41]

Mattock (1968) also edited and translated the Arabic version of *Superfoetation* (*Fī l-Ḥabal 'alā l-ḥabal*), a text that posed particular problems.[42] This is just one of the Hippocratic works on which Galen did not write a commentary, but that were still translated into Arabic. The modalities of this transmission remain, however, much more difficult to determine. For some texts, it is doubtful whether they ever made it into the Arabic tradition. This is the case for the *Coan Prognoses*, but also for *Ancient Medicine*.[43] Undoubtedly, this is linked to Galen's low opinion of these works. For instance, in the extant Greek works by Galen, he mentions *Ancient Medicine* only once, and clearly regards it as spurious, as its main message runs counter to Galen's own opinions.[44]

Hippocrates is thus often viewed through the prism of Galen's explanations and interpretations. This is also true for how Hippocrates was translated. We have already seen that many Arabic

---

[35] Ed. Lyons (1966).   [36] Ed. Mattock and Lyons (1968).
[37] Ed. Mattock and Lyons (1969).   [38] Ed. Mattock (1971).
[39] Ed. Lyons and Mattock (1978).
[40] Rosenthal (1966); new English article by Magdelaine and Mouton (in press).
[41] See Vagelpohl (2014, 2016).   [42] See Ullmann (1974).
[43] The quotations in al-Rāzī and other authors listed by Ullmann (1970), 31, and Sezgin (1970), 43, do not come from the Hippocratic work, but from an anonymous pharmacological treatise, also called the *Ancient Formulary* (*al-Aqrābāḏin al-qadīm/al-'atīq*); see Kahl (2015).
[44] Schiefsky (2005), 65–6.

Hippocratic texts were extracted from the lemmas of Galenic commentaries. But how the translators understood and rendered these lemmas also depended on Galen.[45] Where the Greek Hippocratic text was obscure or difficult, Galen's discussion often decided how Ḥunayn and others translated it. This can best be illustrated by a famous example, namely aphorism 5.22; in the Greek, it runs as follows: '*Fractures that come down from the back to the elbows are resolved by phlebotomy.*' Ḥunayn's translation of the lemma has 'pains (*awǧāʾ*)' instead of 'fractures (*rhḗgmata*)', because Galen says in his explanation of the lemma that 'pains (*algḗmata*)' is the better reading. After all, it is the pain caused by the fracture that descends from the shoulder to the elbow and not the fracture itself. In this way, Galen's understanding of the text flows into the Arabic translations. And these translations had a significant impact in the Arabic tradition.

IMPACT OF THE HIPPOCRATIC CORPUS: THREE CASE STUDIES

So far, we have looked mainly at how the various Hippocratic texts were rendered into Syriac and Arabic. It is hard, however, to overestimate the impact of these texts on the development of medicine in the Arabo-Islamic tradition. This impact is best illustrated by three concrete examples of central texts that already occupied a prominent position in the late Alexandrian curriculum: the *Aphorisms*, the *Prognostic*, and the *Epidemics*.

APHORISMS

The *Aphorisms* are probably the most popular Hippocratic text of all times, perhaps with the exception of the Oath, which is relatively short. No other Hippocratic text spawned more commentaries in the Arabic tradition; in fact, no other Greek text attracted more exegetes.[46] For we have no fewer than twenty commentaries of which we know, and many of them have come down to us. Some

---

[45]   Overwien (2012c).   [46]   See Pormann and Karimullah (2017).

survive in more than forty manuscripts, whereas others are transmitted by a single one or just a few. Yet the whole tradition of Arabic commentaries on the *Aphorisms* spans more than a hundred manuscripts in numerous libraries, with many more yet to be discovered.[47]

To begin with, we have not only the Arabic translation by Ḥunayn of Galen's commentary, but also an older Arabic translation by al-Biṭrīq, as we have seen earlier. Likewise, there was more than one Syriac version of the lemmas. Then physicians in the Arabo-Islamic tradition began to comment on the *Aphorisms* shortly after they became available in Arabic. One of the earliest examples is Abū Bakr Muḥammad ibn Zakarīyāʾ al-Rāzī (d. ca. 925), who wrote a commentary that does not survive in manuscript, but which is often referred to by later commentators such as Ibn Abī Ṣādiq (d. after 1068). Al-Rāzī was a famous physician and can rightly be regarded as the greatest clinician of the medieval period. In his commentary, he appears to discuss matters of medical epistemology, especially the relation between experience and reason, a topic in which he had a keen interest.[48]

Another earlier commentator is the already mentioned Ibn Abī Ṣādiq (d. after 1068), known as the 'second Hippocrates (*Buqrāṭ al-ṯānī*)'. His commentary was in great circulation and survives even today in some forty manuscripts, the oldest dating back to his lifetime and the youngest produced in 1942 [Cairo, Dār al-Kutub, MS 4751/2 ṭibb]. Moreover, it would appear that Ibn Abī Ṣādiq took the trouble to rearrange his commentary thematically. In other words, the main part of the manuscript tradition roughly follows the arrangement that we know from the Greek manuscripts and the Arabic translations, namely in seven sections (*tmḗmata* in Greek) or books (*maqālāt* in Arabic). Yet a number of manuscripts also have a thematic arrangement in twenty chapters (*abwāb* in Arabic), ranging from the preservation of health and diet to colic, haemorrhoids, and gout.

---

[47]   Rosenthal (1966); Pormann and Joosse (2012); Pormann and Karimullah (2017).
[48]   Pormann (in press); Carpentieri and Mimura (2017).

Ibn Abī Ṣādiq expresses his appreciation for the Hippocratic *Aphorisms* in the preface to his commentary, where he waxes lyrical about the quality of this text[49]:

> [The *Aphorisms*] is one of the books that anyone wanting to master this art must commit to memory, for each aphorism contains a principle that could only have come from someone who obtained it with help from heaven [*ta'yīd samāwī*] and divine support [*tawfīq ilāhī*]. Anybody who would criticise it [the *Book of Aphorisms*] by saying that it is confused and unorganised has only a small and vile share in excellence. For such talk should not be uttered by recent physicians. Indeed, I say that Hippocrates was [divinely] inspired to collect [the *Book of Aphorisms*] and rightly guided to compose it. Therefore, not one word in this excellent work is wrong, nor did he make any missteps in it.

From this quotation, we can appreciate the great esteem that Ibn Abī Ṣādiq, the 'second Hippocrates', attaches to this work: its quality is such that it must have been divinely inspired. No wonder then that generations of physicians after him used it as a source of inspiration in their turn.

From the eleventh to the sixteenth century, there are roughly a dozen commentaries on the *Aphorisms* that have come down to us. Their authors come from many different backgrounds. For instance, Maimonides (Mūsā ibn 'Ubayd Allāh, d. 1204), the greatest Jewish thinker of the Middle Ages, wrote not only a short commentary on the *Aphorisms*, but also a *Book of Aphorisms* in its own right.[50] Maimonides hailed from Muslim Spain (al-Andalus), but spent most of his professional life in Cairo, where he served as personal physician to the Ayyubid rulers, including Saladin's son al-Afḍal, who suffered

---

49   Ed. Pormann et al. DOI:10.3927/51931955; see also Istanbul Beyazid Devlet Kütüphanesi, MS Veliyeddin Efendi 2508: fol. 1b. and Harvard, Houghton Library, MS Arab. SM 4272, 1–2.

50   The former was edited and translated into English by Rosner (1987), and Gerrit Bos is currently working a multi-volume edition and English translation; see also Bos (2004, 2007, 2010, 2013, 2015).

from melancholy. Other commentators came from Muslim Spain, such as Avempace (Ibn Bāǧǧa, fl. twelfth century), from Baghdad, such as ʿAbd al-Laṭīf al-Baġdādī (d. 1231), who lived for many years in Egypt and Syria, from Sīwās in central Turkey, such as ʿAbdallāh ibn ʿAbd al-ʿAzīz ibn Mūsā al-Sīwāsī (fl. 14th century), and Greater Syria, such as Ibn al-Quff. Whereas Maimonides was Jewish and Ibn al-Quff was Christian, many other commentators were Muslim. For example, Ibn al-Nafīs, author of yet another commentary, gained equal fame as a theologian and as a medical writer.[51]

By looking at just one aphorism, a preliminary study of this tradition has shown that we also find innovation or further development of medical theory in most of these commentaries. This aphorism, 6.23, says: "When fear and despondency (dusthumía, ḥubṭ al-nafs) last for a long time, this is something melancholic." In commenting on it, Ibn ʾAbī Ṣādiq introduced the idea that black vapours ascending to the brain cause melancholy, an idea already expressed in Galen's *On the Affected Parts*, and probably going back to Rufus of Ephesus. Al-Sinǧārī talks about scholarly melancholy, again a notion probably first formulated by Rufus. ʿAbd al-Laṭīf brings in Galen's theory of causation. Ibn al-Quff discusses melancholic disease matter and pneumas. Al-Kīlānī relate melancholy to luminous pneuma turning dark. And al-Sīwāsī misunderstands the term 'ḥubṭ al-nafs (despondency)' as 'ḥubṭ al-nafas (dyspnoea)' in a creative way.

PROGNOSTIC

The *Prognostic* is the second Hippocratic text in the Late Antique canon, as described by Ibn Riḍwān. It deals with the question of how to deduce past, present, and future bodily states of the patient from outward signs. As such, it was of tremendous relevance to practising physicians not only in the Greek, but also the Arabic tradition.[52] Galen wrote a commentary on it, as did probably the Alexandrian iatrosophist Gesius (fl. fifth century?). Like the *Aphorisms*, the

---

[51] Fancy (2013, 2017, 2018).
[52] See Pormann and Joosse (2012), on which much of the following sketch is based.

lemmas were translated at least twice into Arabic: there is an older translation and a newer one, and the latter was probably produced in Ḥunayn ibn Isḥāq's circle.[53] Commentaries on the *Prognostic* by four thirteenth-century intellectuals have come down to us, namely Muhaḏḏab al-Dīn al-Daḫwār (d. 1230), ʿAbd al-Laṭīf al-Baġdādī (d. 1231) and Ibn al-Nafīs (both of whom also authored commentaries on the *Aphorisms* which still survive), and Mar Gregory Abū l-Faraǧ ibn al-ʿIbrī (known as Barhebraeus, d. 1289).

Al-Daḫwār's commentary is particularly interesting, as he is associated with setting up the first 'medical school' in the Islamic world: he bequeathed his house and other possessions to found the first *madrasa* (or school) devoted exclusively to teaching medicine. He had been a teacher of medicine himself, and his commentary on the *Prognostic* survives only because one of his students, called Badr al-Dīn al-Baʿlbakkī, memorised it and later wrote it down. Al-Daḫwār insisted, however, that Badr al-Dīn should pass it on only to the deserving and intelligent. Al-Daḫwār's commentary also contains accounts of his own experience as a physician; he relates, for instance, how a colleague erroneously prescribed hot steam baths for a patient, which led to the death of the patient.

Ibn al-Nafīs' commentary is also interesting on many different levels. For instance, he quotes from the Qurʾān in order to underline his points. This, of course, is not surprising, as he was also a noted theologian.

ʿAbd al-Laṭīf explains in the preface to his commentary on the *Prognostic* that he wrote it at the instigation of a friend who had particularly liked his earlier commentary on the *Aphorisms*. At the end of his preface, he describes his own hermeneutic approach as follows[54]:

---

53   Klamroth (1886).

54   Text and translation in Joosse and Pormann (2012), 278, with modifications, based on a fresh reading of the manuscripts.

To comment on Hippocrates' lemmas involves three things. First, one explains strange and confused expressions by well-known and clear ones. Second, one makes apparent the hidden [message] of his thought and the subtleties of his mind.[55] And third, one relates the causes for the things that he discussed superficially and one elucidates[56] a hidden or unmentioned condition in order to be forbearing and to trust the student to obtain it by himself. We shall provide each one of these to the best of our ability and power, as time allows.

Therefore, one can summarise 'Abd al-Laṭīf's stated aims as follows: (1) to explain difficult vocabulary; (2) to contextualise Hippocrates' text; and (3) to make explicit those things that are only stated implicitly in the text, especially in the area of aetiology.

These stated aims can partly be explained by the fact that 'Abd al-Laṭīf excelled not only in medicine and philosophy, but also in philology. His interest in the Arabic language chimes well with the first aim, and also explains more generally his philological methods deployed in his commentaries. For he was aware of, and had access to, the two Arabic translations of the *Prognostic*. Where he found Ḥunayn's version, which he generally followed, to be obscured, he compared it with the older one, in order to establish the correct meaning.

Finally, 'Abd al-Laṭīf mentions students as part of his target audience. This illustrates his interest in the teaching of medicine. In another work, the *Book of the Two Pieces of Advice*, he warns of the danger that students in his day master only a few textbooks (such as the *Generalities* of Avicenna's *Canon of Medicine*), but do not study Galen and Hippocrates in detail. He insisted that students should read whole works by these authors, and not just abridgments or summaries.[57] This again underlines the importance of Hippocrates for

---

[55]   Reading '... ḥabī ati 'aqlihī wa-laṭīfati ḍihnihī '.
[56]   Reading '... mā ḍakarahū ġafalan wa-l-tanbīhu 'alā ...'.
[57]   See Joosse and Pormann (2010), 21–3.

medical teaching in the medieval Arabic tradition. But Hippocrates also occupied a prominent place in medical research, as the example of the *Epidemics* demonstrates.

EPIDEMICS

Unlike the *Aphorisms* and the *Prognostic*, we know of only one Arabic translation of the *Epidemics*, that produced by Ḥunayn ibn Isḥāq himself. This translation marks significant philological progress, as it is the result of an intense effort to improve the underlying Greek text. For instance, in his *Epistle* (*Risāla*) about his translations of Galen, Ḥunayn describes his efforts of producing a good Greek text in the case of Galen's commentary on Book 2 of the *Epidemics* (consisting of six parts)[58]:

> I came across this [second] book in Greek, but it lacked one part, and was, in addition to this, full of mistakes, lacunae, and confusions. I restored it [sc. this faulty Greek manuscript] until I [was able to] produce a [better] copy in Greek. Then I translated it into Syriac, and then into Arabic for Abū Ǧaʿfar Muḥammad ibn Mūsā, except for a small part which remained untranslated.

It is the fifth part of Book 2 that was lacking. When coming to this part in his translation, Ḥunayn speaks eloquently about the difficulties that the Greek manuscripts presented.[59] He had access to two manuscripts, neither of which was particularly good, and one merely represented an abridgment; both manuscripts lacked the fifth part. He took great trouble (*taʿab šadīd*) to improve the text, and hoped that his efforts would stir later scholars to emend it further on the basis of fresh manuscript evidence in Greek.

Like the *Aphorisms* and the *Prognostic*, the *Epidemics* also became a crucial text for medical instruction. Ḥunayn himself produced no fewer than four abridgments of this text, three of which are in the form of questions-and-answers and one in the form of

---

[58]   Trans. Pormann (2008), 253.   [59]   Pormann (2008), 257–9.

'aphorisms'. The question-and-answer genre – that of the catechism – in particular was associated with teaching. Only one of these question-and-answer texts has hitherto been studied, namely the *Summaries ... of Hippocrates' 'Epidemics' (Ǧawāmiʿ ... kitāb Ibīḏīmiyā li-Abuqrāṭ)*; it actually represents an abridgment of Galen's commentary much more than of the Hippocratic lemmas.[60]

The *Epidemics* in the larger sense of both the Hippocratic lemmas and Galen's commentary on them are used and quoted by many subsequent authors writing in Arabic across the different parts of various Islamic empires, from Muslim Spain (al-Andalus) and North Africa (Ifrīqīya) in the West to Egypt, Greater Syria, and Iraq in the Islamic heartlands, to Ḫurāsān and beyond in the East.[61] They were used in sex manuals, medical encyclopaedias, agricultural guides, and specialist medical texts. Moreover, they also spawned further commentaries, such as that by Ibn al-Nafīs, and abridgments, such as that by Ibn Riḍwān.[62]

The *Epidemics* had a profound influence not only on the medical literature, but also on medical practice and research. For the greatest clinician of the medieval Islamic world, Abū Bakr Muḥammad ibn Zakarīyāʾ al-Rāzī (d. ca. 925), they were of crucial importance for his own investigations. At the beginning of his famous case histories, contained in this *Comprehensive Book (al-Kitāb al-Ḥāwī)*, al-Rāzī insists that one ought to cite the case histories contained in the *Questions on the Epidemics* [sc. by Ḥunayn] and the *Epidemics*. "Beware not to neglect them, for they are extremely useful, especially those contained in the *Questions [on the Epidemics]*."[63]

In other words, al-Rāzī sees his own note-taking in the tradition of the Hippocratic *Epidemics* and relates the past case histories to his observations. This process can best be illustrated with a famous example. Already in the 1950s, an Egyptian scholar found an example of al-Rāzī's using a control group in a medical experiment.[64] Al-Rāzī

---

[60] Pormann (2008), 259–63.   [61] Hallum (2012).   [62] Das (2017).

[63] Trans. Pormann (2008), 268. See also Pormann (2013c).

[64] Iskandar (2011 [orig. 1962]); see also Pormann (2008), 268–9.

describes how he phlebotomised one group (ǧamāʿa) of patients suffering from 'brain fever (sirsām)', but deliberately left out another. The latter group contracted the disease, whereas the former group remained unaffected. Although we no longer recognise the connection between bloodletting and treating 'brain fever' (something that one might at least partially equate with modern meningitis), this marks significant methodological progress. Importantly, al-Rāzī tested this treatment in the context of information contained in the *Questions on the Epidemics* by Ḥunayn. Ḥunayn's discussion, which ultimately derives from Hippocrates and Galen, spurred al-Rāzī into conducting this experiment.

CONCLUSIONS

In this way, the historical (and often legendary) figure of Hippocrates, as well as various works contained in the *Hippocratic Corpus*, had a significant impact on the development of theoretical and practical medicine in the medieval Islamic world. In both cases, that is, in the reports about Hippocrates and in the writings attributed to him, the Late Antique tradition wielded significant influence. Many of the anecdotes and utterances in the Arabic bio-bibliographical and gnomological literature have parallels in Late Antique sources. And the Late Antique curriculum also proved instrumental in determining which texts would be translated into Arabic and read by medical students and practitioners alike.

The texts within the *Hippocratic Corpus* that were translated into Syriac and Arabic largely became available in the wake of commentaries on them, and especially those by Galen. Consequently, Galen's approach to Hippocrates shaped much of the Arabic reception. This already begins with the translations themselves, which often reflect Galen's interpretations: Galen moulded Hippocrates in his image, and this image dominated.

Texts like the *Aphorisms*, the *Prognostic*, and the *Epidemics* attracted the attention of not just physicians, but also of a wider public. In medical circles, they constituted part of the core curriculum that any medical student would be expected to master. But they also served as the theoretical backdrop against which clinicians such as al-Rāzī developed new treatments or tested existing ones. In fact, the emphasis on recording the patient's history that we find in al-Rāzī goes back to the model of the *Epidemics*.

To be sure, in some areas such as anatomy and pharmacology, later texts – and not least those by Galen himself – dominated the Arabic tradition. Yet, the example of Hippocrates as the great clinician was held in great esteem, and sometimes, Hippocrates was even elevated above Galen. Perhaps most surprising is the longevity of the interest in certain texts. Generations and generations of physicians from various parts of the Islamic empire commented on the *Aphorisms*, thus returning to this great source for inspiration and discussion. It goes without saying that the Arabic tradition spawned many others. Hippocratic works, for instance, were rendered repeatedly from Arabic into Hebrew, Persian, Latin, and many other languages, but this aspect lies beyond the scope of this chapter.

Whether it is through his example or the works attributed to him, Hippocrates stood tall in the medieval Islamic world. School children learnt some of his most famous aphorisms by heart; doctors used him for teaching, medical practice, and research; and the educated public delighted in the anecdotes about his life. Some thought so highly of him that they believed he must have been divinely inspired. In this way, the heavenly Hippocrates transcends the confines of country and creed, and represents a unifying figure beyond the boundaries of East and West.

16 Western Medicine since the Renaissance

David Cantor

Few individuals from the ancient medical world can rival Hippocrates, the so-called father of medicine, in the approval with which they are remembered in the twenty-first century. He first gained attention in classical antiquity, notably from Galen, whose interpretation of the *Hippocratic Corpus* would dominate elite Western medicine until the Renaissance. He survived medicine's growing disenchantment with Galen, and came to stand for empiricism and practice against Galen, who now stood for rationalism and theory. Hippocrates' popularity has endured ever since, and a profusion of different, sometimes conflicting, visions of the man and his medicine emerged, serving a multitude of distinct, even opposed, purposes. In short, there have been many different Hippocrateses, each created and employed for reasons that may have had little or nothing to do with the historical figure or the various authors of the works collected under his name. This chapter focuses those Hippocrateses invented in Europe and North America, here abbreviated to 'the West'. It does not deal, except in passing, with what happened in the so-called 'Orient'. Peter E. Pormann's contribution to this volume shows that this was also part of the 'Western' medical tradition in that it was Galenic, and reimagined Hippocrates in various ways.

Although the diverse meanings and uses of Hippocrates have long been recognised, their study has tended to be dominated by the question of whether or not they capture something of the original historical figure or his insights. From this perspective, the historian's task is to identify the real Hippocrates, 'genuine Hippocratic texts', or

Parts of this chapter are based on Cantor (2002a).

authentic aspects of his life, and then use such identifications to determine the authenticity of subsequent depictions of the original historical figure or his insights, and by extension the 'errors' or 'aberrations' of other interpretations.[1] Such an approach has provided a means of evaluating and discriminating between the many different versions of Hippocrates and his medicine that have been imagined since the Renaissance. However, by subordinating these many versions to the search for the authentic man and his life, ideas, and practice, it told us less about why they emerged or how they were employed, except insofar as they illuminated the search for the real man and his medicine. As such, it also told us less than we might have wished about the related question of how Hippocrates came to have such a pervasive presence in Western culture.

This chapter seeks to explore the question of Hippocrates' survival and pervasiveness by focussing on the many different meanings and uses of Hippocrates and his medicine, regardless of whether they were true or false, however determined. Rather than telling a tale of decline and degradation, it pays attention to creative reinventions of Hippocrates and his medicine: how they have been represented or read by particular groups and individuals within particular historical, cultural, and social circumstances.[2] The Hippocratic tradition is, from this perspective, an 'invented tradition', constantly reinvented over time and place.[3] It does not follow a linear line, but spreads in many directions, and is layered with competing meanings and approaches. Nor does it lead to a common destination, but goes everywhere that people thought about the ancient (medical) world and what it meant for them and the societies and cultures they lived in.[4] It is part of the histories of morality, of medical ideas and practice, and of the imaginings of the ancient world. It is also a history of inventiveness in moral reasoning, in legitimating medical theory and practice, and in

---

[1]   Ackerknecht (1968), 74, 106; Lindbloom (1968), 55–6; Smith (1979), 7; Rey (1992).
[2]   Slikkerveer (1990), esp. 279; Foster (1993); Jouanna (1999 [orig. 1992]), 364.
[3]   Hobsbawm and Ranger (1983).
[4]   Jenkyns (1980); Turner (1981); Clarke (1989); Stray (1998).

thinking about the past. Hippocrates and Hippocratism turn out to be extremely malleable cultural artefacts, and, I suggest, it is this malleability that allowed their spread within Western culture.

A focus on malleability has been facilitated by scholarship that highlights differences between modern and ancient understandings of Hippocrates and his medicine. For example, although Hippocrates is often portrayed as the founder of modern observational methods, Geoffrey Lloyd has shown that the ancient Greeks had no exact equivalent to our word 'observation': the Greek word *tērēsis* – keeping, guarding, or watching – did not appear until later.[5] Indeed, some ancient observational methods appear to be quite the opposite of those of today. Volker Langholf notes that the verb *skopéomai* used in the *Epidemics* meant to 'consider' in the light of existing rules or theories.[6] Consequently, he argues, the observation of individual cases in the *Epidemics* is not done in order to move from observation to theory, but rather to extend the applicability of existing theories. Thus, Hippocrates the observer is an invention rather than an original, subsequently misrepresented by those who wish him to support their cause.

A similar point can be made about Hippocratic ethics. Today the roots of modern medical ethics are constantly traced to Hippocrates, as if the meaning of Hippocratic ethics is timeless and unproblematic.[7] But there have been many versions of his ethics, including key documents such as the Oath, the original of which is probably not from the Hippocratic period: Vivian Nutton calls it a Renaissance invention.[8] Indeed, some ethical writings such as *Decorum* and *The Physician* can be seen as quite unethical in modern terms. They can be read to advocate a morality of deceit that teaches physicians to use techniques of self-presentation to fool their patients. The notion of a timeless set of Hippocratic ethics is therefore

---

[5]   Lloyd (1979).   [6]   Langholf (1990), 193.
[7]   (Bulger 1973); Parsons and Parsons (1995), 1973.
[8]   Rütten (1993, 1996, 2005); Rütten and Thiermann (1994); Nutton (1995).

problematised, as is the notion of later corruptions of Hippocrates' 'high' ideals.

HIPPOCRATES AND GALEN

The malleability of Hippocrates and his medicine is not a modern invention. It can be traced almost back to the time he lived.[9] Langholf suggests that Plato was the first to interpret 'the available information about Hippocrates' method on the basis of his own system of thought.'[10] Galen followed suit in the second century AD, constructing an image of Hippocratic medicine in the likeness of his own medical views, in part by labelling as 'genuine' those Hippocratic writings that echoed his own ideas.[11] On the basis of such a classification, Galen was able to combine often conflicting Hippocratic writings into a unitary theory of fluids, organs, and *pépsis* ('coction', 'digestion', 'cooking'). According to Vivian Nutton, his methods of determining the authenticity of Hippocratic writings were not seriously challenged or supplemented until the twentieth century.[12]

Galen's approach to the *Hippocratic Corpus* defined for centuries what constituted Hippocratic medicine. Galen was the prism though which Hippocratic works were generally understood and approached in the Arabic tradition as he was in the medieval European world, even if Hippocrates was generally elevated above Galen.[13] Moreover, the subsequent demise of the Galenic Hippocrates was neither quick nor straightforward.[14] Thus when humanist scholars started to study Hippocratic texts in the late

[9]   Smith (1979, 1990); Langholf (1990), 197–8; Temkin (1991); Pinault (1992).

[10]   Langholf (1990), 197–8. On the complexities of the relationship among Plato, other ancient writers, and *Ancient Medicine*, see the introduction to Schiefsky (2005).

[11]   Smith (1979), 121. More generally on Roman approaches to Greek medicine see Nutton (2013 [orig. 2004]). Boudon-Millot discusses Galen's Hippocrates in Chapter 13 in this volume.

[12]   Nutton (2013 [orig. 2004]), 5. See also Nutton (2008).

[13]   On the Arabo-Islamic world, see Chapter 15 by Pormann in this volume.

[14]   Kibre (1985); Wear, French, and Lonie (1985); McVaugh and Siraisi (1990); Wear, French, and Lonie (1985).

fifteenth century, they did not necessarily abandon Galen's interpretation of them.[15] The earliest collections (from 1476) of Hippocratic writings were rarely printed without Galen's commentaries, nor did they use Hippocratic texts that were not available in Galen's manuscripts. An entire Latin printed edition of the *Hippocratic Corpus* appeared in 1525, succeeded by a complete Greek edition the next year. This was followed by the appearance of numerous other new translations, editions, and commentaries.[16] For the first time all the then recognised works by Hippocrates were brought together, systematically edited using the earliest manuscripts then available. Readers now had a much broader range of Hippocratic texts to master, and in two ancient languages, which may help to explain why Hippocrates remained subordinate to Galen until the 1560s. Those who quoted Hippocrates seldom read him, or continued to read him through a Galenic lens. Galen portrayed himself as merely an interpreter of Hippocrates, and subsequent generations accepted his claim so that the two were rarely distinguished.[17]

Hippocrates began to emerge from Galen's shadow in the 1560s, when what Vivian Nutton calls 'our modern picture' of Hippocrates was first created.[18] This change had roots in the development of new medical syllabi at Bologna and at Montpellier at the end of the thirteenth century, which included human dissection.[19] These syllabi had depended heavily on texts of Galen translated into Latin from Greek or, more usually, Arabic. The true anatomist, it was claimed, should be able not only to cut properly into the body, but also to explain lucidly and coherently to his audience what he found there within a learned framework, and this generally meant Galen. Even Vesalius' (1514–64) approach to anatomy – often credited with the debunking of

---

[15] Siraisi (1994); Siraisi (1997), chapter 6.   [16]   Maloney and Savoie (1982).

[17] Nutton (1989), 424. More generally on the 'minor niche' occupied by Greek medical writers in the West until the 1490s see Jackson (2012).

[18] Nutton (1989), 421. See also Nutton (1985, 1986–87, 1988, 1993b). See also King (1996), 387. For the importance of Hippocrates to Renaissance understandings of the origins of Greek language see Grafton (1983), 180–2.

[19] Siraisi (1981).

Galen's anatomy – was informed by a profound knowledge of Galen's writings.

Yet a knowledge of Galen could also be his undoing.[20] In the case of Vesalius, his familiarity with Galen was accompanied by doubts about the Galenic system of human anatomy, as it was based on the dissection (and vivisection) of animal bodies. Vesalius came to this conclusion not only because of his own dissections and observations, but also by his awareness of the weaknesses of the Galenic passages that were used to support explanations that differed from his own observations. Vesalius' deep knowledge of Galenic anatomy thus paradoxically contributed to his own disenchantment with it. Yet even he was unwilling to abandon Galen entirely. Much of the physiological explanation offered in *On the Fabric of the Human Body* (*De humani corporis fabrica*) is taken directly from Galen, and includes several sections from *On the Opinions of Plato and Hippocrates*, a then newly discovered Platonising exposition of anatomy.

The arrival of 'new diseases' for which there was no precedent in Galenic medicine also posed a challenge to Galen and Galen's Hippocrates.[21] Yet their impact was neither obvious nor clear-cut. They could reveal the limitations of Galen's knowledge, and a need to improve on his medicine, but, as with human dissection, they could also promote a deeper study of ancient medical texts. Some early modern scholars doubted the novelty of then new diseases, and scoured ancient texts in the belief they included a description of every disease.[22] Classical authors had also dealt with new diseases: Pliny, for example, blamed the new diseases of his day on the new foodstuffs imported from areas newly conquered by the Romans; Plutarch blamed them on luxury, including diet.[23] The stimulus that 'new diseases' provided to philological study also encouraged some to turn

---

[20]   Nutton (1988). More generally on renaissance anatomy and ancient medicine see Cunningham (1997).

[21]   Arrizabalaga, Henderson, and French (1997); French (1998); Rusnock (2002); Shackelford (2002); King (2004), 58–63; Stein (2009).

[22]   King (1998), 195.   [23]   French (1986); King (2004), 60–3.

to Galen for answers. Equally, it led others to dismiss Galenic medicine as no longer relevant.[24] Yet others oscillated between Galenic and (non-Galenic) Hippocratic readings.[25] The abandonment of Galen was thus a complex process that relied in part on a deep understanding of Galenic texts, and how they related to new practices and new diseases.

The growing interest in Hippocrates was equally complex. If some saw a return to Hippocrates as a chance to clear away centuries of Galenic obfuscation, it was also quite possible to argue that to abandon Galen in favour of Hippocrates was consistent with Galenism. If Galen was simply the mouthpiece of Hippocrates, as he claimed, then a return to Hippocrates could be seen as a Galenic move.[26] As such it was quite possible to portray major change as no change at all. Thus, the Paracelsian physician Petrus Severinus (1542–1602) attempted to silence Galenic physicians by portraying himself as the restorer of Hippocrates, a Hippocrates who endorsed theory rather than practice. As he noted with regard to the doctrine of generation:[27]

> These theories are Paracelsian, they are not inconsistent with
> Christian religion, and they are close to the decrees of the
> Platonists. But if they have been supported by the authority of
> Hippocrates, who can accuse them of novelty?

The nature of the *Corpus* was also important to the shift from Galen to Hippocrates. As others in this book note, the *Corpus* is not the work of one individual: no text in the sixty or so collected under his name can be unequivocally proclaimed as the work of Hippocrates, and the *Corpus* itself is an assortment from different periods that differ in style, method, and in the views they advance.[28] Thus, Hippocrates could be whatever mix of texts a reader determined on, which allowed

---

[24]   Cunningham (2002); King (2002); Martensen (2002); Shackelford (2002).
[25]   King (1998), 195–201.   [26]   King (2002).   [27]   Shackelford (2002), 78.
[28]   On the Hippocratic question see Edelstein (1939); Lloyd (1991); Jouanna (1999 [orig. 1992]). See also Chapter 2 by Craik's and Chapter 3 by Jouanna in this volume.

Galenic readings of the *Corpus*, but also allowed their rejection depending on the selection of works or their interpretation. As such, the *Corpus* also helped to spawn a multitude of different Hippocrateses and their medicines, and so facilitated their spread throughout Western medicine even as Galen's fortunes failed.

THE EMPIRICAL HIPPOCRATES

By the end of the seventeenth century, the separation of Hippocrates from Galen seemed irreversible. For many, Hippocrates had come to be revered as a symbol of empiricism and practice against Galen, who stood for rationalism and theory.[29] Invocations of this sort had been made earlier, notably by Francis Bacon (1561–1626), who argued that Hippocrates' practice of taking a 'history' of an individual patient's illness in the form of notes, later called case notes, might be applied to the study of nature more generally. As part of an argument for the reform of science, and in answer to the Hippocratic aphorism 'life is short, art is long', Bacon urged collaboration over long periods of time so that, in the future, individuals would profit from the experience of earlier scholars captured in notes, long after they had passed from this world. He reassured his readers that this project was not 'beyond the capacity of mere mortals' because 'its completion is not confined entirely to a single age but to a succession of them.'[30]

Bacon's interpretation of Hippocratic method took off in the seventeenth century, when prominent fellows of the Royal Society of London adopted his ideas and applied them to the new empirical sciences, among them Robert Boyle (1627–91), John Evelyn (1620–1706), Robert Hooke (1635–1703), and John Locke (1632–1704). In the view of these thinkers, the new sciences demonstrated the urgency of finding a solution to the conundrum posed by Hippocrates' aphorism because, unlike skills such as the playing of a musical instrument, understanding of nature could never be acquired in a lifetime, but only after several generations. These thinkers, therefore, set themselves

---

[29] Smith (1979); Cook (1986) 185; King (2012).   [30] Yeo (2014), 92.

the task of learning the most trusted knowledge accumulated by earlier scholars, and adding to it by further observation and experiment, all detailed in notes, records, and other documents for the future. The Hippocratic aphorism thus offered a rationale for engaging in research over the long term, ensuring that empirical inquiry could last long beyond a single human lifespan.[31]

If Bacon's Hippocrates helped to reform approaches to the natural world, he also helped to reform clinical practice, notably that of Thomas Sydenham (1624–89) – the English Hippocrates – an associate of Boyle, Locke, and other founding members of the Royal Society. Harold Cook has suggested that Sydenham's Hippocrates was a Baconian collector of case studies, a compiler of medical detail, an inductivist, and the early founder of the true methods of natural history whose achievements had been devalued by rationalist practitioners such as Galen who followed him. He was, according to Cook, an empiricist, averse to theory (much like Sydenham himself), an observer, who built cures on what he could see and not on what he could not, who considered the effects of environment on the appearance and nature of disease. He was, in particular, a historian of diseases.[32]

Hippocrates the empiricist took on many different forms and meanings in succeeding centuries. Thus, the Italian Hippocrates, Giorgio Baglavi (1668–1707), retained Hippocrates as a model of practice at the same time as he criticised much of ancient Greek theory as chaotic. In Baglavi's view, practical medicine involved studying diseases as entities in a Baconian way, compiling histories of them over a long period of time, all in order to produce aphorisms, modelled on the Hippocratic, but that Baglavi held to be capable of giving causes of disease, as many of the old rational systems also did.[33] In the Netherlands, Hermann Boerhaave (1668–1738) recommended

---

[31]   Yeo (2014), 92. For another Baconian Hippocrates in the Royal Society, see Rusnock (2002).

[32]   Cook (1986), 185; Cunningham (2002). More generally, Anstey (2011).

[33]   French (2003), 207–12.

practising chemistry 'after the Hippocratical manner'.[34] Boerhaave's Hippocrates turns out to have been an adherent of seventeenth century mechanical philosophy and its guiding principles of simplicity, purity, and observation, and the need to avoid speculation. He was also a Calvinist: Hippocrates, according to Boerhaave, viewed nature as providential, a meaning that was strikingly similar to Boerhaave's own Calvinist understanding of the category 'Nature'.[35] It was this view of Hippocrates that allowed Boerhaave to challenge chemists in the tradition of Paracelsus (1493–1541) and Van Helmont (1580–1644), who had themselves invented a chemical Hippocrates in the likeness of their own ideas, but very different from the Hippocrates of Boerhaave.[36]

Hippocrates the empiricist continued to mutate. In eighteenth-century France, Pierre-Jean-Georges Cabanis (1757–1808) saw Hippocrates as a 'philosopher-physician' (*médecin-philosophe*), someone who combined the empirical and the rational to produce the original and true observational method.[37] The Anglophile Philippe Pinel (1745–1826) saw him as a Baconian or Sydenhamian empiricist, someone who emphasised observation, description of diseases, and respect for nature in his therapy.[38] Paul-Joseph Barthez (1734–1806) saw him as an opponent of a simple faith in the healing power of nature, someone who demonstrated through his close observation of individual patients a view of disease as infinitely variable and individual in character.[39] Georges-Louis Leclerc, Comte de Buffon (1707–88), saw Hippocrates, the practical physician, as a model for the natural historian given his practical interest in careful observation, comparison, and judgement: he was an opponent of the abstract philosopher favoured by mechanists. Buffon, in fact, used Hippocrates to reintroduce the concept of living nature into natural philosophy, to criticise system builders and Aristotelian natural philosophers, even

---

[34] Knoeff (2007).

[35] Cunningham (1990), 54. On Hippocrates' Calvinist leaning, see Knoeff (2007) and Lo Presti (2010).

[36] Smith (1979), 14–18, 23–7; Shackelford (2002); Hedesan (2016).

[37] La Berge (2002).   [38] Ibid.   [39] Rey (1992); Williams (2002).

as he sought to correct his (Hippocrates') errors. His improved Hippocrates, Peter Reill suggests, set the parameters for late eighteenth century debates over generation.[40]

Buffon would criticise the degeneracy of American environments, animals, and peoples, prompting American naturalists to turn to the empirical Hippocrates to argue against him, demonstrating the healthiness of the climate and the lack of diseases that affected the Old World.[41] In addition, in Antebellum America he was variously an advocate of French medicine, an opponent of French medicine, and an advocate of a distinctive identity for Southern physicians and Southern nationalism.[42] In the twentieth century, the empirical Hippocrates was also invoked by clinical holists. This Hippocrates was opposed to reductionism, specialisation, standardisation, and bureaucratisation. He was in favour of generalism, the primacy of the physician over the laboratory scientist, and a focus on the patient as a whole.[43] For some he was the opponent of state medicine; for others he was in favour of it.[44] Some continued to cast their clinical observations as aphorisms in imitation of Hippocrates, a style of transmitting knowledge and wisdom, they suggested, that was grounded in empiricism and a rejection of theory.[45]

THE USES AND PROBLEMS OF EMPIRICISM

Hippocrates the empiricist helps to explain his pervasive presence in European medicine. People of radically different persuasions could express allegiance to him without having to agree on what he stood for, what the practice of observation meant, or how to interpret an observation. Thus, for example, Thomas Apel has shown that during the 1793 epidemic of yellow fever in Philadelphia, most physicians turned to Hippocratic empiricism to understand the disease: they agreed that it was a local condition, largely limited to the city boundaries, and that it tended to emerge in late summer continuing into

[40]   Reill (2005), 65–6.   [41]   Apel (2016), 21.   [42]   Warner (2002).
[43]   Lawrence (1985, 1998); Cantor (2002b); Weisz (2002).   [44]   Sturdy (1998).
[45]   Lawrence (1999).

autumn, a period of heat, humidity, and torrential rain. However, those in favour of miasmatic and contagionist explanations of the disease came to quite different conclusions about what these observations meant. The former argued that the spatial dimensions of the disease meant that it was caused by miasmatic vapours local to the city, and brought on by the particular climatic conditions of the season. Contagionists argued, however, that it could not be caused by miasmas, because its symptoms were unlike any other diseases endemic to the American South or the West Indies. These physicians accepted the need for the practice of observation, that its roots were Hippocratic, and they often concurred on the nature of what was observed. However, they explained these observations in very different ways.[46]

Nevertheless, Hippocrates the empiricist was not without his problems. In the first place, as Dimitri Levitin has shown, a focus on the empirical Hippocratism of Restoration physicians did not go unchallenged.[47] Learned physicians sought to reconfigure Hippocrates as a rationalist, a rationalist Hippocratic method often defended by abandoning Galenic doctrine. Galen was not, to these physicians, the symbol of rationalism and theory that advocates of the empirical Hippocrates claimed. Indeed, Levitin, arguing against Harold Cook, suggests that Sydenham was not opposed to rationalism. On the contrary, for Sydenham Hippocrates was the founder of the true rationalism: his interest in systematic not observation distanced him from empirics. And Sydenham was not alone in situating Hippocrates somewhere between empiric and speculative traditions. Others arguing along similar lines suggested that empirics' refusal to search for causes made them a poor grounding for a 'method of healing' (methodus medendi); rationalism was the position most safely grounded in experience and experiment.[48] Sydenham, in Levitin's view, was in fact part of a broader ongoing effort to reconfigure the identity of traditional medicine, which folded experimentalism and

---

[46]   Apel (2016).   [47]   Levitin (2015), 293–4.   [48]   Ibid., 281.

rationalism together, and promoted experimental method as a respectable tradition.[49] Sydenham, the Hippocratic empiricist, may thus be an anachronism, a later reconstruction of Sydenham's view of the Hippocratic method.

Thus alongside a view of Hippocrates as an empiricist, there was also a tradition of Hippocrates as an experimentalist, opposed to Galen. Van Helmont, for example, claimed that Hippocrates was the first to leave a record of useful experimental practice: Galen, he claimed, had taken the Hippocratic art and turned it into idle speculation through his method, and eventually 'one aery lump of Natural Philosophy'.[50] Similarly, the nineteenth-century editor and translator of the *Hippocratic Corpus*, Emile Littré (1801–81), noted that although the progress of the medical art had improved on Hippocrates, his method and the method of modern medicine did not differ in their essence, as both were the experimental method.[51] What counted as the Hippocratic method was thus quite fluid; it could be clinical observation or it could be the experimental method, each of which concepts was in turn malleable. Such fluidity also helps to explain Hippocrates' pervasiveness. One could retain allegiance to him by redefining what was meant by observation or experiment, and describing these meanings as examples of the Hippocratic method.[52]

In the second place, there was a further problem with the empirical (and indeed the experimental) Hippocrates. The difficulty with a Hippocrates who supported experience and observation – be it empirical or experimental – was that, logically, it could become his downfall. If observation was so important, then the accumulated experience since Hippocrates also had claim to a place in medicine. Thus a theme of improvement emerged in empiricist and experimentalist visions of Hippocrates.[53] Those who wanted to improve on Hippocrates argued that his writings should not be turned into an

---

[49]   Ibid., 282.   [50]   Levitin (2015), 262.   [51]   Osborne (1996), 86.
[52]   On the varied and changing meanings of observation, see Daston and Lunbeck (2011).
[53]   Cunningham (2002).

unchallengeable canon of sacred work.[54] He should not be elevated to the level of scriptural authority.[55]

This is not to say that everyone who wanted to improve on Hippocrates also wanted to keep him. Even within the seventeenth-century Royal Society – that bastion of the Baconian Hippocrates – there were experimentalists indifferent to him.[56] Others sought to improve not only on his knowledge, but also his method, as when the eighteenth-century English physician Francis Clifton (d. 1736) attempted to improve on the Hippocratic method of clinical observation in line with the precepts of the new natural philosophy promoted by the Royal Society.[57]

Finally, it should also be noted that not everyone wanted to improve on Hippocrates. Despite the growing tendency to portray him as an empiricist or an experimentalist, some practitioners continued to turn to Hippocrates not as a source of method but of substantive ways of thinking about the body, health, and disease. In the nineteenth and twentieth centuries such approaches were particularly common among heterodox practitioners, who sometimes turned to Hippocrates as a justification for their medical systems. Thus, Samuel Thomson (1769–1843), the herbalist founder of the Thomsonian medical system, found analogues of many of his ideas scattered throughout the Hippocratic corpus, while today, the US-based Hippocrates Health Institute traces its practice to an idea that it claims was first voiced by Hippocrates: "Let food be thy medicine and medicine be thy food."[58] Some of these ways of thinking about the body, health, and disease had roots in the *Hippocratic Corpus*, while others had more tenuous connections. Either way, Hippocrates was routinely invoked as an ancient source of lost wisdom, ignored by regular physicians at their peril.

---

[54] Broman (1996), 140–1. [55] Warner (2002). [56] Martensen (2002).
[57] Rusnock (2002).
[58] Estes (1990); Hippocrates Health Institute, http://hippocratesinst.org (accessed 21 July 2017).

CONDUCT AND ETHICS

If Hippocrates' pervasive presence in Western medicine and culture owed much to the malleability of his medicine and method, it also owed much to the variety of conduct and ethics justified in his name, and to the fact that the Hippocratic texts themselves could be read in very different ways. For example, physicians in the medieval scholastic medical tradition found that the *Aphorisms* provided wisdom about conduct and outlook, including a justification for seeking monetary reward for medical care, and that *Decorum* offered a justification for glory as a reward for proper behaviour.[59] It was, however, also the case that in the process of condemning deception, *Decorum* also taught about it, describing how a true doctor (and a false one) should look, and hence providing clues for those who might wish to imitate such a presentation.[60] Thus the same Hippocratic texts might be used both to distinguish a physician from his or her competitors and also to erase that difference.

If Hippocratic guides to conduct could be read in different ways, they could also be ignored. For example, although it is possible to read a justification of doctor–patient confidentiality in the Oath, it was a common complaint that early modern English physicians constantly talked publicly about their patients, and that medical concerns about conduct tended to concentrate on accusations of quackery and malpractice rather than privacy.[61] Indeed, Mary Fissell argues that in the English-speaking world prior to the 1770s no ethics particular to the profession or vocation of early modern English medical practitioners governed conduct, and they rarely looked back to antiquity for guidance. Instead, appropriate behaviour was inculcated through the institution of apprenticeship, shaped by general norms of interactions between master and servant, and client and patron, and recommendations as to the proper conduct of physicians were often difficult to separate out from the much broader genre of advice to gentlemen in

---

59   French (2003), chapter 1.   60   King (1998), 42.
61   Porter (1989), 154; Wear (1993).

general conduct manuals. It was only in the 1770s, she argues, that medical ethics became possible or desirable, following changes in the structure of medical practice and a crisis in gentlemanly codes, prompted by Evangelical attacks on the noble code of honour, and Lord Chesterfield's cynical reading of the code of a gentleman, all set against the emergence of a more independent and insistent bourgeois identity that was often marked by opposition to gentlemanly conduct.[62] Hippocratic medical ethics are thus recent in a sense because medical ethics itself is recent.

It might be supposed that the range of medical conduct justified by Hippocrates would stabilise with the creation of medical ethics. But this is not the case. The Oath, for example, has often been adapted and readapted to suit contemporary sensibilities and clauses changed or dropped, such as the religious introduction, the injunction to refuse a request to provide a lethal drug (often interpreted as a ban on suicide or euthanasia, rather than an effort to control a dangerous drug),[63] or from the 1960s the injunction not to provide an abortive pessary (often interpreted as banning all abortive methods, rather than another effort to control a dangerous drug, which left open the possibility of using mechanical measures and orally administered drugs for abortion),[64] and physicians have often found themselves struggling to live up to its shifting standards. Thus, when early twentieth century American physicians invoked Hippocrates as a standard to which they should aspire, critics of the profession used the Oath to show how modern doctors had fallen from the standards set by the physician of Cos.[65] Then again, in the aftermath of the Second World War, critics would argue that Nazi physicians had strayed far from the Hippocratic invocation to do no harm: yet National Socialist physicians had in fact turned to Hippocrates (and to Paracelsus) to justify their actions: doing no harm to the individual body often took second place to doing no

---

[62]   Fissell (1993).
[63]   King (2001), 14. The classic statement of this interpretation is Edelstein (1987 [orig. 1943]); see Chapter 7 by Leven in this volume for further discussion.
[64]   Edelstein (1987 [orig. 1943]); Riddle (1992), 7–8; King (1998), 139.
[65]   Lederer (2002).

harm to the social body as understood through Nazi racial ideology.[66] The Second World War marked a revival of interest in the Oath, especially following the revelations of Nazi medical atrocities. The Geneva Declaration of 1948 adapted the Oath once again, this time to post-war concerns, and the numbers of medical schools in the United States, Canada, and the United Kingdom using some variant of the Oath rose substantially. It remains one of the best known Hippocratic texts. However, Robert Baker argues for an important difference between post–Second World War American and European medicine, namely the extent to which organised American medicine abandoned authoritative ethical statements and standards including the Oath, in favour of watered-down guidelines and suggestions. He suggests that bioethics developed as a reaction to this abandonment.[67]

IMAGINATIVE AND LOST WORLDS

A final reason for the survival and spread of Hippocrates were the limited details of his 'real' life. Plato and Aristotle suggest that the historical Hippocrates was born in or around 460 BC on the Greek island of Cos, a member of the Asclepiads who claimed to be descendants of Asclepius. His height was short, he was willing to charge for teaching medicine, and he seems to have been well known before his death; and that is about all they have to say.[68] These meagre details have left ample room for imaginative constructions of his life and works, and tales about them began to appear in the ancient world, notably in the various version of the 'Life' (*Vita*) of Hippocrates and writings falsely attributed to him, the so-called *Pseudepigrapha*.[69] Among the more famous were stories that he burned the library of Cos, that he cured King Perdiccas of love-sickness, that he patriotically refused the gold of the Persian King Artaxerxes, that he cured the Athenian plague, and that he died in Larrissa in Thessaly. But the

---

[66] Timmermann (2002); Bruns (2014).   [67]   Baker (2013), chapter 10.
[68] Plato, *Protagoras*, 311b–c and *Phaedrus* 270c–d; Aristotle, *Politics* 7, 1326a15–16.
[69] Smith (1979, 1990); Temkin (1991); Pinault (1992); see also Chapter 14 by Manetti and Chapter 15 by Pormann in this volume.

sources for these accounts emerged several hundred years after his death, perhaps in part as a means of creating authority for the Coan medical school, and were read in different ways. To ancient Greeks, Hippocrates' refusal of barbarian gold was a sign of his patriotism; to later Roman commentators it was a sign of the untrustworthiness of Greek physicians.[70]

Such stories had a long afterlife. For example, the story of Hippocrates' refusal of barbarian gold was a staple of later accounts of Hippocrates, where its political message about despotism and tyranny was often linked to the passage in *Airs, Waters, Places* where Hippocrates contrasts Asiatic despotism and Greek freedom.[71] A central idea in *Airs, Waters, Places* is that the climate, season, water, and food of a specific place shape the physical and mental make-up of people born into it and their health and the ills that afflict them. As early modern European explorers and colonisers came in contact with places outside of Europe, such a perspective also provided an explanation of why the peoples in distant lands were different to Europeans and why Europeans often seemed maladapted to such places. The bodily constitutions produced in European places were often deemed to be unsuited to the very different environments of the tropics. Diseases that might be mild in Europe were often much more virulent and dangerous to Europeans in the tropics.[72]

For eighteenth- and nineteenth-century European travel writers *Airs, Waters, Places* provided an explanation not only of the bodily constitution, but also of the characters of the peoples and the political regimes of Asia Minor.[73] Following Hippocrates, these writers

---

[70]   Temkin (1991), 57–61.

[71]   For the use of this story in France, see the account in Crow (1995), 140–4 of Girodet's painting of *Hippocrates Refusing the Gifts of Artaxerxes* (1792). The painting is also causally referenced by Victor Hugo and Honore de Balzac: see de Balzac (1972) and Hugo (1995), 841. For another account of this painting, see Pellicer (2000). More generally on French views of Asiatic deposition inflected through the *Airs, Waters Places* tradition see Kitromilides (2013), 186.

[72]   Wear (2008). For later uses of the *Airs, Waters, Places* see Bashford and Tracy (2012); Osborne and Fogarty (2012).

[73]   Schiffer (1999), 234–9.

claimed that the temperate climates of Asia Minor, with no extreme variations in temperature, made Asiatics less belligerent, more docile, and weaker in character than northern Europeans, more robust races created by more varied and severe climates. Such an account helped to explain and justify northern European imperialism in Asia and elsewhere, as did the sclerotic political systems of Asia, both modern and ancient. The despotic regimes of Asia, these northern European writers suggested, did not encourage courage in combat, as armies were recruited primarily for the benefit of their leaders rather than the recruits. In Britain, the liberal reformer William Farr extended the point, reading in *Airs, Waters, Places* an indictment of the 'very nerve and withering arm' of despotism.[74] For Farr, Hippocrates attributed the unenergetic character of Asiatics to their laws: the great part of Asia being governed by despotic kings. 'Independence', he claimed,[75] 'enlarges, and gives energy to, all the faculties; it is the vital breath of the mind; it gives health to a nation.'

It was here that the story of Hippocrates' refusal of barbarian gold seemed to some commentators to add fuel to the condemnation of Asian and despotic political systems more generally. 'What a noble picture of a free over a slave State!'[76], commented J. Rutherfurd Russell in 1861 of this passage in *Airs, Waters and Places*, echoing Farr, and concluding with a reference to the Artaxerxes story: "No wonder that the mind which conceived it should revolt from the idea of serving a tyrant."[77] For Russell the modern parallel with Persia was the France of Napoleon III.[78] Francis Adams, the English translator of the *Hippocratic Corpus*, saw the invitation itself as an acknowledgement by the Persians of Greek superiority.[79] For the Edinburgh physician J. Warburton Begbie, writing in 1872, the story

---

[74]   On Farr, see Eyler (1979).   [75]   Farr (1835–6), 779.

[76]   Russell (1861), 25.   [77]   Ibid., 25–6.

[78]   Ibid., 26. The 'free' state in this example, however, was America, and Russell cites a modern parallel to the story of Hippocrates and Artaxerxes. In the modern example, an unnamed French geologist refused to return to France from America, his adopted country, although tempted by a personal and flattering invitation from Napoleon III.

[79]   Adams (1849), 14–15.

indicated the reasons why free Greece averted a Persian invasion, and the pride in which the Coans viewed Hippocrates. According to Begbie, Artaxerxes demanded that the Coans hand over the insolent Hippocrates, but they refused to hand over a man of whom they were proud and owed so much. "The firmness of the attitude which these patriots assumed, and the unity by which at that time the different Grecian states asserted their common independence averted in all probability a Persian invasion."[80]

In the late nineteenth and twentieth centuries, Hippocrates also came to be employed to organise a longing for a lost organic world where the doctor was treated with almost religious deference and the healing power of nature had yet to be displaced by modern science and technology. The doctors who wrote on Hippocrates at this time comprised the last generation to be schooled in the classics. They were critical of mass production and culture, of standardisation and specialisation in medicine, the threat (as they saw it) posed to clinical practice by reductive laboratory science, and the tendency to reify diseases as entities – and Hippocrates, in their view, was also opposed to these developments. For example, Arthur John Brock, the physician translator of Galen's *On the Natural Faculties*, argued that Hippocrates' organic and vitalistic view of the body and disease was the medical representative of the sanity, balance, and common sense that had characterised ancient Greek cultural life. In his view, Hippocrates saw disease as a process, and the practical problem was to follow its natural course through clinical observation. Brock's Hippocrates also believed in the healing power of nature: the organism – much like Greek society, in Brock's view – was able to adjust to changes in the environment by its own inherent powers. By contrast, Brock associated a materialist tendency to regard diseases as real things (entities) with conditions of political or social oppression. If Hippocrates enjoyed the relative freedom of the island of Cos, he noted, the situation in Cnidus a few miles away on the mainland of

[80]   Begbie (1872), 676.

what is now Turkey was very different. Brock speculated that the Cnidian tendency to regard diseases as things was in part a product of their political subordination to nearby Carian and Lydian despots.[81]

With perhaps the exception of the field of ethics, Hippocrates is no longer the point of reference in medical debates and training that he was in previous centuries. Hippocrates lives on, however, elsewhere in popular culture. Computer games that need a doctor often label him Hippocrates, and he has appeared in numerous television programmes and in movies.[82] In the 1942 film *The Perils of Nyoka*, Nyoka battles the evil Vultura to find the lost tablets of Hippocrates, a cure for cancer.[83] Hippocrates himself has a walk-on part in the 1957 Marx Brothers motion picture *The Story of Mankind*.[84] In 1996 he learned techniques of tracheotomy, CPR, and the birthing of a centaur from Xena, television's eponymous Warrior Princess, who also encouraged him to rebel against Galen.[85] He is the all-seeing, all-knowing medical computer in the science fiction series *Mercy Point* (1998)[86]; a cartoon character in *Hercules* (1998), the Disney television series[87]; the devoted four-armed alien companion of L. Ron Hubbard's 'Ole Doc Methuselah'[88]; and the *Goofy Hippocrates* (1990), a composite of the father of medicine and the Disney dog character.[89] He gives his name to Dr Hippocrates Noah in television's *Deep Space Nine* and to an

---

[81]   Cantor (2005). See also Lawrence (1985, 1998) and Cantor (2002b).

[82]   Cantor (2002a).

[83]   The movie was re-released as a TV movie *Nyoka and the Lost Secrets of Hippocrates* in 1966.

[84]   This was a Warner Brothers movie, produced by Irwin Allen and based on Hendrick van Loon's (1922) best seller. See Solomon (1978), 189–90 and Solomon (1996) 124 n. 34.

[85]   *Xena: Warrior Princess*: Season 1, Episode 24, 'Is There a Doctor in the House?' written by Patricia Manney and directed by T. J. Scott for Renaissance Pictures. Released in the United States: 29 July 1996.

[86]   Garcia and Garcia (2012), 147–53.

[87]   *Hercules*: Season 1, Episode 8, 'Hercules and the World's First Doctor', first broadcast 9 September 1998.

[88]   Miller (1987), 135. Ole Doc Methuselah appears in many stories; see, for example, Hubbard (1992).

[89]   Ferguson et al. (1990).

episode called 'The Hippocratic Oath'[90]; to *The Hippocrates*, a 1988 movie about the life of a young Japanese doctor[91]; to *The Tree of Hippocrates* (1985), a romantic novel set partly on the island of Cos[92] ;and to an episode of children's cartoon series *Baby Huey*, entitled 'The Hippocratic Oaf'.[93] There is a song by Hoagy Carmichael called 'The Army of Hippocrates' (1942).[94] And, Country Joe MacDonald sang the praises of 'Dr Hip', also known as Dr Hip Pocrates, the pseudonym of Eugene Schoenfeld, a San Francisco Bay area alternative psychiatrist, who according to Country Joe 'could help you make your trip'.[95]

Dr Hip captures something of the playful flexibility of Hippocratic medicine and ideas in the twentieth century. It was flexibility that had helped to ensure he survived the decline of Galenic medicine in the sixteenth century and that he survived the demise of humoral pathology, criticism of his supposed atheism, and the decline of the classics and classical languages. Hippocrates the shape-shifter has taken on different identities over the millennia, reflecting ever changing medical, political, religious, and cultural interests and agendas. In the world of Dr Hip, and now the Internet, he has finally severed all but the most tenuous of connections to the ancient medical world, yet remains the personification of medicine, even if there is disagreement as to what constitutes this medicine.

90   *Star Trek: Deep Space Nine*: Season 4, Episode 9, 'Our Man Bashir', first broadcast 27 November 1995 and Season 4, Episode 3, 'Hippocratic Oath', first broadcast 16 October 1995.

91   www.clip.co.jp/ (accessed 3 December 1997). Thanks to Takashi Asanuma for an email 16 December 1997.

92   Ellis (1985), 36.

93   *The Baby Huey Show*: Season 1, Episode 7, 'The Hippocratic Oaf', first broadcast 30 October 1994.

94   Carmichael (1942), 2–3.

95   The song – Dr Hip – is on his album, *Country Joe* (New York, NY: Vanguard, 1974). My thanks to Country Joe McDonald for his emails and the lyrics to the song, 14 April 1998. See Schoenfeld (1968, 1974, 1980).

English Title	Latin Title	Abbr.
Affections	*De affectionibus*	Aff.
Airs, Waters, Places	*De aere aquis locis*	Aer.
Anatomy	*De anatome*	Anat.
Ancient Medicine	*De prisca medicina / De vetere medicina*	VM / Vet. med.
Aphorisms	*Aphorismi*	Aph.
Art	*de Arte*	
Breaths	*De flatibus*	Flat.
Coan Prognoses	*Coacae praenotiones*	Coac.
Crises	*De iudicationibus*	Judic.
Days of Crisis	*De diebus iudicatoriis*	Dieb. iudic.
Decorum	*De decenti habitu*	Decent.
Decree	*Decretum*	Decr. ath.
Dentition	*De dentitione*	Dent.
Diseases 1	*De morbis I*	Morb. I
Diseases 2	*De morbis II*	Morb. II
Diseases 3	*De morbis III*	Morb. III
Diseases 4	*De morbis IV*	Morb. IV
Diseases of Girls	*De virginum morbis*	Virg.
Diseases of Women 1	*De morbis mulierum I*	Mul. I
Diseases of Women 2	*De morbis mulierum II*	Mul II
Eight-Month Infant	*De octimestri partu*	Oct.
Epidemics 1	*Epidemiarum I*	Epid. I
Epidemics 2	*Epidemiarum II*	Epid. II
Epidemics 3	*Epidemiarum III*	Epid. III
Epidemics 4	*Epidemiarum IV*	Epid. IV
Epidemics 5	*Epidemiarum V*	Epid. V
Epidemics 6	*Epidemiarum VI*	Epid. VI
Epidemics 7	*Epidemiarum VII*	Epid. VII
Excision of the Foetus	*De foetus exsectione*	Foet. exsect.

Craik	Jouanna		Littré	Translations
3	4	VI	208–270	Loeb: Potter V (1988) 1–81
2	3	II	12–92	Loeb: Jones I (1923) 65–137
5	6	VIII	530–540	Loeb: Potter IX (2010) 1–7
51	71	I	570–636	Loeb: Jones I (1923) 1–64
6	7	IV	458–608	Loeb: Jones IV (1931) 97–221
7	9	VI	2–26	Loeb: Jones II (1923) 185–217
15	26	VI	90–114	Loeb: Jones II (1923) 219–253
9	11	V	588–732	Loeb: Potter IX (2010) 103–269
23a	35	IX	276–294	Loeb: Potter IX (2010) 271–298
23b	16	IX	298–306	Loeb: Potter IX (2010) 300–311
11	13	IX	226–245	Loeb: Jones II (1923) 267–301
/	14	IX	400, 15–402, 12	Smith 1990
12	15	VIII	544–548	Loeb: Jones II (1923) 315–329
30	42	VI	140–204	Loeb: Potter V (1988) 83–163
31	43	VII	8–114	Loeb: Potter V (1988) 165–293
32	44	VII	118–160	Loeb: Potter VI (1988) 1–57
33	45	VII	542–614	Loeb: Potter X (2012) 95–185
50	70	VIII	466–470	Loeb: Potter IX (2010) 355–363
35a	47	VIII	10–232	
35b	48	VIII	234–406	
44b	52	VII	436–460	Loeb: Potter IX (2010) 71–101
13a	18	II	598–716	Loeb: Jones I (1923) 139–211
13b	19	V	72–138	Loeb: Smith VII (1994) 18–83
13c	20	III	24–148	Loeb: Jones I (1923) 218–287
13d	21	V	144–196	Loeb: Smith VII (1994) 86–140
13e	22	V	204–258	Loeb: Smith VII (1994) 142–206
13f	23	V	266–356	Loeb: Smith VII (1994) 206–274
13g	24	V	364–468	Loeb: Smith VII (1994) 276–390
16	27	VIII	512–518	Loeb: Potter IX (2010) 365–373

English Title	Latin Title	Abbr.
Fistulas	*De fistulis*	Fist.
Flesh	*De carnibus*	Carn.
Fractures	*De fracturis*	Fract.
Generation	*De genitura*	Genit.
Glands	*De glandulis*	Gland.
Haemorrhoids	*De haemorrhoidibus*	Haem.
Heart	*De corde*	Cord.
Humours	*De humoribus*	Hum.
Internal Affections	*De internis affectionibus*	Int.
Joints	*De articulis*	Art.
Law	*Lex*	Lex
Letters	*Epistulae*	Epist.
Mochlicon	*Mochlicum*	Mochl.
Nature of Bones	*De ossium natura*	Oss.
Nature of Man	*De natura hominis*	Nat. hom.
Nature of The Child	*De natura pueri*	Nat. puer.
Nature of Woman	*De natura muliebri*	Nat. mul.
Nutriment	*De alimento*	Alim.
Oath	*Iusiurandum*	Jusj.
Physician	*De medico*	Medic.
Places in Man	*De locis in homine*	Loc. hom.
Precepts	*Praecepta*	Praec.
Prognostic	*Prognosticum*	Progn.
Prorrhetic 1	*Prorrheticus I*	Prorrh. I
Prorrhetic 2	*Prorrheticus II*	Prorrh. II
Regimen	*De victu*	Vict.
Regimen in Acute Diseases	*De victu acutorum*	Acut.
Regimen in acute Diseases (App.)	*De victu acutorum (Spuria)*	Acut. (Sp.)
Regimen in Health	*De salubri diaeta*	Salubr.

Craik	Jouanna		Littré	Translations
14a	25	VI	448–460	Loeb: Potter VIII (1995) 386–402
8	10	VIII	584–614	Loeb: Potter VIII (1995) 125–165
17a	28	III	412–562	Loeb: Withington III (1928) 95–199
18a	29	VII	470–484	Loeb: Potter X (2012) 1–23
19	30	VIII	556–574	Loeb: Potter VIII (1995) 101–125
14b	31	VI	436–444	Loeb: Potter VIII (1995) 376–386
10	12	IX	80–92	Loeb: Potter IX (2010) 51–69
21	33	V	476–502	Loeb: Jones IV (1931) 61–95
22	34	VII	166–302	Loeb: Potter VI (1988) 59–221
17b	8	IV	78–326	Loeb: Withington III (1928) 201–397
25	37	IV	638–642	Loeb: Jones II (1923) 255–265
/	17	IX	312–400	Smith 1990
29	41	IV	340–394	Loeb: Withington III (1928) 399–449
39	56	IX	168–196	Loeb: Potter IX (2010) 11–49
36a	49	VI	32–86	Loeb: Jones IV (1931) 1–59
18b	51	VII	486–542	Loeb: Potter X (2012) 25–93
37	50	VII	312–430	Loeb: Potter X (2012) 187–323
4	5	IX	98–120	Loeb: Jones I (1923) 335–361
24	36	IV	628–632	Loeb: Jones I (1923) 289–301
28	40	IX	204–220	Loeb: Jones II (1923) 303–313 (1 only); Potter VIII (1995) 291–313
27	39	VI	276–348	Loeb: Potter VIII (1995) 13–101
40	57	IX	250–272	Loeb: Jones I (1923) 303–332
41	58	II	110–190	Loeb: Jones II (1923) 1–55
42	59	V	510–572	Loeb: Potter VIII (1995) 165–211
43	60	IX	6–74	Loeb: Potter VIII (1995) 213–293
49	68	VI	466–662	Loeb: Jones IV (1931) 223–447
1a	1	II	224–376	Loeb: Jones II (1923) 57–125
1b	2	VI	394–528	Loeb: Potter VI (1988) 223–287
36b	61b	VII	72–87	Loeb: Jones IV (1931) 43–59

English Title	Latin Title	Abbr.
Sacred Disease	*De morbo sacro*	Morb. sacr.
Seven-Month Infant	*De septimestri partu (spurium)*	Sept. (Sp.)
Sevens	*De hebdomadibus*	Hebd.
Sight	*De videndi acie*	Vid. Ac.
Sores	*De ulceribus*	Ulc.
Sterility	*De sterilibus*	Mul. III
Superfetation	*De superfetatione*	Superf.
Surgery	*De officina medici*	Off.
Use of Liquids	*De liquidorum usu*	Liqu.
Wounds in the Head	*De vulneribus in capite*	VC

TEXTS NOT PRINTED IN LITTRÉ

English Title	Latin Title	Abbr.
Embassy	*Thessali legati oratio*	Or. thess.
Remedies	*De remediis*	De purg.
Speech from the Altar	*Oratio ad aram*	Or. ad ar.
Testament	*Testamentum / Qualem oportet esse discipulum*	Testam.
Wounds and Missiles	*De vulneribus et telis [lost treatise]*	VT / Vuln.

This Appendix provides an alphabetical list of the works contained in the Hippocratic Corpus. It gives the English title; the standard Latin title and abbreviation; the number of the work in two recent surveys of the Hippocratic Corpus (Craik 2015, Jouanna 2017); the volume and page numbers in the standard edition by Littré (1839–61); and English translations where available.

Craik	Jouanna		Littré	Translations
34	46	VI	352–396	Loeb: Jones II (1923) 127–183
44a	62	VII	436–453	Loeb: Potter IX (2010) 71–101
20	32	VIII, IX	634, 433	
47	69	IX	152–160	Loeb: Potter IX (2010) 375–387
46	66	VI	400–432	Loeb: Potter VIII (1995) 335–376
35c	63	VIII	408–462	Loeb: Potter X (2012) 325–395
45	64	VIII	476–508	Loeb: Potter IX (2010) 313–353
38	53	III	272–336	Loeb: Withington III (1928) 53–82
26	38	VI	118–136	Loeb: Potter VIII (1995) 313–335
48	67	III	182–260	Loeb: Withington III (1928) 1–51

TEXTS NOT PRINTED IN LITTRÉ

Craik	Jouanna	Translations
/	55	Smith 1990
/	61a	
/	54	Smith 1990
/	65	
/	72	See Witt (2009)

References

Ackerknecht, E. (1968). *A Short History of Medicine*, Baltimore.

   (1973). *Therapeutics from the Primitives to the 20th Century (with an Appendix: History of Dietetics)*, New York, N.Y.

Adams, F. (1849). *The Genuine Works of Hippocrates Translated from the Greek with a Preliminary Discourse and Annotation*, Vol. 1, London.

Adamson, P. (2002). *The Arabic Plotinus: A Philosophical Study of the 'Theology of Aristotle'*, London.

   (2007). *Al-Kindī*, New York, N.Y.

Adamson, P., and P. E. Pormann. (2012). *The Philosophical Works of al-Kindī*, Karachi.

Adorno, F., and Accademia Toscana Di Scienze e Lettere La Colombaria, eds. (2008). *Corpus dei Papiri Filosofici Greci e Latini : Testi e lessico nei papiri di cultura greca e latina, Parte I.2: Cultura e Filosofia (Galenus-Isocrates)*, Florence.

Alessi, R. (forthcoming). 'Hippocrates' Sayings in Ibn Abi Usaibi'ia'. In Peter E. Pormann (ed.), *Proceedings of the 15th Colloque Hippocratique, Manchester, 28–30 October 2015*.

Amundsen, D. W. (1974). 'Romanticizing the Ancient Medical Profession'. *BHM* 48, 320–37.

Anastassiou, A. (2010). 'Unbekannte hippokratische Aphorismen bei Theophilos Protospatharios' *De urinis'. RhM* 153, 92–107.

   ed. (2014). *Index Hippocraticus: Neue Nachträge*, Göttingen.

Anastassiou, A., and D. Irmer, eds. (1997–2012). *Testimonien zum Corpus Hippocraticum*, Göttingen.

   eds. (1999). *Index Hippocraticus: Supplement*, Göttingen.

   eds. (2007). *Index Hippocraticus: Nachträge*, Göttingen.

Andò, V. (2002). 'La φύσις tra normale e patologico'. In Antoine Thivel and Arnaud Zucker (eds.), *Le normal et le pathologique dans la Collection Hippocratique. Actes du Xe Colloque international hippocratique, Nice, 6–8 octobre 1999*, 97–122.

   ed. (2000). *Ippocrate, Natura della donna*, Milan.

Andorlini, I. (2014). 'Ippocratismo e medicina ellenistica in un trattato medico su papiro'. In J. Jouanna and Michel Zink (eds.), *Hippocrate et les hippocratismes: Médecine, religion, société, XIV Colloque International Hippocratique, Paris, 8–10 November 2012*, 217–29.

Andorlini, I., and R. W. Daniel, eds. (2016). *Two Hellenistic Medical Papyri of the Ärztekammer Nordrhein (P. ÄkNo1 and 2)*. Papyrologica Coloniensia, Vol. 38, Paderborn.

Angeletti, L. R. (1991). 'The Origin of the Corpus Hippocraticum from Ancestors to Codices Antiqui: The Codex Vaticanus Graecus 276'. *Medicina nei Secoli. Arte e Scienza* 3, 99–151.

Anstey, P. (2011). 'The Creation of the English Hippocrates'. *Medical History* 55, 457–78.

Apel, T. (2016). *Feverish Bodies, Enlightened Minds: Science and the Yellow Fever Controversy in the Early American Republic*, Stanford, Calif.

Arrizabalaga, J. (1998). *The Articella in the Early Press, c. 1476–1534*, Cambridge.

Arrizabalaga, J., J. Henderson, and R. French. (1997). *The Great Pox: The French Disease in Renaissance Europe*, New Haven, Conn.

Artelt, W. (1968). *Studien zur Geschichte der Begriffe 'Heilmittel' und 'Gift'*, Darmstadt.

Asper. M (2007), *Griechische Wissenschaftstexte: Formen, Funktionen, Differenzierungsgeschichten*, Stuttgart: Franz Steiner.

(2015). 'Medical Acculturation?: Early Greek Texts and the Question of Near Eastern Literature'. In B. Holmes and K. D. Fischer (eds.), *The Frontiers of Ancient Science: Essays in Honor of Heinrich von Staden*, Berlin, 19–46.

Asulanus, F., ed. (1526). *Opera omnia Hippocratis*, Venice.

Ayache, L. (1992). 'Hippocrate laissait-t-il la nature agir?' In J. A. López Férez (ed.), *Tratados Hipocráticos: Actas del VIIe colloque international hippocratique, Madrid, 24–29 September 1990*, Madrid, 19–35.

Baader, G., and R. Winau, eds. (1989). *Die hippokratischen Epidemien: Theorie–Praxis–Tradition. Verhandlungen des Ve Colloque International Hippocratique (Berlin, 10.–15.9.1984)*, Sudhoffs Archiv 27, Stuttgart.

Baker, R. (1993). 'The History of Medical Ethics'. In W. F. Bynum and R. Porter (eds.), *Companion Encyclopedia of the History of Medicine*, London, 852–7.

(2013). *Before Bioethics: A History of American Medical Ethics from the Colonial Period to the Bioethics Revolution*, New York, N.Y.

Baker, R. B., and L. B. McCullough. (2009). 'What Is the History of Medical Ethics?' In R. B. Baker and L. B. McCullough (eds.), *The Cambridge World History of Medical Ethics*, Cambridge, 3–15.

de Balzac, H. (1972). *Illusions Perdues*, Paris.

Barry, Samuel Chew. (2016). *The Question of Syriac Influence upon Early Arabic Translations of the Aphorisms of Hippocrates.* PhD dissertation, University of Manchester.

(2018). *Syriac Medicine and Ḥunayn ibn 'Isḥāq's Arabic Translation of the Hippocratic Aphorisms.* Journal of Semitic Studies Supplement Series 40, Oxford.

Bashford, A., and S. Tracy. (2012). 'Modern Airs, Waters, and Places'. *Bulletin of the History of Medicine* 86, 495–514.

Bass, H. (1720). *Gründlicher Bericht von Bandagen*, Leipzig.

Beardslee, J. W. (1918). *The Use of ΦΥΣΙΣ in Fifth-Century Greek Literature*, Chicago, Ill.

Beccaria, A. (1959). 'Sulle tracce di un antico canone latino di Ippocrate e Galeno I'. *Italia medioevale e umanistica* 2, 1–56.

(1961). 'Sulle tracce di un antico canone latino di Ippocrate e Galeno II'. *Italia medioevale e umanistica* 4, 1–75.

(1971). 'Sulle tracce di un antico canone latino di Ippocrate e Galeno III'. *Italia medioevale e umanistica* 14, 1–24.

Beck, L. Y. (2005). *Pedanius Dioscorides of Anazarbus De materia medica*, translated by L. Y. Beck, Hildesheim.

Begbie, J. (1872). 'Hippocrates: His Life and Writings'. *British Medical Journal* 21 (December), 674–7.

Bendz, G., ed. (1990–93). *Caelii Aureliani Celerum passionum libri III, Tardarum passionum libri V*, CML VI 1–2, Berlin.

Benveniste, E. (1945). 'La doctrine medicale des indo-européens'. *Revue de l'histoire des religions* 130, 5–12.

Bergsträsser, G., ed. (1925). *Hunain ibn Ishaq: Über die Syrischen und Arabischen Galen-Übersetzungen*, Vol. 17.2, Abh. für die Kunde des Morgenlands, Leipzig.

Berrey, M. (2014). 'The Hippocratics on Male Erotic Desire'. *Arethusa* 47, 287–301.

Biesterfeldt, H. (2007). 'Palladius on the Hippocratic Aphorisms'. In C. D'Ancona (ed.), *The Libraries of the Neoplatonists*. Philosophia Antiqua, Leiden, 385–97.

Boissonade, J. (1831). *Anecdota Graeca e codibus Regiis*, Vol. 3, Paris.

Bolnick, D. I., L. K. Snowberg, P. E. Hirsch, et al. (2014). 'Individual Diet Has Sex-Dependent Effects on Vertebrate Gut Microbiota'. *Nature Communications* 5, 4500.

Bos, G., ed. (2004). *Maimonides. Medical aphorisms. Treatises 1–5 : A parallel Arabic-English edition = Kitāb al-fuṣūl fī al-ṭibb*, Provo, Utah.

ed. (2007). *Maimonides. Medical aphorisms. Treatises 6–9 : A parallel Arabic-English edition = Kitāb al-fuṣūl fī al-ṭibb*, Provo, Utah.

ed. (2010). *Maimonides. Medical aphorisms. Treatises 10–15 : A parallel Arabic-English edition = Kitāb al-fuṣūl fī al-ṭibb*, Provo, Utah.

ed. (2013). *Maimonides. Medical Aphorisms: Treatises 16–21: A parallel Arabic-English edition = Kitāb al-fuṣūl fī al-ṭibb*, Provo, Utah.

ed. (2015). *Maimonides. Medical Aphorisms: Treatises 22–25: A parallel Arabic-English edition = Kitāb al-fuṣūl fī al-ṭibb*, Provo, Utah.

Boudon-Millot, V. (2003). 'Aux marges de la médecine rationnelle: Médecins et charlatans à Rome au temps de Galien'. *Revue des Études Grecques* 116, 109–31.

(2006). 'Figures du maître chez Galien'. In J. Boulogne and A. Drizenko (eds.), *L'enseignement de la médecine selon Galien, Actes des Journées d'Etude organisées à Lille les 22–23 octobre 2003, Université Lille 3*, Villeneuve-d'Ascq, 15–30.

(2014). 'Le divin Hippocrate de Galien'. In J. Jouanna and Michel Zink (eds.), *Hippocrate et les hippocratismes: médecine, religion, société, XIV Colloque International Hippocratique, Paris, 8–10 November 2012*, Paris, 253–69.

(2016). 'Ce qu' "hippocratique" (ἱπποκράτειος) veut dire: La réponse de Galien'. In L. Dean-Jones and R. Rosen (eds.), *Ancient Concepts of the Hippocratic. Papers.* Presented at the XIIIth International Hippocratic Colloquium Austin, Texas, August 2008, Leiden, 362–82.

ed. (2007). *Galien, Vol. I. Introduction générale. Sur l'ordre de ses propres livres. Sur ses propres livres. Que l'excellent médecin est aussi philosophe*, Paris.

Boudon-Millot, V., and A. Pietrobelli (2005). 'Galien ressuscité: Édition princeps du texte grec du De propriis placitis'. *Revue des Études Grecques Année* 118, 168–213.

Bourbon, F. (2008). 'Nature de femmes dans les traités gynécologiques hippocratiques'. In V. Boudon-Millot, V. Dasen and B. Maire (eds.), *Femmes en médecine; actes de la journée internationale d'étude organisée à l'Université René-Descartes-Paris V, le 17 mars 2006: En l'honneur de Danielle Gourevitch*, Paris, 29–38.

Bräutigam, W. (1908). *'De Hippocratis Epidemiarum libri sexti commentatoribus'.* PhD thesis, University of Königsberg.

Bremmer, J. N. (2002). 'How Old is the Ideal of Holiness (of Mind) in the Epidaurian Temple Inscription and in the Hippocratic Oath?' *Zeitschrift für Papyrologie und Epigraphik* 141, 106–8.

Brockmann, C. (2008). *'Die hippokratischen Schriften De fracturis und De articulis im kulturellen Kontext des 5. Jahrhunderts.'* In V. Boudon-Millot, A. Guardasole and C. Magdelaine (eds.), *La science médicale antique: Nouveaux regards, publié en l'honneur de Jacques Jouanna*, Paris, 119–37.

Brody, H. (2003). *Stories of Sickness*, Oxford.

Broman, T. (1996). *The Transformation of German Academic Medicine, 1750–1820*, Cambridge.

Bruns, F. (2014). 'Turning Away from the Individual. Medicine and Morality under the Nazis'. In W. Bialas and L. Fritze (eds.), *Nazi Ideology and Ethics*, Newcastle-upon-Tyne, 211–36.

Buchdal, G. (1987). 'Philosophy of Science: Its Historical Roots'. *Epistemologia* 10, 39–56.

Bulger, R., ed. (1973). *Hippocrates Revisited: A Search for Meaning*, New York, N.Y.

Burckhardt, R. (1904). 'Das koische Tiersystem, eine Vorstufe der zoologischen Systematik des Aristoteles'. *Verhandlungen der naturforschenden Gesellschaft in Basel* 15, 377–414.

Burkert, W. (1992). *The Orientalizing Revolution: Near-Eastern Influence on Greek Culture in the Early Archaic Age*, Cambridge, Mass.

Bynum, C. W. (1995). 'Why All the Fuss About the Body?: A Medievalist's Perspective'. *Critical Inquiry* 22, 1–33.

Calogero, G. (1967). *Storia della logica antica, Vol. I – L'età arcaica*, Bari.

Calvus, F.M., ed. (1525). *Hippocratis Coi ... octoginta volumina.*

Cantor, D. (2002a). 'Introduction: The Uses and Meanings of Hippocrates.'. In D. Cantor (ed.), *Reinventing Hippocrates*, Aldershot, 1–18.

(2002b). 'The NAME and the WORD: Neo-Hippocratism and Language in Inter-War Britain'. In D. Cantor (ed.), *Reinventing Hippocrates*, Aldershot, 280–301.

(2005). 'Between Galen, Geddes and the Gael: Arthur Brock, Modernity and Medical Humanism in Early-Twentieth-Century Scotland'. *Journal of the History of Medicine and Allied Sciences* 60, 1–41.

Carmichael, H. (1942). *The Army of Hippocrates*, New York, N.Y.

Carpentieri, N., and T. Mimura. (2017). 'Arabic Commentaries on the Hippocratic Aphorisms, vi.11: A Medieval Medical Debate on Phrenitis'. *Oriens* 45.1–2, 176–202.

Cassell, E. J. (1976). *The Healer's Art*, Philadelphia, Penn.

Cavenaille, R. (2001). 'L'anesthésie chirurgicale dans l'antiquité gréco-romaine'. *Medicina nei Secoli. Arte e Scienza* 13.1, 25–46.

Chamoux, F. (1962). 'Perdiccas'. In M. Renard (ed.), *Hommages à Albert Grenier*. Collection Latomus, Brussels, 386–96.

Ciani, M. G. (1987). 'The Silences of the Body: Defect and Absence of Voice in Hippocrates'. In M. G. Ciani (ed.), *The Regions of Silence: Studies on the Difficulty of Communicating*, Amsterdam, 145–60.

Cilliers, L. (2010). 'The Didactic Letters Prefacing Marcellus' On Drugs as Evidence for the Expertise and Reputation of Doctors in the Late Roman Empire'. In H. F. J. Horstmanshoff and C. Van Tilburg (eds.), *Hippocrates and Medical Education: Selected Papers Read at the XIIth International Hippocrates Colloquium, Universiteit Leiden, 24–26 August 2005*. Studies in Ancient Medicine, Leiden, 401–18.

Clarke, G., ed. (1989). *Rediscovering Hellenism: The Hellenic Inheritance and the English Imagination*, Cambridge.

Clarke, M. (1999). *Flesh and Spirit in the Songs of Homer*, Oxford.

Conrad, L.I., et al., eds. (1995). *Western Medical Tradition: 800 BC to AD 1800*, Cambridge.

Cook, H. (1986). *The Decline of the Old Medical Regime in Stuart London*, Ithaca, N.Y.

Cordes, P. (1994). *Iatros. Das Bild des Arztes in der griechischen Literatur von Homer bis Aristoteles*, Stuttgart.

Cornarius, J., ed. (1538). *Hippocratis Coi medici . . . libri omnes*, Basel.

Cottrell, E. (2016). 'La figure d'Hippocrate dans les sources arabes: Sa vie, son oeuvre, ses lettres, et le célèbre Serment.' In Pauline Koetschet and Peter E. Pormann (eds.), *Naš at al-Ṭibb al–'Arabī fī l-qurūn al-wusṭā (La construction de la médecine arabe médiévale)*, Cairo, 131–42.

Craik, E.M. (1995a). 'Diet, Diaita and Dietetics'. In A. Powell (ed.), *The Greek World*, London, 387–402.

(1995b). 'Hippokratic Diaita'. In J. Wilkins, D. Harvey and M. Dobson (eds.), *Food in Antiquity*, Exeter, 343–50.

(2009). *The Hippocratic Treatise: On Glands*, Leiden.

(2015). *The Hippocratic Corpus. Content and Context*, London.

ed. (1998). *Hippocrates: Places in Man*, Oxford.

ed. (2006). *Two Hippocratic Treatises: On Sight and On Anatomy*, Leiden.

Crow, T. (1995). *Emulation: Making Artists for Revolutionary France*, New Haven, Conn.

Csordas, T. (1990). 'Embodiment as a Paradigm for Anthropology'. *Ethos* 18, 5–47.

Cunningham, A. (1990). 'Medicine to Calm the Mind: Boerhaave's Medical System, and Why it was Adopted in Edinburgh.' In A. Cunningham and R. French (eds.), *The Medical Enlightenment of the Eighteenth Century*, Cambridge, 40–66.

(1997). *The Anatomical Renaissance: The Resurrection of the Anatomical Projects of the Ancients*, Aldershot.

(2002). 'The Transformation of Hippocrates in Seventeenth-Century Britain'. In D. Cantor (ed.), *Reinventing Hippocrates*, Aldershot, 92–115.

Daremberg, C. (1854). *Œuvres . . . de Galien*, Vol. 1, Paris.

Das, A. (2017). 'The Hippocratism of ʿAlī ibn Riḍwān: Autodidacticism and the Creation of Medical Isnād'. *Journal of Islamic Studies*.

Daston, L., and E. Lunbeck, eds. (2011). *Histories of Scientific Observation*, Chicago, Ill.

Davies, M. (1989), *The Epic Cycle*, Bristol.

De Lacy, P., ed. (1978–84). *Galeni De placitis Hippocratis et Platonis*. 3 vols., Berlin.

Dean-Jones, L. (1992). 'The Politics of Pleasure: Female Sexual Appetite in the Hippocratic Corpus'. *Helios* 19, 72–91.

(1994). *Women's Bodies in Classical Greek Science*, Oxford.

(1995). 'Autopsia, Historia and What Women Know: The Authority of Women in Hippocratic Gynaecology'. In D. Bates (ed.), *Knowledge and the Scholarly Medical Traditions: A Comparative Study*, Cambridge, 41–58.

(2013). 'The Child Patient of the Hippocratics: Early Pediatrics?' In J. Evans Grubbs, T. Parkin and R. Bell (eds.), *Oxford Handbook of Childhood and Education in the Ancient World*, Oxford, 108–24.

Dean-Jones, L., and R. Rosen, eds. (2016). *Ancient Concepts of the Hippocratic*, Leiden.

Debru, A. (1987). 'Galien commentateur d'Hippocrate : le canon hippocratique'. In *Hippocrate et son Héritage: Colloque franco-hellénique d'histoire de la médecine (Fondation Marcel Mérieux, Lyon, 9–12 octobre 1985)*, Lyon, 51–6.

(1997). *Galen on Pharmacology. Philosophy, History and Medicine*, Leiden.

Deichgräber, K. (1970). *Medicus gratiosus. Untersuchungen zu einem griechischen Arztbild. Mit dem Anhang Testamentum Hippocratis und Rhazes' De indulgentia medici*, Wiesbaden.

Delatte, A., ed. (1939). *Anecdota Atheniensia et alia*, Liège.

Demand, N. H. (1994). *Birth, Death, and Motherhood in Classical Greece*, Baltimore, Md.

Denoyelle, M. (1994). *Chefs-d'oeuvre de la céramique grecque dans les collections du Louvre*, Paris.

Descola, P. (2012). *The Ecology of Others*, translated by G. Godbout and B. P. Luley, Chicago.

(2013). *Beyond Nature and Culture*, translated by J. Lloyd, Chicago, Ill.

Detienne, M., and J.-P. Vernant. (1991 [orig. 1974]). *Cunning Intelligence in Greek Culture and Society*, translated by Janet Lloyd, Chicago, Ill.

Di Benedetto, V. (1986). *Il medico e la malattia: La scienza di Ippocrate*, Turin.

Diels, H. (1905). *Die Handschriften der antiken Ärzte*. Vol. I : *Hippokrates und Galenos*, Berlin.

(1907). *Bericht über den Stand des interakademischen Corpus medicorum antiquorum und Erster Nachtrag zu den in den Abhandlungen 1905 und 1906 veröffentlichen Katalogen: Die Handschriften der antiken Ärzte*, Berlin.

Diels, H., and W. Kranz. (1964). *Die Fragmente der Vorsokratiker*, Berlin.

Dietz, F. R., ed. (1834). *Scholia in Hippocratem et Galenum*, Vol. I–II, Königsberg.

Diller, H., ed. (1970). *Hippocratis De aere aquis locis*, CMG I 1.2, Berlin.

Duffy, J.M. (1984). 'Byzantine Medicine in the Sixth and Seventh Centuries: Aspects of Teaching and Practice'. *Dumbarton Oaks Papers* 38, 21–7.

ed. (1983). *Stephani Philosophi In Hippocratis Prognosticum commentaria III*, CMG 11.1.2, Berlin.

ed. (1997). *Ioannis Alexandrini In Hippocratis Epidemiarum librum VI commentarii fragmenta, Anonymi In Hippocratis Epidemiarum librum VI commentarii fragmenta [Duffy]; Ioannis Alexandrini In Hippocratis De natura pueri commentarium*, CMG 11.1.4, Berlin.

Duminil, M.-P. (1983). *Le sang, les vaisseaux, le cœur dans la collection hippocratique*, Paris.

Ecca, G., ed. (2016). *Die hippokratische Schrift Praecepta. Kritische Edition, Übersetzung und Kommentar*, Wiesbaden.

Edelstein, L. (1937). 'Greek Medicine in Its Relation to Religion and Magic'. *Bulletin of the History of Medicine* 5, 201–46.

(1939). 'The Genuine Works of Hippocrates'. *Bulletin of the History of Medicine* 7, 236–48.

(1987 [orig. 1931]). 'The Dietetics in Antiquity.' In O. Temkin and C. L. Temkin (eds.), *Ancient Medicine: Selected Papers of Ludwig Edelstein*, Baltimore, Md., 303–16.

(1987 [orig. 1943]). 'The Hippocratic Oath: Text, Translation and Interpretation'. In O. Temkin and C. L. Temkin (eds.), *Ancient Medicine: Selected Papers of Ludwig Edelstein*, Baltimore, Md., 3–64.

(1987 [orig. 1956]). 'The Professional Ethics of the Greek Physician'. In O. Temkin and C. L. Temkin (eds.), *Ancient Medicine: Selected Papers of Ludwig Edelstein*, Baltimore, Md., 319–48.

(1987 [orig. 1967]). 'Hippocratic Prognosis'. In O. Temkin and C. L. Temkin (eds.), *Ancient Medicine: Selected Papers of Ludwig Edelstein*, Baltimore, Md., 65–85.

van der Eijk, P. (1997). 'Towards a Rhetoric of Ancient Scientific Discourse – Some Formal Characteristics of Greek Medical and Philosophical Texts (*Hippocratic Corpus*, Aristotle)'. In E. J. Bakker (ed.), *Grammar as Interpretation*, Leiden, 77–129.

(2004a). 'Introduction'. In H. F. J. Horstmanshoff and M. Stol (eds.), *Magic and Rationality in Ancient Near Eastern and Greco-Roman Medicine*, Leiden, 1–10.

(2004b). 'Divination, Prognosis and Prophylaxis: The Hippocratic Work 'on dreams' (De victu 4) and Its Near Eastern background'. In H. F. J. Horstmanshoff and M. Stol (eds.), *Magic and Rationality in Ancient Near Eastern and Greco-Roman Medicine*, Leiden, 187–218.

(2005a). *Medicine and Philosophy in Classical Antiquity: Doctors and Philosophers on Nature, Soul, Health and Disease*, Cambridge.

(2008). 'The Role of Medicine in the Formation of Early Greek Philosophical Thought'. In P. Curd and D. Graham (eds.), *Oxford Guide to Pre-Socratic Philosophy*,. Oxford, 385–412.

(2012). 'Exegesis, Explanation, Epistemology in Galen's Commentaries on *Epidemics*, Books One and Two'. In Peter E. Pormann (ed.), *Epidemics in Context. Greek Commentaries on Hippocrates in the Arabic Translation*. Scientia Graeco-Arabica, Berlin, 25–47.

(2014). 'Hippocrate aristotélicien'. In J. Jouanna and Michel Zink (eds.), *Hippocrate et les hippocratismes: Médecine, religion, société, XIV Colloque International Hippocratique*, Paris, 8–10 November 2012, Paris, 347–68.

(2016). 'On "Hippocratic" and "Non-Hippocratic" medical writings'. In L. Dean-Jones and R. Rosen (eds.), *Ancient Concepts of the Hippocratic*, Leiden, 15–47.

ed. (2005b). *Hippocrates in Context. Papers read at the XIth International Hippocrates Colloquium. University of Newcastle upon Tyne, 27–31 August 2002*, Leiden.

Einstein, A. (1949). 'Remarks Concerning the Essays Brought Together in this Co-operative volume'. In P. A. Schlipp (ed.), *Albert Einstein, Philosopher-Scientist*, Evanston, Ill., 665–88.

Ellis, C. (1985). *The Tree of Hippocrates*, London.

Endress, G. (1987). 'Die wissenschaftliche Literatur'. In Helmut Gätje (ed.), *Grundriss der arabischen Philologie*, Wiesbaden, 400–506.

(1992). 'Die wissenschaftliche Literatur'. In Helmut Gätje (ed.), *Grundriss der arabischen Philologie*, Wiesbaden, 3–152.

Entralgo, P. L. (1970). *The Therapy of the Word in Classical Antiquity*, New Haven, Conn.

Ermerins, F. Z. (1840). *Anecdota medica graeca*, Amsterdam.

ed. (1859–64). *Hippocratis et aliorum medicorum veterum reliquiae*. 3 vols., Utrecht.

Estes, J. (1990). 'Samuel Thomson Rewrites Hippocrates'. In P. Benes (ed.), *Medicine and Healing: The Dublin Seminar for New England Folklife. Annual Proceedings*, Boston, Mass., 113–32.

Etkins, N. L. (2008). *Edible Medicines: An Ethnopharmacology of Food*, Tucson, Ariz.

Etkins, N. L., and P. J. Ross. (1982). 'Food as Medicine and Medicine as Food: An Adaptive Framework for the Interpretation of Plant Utilization Among the Hausa of Northern Nigeria'. *Social Science & Medicine* 16.17, 1559–73.

(1991). 'Should We Set a Place for Diet in Ethnopharmacology?' *Journal of Ethnopharmacology* 32.1, 25–36.

Eyler, J. (1979). *Victorian Social Medicine: The Ideas and Methods of William Farr*, Baltimore, Md.

Fancy, N. (2013). 'Medical Commentaries: A Preliminary Examination of Ibn al-Nafīs's Shurūḥ, the Mūjaz and Commentaries on the Mūjaz'. *Oriens* 41, 525–45.

(2017). 'Womb Heat versus Sperm Heat: Hippocrates against Galen and Ibn Sīnā in Ibn al-Nafīs's Commentaries'. *Oriens* 45, 150–75.

(2018). 'Post-Avicennan Physics in the Medical Commentaries of the Mamluk Period'. *Intellectual History of the Islamicate World* 63, 55–81.

Faraone, C. (2011). 'Magical and Medical Approaches to the Wandering Womb in the Ancient Greek World'. *Classical Antiquity* 30, 1–32.

Farr, W. (1835–36). 'Lecture on the History of Hygiene'. *Lancet* 1, 773–80.

Fasbender, H. (1897). *Entwicklungslehre, Geburtshülfe und Gynäkologie in den hippokratischen Schriften*, Stuttgart.

Ferguson, D., et al. (1990). 'Walt Disney's Goofy Hippocrates: The Father of Modern Medicine'. *Walt Disney's Goofy Adventures #6*.

Ferrier, J.F. (1854). *Institutes of Metaphysic: The Theory of Knowing and Being*, Edinburgh.

Fischer, K.D. (2000). 'The *Isagoge* of Pseudo-Soranus: An Analysis of the Contents of a Medieval Introduction to the Art of Medicine'. *MHJ* 35, 3–30.

(2002). '"Zu des Hippokrates gedeckter Tafel sind alle eingeladen". Bemerkungen zu den beiden vorsalernitanischen Lateinischen Aphorismenkommentaren'. In W. Geerlings and C. Schulze (eds.), *Der Kommentar in Antike und Mittelalter: Beiträge zu seiner Erforschung*. Clavis Commentariorum Antiquitatis et Medii Aevi, Leiden, 275–313.

Fissell, M. (1993). 'Innocent and Honorable Bribes: Medical Manners in Eighteenth-Century Britain'. *Philosophy and Medicine* 45, 19–45.

Flashar, H. (1962). 'Beiträge zur spätantiken Hippokratesdeutung'. *Hermes* 90, 402–18.

(1997). 'Ethik und Medizin. Moderne Probleme und alte Wurzeln'. In H. Flashar and J. Jouanna (eds.), *Médecine et Morale dans l'Antiquité*, Geneva, 1–29.

(2005). 'Ethik'. In K.-H. Leven (ed.), *Antike Medizin: Ein Lexikon*, Munich, 275–77.

Fleischer, U. (1939). *Untersuchungen zu den pseudohippokratischen Schriften ΠΑΡΑΓΓΕΛΙΑΙ, ΠΕΡΙ ΙΗΤΡΟΥ und ΠΕΡΙ ΕΥΣΧΗΜΟΣΥΝΗΣ*, Berlin.

Flemming, R. (2000). *Medicine and the Making of Roman Women*, Oxford.

(2008). 'Commentary'. In R. J. Hankinson (ed.), *The Cambridge Companion to Galen*, Cambridge, 323–54.

Foesius, A., ed. (1595). *Magni Hippocratis ... opera omnia*, Geneva.

Foster, G. (1993). *Hippocrates' Latin American Legacy: Humoral Medicine in the New World*, Langhorne, Penn.

Foucault, M. (1985). *The History of Sexuality Vol. 2: The Use of Pleasure*, Vol. 2, translated by R. Hurley, New York, N.Y.

(1986). *The History of Sexuality Vol. 3: The Care of the Self*, New York, N.Y.

French, R. (1986). 'Pliny and Renaissance Medicine'. In R. French and F. Greenaway (eds.), *Science in the Early Roman Empire: Pliny the Elder, His Sources and Influence*, London, 252–81.

(1998). *Medicine from the Black Death to the French Disease*, Aldershot.

(2003). *Medicine before Science: The Rational and Learned Doctor from the Middle Ages to the Enlightenment*, Cambridge.

Friedrich, P., and J. Redfield. (1978). 'Speech as a Personality Symbol: The Case of Achilles'. *Language* 54.2, 263–88.

von Fritz, K. (1994 [orig. 1945]). 'ΝΟΥΣ, NOEIN, and Their Derivatives in Pre-Socratic philosophy (excluding Anaxagoras) – Part I. From the Beginnings to Parmenides'. In A. Mourelatos (ed.), *The Pre-Socratics: A Collection of Critical Essays*, Princeton, N.J., 23–85.

Garcia, F., and M. Garcia. (2012). *Science Fiction Television Series, 1990–2004: Histories, Casts and Credits for 58 Shows*, Jefferson, Ga.

Garofalo, I. (2000). 'Il Sunto di Ioannes "Grammatikos" delle opere del Canone di Galeno'. In D. Manetti (ed.), *Studi su Galeno. Scienza, filosofia, retorica e filologia Atti del seminario, Firenze 13 novembre 1998*. Florence, 135–51.

(2003). 'I sommari degli Alessandrini'. In I. Garofalo and A. Roselli (eds.), *Galenismo e medicina tardoantica. Fonti greche, latine e arabe*, Naples, 203–31.

ed. (1986, 2000). *Galenus: Anatomicarum administrationum libri qui supersunt novem, Earundem interpretatio arabica Hunaino Isaaci filio ascripta*. 2 vols., Naples.

Garofalo, I., A. Lami, D. Manetti, and A. Roselli, eds. (1999). *Aspetti della terapia nel Corpus Hippocraticum. Atti del IXe Colloque International Hippocratique, Pisa 25–29 settembre 1996*, Florence.

Gell, A. (1998). *Art and Agency*, Oxford.

Geller, M.J. (2004). 'West Meets East: Early Greek and Babylonian Diagnosis'. In H. F. J. Horstmanshoff and M. Stol (eds.), *Magic and Rationality in Ancient Near Eastern and Greco-Roman Medicine*, Leiden, 11–61.

(2010). *Ancient Babylonian Medicine. Theory and Practice*, Chichester.

Gemelli Marciano, L. (2017). 'East and West'. In L. Perilli and D. P. Taormina (eds.), *Ancient Philosophy: Textual Paths and Historical Explorations*, London.

Gill, C. (1996). *Personality in Greek Epic, Tragedy, and Philosophy*, Oxford.

Ginzburg, C. (1989). 'Clues: Roots of an Evidential Paradigm'. In C. Ginzburg, *Clues, Myths, and the Historical Method*, Baltimore, Md., 96–125.

Giogianni, F., ed. (2006). *Hippokrates. Über die Natur des Kindes ("De genitura" und "De natura pueri")*, Serta Graeca 23, Wiesbaden.

Goldhill, S. (2002). *The Invention of Prose*, Oxford.

Goltz, D. (1974). *Studien zur altorientalischen und griechischen Heilkunde, Therapie – Arzneibereitung – Rezeptstruktur*, Wiesbaden.

Gourevitch, D. (1983). 'L'aphonie hippocratique'. In F. Lasserre and P. Mudry (eds.), *Formes de pensée dans la Collection hippocratique. Actes du IVe Colloque international hippocratique, Lausanne 21–26 septembre 1981*, Geneva, 297–305.

(1984). *Le triangle hippocratique dans le monde gréco-romain: Le malade, sa maladie et son médecin*, Paris.

(1999). 'Fumigation et fomentation gynécologiques'. In I. Garofalo, A. Lami, D. Manetti and A. Roselli (eds.), *Aspetti della terapia nel Corpus Hippocraticum. Atti del IXe Colloque International Hippocratique, Pisa 25–29 settembre 1996*, Florence, 203–17.

Grafton, A. (1983). *Joseph Scaliger: A Study in the History of Classical Scholarship*, Vol. 1: Critics and Exegesis, Oxford.

Grant, M. (1997). *Dieting for an Emperor: A Translation of Books 1 and 4 of Oribasius' Medical Compilations with an Introduction and Commentary*, Leiden.

Graumann, L. A. (2000). *Die Krankengeschichten der Epidemienbücher des Corpus Hippocraticum*, Aachen.

Greenhill, W.A. (1862–64). 'Hippocrates, Euryphon, etc.'. In W. Smith (ed.), *Dictionary of Greek and Roman Biography and Mythology*, London.

Grensemann, H. (1970). 'Hypothesen zur ursprünglich geplanten Ordnung der hippokratischen Schriften De fracturis and De articulis'. *Medizinhistorisches Journal* 5, 217–35.

(1975). *Knidische Medizin, Teil I: Die Testimonien zur ältesten knidischen Lehre und Analysen knidischer Schriften im Corpus Hippocraticum*, Berlin.

(1982). *Hippokratische Gynäkologie. Die gynäkologischen Texte des Autors C nach den pseudohippokratischen Schriften De muliebribus I, II und De sterilibus*, Wiesbaden.

(1987). *Knidische Medizin, Teil II: Versuch einer weiteren Analyse der Schicht A in den pseudohippokratischen Schriften De natura muliebri und De muliebribus I und II*, Vol. 51, Stuttgart.

(1989). 'Kennzeichnet der erste Teil von De natura muliebri eine selbständige Stufe der griechischen Medizin?' *Medizinhistorisches Journal* 24, 3–24.

Grmek, M. D. (1980). *Hippocratica: Actes du Colloque hippocratique de Paris, 4–9 septembre 1978*. Colloques internationaux du Centre national de la recherche scientifique, 583. Paris.

(1983a). 'Ancienneté de la chirurgie hippocratique'. In F. Lasserre and P. Mudry (eds.), *Formes de pensée dans la Collection hippocratique: Actes du IVe Colloque international hippocratique, Lausanne 21–26 septembre 1981*, Geneva, 285–95.

(1983b). *Diseases in the Ancient Greek World*, Baltimore, Md.

Guardasole, A. (2003). 'Prose rythmique et ecdotique médicale: Le cas des Problèmes "hippocratiques"'. In A. Garzya and J. Jouanna (eds.), *Trasmissione e ecdotica dei testi medici greci, Atti del Convegno Internazionale, Parigi 17–19 maggio 2001*. Naples, 187–97.

(2007). 'Les "Problemata hippocratiques": Un exemple original de catéchisme et commentaire dans la tradition médicale et religieuse'. *REG* 120, 142–60.

(2014). 'L'image de l'"autre" Hippocrate dans le milieu chrétien'. In J. Jouanna and Michel Zink (eds.), *Hippocrate et les hippocratismes: Médecine, religion, société, XIV Colloque International Hippocratique, Paris, 8–10 November 2012*, Paris, 369–74.

Gundert, B. (1992). 'Parts and Their Roles in Hippocratic Medicine'. *Isis* 83, 453–65.

(2000). 'Soma and Psyche in Hippocratic Medicine'. In J. P. Wright and P. Potter (eds.), *Psyche and Soma: Physicians and Metaphysicians on the Mind-Body Problem from Antiquity to Enlightenment*, Oxford, 13–36.

Gurlt, E. (1898). *Geschichte der Chirurgie*, Berlin.

Gutas, D. (1975). *Greek Wisdom Literature in Arabic Translation: A Study of the Graeco-Arabic Gnomologia*, New Haven, Conn.

(1981). 'Classic Arabic Wisdom Literature: Nature and Scope'. *Journal of the American Oriental Society* 101.1, 49–86.

(1998). *Greek Thought, Arabic Culture: The Graeco-Arabic Translation Movement in Baghdad and Early 'Abbāsid Society. (2nd–4th / 8th–10th centuries)*, London.

(2012). 'The *Poetics* in Syriac and Arabic Transmission'. In L. Tarán and D. Gutas (eds.), *Aristotle: Poetics. Editio Maior of the Greek Text with Historial Introductions and Philological Commentaries.* Mnemosyne Supplements 338, Leiden, 77–128.

ed. (2010). *Theophrastus, On First Principles (Transmitted as His Metaphysics). Greek text and Medieval Arabic translation, edited and translated, with Excursus on Graeco-Arabic Editorial Technique*, Leiden.

Hallum, B. (2012). 'The Arabic Reception of Galen's *Commentary on Hippocrates'* 'Epidemics''. In Peter E. Pormann (ed.), *Epidemics in Context. Greek Commentaries on Hippocrates in the Arabic Translation*, Berlin, 185–210.

Hankinson, R. J. (1992). 'Doing without Hypotheses: The Nature of *Ancient Medicine*'. In J. A. López Férez (ed.), *Tratados Hipocráticos: Actas del VIIe colloque international hippocratique, Madrid, 24–29 Septiembre 1990*, Madrid, 55–67.

(1995). 'Pollution and Infection: An Hypothesis Still-born'. *Apeiron* 28.1, 25–65.

(1998). 'Magic, Religion and Science: Divine and Human in the Hippocratic corpus', *Apeiron* 31.1, 1–34.

(2008). 'The Man and His Work'. In R. J. Hankinson (ed.), *Cambridge Companion to Galen*, Cambridge, 1–33.

Hanson, A. E. (1975). 'Hippocrates: Diseases of Women I'. *Signs* 1, 567–84.

(1990). 'The Medical Writer's Woman'. In D. M. Halperin, J. J. Winkler and F. I. Zeitlin (eds.), *Before Sexuality: The Construction of Erotic Experience in the Ancient Greek World*, Princeton, N.J., 309–37.

(1991). 'Continuity and Change: Three Case Studies in Hippocratic Gynecological Therapy and Theory'. In S. B. Pomeroy (ed.), *Women's History and Ancient History*, Chapel Hill, N. Car., 73–110.

(1992a). 'Conception, Gestation and the Origin of Female Nature in the *Corpus Hippocraticum*'. *Helios* 19, 31–71.

(1992b). 'The Logic of the Gynecological Prescriptions.'. In J. A. López Férez (ed.), *Tratados Hipocráticos: Actas del VIIe colloque international hippocratique, Madrid, 24–29 September 1990*, Madrid, 235–50.

(1995). 'Uterine Amulets and Greek Uterine Medicine'. *Medicina nei Secoli. Arte e Scienza* 7, 281–99.

(1997). 'Fragmentation and the Greek Medical Writers.'. In G. W. Most (ed.), *Collecting Fragments: Fragmente sammeln*, Göttingen.

(1998). 'Talking Recipes in the Gynaecological Texts of the Hippocratic Corpus'. In M. Wyke (ed.), *Parchments of Gender: Deciphering the Bodies of Antiquity*, Oxford, 71–94.

(1999). 'A Hair on her Liver has been Lacerated …,'. In I. Garofalo, A. Lami, D. Manetti and A. Roselli (eds.), *Aspetti della terapia nel Corpus Hippocraticum. Atti del IXe Colloque International Hippocratique, Pisa 25–29 settembre 1996*, Florence, 235–54.

(2004). 'A Long-Lived "Quick-Birther" (Okytokion)'. In V. Dasen (ed.), *Naissance et petite enfance dans l'antiquité*, Fribourg, 265–80.

Hanson, M., ed. (1999). *Hippocratis De capitis vulneribus*, CMG I 4.1, Berlin.

Harig, G., and J. Kollesch. (1974). 'Diokles von Karystos und die zoologische Systematik'. *NTM –Schriftenreihe Geschichte, Naturwissenschaft, Technik, Medizin* 11.1, 24–31.

Harris, C. R. S. (1973). *The Heart and Vascular System in Ancient Greek Medicine, from Alcmaeon to Galen*, Oxford.

Härtel, F., and F. Loeffler. (1922). *Der Verband, Lehrbuch der chirurgischen und orthopädischen Verbandbehandlung*, Berlin.

Hasse, D. N. (2016). *Success and Suppression: Arabic Sciences and Philosophy in the Renaissance*, Cambridge, Mass.

Haverling, G. (1995). 'Un nuovo frammento della traduzione "ravennate" degli Aforismi di Ippocrate e del vecchio commento cosiddetto "oribasiano"'. *Italia medioevale e umanistica* 38, 307–17.

Hedesan, G. (2016). *An Alchemical Quest for Universal Knowledge: The 'Christian Philosophy' of Jan Baptist Van Helmont (1579–1644)*, London.

Heessel, N. P. (2004). 'Diagnosis, Divination and Disease: Towards an Understanding of the Rationale Behind the Babylonian Diagnostic Handbook'. In H. F. J. Horstmanshoff and M. Stol (eds.), *Magic and Rationality in Ancient Near Eastern and Greco-Roman Medicine*, Leiden, 97–116.

Heiberg, J., ed. (1927). *Hippocratis Indices librorum, Iusiurandum, Lex, De arte, De medico, De decente habitu, Praeceptiones, De prisca medicina, De aere locis aquis, De alimento, De liquidorum usu, De flatibus*, CMG I.1, Berlin.

Hellweg, R. (1985). *Stilistische Untersuchungen zu den Krankengeschichten der Epidemien Bücher I und III des Corpus Hippocraticum*, Bonn.

von Helmholtz, H. (1873 [orig. 1847]). 'On the Conservation of Force,' translated by E. Atkinson, *Popular Lectures on Scientific Subjects*, New York, N.Y., 317–62.

Hippocrates Health Institute. (2017). Retrieved from: http://hippocratesinst.org (accessed 15 May 2017).

Hobsbawm, E., and T. Ranger, eds. (1983). *The Invention of Tradition*, Cambridge.

Holmes, Brooke. "In Strange Lands: Disembodied Authority and the Physician Role in the Hippocratic Corpus and Beyond". Writing Science: Medical and Mathematical Authorship in Ancient Greece. Ed. Markus Asper. Berlin: de Gruyter, 2013. Print.

Holmes, B. (2010a). 'Body, Soul, and the Medical Analogy in Plato'. In J. P. Euben and K. Bassi (eds.), *When Worlds Elide: Classics, Politics, Culture*. Lanham, Md., 345–85.

(2010b). *The Symptom and the Subject. The Emergence of the Physical Body in Ancient Greece*, Princeton, N.J.

(2012). 'Sympathy between Hippocrates and Galen: The Case of Galen's Commentary on Hippocrates' 'Epidemics', Book Two'. In Peter E. Pormann (ed.), *Epidemics in Context: Greek Commentaries on Hippocrates in the Arabic Translation*, Vol. 8, Berlin, 49–70.

(2013). 'In Strange Lands: Disembodied Authority and the Role of the Physician in the Hippocratic Corpus and Beyond'. In M. Asper (ed.), *Writing Science. Mathematical and Medical Authorship in Ancient Greece*. Science, Technology and Medicine in Ancient Cultures, Berlin, 431–72.

(2014). 'Proto-sympathy in the *Hippocratic* Corpus'. In J. Jouanna and Michel Zink (eds.), *Hippocrate et les hippocratismes: Médecine, religion, société, XIV Colloque International Hippocratique, Paris, 8–10 November 2012*, Paris, 123–38.

Horstmanshoff, H. F. J. (1990). 'The Ancient Physician: Craftsman or Scientist?', *Journal of the History of Medicine* 45, 176–97.

(1999). 'Ancient Medicine between Hope and Fear: Medicament, Magic and Poison in the Roman Empire'. *European Review* 7.1, 37–51.

ed. (2010). *Hippocrates and Medical Education: Selected Papers Read at the XIIth International Hippocrates Colloquium, Universiteit Leiden, 24–26 August 2005*, Studies in Ancient Medicine, Vol. 35, Leiden.

Horstmanshoff, H. F. J., and M. Stol, eds. (2004). *Magic and Rationality in Ancient Near Eastern and Greco-Roman Medicine*, Leiden.

Horstmanshoff, H. F. J., and C. van Tilburg, eds. (2010). *Hippocrates and Medical Education: Selected Papers Read at the XIIth International Hippocrates Colloquium, Universiteit Leiden, 24–26 August 2005*, Leiden.

Hubbard, L. (1992). *Ole Doc Methuselah*, Los Angeles, Calif.

Hugo, V. (1995). *Les Misérables*, Vol. I, Paris.

Ideler, J.L., ed. (1841). *Physici et medici Graeci minores*, Vol. 1, Berlin.

Ieraci Bio, A.M. (1994). 'La cultura medica a Ravenna nel VI secolo d.C.', *Atti Accademia Pontaniana* 43, 279–308.

(1998). 'Continuità e innovazione nella letteratura medica tardoantica e bizantina'. In F. Conca and R. Maisano (eds.), *La mimesi bizantina*, Naples, 99–119.

(2003). 'Disiecta membra della scuola iatrosofistica alessandrina'. In I. Garofalo and A. Roselli (eds.), *Galenismo e medicina tardoantica: Fonti greche, latine e arabe*. Naples, 9–51.

(2007). 'Dihaireseis relative all'Ars medica di Galeno nel Neap. Orat. gr. CF 2. 11 (olim XXII–1)'. *Galenos* 1, 149–61.

(2012). 'Un inedito commento anonimo ad Ippocrate (epid. VI 4, 18 = V 312 Littré) nel Laur. LXXV 19 (ff. 140 v–141 r) e la tradizione di Suida u 52 (= IV 635 Adler)'. In R. Grisolia and G. Matino (eds.), *Forme e modi delle lingue e dei testi tecnici antichi*, Naples, 215–23.

(2014). 'Nuovi apporti sull'ippocratismo a Bisanzio'. In J. Jouanna and Michel Zink (eds.), *Hippocrate et les hippocratismes: Médecine, religion, société, XIV Colloque International Hippocratique, Paris, 8–10 November 2012*, Paris, 401–20.

Ihm, S. (2002). *Clavis Commentariorum der antiken medizinischen Texte*, Leiden.

Ilberg, J. (1893). 'Das Hippokratesglossar des Erotianos'. *Abhandlungen der sächsischen Akademie der Wissenschaften* 14, 101–47.

ed. (1927). *Sorani Gynaeciorum libri IV, De signis fracturarum, De fasciis, Vita Hippocratis secundum Soranum*, CMG IV, Berlin.

Irigoin, J. (1975). 'Tradition manuscrite et histoire du texte: Quelques problèmes relatifs à la collection hippocratique'. In L. Bourgey and J. Jouanna (eds.), *La collection hippocratique et son rôle dans l'histoire de la médicine*, Leiden, 3–18.

(1997). *Tradition et critique des textes grecs*, Paris.

(2003). *La tradition des textes grecs: Pour une critique historique*, Paris.

Irmer, D. (1975). 'Palladius' Kommentarfragment zur hippokratischen Schrift "De fracturis" und seine Parallelversion'. *QS* 2, 171–93.

(1987). 'Welcher Hippokrateskommentar des Palladius stammt (nicht) von Palladius?' *MHJ* 22, 164–73.

ed. (1977). *Kommentar zu Hippokrates "De fracturis" und seine Parallelversion unter dem Namen des Stephanus von Alexandria*, Hamburg.

Iskandar, A. Z. (1976). 'An Attempted Reconstruction of the Late Alexandrian Medical Curriculum'. *Medical History* 20, 235–58.

(2011 [orig. 1962]). 'Ar-Razi, the Clinical Physician (Ar-Razi al-tabib al-Ikliniki)'. In Peter E. Pormann (ed.), *Islamic Medical and Scientific Tradition*, London, 207–53.

Jackson, D. (2012). 'Greek Medicine in the Fifteenth Century'. *Early Science and Medicine* 17, 378–90.

Jenkyns, R. (1980). *The Victorians and Ancient Greece*, Cambridge, Mass.

Johns, T. (1990). *With Bitter Herbs They Shall Eat It: Chemical Ecology and the Origins of Human Diet and Medicine*, Tucson, Ariz.

Johnston, I., and G. H. R. Horsley, eds. (2011). *Galen. Method of Medicine, Vol. I: Books 1–4*, Cambridge, Mass.

Joly, R. (1960). *Recherches sur le traité pseudo-hippocratique du régime*, Paris.

ed. (1970). *Hippocrate Genit. Nat.Pue. Morb. 4, Oct.*, CUF 11, Paris.

ed. (1972). *Hippocrate Acut., Acut. Sp., Alim., Liqu.*, CUF 6.2, Paris.

ed. (1977). *Corpus Hippocraticum: Actes du Colloque Hippocratique de Mons (22–26 septembre 1975)*, Mons.

Joly, R., and S. Byl, eds. (2003 [orig. 1984]). *Hippocratis De diaeta*, CMG I.2.4, Berlin.

Jones, W. H. S. (1947). *The Medical Writings of Anonymous Londinensis*, Cambridge.

ed. (1923a). *Hippocrates Vol. 1: Ancient Medicine, Airs, Waters, Places, Epidemics I & III, The Oath, Precepts, Nutriment*, London.

ed. (1923b). *Hippocrates Vol. 2: Prognostic, Regimen in Acute Diseases, The Sacred Disease, The Art, Breaths, Law, Decorum, Physician, Dentition*, London.

ed. (1931). *Hippocrates Vol. 4: Nature of Man, Regimen in Health, Humours, Aphorisms, Regimen I–III, Dreams. Heracleitus: On the Universe*. Loeb Classical Library 150, Cambridge, Mass.

Joosse, N. P., and P. E. Pormann. (2010). 'Decline and Decadence in Iraq and Syria after the Age of Avicenna? ʿAbd al-Laṭīf al-Baghdādī (1162–1231) between Myth and History', *Bulletin of the History of Medicine* 84, 1–29.

(2012). 'Abd al-Latif al-Bagdadi's Commentary on Hippocrates' Prognostic. A preliminary Exploration.' In Peter E. Pormann (ed.), *Epidemics in Context. Greek Commentaries on Hippocrates in the Arabic Translation*, Berlin, 251–83.

Jori, A. (1993). 'Platone e la 'svolta dietetica' della medicina greca. Erodico di Selimbria e le insidie della techne'. *Studi italiani di filologia classica* 11, 157–95.

(1997). 'Il medico e il suo rapporto con il paziente nella Grecia dei secoli V e IV A.C.'. *Medicina nei Secoli. Arte e Scienza* 9.2, 189–222.

Jouanna, J. (1974). *Hippocrate. Pour une archéologie de l'Ecole de Cnide*, Paris.

(1980). 'Politique et médecine: La problématique du changement dans le Régime des maladies aigues et chez Thucydide (livre VI)'. In M. D. Grmek (ed.),

Hippocratica: Actes du Colloque Hippocratique de Paris, 4–9 septembre 1978, Paris, 299–318.

(1993). 'La nascita dell'arte medica occidentale'. In M. Grmek (ed.), *Storia del pensiero medico occidentale*, Rome, 3–72.

(1996). 'Un témoin méconnu de la tradition Hippocratique. L'Ambrosianus gr. 134 (B 113 Sup.), fol. 1–2 (avec une nouvelle édition du serment et de la loi)'. In A. Garzya (ed.), *Histoire et ecdotique des textes médicaux Grecs: Actes du IIe colloque international, Paris 24–26 mai 1994*, Naples, 253–72.

(1997). 'Présentation d'un nouveau corpus de Problemata médicaux et physiques: les Problèmes hippocratiques'. In U. Criscuolo and R. Maisano (eds.), *Synodia, Studia humanitatis Antonio Garzya septuagenario ab amicis atque discipulis dicata*, Naples, 511–39.

(1999 [orig. 1992]). *Hippocrates*, translated by M. B. DeBevoise, Baltimore.

(2000a). 'La lecture du traité hippocratique de la nature de l'homme par Galien: les fondements de l'hippocratisme de Galien'. In M.-O Goulet-Cazé, T. Dorandi, R. Goulet, H. Hugonnard-Roche, A. Le Boulluec and E. Ornato (eds.), *Le commentaire entre tradition et innovation*, Paris, 273–92.

(2000b). 'Maladies et médecine chez Aristophane'. In J. Leclant and J. Jouanna (eds.), *Le théâtre grec antique: La comédie. Actes du 10ème colloque de la Villa Kérylos à Beaulieu-sur-Mer les 1er et 2 octobre 1999*, Paris, 171–95.

(2004). 'L'archéologie de l'Ecole de Cnide et le nouveau témoignage du PKöln 356 (inv. 6067)'. In I. Andorlini (ed.), *Testi medici su papiro, Atti del Seminario di studio (Firenze 3–4 giugno 2002)*. Florence, 221–36. Reprint, J. Jouanna, Hippocrate. Pour une archéologie de l'Ecole de Cnide, Paris 1974; 2e édition augmentée d'un article (2004) et d'une Postface (2009), Paris, Les Belles Lettres, 2009.

(2005a). 'La théorie des quatre humeurs et des quatre tempéraments dans la tradition latine (Vindicien, Pseudo-Soranos) et une source grecque retrouvée'. *REG* 118, 1–27.

(2005b). 'Le Pseudo-Jean Damascène "Quid est homo?"' In V. Boudon-Millot and B. Pouderon (eds.), *Les Pères de l'Église face à la science médicale de leur temps*, Théologie historique, Paris.

(2005c). 'Un traité pseudohippocratique inédit sur les quatre humeurs: ("Sur le pouls et sur le tempérament humain")'. In A. Kolde, A. Lukinovich and A.-L. Rey (eds.), Κορυφαίῳ ἀνδρί. *Mélanges offerts à A. Hurst*, Geneva, 449–61.

(2006a). 'La posterité du traité hippocratique La nature de l'homme: La théorie des quatre humeurs'. In Carl Werner Müller, Christian Brockmann and Carl Wolfram Brunschön (eds.), *Ärzte und ihre Interpreten*, Munich, 117–41.

(2006b). 'Un traité inédit attribué à Hippocrate Sur la formation de l'homme: Editio princeps'. In V. Boudon-Millot, A. Garzya, J. Jouanna and A. Roselli (eds.), *Ecdotica e ricezione dei testi medici greci, Atti del Convegno Internazionale, Napoli, 1–2 ottobre 2004*, Naples, 273–319.

(2007). 'Un pseudo-Galien inédit: Le "Pronostic sur l'homme" : Contribution à l'histoire de la théorie quaternaire dans la médecine grecque tardive: L'insertion des quatre vents.' In S. David and É. Geny (eds.), *Troïka, parcours antiques, Mélanges offerts à M. Woronoff*, Besançon, 303–22.

(2008). 'La posterité de l'embriologie d'Hippocrate dans deux traitées pseudo-hippocratiques de la médecine tardive: Sur la formation de l'homme et Sur la géneration de l'homme et la sémence'. In L. Brisson, M.-H. Congourdeau and J.-L. Solère (eds.), *L'embryon: Formation et animation : Antiquité grecque et latine, tradition [sic] hébraïque, chrétienne et islamique*, Paris, 15–41.

(2009). 'Anonyme Sur les quatre éléments (Laur. Plut. 75.19, fol. 26 v–27 r): Publication d'un nouveau témoignage sur la chronobiologie quotidienne des quatre humeurs'. *Galenos* 3, 75–89.

(2009 [orig. 1974]). *Hippocrate: Pour une archéologie de l'Ecole de Cnide*, Paris.

(2010). 'Un Galien oublié: Caractéristiques propres à Hippocrate (Stobée, Anthologie 4.37.14), avec une nouvelle édition'. In V. Boudon-Millot, A. Garzya and A. Roselli (eds.), *Storia della tradizione e edizione dei testi medici greci, Atti del VI Colloquio internazionale Paris 12–14 aprile 2008*, Naples, 199–229.

(2012). 'The Theory of Sensation, Thought and the Soul in the Hippocratic Treatise Regimen: Its Connections with Empedocles and Plato's Timaeus'. Translated by N. Allies. In P. van der Eijk (ed.), *Greek Medicine from Hippocrates to Galen: Selected Papers*, Leiden, 195–228.

(2012 [orig. 1997]). 'La lecture de l'éthique Hippocratique chez Galien.' In J. Jouanna and P. van der Eijk (eds.), *Greek Medicine from Hippocrates to Galen. Selected Papers*, Leiden, 261–85.

(2014). 'L'historien Thucydide vu par le médecin Gallon'. In M. Fumaroli, J. Jouanna, M. Trédé and M. Zink (eds.), *Hommage à Jacqueline de Romilly. L'empreinte de son œuvre*, Paris, 309–40.

(2016). 'Regimen in the *Hippocratic* Corpus: Diata and Its Problems'. In L. Dean-Jones and R. Rosen (eds.), *Ancient Concepts of the Hippocratic. Papers presented at the XIIIth International Hippocratic Colloquium Austin, Texas, August 2008*, Leiden, 209–41.

(2017). 'L'histoire textuelle du Corpus hippocratique'. *Journal des Savants*, Année 2016, Juillet-Décembre.

ed. (1983). *Hippocrate, Tome X 2e partie, Maladies II*, CUF, Vol. X.2, Paris.

ed. (1988). *Hippocrate, Des vents; De l'art.*, CUF, Vol. 5.1, Paris.

ed. (1990). *Hippocrate: Tome II 1e partie, L'ancienne médecine*, Vol. II.1, CUF, Paris.

ed. (2002 [orig. 1975]). *Hippocratis De natura hominis*, CMG I 1,3, Berlin.

ed. (2013), *Prognosticon (Progn.)*, Paris.

ed. (2016). *Épidémies I et III*, Paris.

Jouanna, J., and K. D. Fischer. (2007). 'Chronobiologie dans la médecine tardive: La variation quotidienne des quatre humeurs. Nouveau témoignages grecs et latins'. *Galenos* 1, 175–86.

Jouanna, J., and A. Guardasole, eds. (2017). *Problèmes hippocratiques*, Paris.

Jouanna, J., and J. P. Mahé. (2004). 'Une anthologie arménienne et ses parallèles grecs'. *CRAI* 148.2, 549–98.

Jouanna, J., and M. Zink, eds. (2014). *Hippocrate et les hippocratismes: Médecine, religion, société, XIV Colloque International Hippocratique, Paris, 8–10 Novembre 2012*, Paris.

Kahl, O. (2015). *The Sanskrit, Syriac and Persian Sources in the Comprehensive Book of Rhazes*, Leiden.

Kanhak, A.-M. (2014). 'Περὶ τροφῆς oder: Über Form'. *Antike Naturwissenschaft und ihre Rezeption* 24, 9–45.

Kant, I. (1787). *Kritik der reinen Vernunft B [Critique of Pure Reason, 2nd ed.]*, Riga.

Kapetanaki, S., and R. W. Sharples, eds. (2006). *Pseudo-Aristoteles (Pseudo-Alexander), Supplementa problematorum*, Peripatoi, Vol. 20, Berlin.

Karimullah, K. I. (in press). 'On the Authorship of the Syriac Prognostic'. In Peter E. Pormann (ed.), *Hippocrates East and West: Proceedings of the Fifteenth "Colloque hippocratique"*, Leiden.

Kazantzidis, G. (2016). 'Empathy and the Limits of Disgust in the Hippocratic Corpus'. In D. Lateiner and D. Spatharas (eds.), *The Ancient Emotion of Disgust*, Oxford, 45–68.

Kessel, G. (2012a). 'The Syriac Epidemics and the Problem of Identification'. In Peter E. Pormann (ed.), *Epidemics in Context. Greek Commentaries on Hippocrates in the Arabic Translation*, Berlin, 93–123.

(2012b). '"Triseudaimon maximus noster sophista". The Evidence of One Syriac Text for the Identification of a Source Used in John of Alexandria's in Epid. VI'. In S. Fortuna, I. Garofalo, A. Lami and A. Roselli (eds.), *Sulla tradizione indiretta dei testi medici greci: I commenti, Atti del seminario internazionale di Siena, Certosa di Pontignano, 3–4 giugno 2011*, Pisa, 123–38.

Kibre, P. (1985). *Hippocrates Latinus. Repertorium of Hippocratic Writings in the Latin Middle Ages*, New York, N.Y.

King, H. (1989). 'The Daughter of Leonides: Reading the Hippocratic Corpus'. In A. Cameron (ed.), *History as Text.* London, 13–32.

(1995a). 'Food and Blood in Hippokratic Gynaecology'. In J. Wilkins, D. Harvey and M. Dobson (eds.), *Food in Antiquity*, Exeter, 351–8.

(1995b). 'Self-help, Self-knowledge: In Search of the Patient in Hippocratic gynecology''. In R. Hawley and B. Levick (eds.), *Women in Antiquity: New Assessments*, London, 135–48.

(1996). 'Green Sickness: Hippocrates, Galen and the origins of "The Disease of Virgins"'. *International Journal of the Classical Tradition* 2, 372–87.

(1998). *Hippocrates' Woman: Reading the Female Body in Ancient Greece*, London.

(2001). *Greek and Roman Medicine*, London.

(2002). 'The Power of Paternity: The Father of Medicine Meets the Prince of Physicians'. In D. Cantor (ed.), *Reinventing Hippocrates*, Aldershot, 21–36.

(2004). *The Disease of Virgins: Green Sickness, Chlorosis and the Problems of Puberty*, London.

(2005). 'Women's Health and Recovery in the Hippocratic Corpus'. In H. King (ed.), *Health in Antiquity*, London, 150–61.

(2012). 'Knowing the Body: Renaissance Medicine and the Classics'. In P. Olmos (ed.), *Greek Science in the Long Run: Essays on the Greek Scientific Tradition (4th c. BCE – 16th c. CE)*, Newcastle, 281–300.

(2013). *The One-Sex Body on Trial: The Classical and Early Modern Evidence*, Farnham.

Kitromilides, P. (2013). *Enlightenment and Revolution: The Making of Modern Greece*, Cambridge, Mass.

Klamroth, M. (1886). 'Ueber die Auszüge aus griechischen Schriftstellern bei al-Ja ʿqûbî'. *Zeitschrift der Deutschen Morgenländischen Gesellschaft* 40, 189–233.

Kleinknecht, H. (1942). 'Der Logos in Griechentum und Hellenismus'. In G. Kittel and G. Friedrich (eds.), *Theologisches Wörterbuch zum Neuen Testament*, Stuttgart, 76–89.

Knoeff, R. (2007). 'Practicing Chemistry "After the Hippocratical Manner": Hippocrates and the Importance of Chemistry for Boerhaave's Medicine'. In L. Principe (ed.), *New Narratives in Eighteenth-century Chemistry: Contributions from the First Francis Bacon Workshop, 21–23 April 2005, California Institute of Technology, Pasadena, Calif*, Dordrecht, 63–76.

Knutzen, G.-H. (1964). *Technologie in den hippokratischen Schriften* περὶ διαίτης ὀξέων, περὶ ἀγμῶν, περὶ ἄρθρων ἐμβολῆς, Wiesbaden.

Kosak, J.C. (2005). 'A Crying Shame: Pitying the Sick in the Hippocratic Corpus and Greek Tragedy'. In R. H. Steinberg (ed.), *Pity and Power in Ancient Athens*, Cambridge, 253–76.

Kudlien, F. (1961). 'Wissenschaftlicher und instrumenteller Fortschritt in ihrer Wechselwirkung in der antiken Chirurgie'. *Sudhoffs Archiv* 45, 329–33.

(1967). *Der Beginn des medizinischen Denkens bei den Griechen von Homer bis Hippokrates*, Zurich.

(1968a). 'Early Greek Primitive Medicine'. *Clio Medica* 3, 305–36.

(1968b). 'The Third Century A.D. A Blank Spot in the History of Medicine?' In L. G. Stevenson and R. P. Multhauf (eds.), *Medicine, Science and Culture. Essays in honor of Owsei Temkin*, Baltimore, Md., 25–34.

(1978). 'Zwei Interpretationen zum Hippokratischen Eid'. *Gesnerus* 35, 253–63.

(1988). 'Der ärztliche Beruf in Staat und Gesellschaft der Antike'. *Jahrbuch des Instituts für Geschichte der Medizin der Robert-Bosch-Stiftung* 7, 41–73.

Kühn, J. H., and U. Fleischer. (1986–9). *Index Hippocraticus, Cui elaborando interfuerunt sodales Thesauri linguae graecae Hamburgensis, Curas postremas adhibuerunt K. Alpers, A. Anastassiou, D. Irmer, V. Schmidt*, Göttingen.

Kuriyama, S. (1999). *The Expressiveness of the Body and the Divergence of Greek and Chinese Medicine*, New York, N.Y.

La Berge, A. (2002). 'The Rhetoric of Hippocrates at the Paris School'. In D. Cantor (ed.), *Reinventing Hippocrates*, Aldershot, 178–99.

Labiano, M. (2014). 'The Surgical Treatises of the Corpus Hippocraticum: Statistical Linguistics and Authorship'. In J. Martínez (ed.), *Fakes and Forgers of Classical Literature: Ergo decipiatur!* Leiden, 109–24.

De Lacy, P., ed. (1978–1984). *Galeni De placitis Hippocratis et Platonis*. CMG 5 4.1.2, 3 vols., Berlin.

ed. (1996). *Galeni De elementis ex Hippocratis sententia*, CMG 5 I.2, Berlin.

Laks, A., and G. W. Most, eds. (2016). *Early Greek Philosophy*. 9 vols., Cambridge, Mass.

Lamberz, E. (1987). 'Proklos und die Form des philosophischen Kommentars'. In J. Pépin and H. D. Saffrey (eds.), *Proclus lecteur et interprète des anciens*, Paris, 1–20.

Lami, A. (2002). 'L'inizio di Affezioni interne'. *Filologia Antica e Moderna* 12, 5–22.

(2007). '[Ippocrate.] Sui disturbi virginali. Testo, traduzione e commento'. *Galenos* 1, 15–59.

(2010). 'Una spolverata di farina d'orzo. Hipp. Int. 21'. In V. Boudon-Millot, A. Garzya and A. Roselli (eds.), *Storia della tradizione e edizione dei testi medici greci*, Atti del VI Colloquio internazionale, Paris 12–14 aprile 2008, Naples, 33–42.

Lamoraux, J., ed. (2016). *Hunayn Ibn Ishaq on His Galen Translations*, Provo, Utah.

Lang, H. (2015). 'Plato on Divine Art and the Production of Body'. In B. Holmes and K.D. Fischer (eds.), *The Frontiers of Ancient Science: Essays in Honor of Heinrich von Staden*, Berlin, 307–38.

Langholf, V. (1990). *Medical Theories in Hippocrates. Early Texts and the 'Epidemics'*, Berlin.

(2004). 'Structure and Genesis of Some Hippocratic Treatises'. In H. F. J. Horstmanshoff and M. Stol (eds.), *Magic and Rationality in Ancient Near Eastern and Greco-Roman Medicine*, Leiden, 218–75.

Laqueur, T. (1990). *Making Sex: Body and Gender from the Greeks to Freud*, Cambridge, Mass.

Laskaris, J. (1999). 'Archaic Healing Cults as a Source for Hippocratic Pharmacology'. In I. Garofalo, A. Lami, D. Manetti and A. Roselli (eds.), *Aspetti della terapia nel Corpus Hippocraticum. Atti del IXe Colloque International Hippocratique, Pisa 25–29 settembre 1996*, Florence, 1–12.

(2002). *The Art Is Long: On the Sacred Disease and the Scientific Tradition*, Leiden.

Lasserre, F., and P. Mudry, eds. (1983). *Formes de pensée dans la Collection hippocratique. Actes du IVe Colloque international hippocratique, Lausanne 21–26 septembre 1981*, Geneva.

Lautner, P. (1992). 'Philoponus, *In De Anima* : Quest for an author'. *CQ* 42, 510–22.

Lawrence, C. (1985). 'Incommunicable Knowledge: Science, Technology and the Clinical Art in Britain, 1850–1914'. *Journal of Contemporary History* 20, 503–20.

(1998). 'Still Incommunicable: Clinical Holists and Medical Knowledge in Interwar Britain'. In C. Laurence and G. Weisz (eds.), *Greater Than the Parts. Holism in Biomedicine, 1920–1950*, New York, N.Y., 94–111.

(1999). 'A Tale of Two Sciences: Bedside and Bench in Twentieth-Century Britain'. *Medical History* 43, 421–49.

Lederer, L. (2002). 'Hippocrates American Style; Representing Professional Morality in Early Twentieth-Century America'. In D. Cantor (ed.), *Reinventing Hippocrates*, Aldershot, 239–56.

Lefkowitz, M. (1981). *Lives of the Greek Poets*, Baltimore, Md.

Lefkowitz, M., and M. B. Fant. (2005). *Women's Life in Greece and Rome*, Baltimore, Md.

Leith, D., et al., eds. (2009). *The Oxyrhynchus Papyri*, Vol. 74, London.

Leonti, M. (2012). 'The Co-evolutionary Perspective of the Food–Medicine Continuum and Wild Gathered and Cultivated Vegetables'. *Genetic Resources and Crop Evolution* 59.7, 1295–302.

Letts, M. (2015). 'Questioning the Patient, Questioning Hippocrates: Rufus of Ephesus and the Pursuit of Knowledge'. In G. Petridou and C. Thumiger (eds.), *Homo Patiens. Approaches to the Patient in the Ancient World*, Leiden, 304–22.

Leven, K.-H. (1998). 'The Invention of Hippocrates: Oath, Letters and *Hippocratic Corpus*'. In U. Tröhler and S. Reiter-Theil (eds.), *Ethics Codes in Medicine: Foundations and Achievements of Codification since 1947*, Aldershot, 3–23.

(2007). '"Mit Laien soll man nicht viel schwatzen, sondern nur das Notwendige": Arzt und Patient in der hippokratischen Medizin'. In W. Reinhard (ed.), *"Krumme Touren": Anthropologie kommunikativer Umwege*. Veröffentlichungen des Instituts für Historische Anthropologie e.V., Vienna, 47–61.

Lewis, W. J., and J. A. Beach. (n.d.) *Galen on Hippocrates' On the Nature of Man*. Retrieved from: www.ucl.ac.uk/~ucgajpd/medicina%20antiqua/tr_GNatHom .html (accessed 26 July 2017).

Levitin, D. (2015). *Ancient Wisdom in the Age of the New Science: Histories of Philosophy in England, c. 1640–1700*, Cambridge.

Lichtenthaeler, C. (1984). *Der Eid des Hippokrates. Ursprung und Bedeutung*, Cologne.

Lieber, E. (1981). 'Galen in Hebrew: The transmission of Galen's works in the mediaeval Islamic world'. In V. Nutton (ed.), *Galen: Problems and Prospects*, London, 167–85.

Lightfoot, J. L., ed. (2003). *Lucian: On the Syrian Goddess*, Oxford.

Lindbloom, G. (1968). *Herman Boerhavve: The Man and His Work*, London.

van der Linden, J. A., ed. (1665). *Magni Hippocratis Coi omnia opera . . .*, Leiden.

Lippert, J., ed. (1903). *Ta'rikh al-hukama'*, Leipzig.

Littré, E., ed. (1839–61). *Oeuvres completes d'Hippocrate*. 10 vols., Paris.

Lloyd, G. E. R. (1975). 'The Hippocratic Question'. *CQ* 25, 171–92.

(1979). *Magic, Reason and Experience: Studies in the Origin and Development of Greek Science*, Cambridge.

(1983). *Science, Folklore and Ideology: Studies in the Life Sciences in Ancient Greece*, Cambridge.

(1984). 'Aspects of Science, Folklore and Ideology in the Ancient World'. In G. Giannantoni and M. Vegetti (eds.), *La scienza ellenistica*, Rome, 395–426.

(1987). *The Revolutions of Wisdom: Studies in the Claims and Practices of Greek Science*, Berkeley, Calif.

(1991). 'The Hippocratic Question'. In G. E. R. Lloyd (ed.), *Methods and Problems in Greek Science*, Cambridge, 194–223.

(1996). 'Theories and Practices of Demonstration in Galen'. In M. Frede and G. Striker (eds.), *Rationality in Greek Thought*, Oxford, 255–78.

(2003). *In the Grip of Disease: Studies in the Greek Imagination*, Oxford.

(2007). 'The Wife of Philinus, or the Doctors' Dilemma: Medical Signs and Cases and Non-deductive Inference'. In D. Scott (ed.), *Maieusis*, Oxford, 355–50.

(2008). 'Galen and his Contemporaries'. In R. J. Hankinson (ed.), *Cambridge Companion to Galen*, Cambridge, 34–48.

Lo Presti, R. (2008). *In forma di senso: La dottrina encefalocentrica del trattato ippocratico 'Sulla malattia sacra' nel suo contesto epistemologico*, Rome.

(2010). 'Tradition as Genealogy of "Truth": Hippocrates and Boerhaave between Assimilation, Variation and Deviation'. In H. F. J. Horstmanshoff and C. van Tilburg (eds.), *Hippocrates and Medical Education: Selected Papers Read at the XIIth International Hippocrates Colloquium, Universiteit Leiden, 24–26 August 2005*, Leiden, 475–522.

(2012). 'La notion d'automaton dans les textes médicaux (Hippocrate et Galien) et la Physique d'Aristote: hasard, spontanéité de la nature, et téléologie du comme si'. In K. D. Fischer (ed.), *30 Jahre Arbeitskreis Alte Medizin in Mainz. Beiträge der Tagung 2010, special issue of Les Etudes Classiques 80*, 25–54.

(2016). 'Perceiving the Coherence of the Perceiving Body: Is There Such a Thing as a 'Hippocratic' View on Sense Perception and Cognition?' In L. Dean-Jones and R. Rosen (eds.), *Ancient Concepts of the Hippocratic: Papers Presented at the XIIIth International Hippocrates Colloquium, Austin, Texas, August 2008*, Leiden, 163–94.

Longrigg, J. (1998). *Greek Medicine from the Heroic to the Hellenistic Age: A Source Book*, London.

(1999). 'Presocratic Philosophy and Hippocratic Dietetic Therapy'. In I. Garofalo, A. Lami, D. Manetti and A. Roselli (eds.), *Aspetti della terapia nel Corpus Hippocraticum. Atti del IXe Colloque International Hippocratique, Pisa 25–29 settembre 1996*, Florence, 43–50.

Lonie, I. M. (1965). 'The Cnidian Treatises of the Corpus Hippocraticum'. *CQ* 59, 1–30.

(1977). 'A Structural Pattern in Greek Dietetics and the Early History of Greek Medicine'. *Medical History* 21, 235–60.

(1978). 'Cos versus Cnidus and the Historians'. *History of Science* 16, 42–75, 77–92.

(1983). 'Literacy and the Development of Hippocratic Medicine'. In F. Lasserre and P. Mudry (eds.), *Formes de pensée dans la Collection hippocratique. Actes du IVe Colloque international hippocratique, Lausanne 21–26 septembre 1981*, Geneva, 145–61.

ed. (1981). *The Hippocratic Treatises 'On Generation'; 'On the Nature of the Child'; 'Diseases IV'*, Berlin.

López Férez, J. A., ed. (1992). *Tratados Hipocráticos: Actas del VIIe colloque international hippocratique, Madrid, 24–29 September 1990*, Madrid.

Lorusso, V. (2004). 'Il trattato pseudogalenico De urinis del Paris. Suppl. gr. 634'. *Bollettino dei classici* 25, 5–43.

Losemann, V. (2001). 'Nationalsozialismus. NS-Ideologie und die Altertumswissenschaften'. *Der Neue Pauly* 15, 723–54.

Lyons, M.C., ed. (1966). *Hippocrates. Kitāb tadbīr al-amrāḍ al-hādda li-Buqrāṭ: (Regimen in acute diseases)*, Cambridge.

Lyons, M. C., and J. N. Mattock, eds. (1978). *Kitāb al-Ajinna li-Buqrāṭ: Hippocrates: On embryos (On the sperm & On the nature of the child)*, Cambridge.

Mach, E. (1914 [orig. 1886]). *The Analysis of Sensations and the Relation of the Physical to the Psychical*, translated by C. M. Williams, Chicago, Ill.

(1919 [orig. 1883]). *The Science of Mechanics, a Critical and Historical Account of Its Development*, translated by T. J. McCormack, Chicago, Ill.

Magdelaine, C. (1994). 'Histoire du texte et édition critique, traduite et commentée, des Aphorismes d'Hippocrate'. Doctoral dissertation, Paris IV (Sorbonne).

(2003). 'Le commentaire de Palladius aux Aphorismes d'Hippocrate et le citations d'al-Ya'qubi'. In A. Garzya and J. Jouanna (eds.), *Trasmissione e ecdotica dei testi medici greci, Atti del Convegno Internazionale, Parigi 17–19 maggio 2001*, Naples, 321–34.

Magdelaine, C., and J.-M. Mouton. (2017). 'Le Commentaire au Serment hippocratique attribué à Galien retrouvé dans un manuscrit arabe du haut Moyen Âge'. *CRAI* 2016/1, 217–32.

(in press). 'The Rediscovery of the Commentary on the Hippocratic Oath, Attributed to Galen, in the Grand Mosque of Damascus'. In Peter E. Pormann (ed.), *Hippocrates East and West: Proceedings of the Fifteenth 'Colloque hippocratique'*, Leiden.

Maloney, G., and R. Savole. (1982). *Cinq cents ans de bibliographie hippocratique, 1473–1982*, Québec.

Manetti, D. (1973). 'Valore semantico e risonanze culturali della parola φύσις (De genitura, De natura pueri, De morbis IV)'. *La parola del passato* 28, 426–44.

(1992). 'P.Berol. 11739A e i commenti tardoantichi a Galeno'. In A. Garzya (ed.), *Tradizione e ecdotica dei testi medici tardoantichi e bizantini*, Naples, 211–35.

(1995). 'Hippocrates. In De alimento, PFlor 115,' *CPF*, Florence, 39–51.

(2010). *Anonymus Londinensis. De medicina*, Berlin.

(2014). 'Alle origini dell'ippocratismo: Fra IV e III sec.'. In J. Jouanna and Michel Zink (eds.), *Hippocrate et les hippocratismes: Médecine, religion, société, XIV Colloque International Hippocratique, Paris, 8–10 November 2012*, Paris, 231–51.

Manetti, D., and R. Luiselli. (2008). 'PRyl. 530, Aforismi di Ippocrate con parafrasi-commento,' *CPF*, Florence, 180–97.

Manetti, D., and A. Roselli. (1994). 'Galeno commentatore di Ippocrate'. *ANRW* 37.2, 1529–635.

  eds. (1982). *Ippocrate. Epidemie. Libro Sesto*, Florence.

Mann, J. (2012). *Hippocrates, On the Art of Medicine*, translated by J. Mann, Leiden.

Mansfeld, J. (1992). *Heresiography in Context. Hippolytus' Elenchos as a Source for Greek Philosophy*, Leiden.

Manuli, P. (1980). 'Fisiologia e patologia del femminile negli scritti Ippocratici dell'antica ginecologia Greca'. In M. D. Grmek (ed.), *Hippocratica: Actes du Colloque hippocratique de Paris, 4–9 septembre 1978*, Paris, 393–408.

  (1983). 'Donne mascoline, femmine sterili, vergini perpetue: La ginecologia greca tra Ippocrate e Sorano'. In S. Campese, P. Manuli and G. Sissa (eds.), *Madre materia: Sociologia e biologia della donna greca*, Turin, 147–92.

Marasco, G. (2010). 'The Curriculum of Studies in the Roman Empire and the Cultural Role of Physicians'. In H. F. J. Horstmanshoff and C. van Tilburg (eds.), *Hippocrates and Medical Education: Selected Papers Read at the XIIth International Hippocrates Colloquium, Universiteit Leiden, 24–26 August 2005*. Studies in Ancient Medicine, Leiden, 205–19.

Marganne, M.-H. (2014). 'Hippocrate dans un monde de chrétiens: La réception des traités hippocratiques dans la chôra égyptienne à la période byzantine (284–641)'. In J. Jouanna and Michel Zink (eds.), *Hippocrate et les hippocratismes: Médecine, religion, société, XIV Colloque International Hippocratique, Paris, 8–10 November 2012*, Paris, 283–307.

Martensen, R. (2002). 'Hippocrates and the Politics of Medical Knowledge in Early Modern England'. In D. Cantor (ed.), *Reinventing Hippocrates*, Aldershot, 116–35.

Martzavou, P. (2012). 'Dream, Narrative, and the Construction of Hope in the 'Healing Miracles' of Epidauros'. In A. Chaniotis (ed.), *Unveiling Emotions*

Sources and Methods for the Study of Emotions in the Greek World, Stuttgart, 177–204.

Marzullo, B. (1986–7). 'Hippocr. *Progn.* 1 Alex (Prooemium.)'. *Museum Criticum* 21–22, 199–254.

Masullo, R., ed. (1999). *Filagrio, Frammenti*, Naples.

Mattock, J. N. (1968), *Hippocrates. On Superfoetation (Fī l-Habal 'alā l-ḥabal)*. Arabic Technical and Scientific Texts 3, Cambridge.

ed. (1971). *Kitāb Buqrāṭ fiʾl-akhlāt (Hippocrates: On humours); and, Kitāb al-ghidha' li-Buqrāṭ (Hippocrates: On nutriment)*, Cambridge.

Mattock, J. N., and M. C. Lyons, eds. (1968). *Kitāb buqrāṭ fī ṭabīʿat al-insān: (On the nature of man)*, Cambridge.

eds. (1969). *Kitāb buqrāt fiʾl-amrād al-biladiyya. Hippocrates: On endemic diseases (airs, waters and places)*, Cambridge.

Mazzini, I. (1977). '*De observantia ciborum*. 'Un'antica traduzione latina del Peri diaites pseudoippocratico l. II (editio princeps)'. *Romanobarbarica* 2, 287–357.

(1983). 'De natura humana. Estratti di un'antica traduzione parzialmente inedita del περὶ φύσιος ἀνθρώπου di Polibo'. *Romanobarbarica* 7, 265–66.

(1984). *De observantia ciborum. Traduzione tardoantica del* περὶ διαίτης *pseudoippocratico*, Rome.

(1989). 'Alimentazione e salute secondo i medici del mondo antico: Teoria e realtà'. In O. Longo and P. Scarpi (eds.), *Homo edens. Regimi, miti e pratiche dell'alimentazione nella civiltà del Mediterraneo. Actas del Congreso "Homo edens". Verona 13–15 aprile 1987*, Milan, 257–64.

(1991). 'Les traductions latines d'Oribase et d'Hippocrate'. In P. Mudry and J. Pigeaud (eds.), *Les écoles médicales à Rome. Actes du 2éme colloque international sur les textes médicaux latins antiques, Lausanne, septembre 1986*, Geneva, 286–93.

Mazzini, I., and G. Flammini, eds. (1983). *De conceptu. Estratti di un'antica traduzione latina del* περὶ γυναικείων *pseudoippocratico*, Bologna.

McDonald, G. C. (2012). 'The "Locus Affectus" in Ancient Medical Theories of Disease'. In P. A. Baker, H. Nijdem and K. van 't Land (eds.), *Medicine and Space: Body, Surroundings and Borders in Antiquity and the Middle Ages*, Leiden, 63–83.

McVaugh, M., and N. Siraisi, eds. (1990). *Renaissance Medical Learning: Evolution of a Tradition*, Osiris, Vol. 6, Philadelphia, Penn.

Mercurialis, G., ed. (1588). *Hippocratis opera quae exstant . . .* Venice.

Mewaldt, J., G. Helmreich, and J. Westenberger, eds. (1914). *Galeni In Hippocratis De natura hominis commentaria III; In Hippocratis De victu acutorum commentaria IV; De diaeta Hippocratis in morbis acutis*, CMG V.9.1, Berlin.

Michler, M. (1962). 'Die praktische Bedeutung des normativen Physis-Begriffes in den hippokratischen Schriften De fracturis-De articulis'. *Hermes* 90, 385–401.

(1963). 'Mädchenfänger einst und jetzt'. *Medizinische Monatsschrift* 10, 649–52.

(1968). *Die Alexandrinischen Chirurgen: Eine Sammlung und Auswertung ihrer Fragmente*, Wiesbaden.

(1969). *Das Spezialisierungsproblem und die antike Chirurgie*, Bern.

Miller, R. (1987). *Bare Faced Messiah: The True Story of L. Ron Hubbard*, London.

Mimura, T. (2017). 'A Reconsideration of the Authorship of the Syriac Hippocratic Aphorisms: The Creation of the Syro-Arabic Bilingual Manuscript of the Aphorisms in the Tradition of Ḥunayn ibn Isḥāq's Arabic Translation'. *Oriens* 45, 80–104.

Mol, A. (2003). *The Body Multiple: Ontology in Medical Practice*, Durham, N. Car.

Monfort, M. L. (2002). 'Quae quibus medicamenta danda: Sur l'interprétation du fragment hippocratique *Peri Pharmakon*'. In Antoine Thivel and Arnaud Zucker (eds.), *Le normal et le pathologique dans la Collection hippocratique. Actes du Xe Colloque international hippocratique, Nice, 6–8 octobre 1999*, Nice, 693–708.

Montanari, F. (2006). 'Glossario, parafrasi, "edizione commentata" nei papiri'. In G. Avezzù and P. Scattolin (eds.), *I classici greci e i loro commentatori. Dai papiri ai marginalia rinascimentali, Atti del Convegno. Rovereto 20 ottobre 2006*, Rovereto, 9–15.

Montiglio, S. (2000). *Silence in the land of logos*, Princeton, N.J.

Mørland, H. (1932). *Die lateinischen Oribasiusübersetzungen*, Oslo.

Mudry, P. (1980). 'Medicus amicus. Un trait romain das la médecine antique'. *Gesnerus* 37, 17–20.

Müller-Rohlfsen, I., ed. (1980). *Die lateinische ravennatische Übersetzung der hippokratischen Aphorismen aus dem 5./6. Jahrhunderts n. Chr. Textkonstitution auf der Basis der Übersetzungcodices*, Hamburg.

Nachmanson, E. (1917). *Erotianstudien*, Uppsala.

(1918). *Erotiani vocum hippocraticarum collectio cum fragmentis*, Uppsala.

(1933). 'Zum Nachleben der Aphorismen'. *Quellen und Studien zur Geschichte der Naturwissenschaften und der Medizin* 3, 92–107.

Norman, J. N., ed. (1991). *Morton's Medical Bibliography: An Annotated Check-List of Texts Illustrating the History of Medicine (Garrison and Morton)*, Cambridge.

Nutton, V. (1984). 'From Galen to Alexander, Aspects of Medicine and Medical Practice in Late Antiquity'. *DOP* 38, 1–14.

(1985). 'John Caius and the Eton Galen: Medical Philology in the Renaissance'. *Medizinhistorisches Journal* 20, 227–52.

(1986–7). 'The Legacy of Hippocrates: Greek Medicine in the Library of the Medical Society of London'. *Transactions of the Medical Society of London* 103, 21–30.

(1988). '"Prisci Dissectionum Professores": Greek texts and Renaissance anatomists'. In A. C. Dionisotti, A. Grafton and J. Kraye (eds.), *The Use of Greek and Latin: Historical Essays*, London, 111–23.

(1988 [orig. 1985]). 'Murders and Miracles. Lay Attitudes to Medicine in Classical Antiquity'. In V. Nutton (ed.), *From Democedes to Harvey. Studies in the History of Medicine*, London, 23–45.

(1989). 'Hippocrates in the Renaissance'. *Sudhoffs Archiv Zeitschrift für Wissenschaftsgeschichte* 27, 420–39.

(1991). 'John of Alexandria Again: Greek Medical Philosophy in Latin Translation". *CQ* n.s. 41, 509–19.

(1992). 'Healers in the Medical Market Place. Towards a Social History of Graeco-Roman Medicine'. In A. Wear (ed.), *Medicine in Society*, Cambridge, 15–59.

(1993a). 'Beyond the Hippocratic Oath'. In A. Wear, J. Geyer-Kordesch and R. French (eds.), *Doctors and Ethics: The Earlier Historical Setting of Professional Ethics*, Amsterdam, 10–37.

(1993b). 'Greek Science in the Sixteenth Century'. In J. V. Field and F. James (eds.), *Renaissance and Revolution: Humanists, Scholars, Craftsman and Natural Philosophers in Early Modern Europe*, Cambridge, 15–28.

(1995). 'What's in an Oath?' *Journal of the Royal College of Physicians of London* 29, 518–24.

(1997). 'Hippocratic Morality and Modern Medicine'. In H. Flashar and J. Jouanna (eds.), *Médecine et Morale dans l'Antiquité*, Geneva, 31–56.

(1998). 'Gesios'. *DNP* 4, 1016–17.

(1999a). 'Magnus von Nisibis'. *DNP* 7, 698.

(1999b). 'Medizinische Ethik'. *Der Neue Pauly* 7, cols. 1117–20.

(2000). 'Philagrios'. *DNP* 9, 778.

(2004). *Ancient Medicine*, London.

(2008). 'The Fortunes of Galen'. In R. J. Hankinson (ed.), *The Cambridge Companion to Galen*, Cambridge, 355–90.

(2012). 'The Commentary on the Hippocratic Oath Ascribed to Galen'. In S. Fortuna, I. Garofalo, A. Lami and A. Roselli (eds.), *Sulla tradizione indiretta dei testi medici greci: I commenti, Atti del seminario internazionale di Siena, Certosa di Pontignano, 3–4 giugno 2011*, Pisa, 91–100.

(2013 [orig. 2004]). *Ancient Medicine*, Oxford.

ed. (1979). *Galeni De praecognitione*, CMG V 8.2, Berlin.

ed. (1999c). *Galeni De propriis placitis*, CMG V 3.2, Berlin.

O'Boyle, C. (1998). *The Art of Medicine. Medical Teaching at the University of Paris, 1250–1400*, Leiden.

O'Rourke Boyle, M. (1998). *Senses of Touch: Human Dignity and Deformity from Michelangelo to Calvin*, Leiden.

Opsomer, C., and R. Halleux. (1985). 'La lettre d'Hippocrate à Mécène et la lettre d'Hippocrate à Antiochus'. In I. Mazzini and F. Fusco (eds.), *I testi di medicina latini antichi. Problemi filologici e storici, Atti del I Convegno Internazionale, 26–28 aprile, Macerata-S. Severino Marche* Rome, 339–64.

Osborne, M. (1996). 'Resurrecting Hippocrates: Hygienic Sciences and the French Scientific Expeditions to Egypt, Morea and Algeria'. In D. Arnold (ed.), *Warm Climates and Western Medicine*, Amsterdam, 80–98.

Osborne, M., and R. Fogarty. (2012). 'Medical Climatology in France: The Persistence of Neo-Hippocratic Ideas in the First Half of the Twentieth Century'. *Bulletin of the History of Medicine* 86, 543–63.

Oser-Grote, C. M. (2004). *Aristoteles und das Corpus Hippocraticum*, Stuttgart.

Overwien, O. (2011). 'Eine Anonyme Vorlesung über das Prognostikon aus dem spätantiken Alexandria'. *Galenos* 5, 91–102.

(2012a). 'Die Bedeutung der orientalischen Tradition für die antike Überlieferung des Hippokratischen Eides'. In I. Garofalo, A. Lami and A. Roselli (eds.), *Sulla tradizione indiretta dei testi medici greci. Atti del II seminario internazionale di Siena, Certosa di Pontignano, 19–20 settembre 2008 (Biblioteca di "Galenos"* 2). Pisa, 79–103.

(2012b). 'Medizinische Lehrwerke aus den spätantiken Alexandria'. *LEC* 80, 157–86.

(2012c). 'The Art of the Translator, or: How did Ḥunayn ibn ʾIsḥāq and his School Translate?' In P. E. Pormann (ed.), *Epidemics in Context. Greek Commentaries on Hippocrates in the Arabic Translation*, Vol. 8, Berlin.

(2015). 'The Paradigmatic Translator and His Method: Ḥunayn ibn Isḥāq's Translations of the Hippocrati Aphorisms from Greek via Syriac into Arabic'. *Intellectual History of the Islamicate World* 3, 158–87.

(2017). 'Hippocrates of Cos in Arabic Gnomologia'. In P. Adamson and Peter E. Pormann (eds.), *Philosophy and Medicine in the Islamic World*, London.

ed. (2014), *Hippocratis De humoribus*, CMG I 3.1, Berlin.

Padel, R. (1992). *In and Out of the Mind: Greek Images of the Tragic Self*, Princeton, N.J.

Palm, A. (1933). *Studien zur hippokratischen Schrift Περὶ Διαίτης*, Tübingen.

Palmieri, N. (1981). 'Un antico commento a Galeno della scuola medica di Ravenna'. *Physis* 23, 197–296.

(1989). *L'antica versione latina del "De sectis" di Galeno (Pal. lat. 1090)*, Pisa.

(1991). 'L'école médicale de Ravenne: Les commentaires de Galien'. In P. Mudry and J. Pigeaud (eds.), *Les écoles médicales à Rome. Actes du 2ème colloque international sur les textes médicaux latins antiques, Lausanne, septembre 1986*, Geneva, 294–310.

(1993). 'Survivance d'une lecture alexandrine de l' "Ars medica" en latin et en arabe'. *Archives d'histoire doctrinale et littéraire du Moyen Age* 60, 57–102.

(1994). 'Il commento latino-ravennate all' "Ars medica" di Galeno e la tradizione alessandrina'. In M. E. Vázquez Buján (ed.), *Tradición e innovación de la medicina latina de la antigüedad y de la alta edad media, Actas del IV coloquio International sobre los textos médicos latinos antiguos*, Santiago de Compostela, 57–75.

(2001). 'Nouvelles remarques sur les commentaires à Galien de l'école médicale de Ravenne'. In A. Debru and N. Palmieri (eds.), *Docente natura, Mélanges de Médecine ancienne et Médiévale offerts à G. Sabbah*, Saint-Etienne, 209–46.

(2002). 'La médecine alexandrine et son rayonnement occidental (VI–VII s. ap. J.–Ch.)', *Lettre d'Informations du Centre Jean Palerne. Médecine antique et médiévale n.s.* 1, 5–23.

(2007). 'Elementi alessandrini in Cassio Felice'. *Galenos* 1, 119–35.

Paré, A., ed. (1585). *Les Œuvres d'Ambroise Paré* . . . . 4th edn., Paris.

Parker, R. (1983). *Miasma: Pollution and Purification in Early Greek Religion*. Oxford.

Parry, A. (1956). 'The Language of Achilles'. *TAPA* 84, 124–34.

Parsons, P., and A. Parsons. (1995). *Hippocrates Now! Is Your Doctor Ethical?* Toronto.

Pellicer, L. (2000), 'A propos d'Hippocrate refusant les présents d'Artaxercès, esquisse de Girodet (Montpellier, Musée Fabre)'. In R. Andréani, H. Michel and E. Pélaquier (eds.), *Hellénisme et hippocratisme dans l'Europe méditerranéenne: Autour de D. Coray: colloque tenu les 20 et 21 mars 1998 à Montpellier*, Montpellier, 195–212.

Percival, T. (1803). *Medical Ethics*, London.

Perilli, L. (1994). 'Il lessico intellettuale di Ippocrate: L'estrapolazione logica'. *Aevum antiquum* 7, 59–99.

(2009). 'Scrivere la medicina. La registrazione dei miracoli di Asclepio e le opere di Ippocrate'. In C. Brockmann, W. Brunschön and O. Overwien (eds.), *Antike Medizin im Schnittpunkt von Geistes- und Naturwissenschaften*, Berlin, 75–120.

ed. (2013). *Logos. Theorie und Begriffsgeschichte*, Darmstadt.

Petit, C. (2009a). 'La place d'Hippocrate dans un manuel medical d'époque romaine: l'"Introductio sive medicus" du Pseudo-Galien'. *LEC* 77, 295–312.

(2010). 'Hippocrates in the Pseudo-Galenic Introduction: Or How Was Medicine Taught in Roman Times?', In H. F. J. Horstmanshoff and C. van Tilburg (eds.), *Hippocrates and Medical Education: Selected Papers Read at the XIIth International Hippocrates Colloquium, Universiteit Leiden, 24–26 August 2005*. Studies in Ancient Medicine, Leiden, 343–59.

(2014). 'What Does Pseudo-Galen Tell Us That Galen Does Not? Ancient Medical Schools in the Roman Empire'. In P. Adamson, R. Hansburger and J. Wilberding (eds.), *Philosophical themes in Galen*, London, 269–90.

ed. (2009b). *Galien. Œuvres. Tome III : Le médecin. Introduction*, Paris.

Pétrequin, J. P. E. (1877–8). *Chirurgie d' Hippocrate*, Paris.

Petridou, G., and C. Thumiger, eds. (2015). *Homo Patiens: Approaches to the Patient in the Ancient World*, Leiden.

Phillips, E. D. (1973). *Greek Medicine*, London.

Piettre, R. (1993). 'Les comptes de Protée'. *Mètis. Anthropologie des mondes grecs anciens* 8.1–2, 129–46.

Pigeaud, J. (1980). 'Quelques aspects du rapport de l'âme et du corps dans le Corpus hippocratique'. In M. D. Grmek (ed.), *Hippocratica: Actes du Colloque hippocratique de Paris, 4–9 septembre 1978*, Paris, 417–32.

Pinault, J. R. (1992). *Hippocratic Lives and Legends*, Leiden.

Pormann, P. E. (2008). 'Case Notes and Clinicians: Galen's Commentary on the Hippocratic Epidemics in the Arabic Tradition'. *Arabic Sciences and Philosophy* 18, 247–84.

(2010a). 'Arabic Astronomy and the Copernican 'Revolution''. Review of George Saliba, Islamic Science and the Making of the European Renaissance (London; Cambridge, Mass., 2007). *Annals of Science* 67, 243–8.

(2010b). 'Medical Education in Late Antiquity: From Alexandria to Montpellier,' In H. F. J. Horstmanshoff and C. van Tilburg (eds.), *Hippocrates and Medical Education: Selected Papers Read at the XIIth International Hippocrates Colloquium, Universiteit Leiden, 24–26 August 2005*, Leiden, 419–41.

(2011). 'The Formation of the Arabic Pharmacology: Between Tradition and Innovation'. *Annals of Science* 68, 493–515.

(2012a). 'The Development of Translation Techniques from Greek into Syriac and Arabic: The Case of Galen's On the Faculties and Powers of Simple Drugs, Book Six'. In R. Hansburger, M. Afifi al-Akiti and C. Burnett (eds.), *Medieval Arabic Thought: Essays in Honour of Fritz Zimmermann*, London, 143–62.

(2013a). 'Avicenna on Medical Practice, Epistemology, and the Physiology of the Inner Senses'. In P. Adamson (ed.), *Interpreting Avicenna*, Cambridge, 91–108.

(2013b). 'The Hippocratic Aphorisms in the Arabic Medical Tradition'. *Aspetar* 2.3, 412–15.

(2013c). 'Qualifying and Quantifying Medical Uncertainty in 10th-century Baghdad: Abu Bakr al-Razi'. *Journal of the Royal Society of Medicine* 106, 370–2.

(2015a). Review of Leonardo Tarán, Dimitri Gutas (eds.), Aristotle: Poetics. Editio Maior of the Greek Text with Historial Introductions and Philological Commentaries, Mnemosyne Supplements 338 (Leiden, 2012), *Journal of the American Oriental Society* 135, 631–3.

(2015b). 'Al-Fārābī: The Melancholic Thinker and Philosopher Poet'. *Journal of the American Oriental Society* 135, 209–24.

(2016). 'Al-Tarǧamāt al-Yūnānīya al-Suryānīya al-ʿArabīya li-l-nuṣūṣ al-ṭibbīya fī awāʾil al-ʿaṣr al-ʿAbbāsī'. In Pauline Koetschet and Peter E. Pormann (eds.), *Naš at al-Ṭibb al-ʿArabī fī l-qurūn al-wusṭā (La construction de la médecine arabe médiévale)*. Publications de l'Institut Français de Damas, Cairo, 43–59.

(2017). 'Philosophical Topics in Medieval Arabic Medical Discourse: Problems and Prospects'. In P. E. Pormann and P. Adamson (eds.), *Philosophy and Medicine in the Formative Period of Islam. Warburg Institute Colloquia 31*, London.

ed. (2012b). *Epidemics in Context. Greek Commentaries on Hippocrates in the Arabic Translation*, Vol. 8, Berlin.

ed. (in press), *Hippocrates East and West: Proceedings of the Fifteenth "Colloque hippocratique"*, Leiden.

Pormann, P. E., S. Barry, N. Carpentieri, et al. (2017). 'The Enigma of Arabic and Hebrew Palladius'. *Intellectual History of the Islamicate World* 5.3, 252–310.

Pormann, P. E., and N. P. Joosse. (2012). 'Commentaries on the Hippocratic Aphorisms in the Arabic Tradition: The Example of Melancholy'. In Peter E. Pormann (ed.), *Epidemics in Context. Greek Commentaries on Hippocrates in the Arabic Translation*, Berlin, 211–49.

Pormann P. E., and K. I. Karimullah, eds. (2017). Special Issue: Arabic Commentaries on the Hippocratic Aphorisms. *Oriens* 45.1–2.

Porter, J. I. (1999). 'Introduction'. In J. I. Porter (ed.), *Constructions of the Classical Body*, Ann Arbor, Mich., 1–18.

Porter, R. (1989). *Health for Sale: Quackery in England,1660–1850*, Manchester.

Potter, P. (1988). *Short Handbook of Hippocratic Medicine*, Quebec.

(1989). 'Epidemien I/III: Form und Absicht der zweiundvierzig Fallbeschreibungen'. In G. Baader and R. Winau (eds.), *Die Hippokratischen Epidemien: Theorie-Praxis-Tradition, Verhandlung des Ve Colloque Hippocratique, Berlin 10–15.9.1984*. Sudhoffs Archiv 27, Stuttgart, 9–19.

(1990). 'Some principles of Hippocratic nosology'. In P. Potter, G. Maloney and J. Desautels (eds.), *La maladie et les maladies dans la Collection Hippocratique, Actes di VIe Colloque international Hippocratique (Québec 28 septembre –3 octobre 1987)*, Québec, 237–54.

(2014). 'Nosology and Organization in Barrenness'. In J. Jouanna and Michel Zink (eds.), *Hippocrate et les hippocratismes: Médecine, religion, société, XIV Colloque International Hippocratique, Paris, 8–10 November 2012*, Paris, 59–68.

ed. (1980). *Hippocratis De morbis III*, CMG 1 2.3, Berlin.

ed. (1988b). *Hippocrates, Vol. 5: Affections, Diseases I & II*, London.

ed. (1988c). *Hippocrates, Vol. 6: Diseases III, Internal Affections, Regimen in Acute Diseases*, London.

ed. (1995). *Hippocrates, Vol. 8: Places in Man, Glands, Fleshes, Prorrhetic I & II, Physician, Use of Liquids, Ulcers, Haemorrhoids, Fistulas*, London.

ed. (2010). *Hippocrates, Vol. 9: Anatomy, Nature of Bones, Heart, Eight Months Child, Coan Prenotions, Crises, Critical Days, Superfetation, Girls, Excision of the Fetus, Sight*, London.

ed. (2012). *Hippocrates, vol. 10: Generation, Nature of the Child, Diseases IV, Nature of Women, Barrenness*, London.

Potter, P., G. Maloney, and J. Desautels, eds. (1990). *La maladie et les maladies dans la Collection Hippocratique, Actes di VIe Colloque international Hippocratique (Québec 28 septembre–3 octobre 1987)*, Québec.

Pritchet, C. D., ed. (1975). *Iohannis Alexandrini Commentaria in sextum librum Hippocratis Epidemiarum*, Leiden.

ed. (1983) *Johanni Alexandrini commentaria in librum De sectis Galeni*, Leiden.

Raeder, J. (1928–33). *Galeni In Hippocratis Epidemiarum*, 4 vols., CMG 6 1.1–2.2, Berlin.

Rechenauer, G. (1991). *Thukydides und die hippokratische Medizin. Naturwissenschaftliche Methodik als Modell für Geschichtsschreibung*, Hildesheim.

Reill, P. (2005). *Vitalizing Nature in the Enlightenment*, Berkeley, Calif.

Renehan, R. (1979). 'The Meaning of ΣΩMA in Homer: A Study in Methodology'. *California Studies in Classical Antiquity* 12, 269–82.

Rey, R. (1992). 'Anamorphoses d'Hippocrate au XVIIIe siècle'. In D. Gourevitch (ed.), *Maladie et Maladies: Histoire et Conceptualisation. Mélanges en l'Honneur de Mirko Grmek*, Geneva, 257–76.

Richard, M. (1950). 'ἀπὸ φωνῆς'. *Byzantion* 20, 191–222.

Riddle, J.M. (1985). *Dioscorides on Pharmacy and Medicine*, Austin, Texas.

(1987). 'Folk Tradition and Folk Medicine: Recognition of Drugs in Classical Antiquity'. In J. Scarborough (ed.), *Folklore and Folk Medicine*, Madison, Wis., 33–61.

(1992). *Contraception and Abortion from the Ancient World to the Renaissance*, Cambridge, Mass.

Robert, F. (1975). 'La prognose hippocratique dans les livres V et VII des Epidémies'. In J. Bingen, J. G. Cambier and G. Nachtergael (eds.), *Le Monde Grec. Pensée, Literature, Histoire, Documents. Hommages à C. Préaux*, Brussels, 257–70.

Roby, C. (2015). 'Galen on the Patient's Role in Pain Diagnosis: Sensation, Consensus, and Metaphor'. In G. Petridou and C. Thumiger (eds.), *Homo Patiens. Approaches to the Patient in the Ancient World*, Leiden, 304–22.

Rose, V., ed. (1894). *Theodoris Prisciani Euporiston Libri III*, Leipzig.

Roselli, A. (1990). 'On Symptoms of Diseases'. In P. Potter, G. Maloney and J. Desautels (eds.), *La maladie et les maladies dans la Collection Hippocratique, Actes di VIe Colloque international Hippocratique (Québec 28 septembre –3 octobre 1987)*, Québec, 237–54.

(1998a). 'L'Anonimo *De medicina* (II 244–245 Dietz): Un *prolegomenon* alla lettura di testi medici?' *Filologia Antica e Moderna* 15, 7–23.

(1998b). *Lettere sulla follia di Democrito*, Naples.

(1999). 'Un commento inedito a Hipp. Epid. VI 2.24 (Epid. II 3.7) nel ms. Par. gr. 2230'. In A. Garzya and J. Jouanna (eds.), *I testi medici greci. Tradizione e ecdotica, Atti del Convegno Internazionale, Napoli 15–18 ottobre 1997*, Naples, 493–508.

(2000). 'Un corpo che prende forma: L'ordine di successione dei trattati ippocratici dall'età ellenistica fino all'età bizantina'. In G. Cerri (ed.), *La letteratura pseudepigrafa nella cultura greca e romana: Atti di un incontro di studi, Napoli, 15–17 gennaio 1998*, Naples, 167–95.

(2002). 'Ek bibliou kubernetes: I limiti dell'apprendimento dai libri nella formazione tecnica e filosofica (Galeno, Polibio, Filodemo)'. *Vichiana* 4, 37–50.

(2011). Review of C. Petit. Galien, Le medicin. Introduction. 2009, Paris: Les Belles Lettres., *RFIC*, 179–87.

(2016). 'The Gynaecological and Nosological Treatises of the *Corpus Hippocraticum*: The Tip of an Iceberg'. In G. Colesanti and L. Lulli (eds.),

Submerged Literature in Ancient Greek Culture, vol. 2: *Case Studies*, Berlin, 187–203.

ed. (1996). *La malattia sacra*, Venice.

Rosen, R. M., and H. F. J. Horstmanshoff. (2003). 'The *andreia* of the Hippocratic Physician and the Problem of Incurables'. In R. M. Rosen and I. Sluiter (eds.), *Studies in Manliness and Courage in Classical Antiquity*, Leiden, 95–114.

Rosenthal, F. (1966). "Life Is Short, the Art Is Long': Arabic Commentaries on the First Hippocratic Aphorism'. *Bulletin of the History of Medicine* 40, 226–45.

Rosner, F., ed. (1987). *Maimonides' Commentary on the Aphorisms of Hippocrates*, Haifa.

Roueché, M. (1990). 'The Definition of Philosophy and a New Fragment of Stephanus the Philosopher'. *JÖByz* 40, 108–28.

(1999). 'Did Medical Students Study Philosophy in Alexandria?' *BICS* 43, 153–69.

Rouselle, A. (1980). 'Images médicales du corps: Observation féminine et idéologie masculine: le corps de la femme d'après les médicins grecs'. *Annales* 35, 1089–115.

Rowe, C. J. (1997). *Plato, Complete Works*, ed. J. M. Cooper, Indianapolis, Ind./ Cambridge.

Ruelle, C. É. (1898). *Les lapidaires du Moyen-Âge*, Paris.

Rusnock, A. (2002). 'Hippocrates, Bacon and Medical Meteorology at the Royal Society, 1700–1750'. In D. Cantor (ed.), *Reinventing Hippocrates*, Aldershot, 136–53.

Russell, J. (1861). *The History and Heroes of the Art of Medicine*, Vol. 1, London.

Rütten, T. (1992). *Demokrit – lachender Philosoph & sanguinischer Melancholiker. Eine pseudohippokratische Geschichte*, Leiden.

(1993). *Hippokrates im Gespräch. Katalog der Aussetellung des Instituts für Theorie und Geschichte der Medizin und der Universitäts- und Landesbibliothek Münster, 10. Dez. 1993 – 8. Jan. 1994*, Muenster.

(1996). 'Receptions of the Hippocratic Oath in the Renaissance: The Prohibition of Abortion as a Case Study in Reception'. *Journal of the History of Medicine and Allied Sciences* 51, 456–83.

(1997). 'Medizinethische Themen in den deontologischen Schriften. Zur Präfigurierung des historischen Feldes durch die zeitgenössische Medizinethik'. In H. Flashar and J. Jouanna (eds.), *Médecine et morale dans l'Antiquité*, Geneva, 65–120.

(2005). 'François Tissard's 1508 edition of the Hippocratic Oath'. In P. van der Eijk (ed.), *Hippocrates in Context. Papers Read at the XIth International Hippocrates Colloquium. University of Newcastle upon Tyne. 27–31 August 2002*, Leiden, 465–91.

Rütten, T., and P. Thiermann. (1994). 'Greek Manuscripts of the Hippocratic Oath'. *Society for Ancient Medicine Review* 22, 93–5.

Salama-Carr, M. (1990). *La traduction à l'époque abbasside: L'école de Ḥunayn Ibn Isḥāq et son importance pour la traduction*, Paris.

Saliba, G. (2007). *Islamic Science and the Making of the European Renaissance*, London.

Sāmarrā'ī, K., ed. (1986). *al-Kitāb al-Nāf 'fī kayfīyat ta 'līm ṣinā 'at al-ṭibb*, Baghdad.

Sassi, M. M. (2001). *The Science of Man in Ancient Greece*, translated by P. Tucker, Chicago, Ill.

Sauneron, S. (1985). *Un traité égyptien d'ophiologie: Papyrus du Brooklyn Museum n. 47.218.48 et 8 85*, Cairo.

Scarborough, J. (1978). 'Theophrastus on Herbals and Herbal Remedies'. *Journal of the history of Biology* 11, 353–85.

   (1982). 'Beans, Pythagoras, taboos, and ancient dietetics'. *The Classical World* 75, 355–8.

   (1983). 'Theoretical Assumptions in Hippocratic Pharmacology'. In F. Lasserre and P. Mudry (eds.), *Formes de pensée dans la Collection hippocratique. Actes du IVe Colloque international hippocratique, Lausanne 21–26 septembre 1981*, Geneva, 307–25.

   (1991). 'The Pharmacology of Sacred Plants, Herbs, and Roots'. In C. A. Faraone and D. Obbink (eds.), *Magika Hiera: Ancient Greek Magic and Religion*, Oxford, 138–74.

Schiefsky, M. J. (2005). *Hippocrates On Ancient Medicine*, Leiden.

Schiffer, R. (1999). *Oriental Panorama: British Travellers in 19th Century Turkey*, Amsterdam.

Schlipp, P. A. (1949). *Albert Einstein, Philosopher-Scientist*, Evanston, Ill.

Schoenfeld, E. (1968). *Dear Doctor Hip Pocrates: Advice Your Family Doctor Never Gave You*, New York, N.Y.

   (1974). *Dr. Hip's Natural Food and Unnatural Acts*, New York, N.Y.

   (1980). *Jealousy. Taming the Green-Eyed Monster*, New York, N.Y.

Schöne, H. I. (1920–24). 'Hippokrates *Peri Pharmakon*'. *Rheinisches Museum für Philologie* 73, 434–48.

Scurlock, J. (1999). 'Physician, Exorcist, Conjurer, Magician: A Tale of Two Healing Professionals'. In T. Abusch and K. van der Toorn (eds.), *Mesopotamian Magic: Textual, Historical, and Interpretive Perspectives*, Groningen, 69–79.

   (2014). *Sourcebook for Ancient Mesopotamian Medicine*, Atlanta, Ga.

Scurlock, J., and B. R. Andersen. (2005). *Diagnoses in Assyrian and Babylonian Medicine*, Urbana, Ill.

Sezgin, F. (1970). *Geschichte des Arabischen Schrifttums*, Leiden.

Shackelford, J. (2002). 'The Chemical Hippocrates: Paracelsian and Hippocratic Theory in Petrus Severinus' Medical Philosophy'. In D. Cantor (ed.), *Reinventing Hippocrates*, Aldershot, 59–88.

van Shaik, C. D. (2015). 'It may not cure you, it may not save your life, but it will help you'. In G. Petridou and C. Thumiger (eds.), *Homo Patiens: Approaches to the Patient in the Ancient World*, Leiden, 471–96.

Sigerist, H. E. (1963). *Anfänge der Medizin*, Zurich.

(1989). 'The History of Dietetics'. *Gesnerus* 46, 249–56.

Singer, C., ed. (1956). *Galen on Anatomical Procedures*, London.

Singer, P., ed. (1997). *Galen. Selected Works*, Oxford.

Siraisi, N. (1981). *Taddeo Alderotti and His Pupils: Two Generations of Italian Medical Learning*, Princeton, N.J.

(1994). 'Cardano, Hippocrates and Criticism of Galen'. In E. Kessler (ed.), *Girolamo Cardano: Philosoph, Naturforscher, Arzt*, Wiesbaden, 131–55.

(1997). *The Clock and the Mirror: Girolamo Cardano and Renaissance Medicine*, Princeton, N.J.

Sissa, G. (1990). 'Maidenhood without Maidenhead: The Female Body in Ancient Greece'. In D. M. Halperin, J. J. Winkler and F. I. Zeitlin (eds.), *Before Sexuality: The Construction of Erotic Experience in the Ancient Greek World*, Princeton, N.J., 339–64.

Slikkerveer, L. (1990). *Plural Medical Systems in the Horn of Africa: The Legacy of 'Sheikh' Hippocrates*, London.

Sluiter, I. (1994). 'Two Problems in Ancient Medical Commentaries. I. An Anonymous Commentary on Hippocrates' Aphorisms', *CQ* 44, 270–3.

Smith, C. F., ed. (1921). *Thucydides. History of the Peloponnesian War*, Vol. III, Cambridge, Mass.

Smith, W. D. (1979). 'The Hippocratic Tradition', Ithaca, N.Y.

(1980). 'The Development of Classical Dietetic Theory'. In M. Grmek (ed.), *Hippocratica*, Paris, 439–48.

(1983). 'Analytical and Catalogue Structure in the Corpus Hippocraticum'. In F. Lasserre and P. Mudry (eds.), *Formes de pensée dans la Collection hippocratique. Actes du IVe Colloque international hippocratique, Lausanne 21–26 septembre 1981*, Geneva, 277–84.

(1989). 'Generic Form in *Epidemics* I to VII'. In G. Baader and R. Winau (eds.), *Die Hippokratischen Epidemien: Theorie-Praxis-Tradition, Verhandlung des Ve Colloque Hippocratique, Berlin 10–15.9.1984*. Sudhoffs Archiv 27, Stuttgart, 144–58.

(1990). *Hippocrates: Pseudepigraphic Writings*, Leiden.

ed. (1994). *Hippocrates, Vol. 7: Epidemics 2 & 4–7*, London.

Snell, B. (1953). *The Discovery of the Mind*, translated by T. Rosenmeyer, Oxford.

Solomon, J. (1978). *The Ancient World in the Cinema*, South Brunswick, N.J.

(1996). 'In the Wake of *Cleopatra*: The Ancient World in the Cinema Since 1963'. *Classical Journal* 91, 113–40.

Speyer, W. (1976). *Die literarische Fälschung im heidnischen und christlichen Altertum*, Munich.

von Staden, H. (1989). *Herophilus: The Art of Medicine in Early Alexandria*, Cambridge.

(1990). 'Incurability and Hopelessness: The Hippocratic Corpus'. In P. Potter, G. Maloney and J. Desautels (eds.), *La maladie et les maladies dans la Collection Hippocratique, Actes du VIe Colloque international Hippocratique (Québec 28 septembre –3 octobre 1987)*, Québec, 75–112.

(1992). 'Women and Dirt'. *Helios* 19, 7–30.

(1996). '"In a Pure and Holy Way": Personal and Professional Conduct in the Hippocratic Oath?' *Journal of the History of Medicine* 51, 404–37.

(1997). 'Character and Competence: Personal and Professional Conduct in Greek Medicine'. In H. Flashar and J. Jouanna (eds.), *Médecine et morale dans l'Antiquité*, Geneva, 157–210.

(1999a) 'Celsus as Historian?' In P. van der Eijk (ed.), *Ancient Histories of Medicine. Essays in Medical Doxography and Historiography in Classical Antiquity*, Leiden, 251–94.

(1999b) 'Reading the Agonal Body: the Hippocratic Corpus'. In Y. Otsuka, S. Sakai and S. Kuriyama (eds.), *Medicine and the History of the Body. Proceedings of the 20th, 21st, and 22nd International Symposium on the Comparative History of Medicine: East and West*, Tokyo, 287–94.

(2007a). '"The Oath', the Oaths, and the *Hippocratic* Corpus'. In V. Boudon-Millot, A. Guardasole and C. Magdelaine (eds.), *La science médicale antique. Nouveaux regards. Études réunies en l'honneur de Jacques Jouanna*, Paris, 425–66.

(2007b). 'Physis and Technê in Greek Medicine'. In B. Bensaude-Vincent and W. R. Newman (eds.), *The Artificial and the Natural: An Evolving Polarity*, Cambridge, Mass., 21–49.

(2008). 'Animals, Woman and 'Pharmaka' in the *Hippocratic Corpus*.'. In V. Boudon-Millot, V. Dasen and B. Maire (eds.), *Femmes en médecine; actes de la journée internationale d'étude organisée à l'Université René-*

Descartes-Paris V, le 17 mars 2006: en l'honneur de Danielle Gourevitch, Paris, 171–204.

(2009). 'The Discourses of Practitioners in Ancient Europe'. In R. B. Baker and L. B. McCullough (eds.), *The Cambridge World History of Medical Ethics*, Cambridge, 352–8.

Stamatu, M. (2005). 'Blasenstein'. In K.-H. Leven (ed.), *Antike Medizin: Ein Lexikon*, Munich, 161.

Stannard, J. (1961). 'Hippocratic Pharmacology'. *Bulletin of the History of Medicine* 35, 497–518.

Steger, F. (2004). 'Antike Diätetik – Lebensweise und Medizin'. *NTM International Journal of History & Ethics of Natural Sciences, Technology & Medicine* 12.3, 146–60.

(2007). 'Patientengeschichte – eine Perspektive für Quellen der Antiken Medizin? Überlegungen zuden Krankengeschichten der Epidemienbücher des Corpus Hippocraticum'. *Sudhoffs Archiv* 91, 230–8.

Stein, C. (2009). *Negotiating the French Pox in Early Modern Germany*, Farnham.

Stok, F. (2009). 'Medicus amicus: La filosofia al servizio della medicina'. *Humana Mente* 9, 77–85.

Stray, C. (1998). *Classics Transformed: Schools, Universities, and Society in England, 1830–1960*, Oxford.

Sturdy, S. (1998). 'Hippocrates and State Medicine: George Newman Outlines the Founding Policy of the Ministry of Health'. In C. Lawrence and G. Weisz (eds.), *Greater Than the Parts. Holism in Biomedicine, 1920–1950*, New York, N.Y., 112–34.

Temkin, O. (1932). 'Geschichte des Hippokratismus im ausgehenden Altertum'. *Kyklos* 4, 1–80.

(1953). 'Greek Medicine as Science and Craft'. *Isis* 44.3, 213–25.

(1973). *Galenism: The Rise and Decline of a Medical Philosophy*, Ithaca, N.Y.

(1991), *Hippocrates in a World of Pagans and Christians*, Baltimore, Md.

(2002). 'What Does the Hippocratic Oath Say? Translation and Interpretation'. In O. Temkin (ed.), *"On Second Thought" and Other Essays in the History of Medicine and Science*, Baltimore, Md., 21–48.

Thivel, A. (1981). *Cnide et Cos? Essai sur les doctrines médicales dans la Collection Hippocratique*, Paris.

(1999). 'Quale scoperta ha reso celebre Ippocrate'. In I. Garofalo, A. Lami, D. Manetti and A. Roselli (eds.), *Aspetti della terapia nel Corpus Hippocraticum: Atti del IXe Colloque International Hippocratique, Pisa 25–29 settembre 1996*, Florence, 149–61.

Thivel, A., and A. Zucker, eds. (2002). *Le normal et le pathologique dans la Collection hippocratique. Actes du Xe Colloque international hippocratique, Nice, 6–8 octobre 1999*. 2 vols., Nice.

Thumiger, C. 'The professional audiences of the Hippocratic Epidemics. Patient cases in Hippocratic scientific communication'. In Petros Bouras-Vallianatos, Sophia Xenophontos (eds.) *Greek Medical Literature and its Readers. From Hippocrates to Islam and Byzantium*. Tauris (2018) 48–64.

A History of the Mind and Mental Health in Classical Greek Medical Thought. Cambridge University Press (2017)

(2015). 'Patient Function and Physician Function in the Epidemics Cases'. In G. Petridou and C. Thumiger (eds.), *Homo Patiens: Approaches to the Patient in the Ancient World*, Leiden, 107–37.

(2016). 'Fear, Hope and the Definition of Hippocratic Medicine'. In W. V. Harris (ed.), *Popular Medicine in the Graeco-Roman World: New Approaches*. Columbia Studies in the Classical Tradition, Leiden, 198–214.

(in press), 'The Professional Audiences of the Hippocratic *Epidemics*: Patient Cases in Ancient Scientific Communication'. In P. Bouras-Vallianatos and S. Xenophontos (eds.), *The Greek Medical Text and Its Audience: Perception, Transmission, Reception*, London.

Timmermann, C. (2002). 'A Model for the New Physician: Hippocrates in Interwar Germany'. In D. Cantor (ed.), *Reinventing Hippocrates*, Aldershot, 302–24.

Totelin, L. (2009). *Hippocratic Recipes: Oral and Written Transmission of Pharmacology Knowledge in Fifth and Fourth Century Greece*, Leiden.

(2014). 'Smell and Epistemology in Ancient Medicine'. In M. Bradley (ed.), *Smell and the Ancient Senses*. The Senses in Antiquity, London, 17–29.

(2015). 'When Foods Become Remedies in Ancient Greece: The Curious Case of Garlic and Other Substances'. *Journal of Ethnopharmacology* 167, 30–37.

Touwaide, A. (1996). 'The Aristotelian School and the Birth of Theoretical Pharmacology in Ancient Greece'. In R. Pötzsch (ed.), *The Pharmacy: Windows on History*, Basel, 11–21.

Turner, F. (1981). *The Greek Heritage in Victorian Britain*, New Haven, Conn.

Tytler, J., ed. (1832). *The Aphorisms of Hippocrates, Translated into Arabic by Honain Ben Ishak*, Calcutta.

Ullmann, M. (1970). *Die Medizin im Islam*, Leiden.

(1974). 'Die arabische Überlieferung der hippokratischen Schrift "De superfetatione"'. *Sudhoffs Archiv* 58.3, 254–75.

(1975). *La Collection hippocratique et son rôle dans l'histoire de la médecine: Colloque de Strasbourg octobre 1972*, Université des sciences humaines de Strasbourg. Centre de recherches sur la Grèce antique, Leiden.

(2002). *Wörterbuch zu den griechisch-arabischen Übersetzungen des 9. Jahrhunderts*, Wiesbaden.

(2006–7). *Wörterbuch zu den griechisch–arabischen Übersetzungen des 9. Jahrhunderts, Supplement*, Wiesbaden.

(2009). *Wörterbuch der Klassischen Arabischen Sprache*, Wiesbaden.

Vagelpohl, U. (2008). *Aristotle's Rhetoric in the East: The Syriac and Arabic Translation and Commentary Tradition*, Leiden.

ed. (2014). *Galeni in Hippocratis Epidemiarum librum I commentariorum I–III versio arabica. Corpus Medicorum Graecorum*, CMG. Supplementum Orientale V,1, Berlin.

ed. (2016). *Galeni In Hippocratis Epidemiarum librum II commentariorum I–VI versionem Arabicam*, CMG. Supplementum Orientale V,2, Berlin.

Vázquez Buján, M. E. (1982). 'La antigua traducción latina del tratado De natura humana del 'Corpus Hippocraticum''. *RHT* 83, 391–2.

(1984). 'Problemas generales de las antiguas traducciones médicas latinas'. *Studi Medievali* 25, 641–80.

(1992). 'El Hipócrates de los comentarios atribuidos al Círculo de Rávena'. In J.A. López Férez (ed.), *Tratados Hipocráticos: Actas del VIIe colloque international hippocratique, Madrid, 24–29 September 1990*, Madrid, 675–85.

(2010). 'Éléments complémentaires en vue de l'edition critique de l'ancienne version latine des "Aphorismes" hippocratiques'. In D. R. Langslow and B. Maire (eds.), *Body, Disease and Treatment in a Changing World: Latin Texts and Contexts in Ancient and Medieval Medicine. Proceedings of the 9th International Conference "Ancient Medical Texts", University of Manchester, 5–8 September 2007*, Lausanne, 119–30.

Vegetti, M. (1999). 'Tradition and Truth. Forms of Philosophical-Scientific Historiography in Galen's *De placitis*'. In P. van der Eijk (ed.), *Ancient Histories of Medicine. Essays in Medical Doxography and Historiography in Classical Antiquity*, Leiden, 333–58.

Viano, C. A. (1984). 'Perché non c'era sangue nelle arterie: La cecità epistemologica degli anatomisti antichi'. In G. Giannantoni and M. Vegetti (eds.), *La scienza ellenistica*, Rome, 297–352.

Vogt, S. (2008). 'Drugs and Pharmacology'. In R. J. Hankinson (ed.), *The Cambridge Companion to Galen*, Cambridge, 304–22.

Wachsmuth, C., and Hense, O. (1912). *Ioannis Stobaei Anthologium*, Vol. 3, Berlin.

Walzer, R., and M. Frede. (1985). *Galen: Three Treatises on the Nature of Science*, Indianapolis, Ind.

Warner, J. (2002). 'Making History in American Medical Culture: The Antebellum Competition for Hippocrates'. In D. Cantor (ed.), *Reinventing Hippocrates*, Aldershot, 200–36.

Watts, E. J. (2009). 'The Enduring Legacy of the Iatrosophist Gessius'. *GRBS* 49, 113–33.

Wear, A. (1993). 'Medical Ethics in Early Modern England'. In A. Wear, J. Geyer-Kordesch and R. French (eds.), *Doctors and Ethics: The Earlier Historical Setting of Professional Ethics*, Amsterdam, 443–65.

  (2008). 'Place, Health, and Disease: The Airs, Waters, Places Tradition in Early Modern England and North America'. *Journal of Medieval and Early Modern Studies* 38, 443–65.

Wear, A., R. French, and I. M. Lonie, eds. (1985). *The Medical Renaissance of the Sixteenth Century*, Cambridge.

Webster, C. (2015). 'Voice Pathologies and the 'Hippocratic Triangle''. In G. Petridou and C. Thumiger (eds.), *Homo Patiens. Approaches to the Patient in the Ancient World*, Leiden, 166–99.

Weiss, G. (1910). 'Die ethischen Anschauungen im Corpus Hippocraticum'. *Archiv für Geschichte der Medizin* 4, 235–62.

Weisser, U. (1989). 'Das Corpus Hippocraticum in der arabischen Medizin'. In G. Baader and R. Winau (eds.), *Die hippokratischen Epidemien: Theorie–Praxis–Tradition. Verhandlungen des Ve Colloque International Hippocratique (Berlin, 10.–15.9.1984)*. Sudhoffs Archiv 27, Stuttgart, 377–408.

Weisz, G. (2002). 'Hippocrates, Holism and Humanism in Interwar France'. In D. Cantor (ed.), *Reinventing Hippocrates*, Aldershot, 257–79.

Wenkebach, E., ed. (1936). *Galeni In Hippocratis Epidemiarum librum III commentaria III*, Leipzig.

  ed. (1951). *Galeni Adversus Lycum et Adversus Iulianum libelli*, CMG 5.10.3, Berlin.

Wenkebach, E., and F. Pfaff, eds. (1934). *Galeni In Hippocratis Epidemiarum librum I commentaria III [Wenkebach]; In Hippocratis Epidemiarum librum II commentaria V, [Pfaff]*, CMG 5.10.1, Berlin.

  eds. (1956). *Galeni In Hippocratis Epidemiarum librum VI commentaria I–VI [Wenkebach]; commentaria VI–VIII [Pfaff]*, CMG 5.10.2.2, Berlin.

Westendorf, W. (1999). *Handbuch der altägyptischen Medizin*, Vol. 1, Leiden.

Westerink, L. G. (1964). 'Philosophy and Medicine in Late Antiquity'. *Janus* 51, 169–77.

  ed. (1985 [2nd. ed. 1998], 1992, 1995), *Stephani Atheniensis In Hippocratis Aphorismos commentaria*. 3 vols., CMG 11.1.3, Berlin.

Wilkins, J., and S. Hill. (1996). 'Mithaikos and other Greek Cooks'. In H. Walker (ed.), *Cooks and Other People: Proceedings of the Oxford Symposium on Food and Cookery 1995*, Totnes, 144–8.

Williams, B. (1993). *Shame and Necessity*, Berkeley, Calif.

Williams, E. (2002). 'Hippocrates and the Montpellier Vitalists in the French Medical Enlightenment'. In D. Cantor (ed.), *Reinventing Hippocrates*, Aldershot, 157–77.

Willis, J., ed. (1963). *Saturnalia*, Leipzig.

Withington, E. T., ed. (1928). *Hippocrates*, Vol. 3: *On Wounds in the Head, In the Surgery, On Fractures, On Joints, Mochlicon*, London.

Witt, M. (2009). *Weichteil- und Viszeralchirurgie bei Hippokrates. Ein Rekonstruktionsversuch der verlorenen Schrift Περὶ τρωμάτων καὶ βελῶν (De vulneribus et telis)*, Berlin.

(2011). 'Die "Zwillinge des Hippokrates". Ein antikes Zeugnis von erblich disponierter Erkrankung (Augustinus, De civitate dei V, 2), seine mögliche Quelle und Rezeption'. In L. Perilli, C. Brockmann, K.D. Fischer and A. Roselli (eds.), *Officina Hippocratica, Beiträge zu Ehren von Anargyros Anastassiou und Dieter Irmer*, Beiträge zur Altertumskunde. Berlin, 271–328.

(2012). 'Galens zweifache Kommentierung zu chirurgischen Schriften des Corpus Hippocraticum (Methodus medendi, Bücher 3–6, und chirurgische Hippokrates-Kommentare)'. *Les Études Classiques* 80, 73–126.

(2014a). 'Die verlorenen Galen-Kommentare zu den hippokratischen Schriften De ulceribus und De vulneribus in capite – Fragmentsammlung und Erläuterungen', *Rheinisches Museum für Philologie* 157, 37–74.

(2014b). 'The 'Egoistic' Physician – Considerations about the 'Dark' Sides of Hippocratic Ethics and Their Possible Aristocratic Background'. In J. Jouanna and Michel Zink (eds.), *Hippocrate et les hippocratismes: médecine, religion, société, XIV Colloque International Hippocratique, Paris, 8–10 November 2012*, Paris, 103–24.

Wittern, R. (1979). 'Die Unterlassung ärztlicher Hilfeleistung in der griechischen Medizin der klassischen Zeit'. *Münchener Medizinische Wochenschrift* 121, 731–4.

(1998). 'Gattungen im Corpus Hippocraticum.'. In W. Kullmann, J. Althoff and M. Asper (eds.), *Gattungen wissenschaftlicher Literatur in der Antike*, Tübingen, 17–36.

ed. (1974). *Die hippokratische Schrift De morbis I*, Hildesheim.

Wittern, R., and P. Pellegrin, eds. (1996). *Hippokratische Medizin und antike Philosophie: Verhandlungen des VIII. Internationalen Hippokrates*

Kolloquiums in Kloster Banz/Staffelstein vom 23. bis 28. September 1993, Hildesheim.

Wolska-Conus, W. (1989). 'Stéphanos d'Athènes et Stéphanos d'Alexandrie. *Essai d'identification et de biographie*', REByz 47, 5–89.

(1992). 'Les commentaires de Stéphanos d'Athènes aux Prognostikon et aux Aphorismes d'Hippocrate: De Galièn à la pratique scolaire alexandrine'. *REByz* 50, 5–86.

(1994). 'Stéphanos d'Athènes (d'Alexandrie) et Théophile le Prótospathaire, commentateurs des 'Aphorismes' d'Hippocrate, sont-ils indépendents l'un de l'autre?'. *REByz* 52, 5–68.

(1996). 'Sources des commentaires de Stéphanos d'Athènes et de Théophile Proto- spathaire aux 'Aphorismes' d'Hippocrate'. *REByz* 54, 5–66.

Wulfsohn, M. (1889). *Studien über Geburtshülfe und Gynäcologie der Hippocraticer*. Dorpat.

Yeo, R. (2014). *Notebooks, English Virtuosi, and Early Modern Science*, Chicago, Ill.

Youtie, L. C. (1996). *P.Michigan XVII: The Michigan Medical Codex (P.Mich. 758 = P.Mich. inv. 21)*, Atlanta, Ga.

Zellini, P. (2010). *Numero e logos*, Milan.

Zuril, L. (1990). 'Cinque Epistulae de tuenda valetudine'. In C. Santini and M. Scivoletto (eds.), *Prefazioni, prologhi, proemi di opere tecnico-scientifiche latine*, Rome, 381–97.

Zwinger, T., ed. (1579). *Hippocratis Coi ... viginti duo commentarii tabulis illustrata*, Basel.

Index